Gower

HANDBOOK
of
MANAGEMENT SKILLS
THIRD EDITION

Gower

HANDBOOK
of
MANAGEMENT SKILLS

THIRD EDITION

edited by
Dorothy M. Stewart

Gower

First published 1987 as *Handbook of Management Skills*
Second edition 1992
This edition published by
Gower Publishing Limited
Gower House
Croft Road
Aldershot
Hampshire GU11 3HR
England

Gower
Old Post Road
Brookfield
Vermont 05036
USA

British Library Cataloguing in Publication Data
Gower handbook of management skills. – 3rd ed.
    1. Industrial management
    I. Stewart, Dorothy M.   II. Handbook of management skills
    658.4

    ISBN 0 566 07889 9

Library of Congress Cataloging-in-Publication Data
Gower handbook of management skills / edited by Dorothy M. Stewart. –
    3rd ed.
        p.   cm.
    Includes index.
    ISBN 0–566–07889–9 (cloth)
        1. Management.   I. Stewart, Dorothy M.
    HD31.G843   1998
    658.4—dc21

                                                                94–12471
                                                                CIP

Typeset in 10pt Cheltenham by Raven Typesetters, Chester, Cheshire
and printed in Great Britain by Biddles Ltd, Guildford and King's Lynn.

Contents

PART I   MANAGING YOURSELF

Introduction: understanding yourself and your skills needs as a manager   3

1   Management self-development   5
Andrew Constable

What is management self-development? – Why is self-development important? – How can I go about developing myself? – For whom is management
self-development relevant? – Areas to which an individual might apply self-
development principles – How organizations are applying this approach in
practice – What are the challenges? – What brings success? – Rewards and
benefits – Further reading

2   Managing your time   13
John W. Rogers

Introduction – Setting objectives – Planning systems – Logging time use –
Individual behaviour: problems and solutions – Managerial styles – Visual
reminders – Summary and check list – Further reading

3 Managing information 51
Feona J. Hamilton

Starting somewhere – Using the computer – Information from the network – Information that you set up and store yourself – Making copies and keeping them – Good old paper – Using the library or information centre – Conclusion and summary – Further reading

4 Information technology 60
Barbara Smolny-Kostrewski

The typewriter – The telephone – Faxes – Computer-based technology – When to install a computer system – Computer technology in the office – Safety – Document preparation – Multimedia – Exchange of information – Electronic mail (E-mail) – Internet – Check list: points to be borne in mind when using IT – Further reading

5 Writing 72
Krystyna Weinstein

Writing is like having a conversation – Writing this chapter – The six stages of writing – Afterthought – Notes – Further reading

6 Speaking in public 90
Brian Sanders

The spoken word – How to make the best use of oneself – Creating a feeling of confidence – Using a microphone – Preparing the material – Notes – A general observation – Using visual aids – Answering questions – Extending the vocal range – Key points – Further reading

7 Managing your health 107
Dr H. Beric Wright

Health and wellbeing – What you have to survive – Managing health – Key points – Further reading

8 Coping with stress 128
Andrew M. Stewart

What is stress? – What does stress cost? – What causes stress? – What are the signs of stress? – What can the individual do about stress – Coping at the top – What can organizations do about stress? – Check list – Further reading

PART II   MANAGING OTHER PEOPLE

9   Recruitment   155
John Courtis

Is there a job, and what is the candidate specification? – How do we find the right people? – Processing the results – Decisions, decisions – Acceptance – Induction – Recruitment check list – Further reading

10   Interviewing   165
John Courtis

Objectives – Abort the abortive – Time flies – Preparation – The interview proper – Body language – The close – Interviews and the law – The secondary objectives – Other kinds of interview – What we have learned – Structured interviewing – Check list of key points – Further reading

11   Listening   179
Meribeth Bunch

Become centred and still – I want to be here – Use 180 degree vision – 'Blank your screen' momentarily – Leave your internal critic out of the conversation – Stop analysing everything that is being said to you – A special note about listening to criticism – Accept what you are hearing – Allow the other person to be him/herself – Summary – Skills check list – Further reading

12   Helping people learn   187
Norman Gealy

What should you help with? – Should you set targets? – What should you do to help? How will you know that what you did helped? – Summary of recommendations – Further reading

13   People skills   199
Peter Honey

What are people skills? – Why the emphasis on behaviour? – What are the advantages of improved people skills? – Can people skills be improved? – What are the fundamental people skills? – Are there alternative people skills? – Conclusion and check list – Further reading

goals – Networking for greater success – Understanding human motivations – Rapport – Styles of influence – Models of strategic influence – Further reading

Why is communication important? – What is communication? – Why communication is not simple – A manager's job is about communicating – How can you manage your communications? – Separation, distance . . . and perspective – Managing yourself . . . your behaviour – The importance of feedback – Check list of key points – Notes – Further reading

Good meetings mean more profit – Why do meetings fail? – People – Planning – Progress – Check lists of seven ways to better meetings – Further reading

The accounting process – Understanding accounting information – Accounting information and managerial decision making – Conclusion – Check list of key points – Further reading

Environmental pressures – Project definition – Developing a project statement – Project appraisal – Project approval – Project implementation – Auditing project performance – Project management check list – Further reading

Decision making, problem solving, contingency planning and creativity – Creativity – Problem solving – Decision making – Contingency planning – Check list – Further reading

25 Negotiating 392
Nicholas Jeffery

Why negotiate? – Preparation – Styles of negotiation – Key negotiating principles – Structure of a negotiation – The skills of negotiation – Check list of key points – Further reading

26 Creativity 405
Victor Newman

Creativity, risk and instability in organizations – Creative problem solving – Introducing 'Problem Solving for Results' – The impact of problem-solving styles – Creativity and teams – Fundamental approaches – Summary – Check list – Further reading

List of figures

Preface

This is the book I wish I'd had in my desk drawer when I was first a manager. Instead I tried to fill the gaps in my knowledge, experience and confidence with short courses, lots of other books, and an MBA course studied in the evenings for three years. The hard way to do it – but only too familiar to today's beleaguered managers.

The drawback with this approach is the gap between the learning process and your daily work. Management is a mass of different things happening, often at once, and all of them with direct repercussions on your future career. Yesterday's elegant theory expounded so convincingly by that self-assured academic just does not stand up to the rigours of life at the coalface.

That course on presentation skills is fine when you are there, supported by that kindly tutor and friendly bunch of co-participants. But it is very different presenting the case for your pet project in front of a sceptical board, with half-a-dozen hostile colleagues sitting round the table with knives sharpened to attack it.

So this book is the one to keep in your desk drawer, out of sight. When you need the information, you will find a chapter to help; no fancy models or useless theories. This is a practical book for real managers, aimed at helping you manage more effectively in the real world of business today. You will find enough background information, but no overwhelming detail, and plenty of 'how-to-do-it' information, soundly based on research and years of experience and practice. This is material you can trust. It is tried and tested.

There are three parts. The first, beginning with a keynote chapter on management self-development by Andrew Constable, covers the main methods of self-development. Part II provides chapters on the key aspects of managing other people. Part III contains a number of techniques chapters for the manager who wants that extra competitive edge. Inevitably, there is some overlap where techniques apply in more than one area. I have tried to keep this to a minimum but since management skills tend to be multipurpose some duplication has been unavoidable.

Of the twenty-six chapters in this edition, twelve are new; the others have been revised and updated. Every chapter contains a check list of key points and suggestions for further reading and details of relevant resources, for when you have time to pursue the subject in more detail.

We know from the sales of the previous editions that this *Handbook* has provided helpful information, in a useful form, to many thousands of managers. I hope that this third edition will prove even more effective.

Dorothy M. Stewart

Notes on contributors

Meribeth Bunch, Ph.D. *(Listening)* works in organizational development, specializing in helping individuals and groups to expand and develop awareness of self and others in order to facilitate improvement in communication and to build positive relationships. Her seminars include a broad range of communication and presentation skills including: confident communication, personal image, voice and presence, creative presentations and interpersonal relations. Recent clients include: Marks & Spencer, ICI, The Prudential Assurance Company, Sears and Hewlett Packard.

Andrew Constable MA(Cantab) MIPD *(Management self-development)* joined Roffey Park in February 1992 and holds the position of Director of International Development. He has worked with many organizations on in-house management development activities and is currently Account Manager for a number of Roffey's major clients including Allied Domecq, ASDA, The British Council, ICL, Coopers and Lybrand, Oracle, Groupe Schneider, Brown and Root, Abbey National, Yellow Pages, Honda, BMW, the NHS, Glaxo Wellcome, PPP Healthcare and BAT Industries. After graduating from Cambridge University, Andrew trained and worked with the Manpower Services Commission in London. His work there embraced both managerial and training responsibilities. He then moved from public to private sector through joining Abbey National, where initially he established and developed the Graduate Recruitment function. Following this he held a variety of management and management development positions and carried out a wide spectrum of work in this field. His work covers a number of projects including Matrix management with a Board of Directors, Workshops on Organizational Culture and Strategy/Leadership Styles, Managing Change, Consultancy and Facilitation Skills programmes and management Development programmes. But his particular areas of interest are managing change at a personal and organizational level, strategy and leadership, managing people and personal development. In addition, Andrew tutors on several of Roffey's open programmes and is Programme Director for *Assessment/Development Centre Design* and *The Enterprising Manager*. He has been Course Director for the Self Managed Learning MBA as well as a Set Adviser on this programme. Andrew has carried out assessment and development work in the United States, Canada, Central/Eastern Europe and Asia.

Alan Cook *(Team building)* recently joined Smythe Dorward Lambert, the Communication Management Consultancy, as a Senior Consultant, specializing in team dynamics and work relationships. He has worked mainly in the public sector – initially as a Personnel Manager in local government, then as a Training and Education Manager at a large London teaching hospital, and finally as an Organization and Management Consultant with the Salomons Centre. While working in the NHS, in conjunction with Salomons, he developed 'The Capable Team', a model of team competencies used for both assessing and developing teams. An experienced group facilitator, he has undertaken a considerable number of team development events at all levels within organizations and with many types of teams, and particularly enjoys finding new and creative ways of working with groups and managers. He also carries out many formal assessments of managers and other staff in both selection and development processes, and is a qualified and experienced therapeutic counsellor.

John Courtis, FCSA, MIPD *(Recruitment; Interviewing)* has been in management search or selection for 20 years. He trained as a chartered accountant, was commissioned in the RAF and then spent five years in Ford Motor Co., before joining Reed Executive in 1967. He was then with EAL for a four-year period before setting up what is now Courtis and McManus in 1974. He has been active in management education since 1972, for the Institute of Chartered Accountants in England and Wales and other bodies and is the author of ten books on management, profit improvement, public relations and recruitment. He is now senior partner of Courtis and McManus and a former chairman both of Deeko plc and the recruitment trade association, FRES. In his spare time he writes more books, searches for the ideal motor car of yesteryear and collects interesting cameras.

Neil Garrod *(Financial information and management)* is currently Professor of Financial Analysis and Head of the Department of Accounting and Finance at the University of Glasgow. He teaches and researches in the general field of accounting, finance and financial analysis. His publications, in both book and research paper form, span issues relating to segmental reporting, accounting regulation and market-based accounting research in general. He is currently working extensively in accounting and regulatory issues in the emerging economies of central and eastern Europe with particular emphasis on issues of corporate governance, and co-edited *Accounting in Transition*, published in

1996, in which the issues of accounting regulatory development in the countries of central and eastern Europe are examined. He holds a visiting professorship at the University of Ljubljana, Slovcnija and has held visiting professorships at Union College in New York, University of British Columbia and Moscow State University. He gained his B.Sc. and Ph.D. from the Department of Management Sciences at the University of Manchester Institute of Science and Technology in 1975 and 1980 respectively, and, before moving to Glasgow, he was Professor of Financial Analysis at the University of Wales, Bangor and lecturer in Business Finance at the University of Wales, Aberystwyth.

Norman Gealy *(Helping people learn)* has over twenty years' experience in training and in assessment. A founding partner of Moloney & Gealy, a London-based consultancy which provides advice to and develops systems for private companies, professional firms, institutions (from trade associations to learned societies), and government departments, he continues to under-take project work, as well as writing and speaking, and takes responsibility for staff development within the firm. He graduated in Experimental Psychology from Oxford University and, while working in New York, studied Educational Measurement at Columbia University. He is a member of the Institute of Personnel and Development and a Chartered Psychologist.

John Gregory *(Meetings)* is enjoying his fourth career – that of a management selection consultant. He joined the accountancy profession straight from school and later joined mechanical handling engineers, Lansing Bagnall Ltd, as a junior accountant. National Service led to a Short Service Commission in the Royal Army Pay Corps and this, indirectly, to a second career in management education because his three years in the army were spent in the RAPC Headquarter Training Unit. A developing interest in training led to him joining the Management School at Portsmouth Polytechnic where he stayed nine years taking leave in 1967 to study for an M.Sc. in Management Control at Bath University. In 1972, he joined the Institute of Chartered Accountants in England and Wales as Assistant Director Post Qualifying Training, becoming Director, Professional Development Services in 1980. Five years later he became a partner in management selection consultants, John Courtis and Partners, and a year later opened their Milton Keynes office, which he managed for four years before joining Breckenridge Consultants Ltd. He is now Chairman of this company.

Feona Hamilton *(Managing information)* is an expert in electronic publishing and corporate information strategy. She is the author of four books and many articles on these and related subjects. She has also designed and run training courses. Feona Hamilton is currently a freelance writer and consultant. She is a Director of the Electronic Information Publishers' Group.

Dr Peter Honey *(People skills)* is a chartered psychologist who works as a   *xix* management consultant. He worked for Ford Motor Company and British Airways before becoming a freelance in 1969. He specializes in anything to do with people's behaviour and its consequences, and divides his work between designing courses, writing and publishing. He has written widely on behavioural topics in over fifty publications. His books include *Face to Face Skills*, *The Manual of Learning Styles*, *Solving People-Problems*, *Improve Your People Skills*, *Problem People ... and How To Manage Them* and *The Manual of Learning Opportunities*. He has advised on the contents of many training films and written the accompanying booklets. He features in the Video Arts production *Talking about Behaviour*. He is an Associate Professor with the International Management Centre, a Fellow of the Institute of Management Consultants and the Institute of Training and Development. He is a chartered psychologist with the British Psychological Society and a member of the Association for Management Education and Development.

Nicholas Jeffery *(Negotiating)* is MBA Programme Director at Roffey Park Management Institute. He has held senior positions at British Airways in industrial relations, customer service and management development, before moving to be Managing Consultant of a training consultancy specializing in sales and customer service. He holds an MBA from Bath University School of Management and is studying for a Ph.D. in Critical Management with the University of Lancaster. Currently, he teaches and consults in strategy, organizational change and negotiating with a variety of blue-chip clients.

Jessica Levant *(Motivation)* has spent the past ten years as Managing Partner of The Pennybank Partnership, a management development and training consultancy based in London, where she has been creating and delivering training and development to managers over a cross-section of industries and sectors in Europe and America. Prior to setting up her own business, Jess was a staff development specialist in New York, working for the local government department where she had previously gained her first-hand management experience. She was also the first Chair of the Central London Branch of the Institute of Personnel and Development. Having co-authored two books – *Marketing the Training Function* (Kogan Page, 1993) and *Managing Your Career* (Institute of Health Service Management, 1994) – and written *Selecting the Right People* (Technical Communications Publishing, 1995). She is currently writing *Don't Waste Money on Training and Development!* (working title), which will be published by Gulf Publications (Texas) in 1998.

John Lewington *(Project management)* is a faculty member of the John E. Simon School of Business, Maryville University, St Louis, Missouri, where he teaches marketing and management courses. He originally trained with the Ever Ready Company (GB) while completing a degree in production engineering. His early career focused on solving operations management problems, which included three years working for General Motors (AC Delco) in project planning, evaluation and control. In 1979 he gained an M.Sc. in Business

Administration from the City University Business School. Subsequently, he became Director of Management Studies at Harrow College of Higher Education (now the University of Westminster). In 1986 he moved to the United States and founded Datafax of St Louis, a database marketing company, which provides marketing and consulting services to a wide variety of businesses. His doctoral research into the structure of database marketing systems was recently published in the *Journal of Marketing Management*. He has designed and taught a wide variety of postgraduate business courses in the United States, Canada, and in the United Kingdom for the Open University, Westminster University and London School of Economics. These courses were adopted for in-house training by such leading companies as Harrods, Kodak, McDonnell Douglas and Maritz.

The late **Mike Megranahan** *(Counselling in the workplace)* was a Director of the Employee Advisory Resource (EAR), based in Uxbridge, which is an employee assistance programme established in the United Kingdom in 1981. He had worked in personnel, consultancy and with a number of counselling agencies. A chartered psychologist and Associate Fellow of the British Psychological Society, he was also editor of *Employee Counselling Today* and past Chair of the Counselling at Work Division.

Victor Newman *(Creativity)* is Head of Organization Development at The CIM Institute, Cranfield University. He consults within leading organizations, facilitating and developing teams to lead, manage and learn from implementing change in their own organizations. His implementation experience spans aerospace, electronics, manufacturing engineering and service organizations, and he has also worked with new forms of organization, including alliance partnerships and joint ventures. He is interested in implementation psychology and developing process leadership in process-based organizations. His first book, *Problem-Solving for Results*, encapsulating some of his experiences, was published by Gower in 1995.

Bill Rees *(Financial information and management)* holds a Chair of Accountancy at the University of Glasgow. After qualifying as a Chartered Accountant and working with Deloitte, Haskins and Sells, he completed an MBA at the University of Liverpool. Subsequent academic appointments included the Universities of Sydney, Kingston, Newcastle and Strathclyde. His lecturing interests cover corporate finance and financial accounting with a specialist interest in financial analysis. The author of *Financial Analysis* (Prentice Hall, 1995), which is now in its second edition, his published academic papers, which have been presented at British, European and American finance and accounting conferences, include studies of accounting choice, earnings forecasting, earnings/returns association tests, valuation models, investment analysts' meetings and IPOs. His ongoing research interests encompass studies of earnings forecasting, accounting choice, foreign exchange exposure, IPOs and valuation models.

Dr John W. Rogers *(Managing your time; Dealing with problem staff)* is a Development Consultant at the Lloyds TSB Group Management Centre in Solihull, and specializes in designing training and development initiatives that lead to company and individual change. He currently leads internally delivered programmes progressing to corporate membership of such organizations as the Institute of Personnel and Development and the Chartered Institute of Marketing. His training and research interests include balancing work/personal/family commitments, what makes successful people successful, designing new flexible careers over the age of 50, and supporting staff into becoming 'assets rather than costs'. He is a Fellow of the Institute of Personnel and Development.

Tim Russell *(Performance appraisal)* is an international management and training consultant advising companies in three important areas: training and development of managers in human problem solving and interpersonal skills; training and development of those staff responsible for training; and setting up customer service training strategies. He consults with top public and private companies, as well as with Institutes of Management worldwide from his offices in London, Malta, Singapore and Australia. The originator of the 'Microskills' system of training managers in interpersonal skills, he has written books and articles and produced a number of videos on management topics. Additionally, he has lectured widely and has appeared on television and radio. His past employment has included Group Management Development Manager for the Berec (Ever Ready) Group of companies, Chief Training Officer for the British Association for Commercial and Industrial Education (BACIE), and chemical engineer with the Esso Petroleum Company Ltd. He is a graduate in Psychology and in Chemical Engineering.

Brian Sanders *(Speaking in public)* has been involved in maximizing the power of the spoken word all his working life. He trained as an actor and toured the British Isles, France, Belgium and Egypt with the Donald Wolfit Shakespeare Company. He left the theatre in 1954 to take up a career in education. He is a qualified teacher of speech, drama and English and for several years was head of the Speech and Drama Department of a constituent college of London University. He first broadcast in 1960 when he wrote and narrated programmes on acting, the theatre and Shakespeare. From 1970 to 1979 he wrote and presented a drama programme for BBC Schools Radio. Nowadays he broadcasts regularly on radio as an actor and narrator. He has extensive experience of teaching professional people in all aspects on communication and presentation. He runs courses on effective speaking and on speaking professionally through the media in which he deals in a practical way with interviews and talks on TV and radio, the phone-in, and discussions. He runs one-, two- and three-day practical workshop courses for the Industrial Society, the Institute of Chartered Accountants, Touche Ross, the CEGB, the Electricity Council, firms of solicitors and actuaries, and the Police Federation. Since

1985 he has devised and run courses for several UK marketing companies. He lectures to large conferences and small groups.

Barbara Smolny-Kostrewski, M.Sc., Ph.D. *(Information Science)* is now a freelance writer and consultant based in London. She has an academic background in university teaching and research, where her principal contributions have been in the field of IT applications in medicine and pharmacy, relating, in particular, to knowledge representation. She has been instrumental in the development of several systems that are currently operational worldwide, and which have benefited many postgraduate students both in Britain and overseas, and was a member of an EEC/AIM funded consortium carrying out research to develop a prescribing system for medicines (OPADE). Sponsored by the British Council, she has lectured and consulted in Poland and Mexico, and she has held a visiting faculty in the United States. As well as publishing and presenting numerous articles and papers, she has been editor of the scientific journal, *Medical Informatics*, and is a member of various professional committees.

The late **Andrew M. Stewart** *(Coping with stress)* was Managing Director of Informed Choice, an organization which applied psychology to business and industry. His activities ranged from diagnosing the characteristics of effective performance, and conducting training needs analyses and employee attitude surveys, to personnel and management selection, performance appraisal, and the identification and development of potential managers and entrepreneurs. He graduated in psychology from Aberdeen University, lectured at Surrey University for two years, and then held personnel and management development posts with IBM. He was then seconded to the Institute of Manpower Studies at Sussex University, where he remained until 1977, developing the research interests which underpinned his later work. He was Managing Director of Macmillan Stewart Ltd until 1986. He published over 40 papers, eleven chapters for various handbooks, and six books, covering assessment centres, performance appraisal, management development, poor performance, and repertory grid.

Richard Storey *(Influencing)* is Director of Sigma Training Services and specializes in communication training, which covers influencing, selling, presenting, interviewing, writing and reading. Originally a systems analyst, he moved to the newspaper industry, starting as a salesman and holding a variety of increasingly senior commercial positions up to Deputy Advertisement Manager, with a team of over 150. His first book, *The Art of Persuasive Communication*, was published by Gower in 1997.

Peter Walker *(Decision making and problem solving)* is a partner at Walker Associates. He has previously held posts of European Training Manager at Texas Instruments, and Manager Organization Development at Rank Xerox. He specializes in providing training and consultancy to organizations in *xxiii* problem-solving approaches, the management of change, people development, and the introduction of total quality management. Much of his work has been with multinational companies, helping country managers and the training function to put in place quality improvement strategies, train in-company staff as instructors, and develop internal consultants capable of providing ongoing support to the organization. As a Chartered Engineer he brings management and business experience to the training function in fields such as technical sales, product support, and services management.

Krystyna Weinstein *(Writing; Communication)* is a freelance trainer and consultant, specializing in issues around non-communication. She has an extensive background as a writer and editor, and has worked in business and other fields – experience which she combines with a knowledge of organizational issues gained while on the staff of Manchester Business School, and an interest in action learning and learner-centred development. Her current work includes editing and writing, and she is a coordinating editor of *Organisations and People*, the journal of the Association for Management Education and Development. She also runs communication and writing workshops, as well as action-learning programmes. Her two most recent books are, *Writing Works: A Manager's Alphabet*, and *Action Learning: A Journey in Discovery and Development*, both published in 1995.

Dr H. Beric Wright *(Managing your health)* retired from his executive role in BUPA in 1983 where he had been Chairman of their Medical Centre and Hospital companies, and a Governor. He retained a non-executive role for a further three years. In 1958, Dr Wright had joined the Institute of Directors to start their medical research unit and in 1964 this became the first specialized executive health centre in Europe. It merged with BUPA in 1970 and has grown steadily ever since. Dr Wright qualified in 1941 from University College and Hospital and spent his RAMC years doing operational research as an applied physiologist. He then trained as a surgeon and worked overseas for Shell International. The early work at the IOD taught him that the diseases people get are largely related to the lives they lead and that a holistic or psychosomatic approach is essential. Dr Wright is a Fellow of University College, London, and for many years was involved in the problems of housing the elderly through the Abbeyfield Society. He was also a founder member of the Pre-Retirement Association. Since 1960 he has been in the forefront of informing the public about medical problems through the media.

Part I
MANAGING YOURSELF

Introduction: understanding yourself and your skills needs as a manager

Among the most bewildering causes of unemployment are shortages of skills. There are plenty of people who want to work and there are people who want to employ workers. But the posts and the people do not match – because the people do not have the skills the employers want.

As business moves into the twenty-first century, the skills that managers need are changing too. A mismatch between posts and people is increasingly likely, especially for people in a post which changes when they do not. In the all too common case of companies that offer no management training, your future is indeed in your own hands.

A personal inventory of your current skills, their strengths and weaknesses, and of the skills demanded currently by your job, will provide a start. But do look ahead to where you think you and your job may be going, and assess your skills needs for the future. Then it is time to get to work on plugging the gaps you see, and polishing up your poorer skills.

Part I of this *Handbook* focuses on your personal skills. Chapter 1 is a key chapter on management self-development – what it is, why it is important, and a review of the main methods available for self-development. Do read this chapter first, before dipping into the rest of the book.

The other chapters in Part I offer guidance on fundamental skills for the manager: managing your time, which provides a review of the main time management systems and methods; managing the information that threatens to overwhelm us all, with guidance on assessing your own information needs and how to control the information when you've got it; and two chapters on the other side of the coin: managing the production of information – effective writing, which aims to help you save time and effort in producing effective written material, and effective speaking, which treats not only the planning and preparation of the material of your presentation but also the technical details of delivery and presentation.

Management is a demanding profession and many managers find that the lifestyle can be damaging in many ways. Dr Beric Wright in Chapter 7 maintains that it is not only possible but necessary that managers manage their own health to achieve a high level of wellbeing, and points out both the dangers and some ways to survive them. Chapter 8 focuses on the effects of stress, its various symptoms and causes, and provides guidelines for its management, both by the individual and by the organization.

1 Management self-development

Andrew Constable

As the first chapter in this new third edition of the *Handbook of Management Skills*, this chapter takes on a particular significance, for it could be viewed as a heading for all the subsequent chapters. I shall therefore start by defining the term 'management self-development' as a basis for my argument, and I shall then move on to discuss why the subject of self-development is so important for managers in today's, and indeed tomorrow's, work environment. Finally, I shall outline some of the specific approaches that one can use to develop oneself.

WHAT IS MANAGEMENT SELF-DEVELOPMENT?

Management self-development is an approach through which individuals – rather than their manager or the organization or indeed anyone else – are the key drivers in developing themselves. That is not to say that those other parties mentioned do not have a role to play in the development of the individual, but simply that development is driven *primarily* by the individual, while others have a supportive and enabling role. The key concept in considering management self-development is the notion of *responsibility*. Certainly in the past the organization has assumed primary responsibility for developing individuals, but thinking changed during the 1980s, and in the 1990s the majority of organizations now expect individuals to drive their own development. This change has come as quite a shock to many managers, particularly in those organizations which have a history of providing structured opportunities for learning for their staff.

People working in smaller, more entrepreneurial organizations may already be applying some of the principles of self-development without necessarily realizing that that is what they are doing. Thus self-development is much more than just a skill: it is more akin to a philosophy and mind-set that the individual adopts. As such, it is not something that can be learned quickly and it will often require considerable perseverance and effort on the part of the individual, supported by the organization in a variety of ways, to bring about this evolution.

In this sense, management self-development can embrace a range of individual approaches. These might include open learning, action learning, accelerated learning, distance-learning courses, self-managed learning and, indeed, more conventional approaches to developing managers. An individual who is comfortable with and has absorbed the principles of self-development is likely to be able to make good use of a number of different learning methods, and we will look at each of these approaches later in this chapter.

WHY IS SELF-DEVELOPMENT IMPORTANT?

Having defined self-development for managers, we must now ask: Why have a chapter on self-development, and why should it be the first chapter in this publication? To answer these questions, we should look first at the external or *environmental* influences on organizations that have encouraged self-development. These factors include the impact of new technology, globilization, pressures to produce short-term profitability, and rising expectations of consumers and customers. For many organizations the impact of these and other forces has caused them to reduce the number of their employees and cut down the number of layers in the organization. There is much talk today of flatter organizational structures, one of the consequences of which is the disappearance of some of the traditional means of motivating employees. Promotion, for example, was long considered one of the chief ways of rewarding successful employees, but if there are no longer as many layers within the organization, where do successful people go?

Pressure to reduce costs has also caused many organizations to move away from what we might refer to as the 'sheep dip' approach to management development, whereby all people at certain levels in the organization went through the same management development processes. The emphasis has switched to individuals identifying their own development needs and then looking personally for suitable ways to satisfy those needs. The more enlightened organizations will of course provide resources – for example, finance, time, programmes – as appropriate to support individuals in their pursuit of self-development. Moreover, the principles outlined in this chapter apply both inside and outside the working environment. Individuals who have already taken these principles to heart are probably applying them in all areas of their life. Indeed, for many people in employment, the boundaries between their work and their life outside work are becoming increasingly blurred.

HOW CAN I GO ABOUT DEVELOPING MYSELF?

Open learning

Of the range of methods one can use to develop oneself as a manager, we will look first at *open learning*. This approach offers easy and open access to a whole range of learning materials, which might include books, journals, audio and video tapes, information files, CD-ROM, and so forth. Many organizations have set up open-learning centres or, as they are sometimes called, *learning resource centres*. Such facilities need not be particularly expensive to establish and can expand over a period of time. All that is required to establish an open-learning or learning-resource centre is a dedicated area of space in which materials can be housed. If this is not feasible, resources can be provided via information technology (IT). Individuals can then access these resources through their PCs.

Action learning

The second approach to examine is *action learning*, which originated from Reg Revans's work in the coal industry. Action learning requires a group of managers to meet together at regular intervals over a period of time. In their meetings they tackle real-life work projects, and work together to help each other complete these projects and to learn in the process. This particular approach was born out of Revans's dissatisfaction with the content, relevance and applicability of many training programmes current at the time. The key vehicle in action learning is the *learning set*. A learning set is different from other groups that may meet in organizations – for example, committees, project teams, task forces – since in this case, learning is given a higher priority than in these other groups.

Accelerated learning

The third approach is *accelerated learning*. As implied in the name, the key to this approach is to speed up the process of learning for individuals, which, in simple terms, is achieved by appealing in the process to all the senses of the individuals. Very often, learning processes only appeal to one sense, or one sense dominates in the process. An example of this would be an individual attempting to impart a great deal of knowledge to a group of people simply by talking to them. Those who are able to absorb much information in this way will find the method highly suitable for themselves, but there are many others who require different kinds of stimulation and instruction. Thus pictures, diagrams and the use of visual aids may appeal to some people; others may need to participate actively in processes in order to fully understand them, and in these instances, rehearsing situations can be of enormous benefit.

Coupled with this appeal to the different senses is the challenge to the individual to use different forms of intelligence, which is based on the work of

7

Howard Gardner, Professor of Education at Harvard University. In the 1980s, Gardner published ground-breaking research that identified seven different forms of intelligence. This study questioned our conventional understanding which tends to view intelligence as a unitary concept. The seven forms of intelligence which Gardner identified were as follows: linguistic, mathematical/logical, visual, spatial, physical, musical, interpersonal and intrapersonal. The principal exponent of accelerated learning techniques in the United Kingdom is Colin Rose, who readily acknowledges his debt to Gardner. Rose has applied the principles very practically in his work in developing accelerated-learning language courses.

Distance learning

Distance learning courses have now become very widespread, and most people have an understanding of what this approach entails, namely, studying at a distance from the supplier of the course materials. The pioneer and one of the leaders in this field is the Open University, although there are now a number of other good providers of distance learning in the United Kingdom. The chief advantages of the approach are that it enables individuals to study at a place, a time and a pace which suits them.

Self-managed learning

Lastly, we come to *self-managed learning* (SML), which, in a way, combines the best elements of the other approaches mentioned above.

1 Open-learning materials are often available as resources to participants on a self-managed learning programme.
2 As in action learning, the key element in the process is the learning set.
3 SML encourages individuals to use different approaches to learning and to present evidence in different forms; there are thus strong connections with the principles of accelerated learning.
4 In an SML programme, much of the learning takes place between learning-set meetings; this learning is carried out at a distance and in this respect resembles the distance-learning approach.

However, one additional element in SML is the use of *learning contracts*, which were first used in the United States. A learning contract is primarily a series of goals or objectives that an individual will pursue over a period of time. In some organizations learning contracts are referred to as *personal development plans* (PDPs), and in the United Kingdom, some higher-education institutions have been making use of learning contracts or PDPs for many years. These contracts enable an individual to focus specifically on what he or she wants to learn.

Another key element of the SML approach is that individuals use on-the-job projects as vehicles for learning. This facilitates the *transfer* of learning, which is often a problem in management development programmes.

Many organizations are using this self-managed learning approach or a variant of it. Although it has been widely copied and imitated, the term was first coined by Ian Cunningham.

This is by no means an exhaustive list of the range of approaches which fall under the umbrella of self-development; others, for example, are self-directed learning and self-organized learning. The essential point, however, is to recognize what all these approaches have in common: namely, they all require the individual to take charge of and be responsible for his or her own development.

FOR WHOM IS MANAGEMENT SELF-DEVELOPMENT RELEVANT?

The term 'management self-development' itself implies that management self-development is relevant for managers, but are they the only group? My response to this question is a resounding *no*! I believe that the principles of self-development are relevant to practically everyone. They are as applicable to chief executives as they are to individuals beginning their careers in an organization, as relevant to someone reaching the end of their working life as they are to someone just starting out. Indeed, it could be argued that the earlier the individual embraces these principles, the more he or she is likely to achieve in life. Therefore these principles are certainly pertinent to the education and upbringing of children. Colin Rose and his colleagues have produced excellent materials to be used by parents during the first few years of a child's life. Once adopted they are likely to yield all sorts of unforeseen benefits.

At a higher level there are links also with Peter Senge's *five disciplines*. In particular, there is a connection with the discipline of *personal mastery*, which is a lifelong process in which individuals seek to master a particular subject. Though it is a journey on which one never reaches the destination, the process enables the individual to focus his or her energy. A helpful analogy may be with the professional musician or professional sportsperson. Both will put in many hours of practice each day to improve their level of performance, and by most people's standards both will be regarded as supreme performers in their field. However, this does not mean that the musician plays every single note correctly or that the professional sportsperson never makes a mistake. The value of these comparisons is that they emphasize the importance of practice and perseverance, two key principles in management self-development.

AREAS TO WHICH AN INDIVIDUAL MIGHT APPLY SELF-DEVELOPMENT PRINCIPLES

First – and perhaps the most obvious – is the area of the *intellect*. This area can be developed through a variety of means: courses, books, audio and video tapes, and journals are just some examples.

9

However, there are other equally important areas of the individual that will benefit from self-development. The *emotions*, for example, have traditionally been neglected in favour of the intellect, and yet emotional blocks are often stronger and more difficult to overcome than intellectual ones. This is a subject which arises frequently on our programmes at Roffey Park. Then there is the *physical* part of ourselves to which we can apply the same principles. Fitness training became very popular in the 1980s and it is now widely accepted that we should keep our bodies in shape as well as our minds. Some people have very demanding and vigorous fitness routines, while others may prefer a more gentle regime. Nevertheless, anyone who has ever embarked on a fitness programme of any description will know the importance of regular practice and discipline if it is to be worthwhile. Finally, there is the *spiritual* area to which an increasing number of people are paying attention. There are many ways in which this can be accessed: for example, through reading, music, prayer, gentle physical exercise and meditation.

By attending to these four different dimensions of the self, therefore, the individual is likely to develop into a much more balanced person. It is a holistic approach to development that produces benefits of greater substance and permanence.

HOW ORGANIZATIONS ARE APPLYING THIS APPROACH IN PRACTICE

One method that is used frequently is to have a launch or start-up event focused on the principles of learning and self-development. As an example, I was recently involved on behalf of an international company in running a programme with the title, 'Learning to Learn'. The programme lasted three days and drew participants from countries all over the world. The content of the programme included such topics as 'What is active learning?' and 'What makes an active learner?' For reference, Kolb's pioneering work on how adults learn and the learning cycle is a valuable piece of theory to support these ideas, while the learning styles questionnaire developed by two Englishmen, Peter Honey and Alan Mumford, identifies individual's preferred learning styles and employs language which is easily accessible and understandable for managers. At this launch event individuals began to put together a learning contract which will cover a period of approximately one year. This contract is developed against a backdrop of management competencies that were themselves developed by the organization a few years ago and which provide a focus for self-development.

In addition, participants each have a personal development programme handbook that provides materials covering the principles of learning and self-development and the management competencies. An interesting additional dimension to this programme is that the participants have each been allocated an individual development budget which they are able to make use of to further their learning and to demonstrate evidence of it. The programme also includes work in challenge and support groups to assist each individual's development. This is a variant of the learning set idea mentioned earlier. Finally, each of the participants on the programme have access to a mentor provided by Roffey Park to aid them with their development over a longer period of time. This is just one example of how an organization is encouraging self-development in its people.

WHAT ARE THE CHALLENGES?

Any organization wishing to further self-development in its people faces a number of challenges. For example, there may be a natural and understandable resistance from long-serving employees for whom training and development opportunities have been planned and structured by the organization in the past. Suddenly they are presented with an approach which demands far more from them personally. It is not simply an approach which is aimed at changing people's language in the organization or, indeed, modifying their behaviour or adding to their skills. It is a far more fundamental process which is targeted at their attitude and outlook on the world, attributes which are far more difficult to influence and change and therefore require more time. However, although the process demands much more effort on the part of the individual, in turn it produces greater rewards.

WHAT BRINGS SUCCESS?

What are some of the ways which offer the best chance of success with this approach? Certainly the use of a variety of the methods available to help people learn will increase the chances of success, and this is linked to tapping the multiple intelligences referred to earlier. One of these is the interpersonal intelligence, which has particular importance here because it can be employed to ensure that self-development is not a selfish activity (an occasional misconception of the nature of self-development). The interpersonal intelligence can be tapped through learning sets, challenge and support groups, and through the use of mentors. Any of these methods will drastically increase the chances of success. The use of learning budgets, development handbooks, and access to a learning resource centre are also important ingredients. Any means of providing support while not taking away responsibility can be considered useful.

REWARDS AND BENEFITS

What, therefore, are the rewards and benefits of management self-development? A long list could be drawn up of what individuals believe they have acquired using this approach, but I consider that the main benefits are:

1   Individuals who have embraced the principles of self-development appear more positive in outlook. They have what is sometimes referred to as a 'can do' attitude to their work.

2   They have high levels of confidence which stands them in good stead when faced with new challenges.
3   Self-development encourages the more entrepreneurial nature of people, which is a quality in increasing demand in organizations both small and large.
4   Individuals develop greater resilience that enables them to cope better with stressful situations and to bounce back quickly from setbacks.
5   Self-development encourages the spirit of *interdependence* in people. This is different from *independence*, which implies a more self-centred approach to work and life. It is also different from *dependence*, which describes the kind of relationship that many employees have had with their organization in the past. The notion of interdependence suggests that we are connected to each other but in a mutual relationship. We can help each other to learn and develop more effectively.
6   The principles and practice of self-development help individuals achieve what Maslow called, in his *Hierarchy of Needs*, the level of *self-actualization*: that is, fulfilling oneself and achieving one's potential.

For these reasons, it is well worth taking time to reflect on the ideas set out in this chapter, which I hope will also serve as a useful framework within which to consider the other chapters of this book.

FURTHER READING

Constable, A., 'Self-managed learning', in S. Crainer (ed.), *Financial Times Handbook of Management*, FT/Pitman, 1995.
Covey, S. R., *The Seven Habits of Highly Effective People*, Simon & Schuster, 1992.
Cunningham, I., *The Wisdom of Strategic Learning*, McGraw-Hill, 1994.
Gardner, H., *Frames of Mind: The theory of multiple intelligences*, Fontana, 1993.
Honey, P. and Mumford, A., *The Manual of Learning Styles*, 3rd edn, Honey, 1992.
Kolb, D. A., *Experiential Learning*, Prentice Hall, 1985.
Revans, R., *Action Learning*, Chartwell Bratt, 1983.
Rose, C., *Accelerated Learning*, Accelerated Learning Systems, 1985.
Senge, P. M., *The Fifth Discipline*, Century Business, 1992.

2 Managing your time

John W. Rogers

This chapter presents guidelines that will help you manage your time better. Six proven approaches are described: setting objectives; planning systems; logging time use; individual behaviours; managerial styles; and visual reminders. The thinking behind each approach is discussed, followed by suggestions and self-assessment exercises. Your strategy in managing your time better is likely to involve a combination of several approaches, specific to your circumstances and preferred ways of 'getting things done'.

INTRODUCTION

Managing the time granted to us continues to be a serious dilemma in the late 1990s despite our apparent familiarity with many of the key practical ideas. Recently, colleagues have exclaimed vehemently to me:

> Yet more paperwork in the post; no wonder I can't get my *proper* job done – whatever happened to computers and the paperless office.

> I've had enough of that phone ringing today; I'm going to lock myself away in a quiet room and send the telephone on holiday.

> If I've told them once, I've told them a dozen times. When will they ever get it right?

> They want me to rewrite it yet again. Why can't they tell me what is wanted in the first place. Another weekend spent on the computer.

> Not another computer print out. Surely they could pick out the key indicators rather than present us with these pages and pages of gobbledygook figures.

Are you surrounded by people making similar comments – or indeed do you make them yourself? What is the common feature about these comments? It seems clear to me that they all relate to how we organize and manage our   *13* time. Furthermore, they say something about how we respect and value the time of other people.

Managing time often appears to be straightforward common sense; after all, it's simply a matter of setting objectives, determining priorities and carrying out tasks systematically. Or is it? If common sense was that common we would all be experts at managing our time, and the above exclamations would become extinct.

Time as a resource

First, we have to recognize that time is a unique resource when compared with other resources we are familiar with in business. Whatever your requirements for time, your race, gender, class and age, time is the limiting factor in achieving anything. You cannot hire it, buy it or rent it (although octogenarians may disagree), and you cannot obtain more than your allocation of 24 hours per day. In the economic sense, you cannot construct a marginal utility curve for time and its supply is totally inelastic – no matter how high the demand, the supply will not and cannot be increased. Time is totally perishable; it cannot be stored in freezers, tins or deposit accounts, or slowed down as with coastal erosion. Time is totally irreplaceable, unlike plastics for steels, bread for potatoes and automated systems for human labour.

Biologically we appear to be ill-equipped to manage the passage of time. Deprived of our main senses and isolated in a darkened room, we quickly lose track of the rate of time passing. Whilst boredom apparently extends time ('When is this meeting ever going to end'), excitement and deadlines compress time ('Phew, it's four o'clock already, we must get these out in tonight's post'). Paradoxically, despite unemployment levels still being comparatively high and the predicted promise during the late 1980s of an age of leisure, many managers still work unnecessarily long hours, often suffering the physical and physiological consequences in the battle 'to get things done'.

Increasingly, it appears that most people are faced with the problem of either having far too much to do in the time available or far too little to do. Creating a satisfying time balance between work, home/family/friends, and personal issues is a worthwhile and attainable goal.

The changing world and time

The context of managerial work continues to change rapidly. The previous cosy paradigm of 'a job for life' has for many been replaced with increased job insecurity and fragmentation as companies fight to remain lean and competitive. So, in addition to managing our time well to carry out our existing roles, we need to adapt, learn and unlearn in order to cope effectively with this 'brave new world'. In the service sector many managers are now responsible for delivering increasing numbers of products and services which they offer to increasingly discerning customers in an increasingly competitive environment, while at the same time adapting to complex technological innovations. Such change is not unique – your context is likely to be changing just as dramatically. But in the final analysis, it is your responsibility to commit yourself to using time well to manage these changes and achieve success.

Surveys over the years show that managers often spend time poorly. Carrying out subordinates' work (lack of delegation) can account for up to 50 per cent of wasted managerial time. Managers constantly try to justify doing the familiar and less threatening activities they themselves *used* to do. The cost effects can be alarming. Consider a salary level of £30,000 per year, for example: this is equivalent to about £130 per day, or £15 per hour (excluding employment costs). The cost of time wasting through bad managerial practices can be readily computed into a fixed overhead, highlighting the need for good time use and often justifying initiatives for time management courses

Areas for improvement	Manager 1	Manager 2	Manager 3
1			
2			
3			
4			

Figure 2.1   Areas for improvement for three managers you know well   *15*

and other interventions. Managers often say to me, 'Oh, I haven't got time to do this or that' and 'I couldn't get round to it'. Rubbish! I suggest as adults we are all responsible for recognizing that we always do what is important to us. If watching the football, plus the extra time, plus the penalty shoot out, plus the experts' comments and – later in the evening – the edited highlights, is more important to you than unscrambling the action points from that two-day career planning workshop, then admit it to yourself. The managers' comments really mean, 'I had other priorities I preferred to spend my time on'.

Exercise: improving managerial effectiveness

Think of three managers you know well. Using the matrix shown in Figure 2.1 insert at least four areas for improvement for each manager that you believe would enable them to operate more effectively. Then look through and analyse your entries. It is most likely that you have included a high proportion of matters relating to time management – organizing themselves, running better meetings, not putting things off, finding time to consult with others. On the other hand, technical subject knowledge is likely to be less well represented – if at all. So the first main message about managing time is that we sometimes need to work on and develop our time managing skills to a much greater extent than our technical skills or knowledge. For most managers, too much energy is spent refining the latter.

SETTING OBJECTIVES

Goals

What are your lifetime goals? Alan Lakein, a time management guru, claims that you should be very clear about them. Writing them down while being selfishly honest with yourself can not only help you to discover what you really want to achieve in the longer term, but will also generate inspiration and motivation, and give meaning to your day-by-day and minute-by-minute use of time. Lifetime goals are related to our visions, dreams, purposes, missions and basic beliefs about what is worth spending time on. Questions that can focus your thinking upon the long term use of time are:

- How would you like to spend the next five years?
- What do you want to achieve in the next five years?
- If you knew now that you would be struck by lightning six months from today, how would you spend your time until then?

Remember, goal setting is an ongoing activity which needs regular recording, updating, prioritizing and reviewing for both long-term and short-term goals. Do it at least every six months. And write the goals down. Show them to others if you need that extra commitment.

Lifegoals Planning – the ultimate exercise

Please prepare your obituary by completing the spaces below. Your entries can include ambitions achieved so far as well as those still to be achieved.

Earlier today the death was announced of _____ *(first name or name you would like to be known as) at the age of* _____ *years in the presence of* _____ *(any person[s] who would be present at your death) in* _____ *(where you would most like to be living at the time).*

_____ (name again) worked as a _____ (your main career or area of work) and achieved the position of _____ (how far you expect to get up the career ladder).

_____ *'s main achievements/enjoyments outside work included*

_____

_____

_____ will always be remembered for _____

_____

_____

Figure 2.2   A lifegoals planning exercise based upon a fantasy obituary

When developing your goals, objectives or key task areas, try to be aware of any inconsistencies or paradoxes: for example, becoming managing director is not usually compatible with having unlimited time with the children or with that new mountain bike. Similarly, to be liked by everyone in the office is not usually compatible with having strong opinions which you voice regularly. Look at your own lifetime goals for any such incompatibilities, but do not stop yourself from starting to achieve lifetime ambitions.

Some people say such questions are difficult to address as there is so much external change now that the future is too unpredictable – so it's probably not worth the effort. There is strong evidence that people who set long-term goals feel more successful and happy with life. One Alan Lakein video starts with a world-weary executive shaving and saying to himself in the mirror: 'I'm 52 years old. Whatever happened to my life. I spend it commuting, going to meetings, commuting again, eating and sleeping.' Clearly this person has no long-term goals, or those ambitions have been blunted. If you are not convinced, spend a few minutes with the obituary exercise in Figure 2.2 and share your results with family, friends and other managers.

Key task areas

Key task areas (KTAs) are primarily applicable to your working life, but they also have applications in other areas of your life. Essentially, KTAs are those areas of work that you 'need to spend your time and energy on in order to be effective and efficient in what you achieve'. So how do you establish your own KTAs? First, you need some information about what you do and how you do it: time logs (see page 29) can be useful in this respect. An alternative approach is to generate your own KTAs: this is a preferred approach for people who are more future oriented, and maybe lack the tolerance and analytical discipline needed for most approaches based on time logs.

Your KTAs can evolve through consideration of the following check list of business-oriented questions:

- Why is the company (or am I) in business?
- What is it in business for?
- What do we need to do to remain in business?
- Where do we need to be in two and five years time?
- How can we get there?
- What parts of the company can I influence directly?
- What are my department's objectives?
- What are my objectives?
- How do my, the department and the company objectives link together?

You may have more personal or local sources to develop KTAs, such as:

- Job descriptions, but beware that these may well be out of date or too static, and may, in any case, say little about your priorities.
- Appraisals and assessment interviews, which indicate potential skill strengths and limitations in achieving goals.
- Colleagues, who will help you understand how you use your time in achieving tasks, and let you know how they think you *should* spend your time.
- Company goals, from annual reports, house journals, top management, and so on.
- Professional journals and databases, which contain factual information about companies and managers in similar fields to yourself .
- Your own life plans, and what you really want to achieve in life through work and other activities.

In many large companies, annual objective setting is part of a performance-related pay (PRP) system, where agreement with the line manager of objectives covering the whole job is essential in order to make a future assessment as to whether goals were attained.

Examples of key task areas

Ideally, key task areas should be results oriented, cover all the tasks you do (or should do), be vividly and concisely expressed, and be of a manageable number (usually about six to eight). As an example, consider a typical assistant manager or supervisor. Typical key areas in such jobs are likely to be based upon these factors:

- Management of staff (staff relations, managerial effectiveness, training and development of others, motivation of staff, coaching, delegation, health and safety).
- Finance administration (budgets, local profitability, costing, income, statistics, routines).
- Clients/customers/accounts (large–small, develop–maintain).
- New business development (new and existing customers).
- Local market information (competitors' performance, business sector developments).
- Premises (building maintenance, equipment, security).
- Internal co-ordination/communications (head office, boss, peers).
- Special projects and big one-off tasks.
- Professional updating and continuous professional development (CPD).

Exercise: time spent in key task areas

This exercise will enable you to determine whether you are spending your time in the right areas. You are invited to develop your own KTAs and insert them in the boxes in the left-hand column of Figure 2.3. In more sophisticated settings you may well have job objectives – these can replace KTAs in most situations. Then complete the column headed 'Past' by inserting your current or recent time allocation as a percentage of total time. The 'Proposed' column should contain the percentage changes you wish to make, together with a deadline date for achieving the changes. The final column, 'Actual', allows you to review in, say, three months' time whether you have achieved the changes you intended.

PLANNING SYSTEMS

The need for information

Managers need a way of capturing, storing and having ready access to important information. In addition to a sensible working environment with well-labelled filing systems for static information, you will need some form of diary/organizer that is designed with both you and good time management principles in mind. The more recent advent of electronic organizers are now a powerful option. Most conventional diaries bought at the start of the year from stationers are inadequate for anything more than appointments.

Ask yourself, what kinds of data and information do I need to refer to on a regular basis? Your answer might include:

- Appointments and other dated deadlines.
- Tasks – 'to do' lists, in progress, and completed.

Key task area	Past	Proposed (state time deadline)	Actual

Figure 2.3   Percentages of time spent in key task areas (your own)

- Ideas and other sudden inspirations.
- Key task areas – keep them 'in sight and in mind'.
- Birthdays, school terms and household jobs.
- Maps and timetables.
- Booklists, films to see and places to visit.
- Expenses, budgets and other financial matters.
- Delegation, crises and interruption logs.

Choosing a diary

When choosing a diary ask yourself :

- What size do I want and need? Sizes range from large wall charts and yearly planners via desk diaries (about 20 by 25 cm) to pocket diaries (about 10 by 15 cm) – but beware of the difficulties caused by running two or more diaries and the perennial problem of double-booking and

Daily plan	Date
	MUST do
8	
9	
10	**Should do**
11	
12	
1	
2	**Could do**
3	
4	
5	

Figure 2.4   Typical planning forms for managing your time

21

	John	Gail	Colin	Helen	Barry	Daniel
Date						
Mon						
Tues						
Wed						
Thurs						
Fri						
Sat						
Sun						

Figure 2.4   **(continued)**

Weekly Plan	Wk No:
	Date:

	MUST do:
Mon	
Tues	**Should do:**
Wed	
Thurs	
Fri	**Could do:**
Sat	
Sun	

Figure 2.4   (continued)

	Wk no: Period:
Objectives of the week	1.
	2.
	3.
	4.

Mon			
Tues			
Wed			
Thurs			
Fri			

24　**Figure 2.4　(continued)**

	Month	

Objectives of the month	1.
	2.
	3.
	4.
	5.
	6.
	7.

1		17	
2		18	
3		19	
4		20	
5		21	
6		22	
7		23	
8		24	
9		25	
10		26	
11		27	
12		28	
13		29	
14		30	
15		31	
16			

Figure 2.4   (concluded)

missing appointments. Popular diary formats include one to seven days per page and one month per page. The increasing use of specially designed loose-leaf time management systems purchased from retail outlets helps you create a system that works for you; some typical page designs people find useful are shown in Figure 2.4. Your choice of size may be influenced by the amount and type of travelling you do in your job; many so-called pocket organizers will only fit into the largest of pockets and it can be inconvenient to have to carry a briefcase everywhere.

- What information do I need a diary or time planner to contain? Traditional diaries usually contain standard information that may or may not be useful – a map of the London Underground system or a listing of the addresses of Asian airports will be of little practical use to someone who travels almost exclusively in Scotland. Loose-leaf diaries designed with time management principles in mind offer a wealth of information that you can choose from to suit your purposes – maybe even a road map of Glasgow and Edinburgh.

Supplies of useful time-planning systems are listed at the end of this chapter, but you can also design your own system if you wish.

At this stage, you should stop and consider the planning systems you use and whether they are adequate. If you find yourself excavating through scraps of paper, missing appointments, losing track of ideas and generally unaware of what you are trying to achieve, you should consider changing to a better system. But beware! If you are by nature a perfectionist, ensure that you spend your time achieving results, rather than spending far too much time keeping the perfectly neat and multicoloured time planner – and achieving mere administrivia.

Determining priorities

Whatever system you choose, it is essential to list all the activities that you need to complete. For many managers this is best carried out daily, either immediately on arriving at work or just before leaving the previous evening. If necessary, try to find the mental space by arriving ten minutes earlier, or leaving ten minutes later. Where life is often less hectic, for a Project Manager for example, the list can be made weekly or monthly and project-planning techniques, such as critical path analysis, become useful.

You will doubtless end up with more activities than time available. Do not become overwhelmed at this stage; you now need to prioritize. Go through your list and pick out priorities using the ABC system: 'A's are priority tasks, 'B's less so, and 'C's not so important. 'A's are usually the hardest, most complex and difficult to achieve – and also the most important! 'C's are often trivial, easy to do, look impressive when crossed off a list, but don't get you anywhere. So start with 'A's, not with 'C's – or 'Z's.

Look at the 'A' priorities. If you have several 'A's, you may like to prioritize

IMPORTANT

MUST BE DONE SOMETIME	MUST BE DONE NOW/SOON
Time consuming and needing careful planning	Key task areas (KTAs) for the manager

NOT URGENT ──────────────────────────────── **URGENT**

DOES NOT NECESSARILY NEED DOING	MUST BE DONE NOW/SOON BUT IN MINIMUM TIME
Hobbies, grapevine, droppers-in and moaning	Emergencies and unforeseeable crises

NOT IMPORTANT

Figure 2.5   Grid showing the time management relationship between important and urgent tasks

again (Al, A2, A3, and so on), and then begin to see the connections between tasks. By now you will probably be crossing off tasks and interlinking them; it may look rather messy, but the left and right sides of your brain will be working away, searching for speedy and effective planning methods to get things done.

If 'ABC's fail to appeal try prioritizing using 'MSC's where there are:

- tasks that *must* be completed;
- tasks that *should* be completed; and
- tasks that *could* be completed (if only I had time).

Avoid generating multiple lists, unmanageable numbers of priorities, items duplicated on several lists, and constantly changing priorities.

The urgency and importance of tasks

Many managers find it useful to look at tasks in terms of their urgency and importance (a grid showing the relationships between urgent and important tasks is given in Figure 2.5). Successful managers often experience a mixture of mostly urgent and non-urgent but still important tasks. If your non-urgent/ non-important area starts to increase noticeably, you may well need to take correcting action.

Using a diary or planner

If you use a traditional diary, ensure that you transfer tasks into it in addition to the usual appointments. Do this by blocking out chunks of time. Take care   27 not to underestimate the amount of time required for project work, such as producing board reports and setting up team-briefing initiatives, and make sure you insert the full-time requirements into your diary. The alternative is bad time planning, plus a bulging briefcase to accompany the trek home and needless burning of midnight oil. Fortunately, I cycle between home and work about 120 days each year, so paperwork has to be completed at work as I like to travel light. On those dark winter nights when I use the car I can sometimes catch myself automatically taking work home that I'm unlikely to look at simply because the car has room for it – and the desire to appear busy to others can be addictive!

Try to become more aware of your regular daily tasks and how long they take, and the average amount of time that must be left unplanned and unallocated to deal with crises, the unexpected and the unreasonable. Your time can be seen as having discretionary and non-discretionary elements: that is, there are those tasks you choose to do (and often, how you do them) and those tasks you are told to do and have no choice but to comply. Any managerial job is going to have elements of both, but a difficulty can occur in planning your time where the non-discretionary area is comparatively high. In this case, try to estimate the non-discretionary level; if it is say about 40 per cent of your total time available, then it makes sense in your planning to leave 40 per cent of future time unplanned so as not to become overloaded.

Another approach is to recognize the job's flexibility by considering the demands, the choices and the constraints (boundaries) within the job. This encourages a more strategic consideration of your job by focusing on how you divide your time up between people in your networks, where you focus your attention most often and where you try to have an impact.

Electronic organizers and personal digital assistants

Filofax-type organizers and their equivalent became a 'yuppie' status symbol during the late 1980s, and everybody who was anybody would be seen carrying one and even occasionally using it. Electronic organizers were seen as rather unfashionable at the time and an obsession of 'tekkies'. They have come of age in recent years and the developments are outstanding, with prices and functionality to suit all pockets and purposes.

If you work with a personal computer by your side, you are likely to have several useful organizing programmes with the software. With Windows-based software these are typically diary, database, notebooks and address books, with easy search facilities and print-out options.

Many people are on the move and prefer something more portable. Portable computers are still hardly pocket-sized and light to carry, unlike today's personal digital assistants. The less expensive electronic organizers tend to replicate the features of most paper-based organizers, but as you invest more, so the facilities increase.

At the higher end of the range, electronic organizers can offer many of the facilities we expect from desktop computers, including word-processing, spreadsheet and database software, automatic telephone/fax dialling, and compatibility with desktop computers. All offer long-life battery operation, can wake you up in the morning, and offer backup facilities (so losing it would not be such a disaster as losing a paper-based system). Top-of-the-range organizers cost about £250 to £500; this cost is tending to fall with time, or improved facilities are offered at the same price. Some recommended suppliers are listed at the end of this chapter, with most products on sale through high-street outlets.

LOGGING TIME USE

Why bother?

Many managers have at some stage in their working lives logged their use of time as it is actually being used up, and analysed it later. But why bother, in view of the effort and dedication involved with time logs? The answer is that you are probably unsure how your time is currently being spent on your various activities. All right, you may have some general ideas about where time goes, but to effect *real* improvements a constructive survey and analysis is critical. Indeed, managers often conclude from a time log that their use of time is even more haphazard and fragmented than they previously believed! This sudden realization can be a poignant lesson and stimulus towards the need for personal change. If a manager delegates more effectively, closes the door when necessary to concentrate and plan, while learning to say 'yes' and 'no' appropriately, then a second log can be completed about four weeks later to determine the relative success of implementing the changes.

The main advantages of the time log approach are:

- It offers self-development opportunities insofar as the results can be used by you personally and revealed only to those you wish to discuss them with. Thus you can be totally honest with yourself.
- It has an in-built logic, that is, it deals with real and indisputable *facts* about how you spend your time.
- You learn through the actual processes. For example, a salesperson may be genuinely surprised at how much time is spent chasing low-yield prospects, or a line manager may learn just how much or little discretionary time is really available.

However, two to four weeks of disciplined logging can become tedious, particularly if your time log design is overcomplicated or if you are too busy or forgetful to record items. In fact, if you really are too busy to consider a time log, then you would be strongly advised to complete one!

Designing and using time logs

In the most straightforward approach you would divide your working life into between six and eight main categories of activities – these may be key task *29* areas, job objectives, areas of activity, and so on. You need to note over two to four weeks the amount of time spent in each category, while time spent on 'other activities' can be recorded in a separate catch-all category.

All time spent *must* be allocated somewhere on your log. Ideally, your notes should be made during or soon after the activity. In the turmoil of managing, a sensible compromise, enabling the log to be useful and accurate without being laboriously detailed, is to complete your prepared sheets as convenient. An hour is regarded as about the maximum amount of time that should elapse between recording – use an alarm, such as the bleep on a digital watch, to assist you as the memory can be notoriously unreliable when completing time logs.

Other useful guidelines

In carrying out your time log and subsequent analysis, bear in mind:

- The log should preferably be kept for a *typical* two- to four-week period of time. You may claim you have no typical period of time and that there is too much variation in your job: often, in fact, if we sense the luxury of a typical and routine week on the horizon, some unexpected pressure or crisis will surely occur. However, this will not invalidate your log: on the contrary, it will enhance your learning with facts about how you coped with unexpected events. Remember that the main purpose of your log is to inspire you to improve your use of time, and not to define some mythical typical week.
- Your designed time log should be easy to understand and should be completed during the course of the day. Do not make it so intricate that completing it every few minutes supersedes your role as a manager and you need an extra key task area entitled 'Filling in my time log'.
- Using symbols and abbreviations where you can is helpful, particularly in the additional notes column.
- On arriving at work each day, you should start your log by confirming in writing your priority tasks and objectives for the day ahead.
- Time spent in travelling, working beyond 'normal hours', and in breaks should all be included.

Sharing your time log with others

While your time log is directly personal to you, it is useful for a group of managers to get together to discuss their completed logs; this is particularly helpful where people are doing similar jobs in different departments or locations. A process that works well is for each manager to take about 20 minutes of group time to give an informal but thorough presentation of his or her time log data. Other people in the group should listen attentively but should also not hesitate to query the manager's explanation of the use of time if that seems necessary. The presenting role is rotated until all managers in the group have experienced the 'hot seat'. Managers should each identify through discussion and commit themselves to at least two specific and significant improvements in their time use by the end of the session.

Some questions that group members should keep in mind during this process are:

- Where has time been used effectively/ineffectively? Why?
- What could/should have been delegated? Up, down or sideways?
- Should 'no' have been said politely but firmly to some activities and interruptions? Why wasn't it? How could it be said in the future?
- Could some tasks (meetings, paperwork, interviews, and so forth) have been carried out more quickly? How?
- Are there any tasks not done that should have been done? What has prevented them from being done? How may this be avoided in future?
- What kinds of decisions are taken? Alone or with others? Who? How often?
- What are the main similarities and differences between the time logs in the group? Why?
- What do you like/dislike about what you have decided or been told about your own use of time?
- What are you going to do about the feedback? How can we help you make those changes?

Examples of time logs

During one development programme a group of managers noted down all the activities on which they spent time, in order to determine categories for their time log analysis. Many managers listed over fifty activities, which they then broke down into about twenty activity areas and finally resolved into seven categories of activity. A typical example is shown in Figure 2.6.

One manager developed a time log together with a section for identifying daily priority objectives as shown in Figure 2.7. The time log axes are in this case one-hour time bands and eight key activity or key task areas. The 'Comments' column was used for noting down issues about levels of effectiveness, thoughts, feelings, and so on. For each daily sheet the columns were totalled and transferred to the time log summary sheet given in Figure 2.8. The overall analysis for the length of the time log can be computed by completing the total figures at the bottom of the summary.

Variations in time spent in key task areas

Comparisons of time use between managerial jobs can be quite useful, particularly where people are doing similar jobs. The minimum, maximum and percentage ranges of time spent in categories of activities for nine managers with the same job title within one company are shown in Figure 2.9. The   *31*

TIME LOG – CATEGORY SUMMARY

A   PLANNING, PREPARATION AND UPDATING

A1   Planning ahead
A2   Preparation for interviews/visits etc.
A3   Keeping your knowledge up to date

B   CUSTOMER INTERVIEWS (IN BRANCH)

B1   Lending interviews – personal and commercial
B2   Other interviews with customers arranged to increase business, etc.
B3   Non-lending/non-business development interviews

C   CUSTOMER CONTACT – INFORMAL (IN BRANCH)

C1   Working at an enquiry desk
C2   Meeting customers informally in the banking hall/casual meetings
C3   Working at a customer point

D   STAFF CONTACT

D1   Checking/advising on the work of others
D2   Briefing staff about changes in working routines/products, etc.
D3   Training staff/discussing progress/coaching others

E   OFFICE – ROUTINES AND PROCEDURES

E1   Dealing with correspondence/telephone calls, etc.
E2   Attending to faults, problems, priorities, administration, etc.
E3   Interpreting/issuing HO advices/procedures

F   ATTENDING MEETINGS

F1   Meetings with Area Manager or equivalent
F2   Attending non-business professional meetings
F3   Meetings with other departments (e.g. Marketing, Personnel)

G   WORKING OUTSIDE THE BRANCH

G1   Seeing customers at their premises
G2   Visiting existing/prospective business clients
G3   Meeting/lunching with professional contacts
G4   Visits/talks/film shows outside the branch

H   OTHER CATEGORIES

H1
H2
H3

Figure 2.6   The 22 main activities and 7 categories of activities for a managerial-type job

Time Log

Priority Objectives   Achieved

| 1 |

Day No

| 2 |

Date

| 3 |

Time	Plan/ Prepare Update			Customer Interviews			Informal Customer Contact (in-branch)			Staff Contact			Office Routines & Procedures			Attend Meetings			Work outside the Office				Other			Comments
	A			B			C			D			E			F			G				H			
	1	2	3	1	2	3	1	2	3	1	2	3	1	2	3	1	2	3	1	2	3	4	1	2	3	
9.00																										
10.00																										
11.00																										
12.00																										
1.00																										
2.00																										
3.00																										
4.00																										
5.00																										
6.00																										
Sub-total																										
Total																										

Figure 2.7 A daily time log for a managerial-type job

Time Log Summary

Date	Plan/ Prepare Update			Customer Interviews			Informal Customer Contact (in-branch)			Staff Contact			Office Routines & Procedures			Attend Meetings			Work outside the Office				Other			Comments
	A			B			C			D			E			F			G				H			
	1	2	3	1	2	3	1	2	3	1	2	3	1	2	3	1	2	3	1	2	3	4	1	2	3	
Sub-total																										
Total																										

Figure 2.8   A summary sheet for collating daily time log data

	Min (%)	Max (%)	Range (%)
Planning–preparing–keeping up to date	3	15	12
Customer interviews (in branch)	14	26	12
Informal customer contact/approaches (in branch)	0	20	20
Staff contact	4	14	10
Office routines and procedures	18	48	30
Working outside the branch	0	27	27
Attending meetings etc.	0	16	16

Figure 2.9   Percentage minimum, maximum, and range of time spent in each key task area for managers doing similar jobs

information was discussed and the differences were explained by the managers in terms of unit size, geographical location, skill and maturity of staff, styles of managing, priorities and differing customer bases – *and the manager's ability to use time effectively!*

People often work closely together in organizations, and one manager and an assistant looked at the overlapping areas of interest in their respective jobs. Four general areas of responsibility were defined and a time log approach used to develop their effectiveness in working together. They recognized a strong need to understand the balance between their work over a timescale. In addition to achieving certain key objectives, the time and energy spent within each of the areas was addressed. As a result, the unit performance improved, as the manager recognized a need to delegate the more routine customer interviews while at the same time developing the assistant's confidence and competencies by supporting more of the staff briefing and development activities.

These examples are described here both to stimulate you into designing a time log for yourself and to demonstrate to you how it can be used, especially in discussion with your boss and other managers.

INDIVIDUAL BEHAVIOUR: PROBLEMS AND SOLUTIONS

The need to develop objectives, assess priorities and measure success in managing your time are well-known requirements and can be usefully practised. But what about all those other behaviours we exhibit, often without being aware of them, that influence our ability to achieve objectives? This section discusses several commonly occurring problems managers experience and some potential solutions.

Don't procrastinate

Do you have a house full of leaking taps, faulty electrical connections and   *35* loose door handles that you have often and in good faith promised to put right? Do you *still* have that difficult customer with the complaint who you really must contact, or that urgent sales report nagging away to be finished rather than staring at you surreptitiously from your pending tray, or that tricky performance review that should have been completed before the end of the month, or that overdue apology? The gentle art of 'putting things off', or procrastination, is an enormous time stealer.

Procrastination is for most people a deep-seated and acquired habit. It is a problem that should be tackled immediately as soon as you decide to improve your time management. Useful first steps in tackling procrastination include:

- Resolve that you are going to change as soon as you can – preferably *now*!
- List all those tasks you have been putting off. Make no exceptions – everything must be on your list.
- Remove one or two items from the list immediately by actually *doing them*. Doing them is often quicker than writing them out again.
- Plan how you will deal with the other items on the list, at a rate of, say, two or three each day. Then implement this plan first thing each morning as this sets a positive tone for the rest of the day. You can tell yourself: 'Great, the day is only 20 minutes old and already I have accomplished the most irritating tasks of the day.'
- If you stick to your plan, reward yourself, maybe with a new time-planning system. If you fail, punish yourself – gently, but in a way that ensures you will make a better effort next time round.

There are positive aspects of procrastination, however, which are determined by the nature of what needs to be done, rather than by a preference for putting things off. If you still require information and skill in order to carry out a complicated and important, but not urgent, task, for example, then you may be better advised to negotiate a postponement. Important decisions may also be delayed where you are suffering from excessive tiredness – from, say, a transatlantic flight – and a fully alert mind is needed. Remember the buyer's slogan, 'If you want a quick answer – it's NO!' In the same vein, decisions may best be left on the back burner where the emotional states and stakes are high; for example, following news that a supplier has let you down or that your job has become redundant. Our first reaction to such news may be to strike out in fitful anger, but a more thoughtful and constructive problem-solving strategy is usually preferable. Similarly, delay low-priority in favour of higher-priority tasks.

Handling interruptions

We have all experienced that feeling of being interrupted and somehow being diverted from what we really need to achieve. In fact, we usually see ourselves as being on the receiving end of other people's interruptions. At such times, inconveniences such as computer downtime or travelling problems appear, to all intents and purposes, to have been deliberately selected to interfere with our work. However, interruptions like these need be put in to perspective: even excellent managers are subject to interruptions. One difference is that successful managers demonstrate a more positive approach in recognizing that interruptions are part of everyday working life. When the phone rings they might say to themselves, 'That's my job calling', and continue to cope without developing undue angst. Another difference is that they tend to be skilled at handling interruptions positively and can usually see their way to reaching a workable compromise.

Two simple techniques for handling interruptions are:

1   Try to keep that interruption short. There are many ways of achieving this, including letting the interrupter know politely about the top priority task you are working on. When people 'drop in' you can either remain standing or sit on your desk while they sit. Alternatively, you can transfer the meeting to the other person's office or to neutral ground such as a reception area, where you can be more in control of when to leave. Stick to time limits whenever you can, maybe by saying 'I don't have a minute but I can give you ten' – and then stick to the ten minutes of undivided attention.

2   Remember that most interruptions involve other people, and therefore we must handle matters sensibly and graciously. That assertiveness course may have taught us to say 'no' to unreasonable demands and interruptions, but at the same time, we must try not to demonstrate irritation with the interrupter that will, in turn, dilute our ability to listen carefully and to help them 'get to the point'. Try to reach a workable compromise and, whether they be colleagues or customers, do not let people go away empty handed: at the least, promise to tackle their problem later, or find a time when you can both talk without time pressures, or share the problem and solution more creatively.

You must also ensure that you are not your own worst interrupter, as interruptions can be consciously and unconsciously set up as excuses to procrastinate. Extroverts particularly can find themselves leaving their office door open deliberately to try to entice interrupters; often they place their desks in a position that makes it easy for them to be seen and invites interruption. Open-plan offices need very careful design, and it is not unusual for managers to invent a system for flagging up their willingness to be interrupted; among various simple but useful systems, yellow and red discs on the corner of the desk can signify 'I can be interrupted if you must' and 'I can only be interrupted if it's really very important'. Introverts, on the other hand, are likely to be most irritated by interruptions, and they must ensure that they maintain momentum and keep on track with that top priority task after dealing with the interruption.

Questions managers can ask themselves when developing skills at handling interruptions include:

- How often am I interrupted or distracted when working on a top priority task?
- How often do I focus upon a task which could or should be delegated?
- How regularly do I change my priorities involuntarily by leaping from one task to another?
- How often would tasks have been completed if more thought had gone into how to do them in the first place?
- How often did I postpone or interrupt myself on a high-priority task in order to fight that same old crisis yet again?

If the level of disruption caused by interruptions is serious, an interruption log can be considered. This would clarify systematically what you may suspect, and is likely to influence you further towards changing your approach to managing interruptions.

Aim for excellence - not perfection

Do you have letters retyped because of one minor error, and never expect to receive customer complaints, or interruptions at work? Do you expect your pre-school children to have impeccable table manners, the garden to be perfect, and every day to be like Christmas?

The pursuit of perfection in most management jobs can be paralysing, whether we experience it personally or from others. There are fundamental differences between striving for excellence and striving for perfection. The former is achievable, realistic, healthy and personally satisfying; the latter can be demoralizing and can lead to stress and frustration. You have to recognize in what areas of your work you really need 'to be perfect', and ensure that such compulsions do not trap you into missing opportunities and achieving excellence elsewhere.

Driver behaviour such as the pursuit of perfection is simply what we feel compelled to do. It is unconscious and beyond our awareness. Five drivers are recognized: to be perfect; to hurry up; to be strong; to try hard; and to please others. We pick up drivers early in life and they remain with us unless we choose to do something about it. Boys are taught not to express feelings or to cry when they are physically or mentally hurt and, as a result, grow up with a 'man's gotta do what a man's gotta do' approach in adult life. Try-harders have been rewarded early in life for effort. 'Never mind that you failed all your GCSEs, at least you tried' they are told, while being rewarded with another plate of ice cream. Rewards here are for effort and not results – in adult life it should be the other way round. Drivers have a strong influence on time management behaviours.

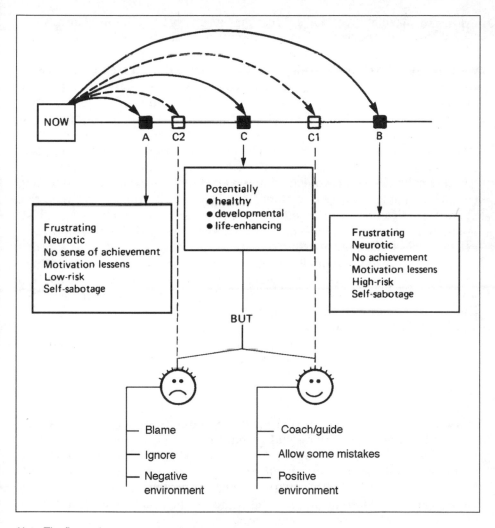

Note: The figure shows the value of challenging but realistic objectives in achievement – A is too low, B too high, with C about right in normal circumstances and C1 where managerial support happens.

Figure 2.10   Setting challenging objectives

Set challenging objectives

Do you find yourself consistently failing to meet objectives and being disappointed, annoyed and frustrated? Do you find yourself regularly underachieving, or meeting objectives without expending much physical or emotional effort?

Imagine an exercise involving throwing tennis balls into a bucket, where your performance is defined by your distance in feet from the bucket when you throw multiplied by the percentage of balls actually landing in the bucket.   *39*

If you set your objectives and success measure very low (by choosing a short distance of, say, one or two feet), then your percentage will be about l00 per cent. You will experience some initial success, but after a few minutes you will probably develop a growing sense of unease due to lack of a sense of achievement, compounded by an absence of risk, plus boredom, annoyance and frustration. This is represented by position 'A' in Figure 2.10. You may well find yourself creating risks that lead to failure: for example, trying to just hit the rim of the bucket, with the ball bouncing on the rim a few times before hopefully dropping into the bucket. The analogies in working life with poorly motivated people seeking attention are readily apparent.

Conversely, if you set your objective very high, for example by selecting a long distance as depicted by point 'B' in Figure 2.10, you set up a high-risk situation that can be encouraged by some initial success which does not last. Again, motivation and achievement are likely to diminish as frustration and lack of success become apparent.

Position 'C' is the potentially healthy performance position and results in optimum success. With good coaching, positive support and recognition (and a few allowable mistakes), position C1 can be reached; with isolation, negative recognition and lack of support, only C2 may be possible.

Have a look at your own objectives. How realistic are they? What happens to you personally when objectives are too difficult or too easy to achieve? And how realistic are your staff's objectives?

Learning how to learn

How children learn is well researched and understood, adult learning less well so. Learning, un-learning and re-learning are key issues in good time management. You can no longer rely upon the occasional off-the-job course or instructions from top management for your own learning. In any case, there is strong evidence that mature adults have a strong need to be self-managing in their learning and to be clear about the practical reasons for the learning. However, you should become aware of:

- the barriers you place in the way of your learning;
- your preferred manner of learning for such situations; and
- what you did that enabled you to learn enjoyably and successfully in the past.

Modern learning methods such as distance learning, action learning, computer-based training (CBT) and activity-based workbooks help you learn at your own pace and in your own style, and thus you can manage your learning time more effectively.

At a company level it has been stated that 'over the long term, the only sustainable competitive advantage may be an organization's ability to learn faster than the competition'. Capital resources, technical innovation and managerial expertise can be rendered obsolete by the competitor who looks from a different perspective, reads the changing environment and learns in more relevant and creative ways. Hence the importance of accelerating the development of new products and services to the market early by simplifying procedures, eliminating steps throughout the phases and adapting just-in-time techniques.

Fighting recurring crises

There is nothing wrong with the occasional crisis, and indeed we cannot escape them. But if it turns out to be the same crisis that occurred last week, the week before and the week before that, you may be looking for someone to blame rather than learning from the crisis experience.

Good practices in a crisis are:

- Use your energies to find solutions (not for shouting or searching for scapegoats).
- Focus on the problem at hand (not your personal performance or how it will look at appraisal time).
- Relax momentarily before considering options and then controlling that crisis.
- Turn the crisis into an opportunity for new ideas and methods. Contingency plans that help avoid future identical crises can be devised.

Other requirements for solving time problems

Six of the most important personal time wasters have been described above together with ways of resolving or at least limiting them. The following requirements are also important to manage your individual behaviour and hence the use of your time:

- Take breaks.
- Avoid clutter (physical and mental).
- Beware of becoming a workaholic.
- Learn to say 'no' firmly but graciously, when appropriate.
- Access and use information well.
- Read and write accurately and quickly.
- Relax and reduce the impact of work pressures.

MANAGERIAL STYLES

Think about the ways people manage in your organization. The amount of time spent working is not usually a measure of effectiveness at work, although managers who work all hours often perceive themselves to be held in high regard by others. Ask yourself who is more highly rated in the following examples:

41

- The manager who explains over and over in detail why a problem cannot be solved, or the manager who solves the problem and then quickly and quietly moves on to other tasks?
- The supervisor who makes few decisions of any kind, even when decisions are urgently needed, or the supervisor who makes the required decisions but occasionally makes a mistake?
- The boss who frantically dashes around solving subordinates' problems again and again, or the boss who develops subordinates so that crises are avoided and they can solve their own problems?

Managerial style and time

One popular and practical model of management describes five styles of managing that may be defined as follows:

1 *Telling* An authoritarian style whereby managers make decisions themselves, announce them, and command that they be carried out.
2 *Selling* A style whereby managers make the decisions with some limited discussion prior to explaining or trying to convince their subordinates.
3 *Consulting* A style whereby managers get suggestions by inviting questions, making suggestions themselves, and consult subordinates before making decisions.
4 *Sharing* A style whereby managers present the problem, define the limits of any solution, and decisions are made jointly.
5 *Delegating* A style whereby managers allow subordinates to function within set limits by defining constraints and by conforming with subordinates' requirements.

As we go down this list, the area of freedom for subordinates to make decisions increases, while the use of authority by the manager decreases.

Your own predominant or preferred style (they should be the same) will influence the amount of time you spend with subordinates and others, and how you spend that time. The *telling* style will save time in the short term – it's easy to tell people what to do if they are willing to do anything you tell them to do. But it could mean extra time eventually being spent dealing with dissatisfactions and the mistakes that occur as the culture matures or the individuals give up trying to have an influence. The *consulting* style will result in more time spent in meeting subordinates, often at their request, to deal with the many ideas and options around; but good time management principles still apply, and subordinates are likely to be more reliable and resourceful.

Exercise: time and managerial styles

You are asked to develop your understanding of the five main styles by inserting the main advantages and disadvantages of each style in the grid in Figure

Style	Time management		% of time spent	
	Advantages	Disadvantages	Actual	Ideal
Telling				
Selling				
Consulting				
Sharing				
Delegating				

Note: The figure shows a matrix where you consider the advantages and disadvantages of several managerial styles in time management terms, before allocating your actual and ideal percentages of time spent in each style.

Figure 2.11   Managerial styles and managing time

2.11 from a time management perspective. Then consider your own styles and the percentage of time spent in each style in the column marked 'Actual'. It is likely that you will have some time spent in each of the styles and that no one style will achieve 100 per cent. The 'Ideal' column should be completed, together with a statement about how you will make the 'Actual' to 'Ideal' changes occur.

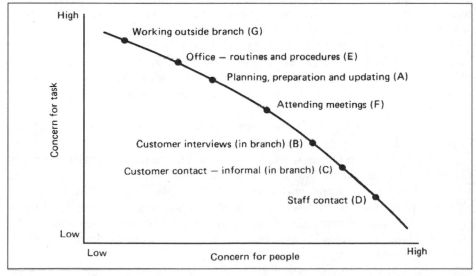

Note: The figure shows how key task areas are related to the popular concept of a manager's concern for task and concern for people. Time spent in our key task areas reflects our managerial styles.

Figure 2.12   Key task areas and managerial concern for task and people   *43*

Key task areas and management styles

Many models of management express style and success in terms of two dimensions: our ability to get things done, and our relationships with people. We can relate key task areas to these models. Figure 2.12 shows how seven key areas of activity in a job relate to a high and low concern for tasks and people by the manager. The manager in this case saw *working outside the branch* and *office routines and procedures* as primarily associated with task activities insofar as they did not involve the staff in any direct way, whereas *staff and customer contact activities* did.

Exercise: tasks and people components of managing time

Consider your own key task areas, objectives or use of time that you developed in an earlier exercise. Plot them on a task/people figure similar to Figure 2.12 and study the profile. Most chief executives claim that 'people are our most important resource'; a popular definition of management over the years has been that it is the ability 'to get things done through other people'. If this is so, then your own objectives as a manager are likely to reflect a balanced spread between predominantly task- and predominantly people-related activities to optimize success.

Functions of management and delegation

Some schools of management look at the functions that management actually perform. One classic framework reduces management to four basic functions: planning, organizing, motivating and controlling (POMC). Other models suggest that the work of a manager is fragmented, varied, subject to continual adjustment, and governed on the whole by having to cope with ambiguity and turbulence. Whatever your understanding, the functions approach again offers much towards improving your time management. The best approach is probably in recognizing the functions that can lead to the most time leverage for you, the most relevant of which is usually delegation.

Delegation can be defined as allocating work to others for them to carry out to your satisfaction; in essence, you have ultimate responsibility, but they are accountable for completing work properly and on time. Delegation certainly does not mean simply 'dishing out the work'. Consideration of the advantages and disadvantages of improving your delegation skills together with how you use your time at work can lead to massive time savings. One manager I work with operates on the principle of 'never doing anything someone else can be persuaded to do' – and what's more, that manager is both extremely effective and highly respected by all.

Why should you be concerned with delegation? Most managers offer good excuses as to why they do not delegate more – few managers willingly admit failings here. It is often claimed that it is simpler just to carry out a task yourself, rather than arrange to meet someone and have to explain, monitor and

BUSINESS REPLY SERVICE
Licence No AT170

Gower Publishing
Gower House
Croft Road
ALDERSHOT
Hampshire
United Kingdom
GU11 3BR

Gower

MANAGEMENT UPDATE

Gower is the leading publisher of business and management books in the UK and with over 400 titles in print it is one of the largest in the world in this area. The range embraces handbooks, practical management guides, reference works, personal skills books, audio manuals, and state-of-the-art studies in specialist areas of business activity. The subjects covered span from training, personnel and management development through manufacturing, sales and marketing to accountancy and finance.

We would be pleased to send you details of our publications in your chosen areas of interest. Just fill in the section below and we will send you the relevant information.

Please send me information on the books and other materials you publish in the following subject areas:
(please write clearly)

Name ....

Job Title ....

Company ....

Address ....

....

.... Postcode ....

If you would like to receive e-mail on our new products, please give your e-mail address below, OR

include the names of any other colleagues in your company who would benefit from being on our mailing list:

....

....

☐ If you do not wish to receive information from other organizations, please tick here

Gower also has offices in Singapore • Sydney • Brookfield, VT, USA

Code: 55004M

then evaluate what is being done. Once or twice this may be an acceptable view, but in the longer term your lack of delegation will cause you time problems, particularly as others learn how to pass tasks back to you to do.

VISUAL REMINDERS

Most successful managers use the analytical methods for managing time, as described in earlier sections, finding customized diaries supportive in the process. However, about 20 per cent of managers are just not able to see the value in this disciplined approach and need broader, more visual reminders to encourage good time use. Such managers often have a very clear picture in their minds of what they want to achieve, with seemingly little need to write it all down.

The right side of the brain is the unconscious creative part that is responsible for visualizing. Operating intuitively, it looks for complete pictures and is non-judgemental. Creative people often see the nuts and bolts of traditional time management approaches as irrelevant: 'After all,' they say, 'no known schedule can make you productive if you don't want to work.' For such people, the solution to better time management is to create a motivating atmosphere that encourages greater productivity, rather than lists and scheduling. Fun, enjoyment, colour and visual reminders are relevant for such managers.

Quotations and slogans

Despite all your good intentions and plans, too much time still gets wasted. Those improvement plans can soon be forgotten at times of interruptions and unexpected happenings, and we can drift back to old ways. One way to remind yourself of good time management principles on such occasions is to carry in your mind or on your desk quotations and slogans that offer a continuing stimulus.

Now, we have all heard of quotations like, 'Time and tide wait for no man', 'To thine own self be true', and one I noticed on a public clock with the hands missing, 'tempus fugit'. One I particularly like is 'Illegitimi non carborundum' (in rough translation, we must not let the antics of others get us down). You can design and display similar slogans for yourself to support your time management changes – and they also flag up your intentions to others when displayed. If you are more creative, a 'slogan of the week' may be preferred.

Your own quotations

You can of course keep your 'slogans' in your head, repeating them like mantras until they reach an almost spiritual significance. Better locations could include your wall chart, inside your desk blotter, in a photographic frame on your desk, in your time planner in bold letters where they will be noticed, and on the telephone, especially if the telephone is your favourite time management problem. You may prefer initials, such as DIBS ('Do it

Figure 2.13   Test your skills with the principles of good time management

---

1   Sounds like little sister is shouting for help   (6)

2   Is ma aware of her target?   (4)

3   Sounds like defect minus an old penny   (6)

4   Mind a small head office   (5)

5   One at each end at Wembley   (5)

6   Architects are always doing this   (8)

7   Door locks   (3, 5)

8   Change your system   (10)

9   Sounds like the entrance to Indian capital city   (8)

10   Test   (7)

11   Print a negative   (7)

12   After deuce   (9)

13   First notice P.E.   (13)

14   Don't put off until tomorrow, what can be done today   (13)

15   Sounds like the national drink   (1)

Figure 2.13   (concluded)

before sunset') – they are certainly more private and mysterious. On one December course a manager designed the Christmas crossword shown in Figure 2.13 to stimulate good time management in his department. Remember, if it works for you, it works for you!

An organized work area

More naturally occurring visual reminders about your attitudes to good time use will abound in your work area or office anyway. Whatever the slogans you select, if your office looks a mess, your time management is likely to be a mess too. Bear in mind the following general points:

- Keep your paperwork under control. Whenever possible, handle each piece of paper once and once only. Decide what action to take at the time: do something and pass it into the out tray; start some action and place in a pending tray; read and file; or GROAN ('get rid of it now' – *any way!*).
- Choose and site your furniture with good time management principles in view. Filing cabinets should be well organized, regularly updated, and work well for you, especially if secretarial and clerical support from others is limited. Certainly your files should not involve an exploration

or paper safari every time you look for an item – nor should they challenge the exhibits in the local museum or company archives. Desks and chairs should preferably be ergonomically matched and sited in positions that give you maximum privacy when you need it – don't be your own worst interrupter and catch the eye of every passer-by when you look up, especially in open-plan work areas.

SUMMARY AND CHECK LIST

The main purpose and ultimate reward for managing your time well is the feeling of wellbeing, relative freedom, and control over your life that follows. In this chapter we have discussed six successful approaches, some of which will appeal more or be more relevant to you as a manager than others. Consider the following questions:

- Am I clear and up to date with my lifetime goals, objectives and key task areas?
- Are my time-planning systems (diaries, ABC priorities, electronic organizers, and so on) working well for me?
- Do I understand where my time is being spent in sufficient detail to be able to say conclusively that I do not need to change?
- Do I operate with excellent behavioural skills that support my time management?
- Is my flexibility of managerial style (concerns for task/people, delegation, and so forth) optimized to make maximum use of time?
- Does my working area support and reflect good time use? Would revised systems and visual reminders help?

Improvement areas	Objectives	Stages toward objectives	Possible problems	Achievement date

Note: The figure leads into developing an action plan that you can use to monitor your improvement in managing your time.

Figure 2.14   Action plan for managing your time

While answering these questions remember that:

Excellence (doing the right things right)

=

Effectiveness (doing the right things)

×

Efficiency (doing things right)

If you can answer an honest 'yes' to all these questions, you can move on to the next chapter. Otherwise, the final action planning exercise shown in Figure 2.14 should be completed to bring together the themes of managing your time. Where you identify an area for improvement, try to put the outcome you desire in the 'Objective' column, using SMART (*specific, measurable, achievable, realistic and timely*) principles where possible. Then break the change into stages and determine a date for final achievement.

Finally, will you complete the action plan? Or has that alternative and vital priority loomed up from the nether reaches of your in tray? Or are you procrastinating by reading this? As Lakein asks: '*What is the best use of your time right now?*'

FURTHER READING

Buzan T., *The Mind Map Book*, BBC Books, 1993. Explains thinking processes in terms of how the brain works to enable better memory and creativity in planning and structuring thought at all levels.

Gibbons B., *This Indecision is Final*, Irwin, 1996. Thirty-two management secrets of Albert Einstein, Billie Holliday and other diverse people who never worked 9 to 5.

Handy, C., *Beyond Certainty*, Hutchinson, 1995. In the changing world of organizations we must not let our past, no matter how glorious, get in the way of our future.

Jeffers, S., *Feel the Fear and Do It Anyway*, Arrow, 1991. How to turn your fear and indecision into confidence and action.

Jeffers, S., *End the Struggle and Dance With Life*, Hodder & Stoughton, 1996.

Lakein, A., *How to Get Control of Your Time and Your Life*, Gower, 1984. A classic book describing the author's system of time management, which includes simple but powerful techniques that succeed in life, work and in leisure.

Skopec, E. and Kiely, L., *Taking Charge,* Addison-Wesley, 1991. Time management techniques for personal and professional productivity.

Electronic organizers and personal digital assistants from:

Hewlett Packard Ltd
Cain Road
Bracknell
Berks RGl2 lHN
Tel: 01344 360000

Psion
1 Red Place
London W1Y 3RE
Tel: 0990 143050

Sharp Electronics UK Ltd
Sharp House
Thorp Road
Newton Heath
Manchester M40 5BE
Tel: 0161 205 2333

3 Managing information

Feona J. Hamilton

Information is one of your most important assets, together with money and staff. Many people would argue that information is the core commodity of any organization, however large or small. It makes a great deal of sense, therefore, both to manage it properly, so that you can make the most effective and efficient use of what is available to you, and to get a little training and knowledge about where to find the information that you need.

My objective in this chapter is to give you some good, basic advice on how to organize the information you use *according to your own needs*. There is no such thing as a blueprint that will suit everyone, but guidelines can certainly be given. Whether you apply them or not is up to you. There is a saying that the greater the muddle on someone's desktop, the more creative and imaginative that person is – but that was probably originally an imaginative excuse used by a deeply untidy person, when called on by his or her manager to explain the mess.

There is a current myth that everyone is now using sophisticated computer networks, surfing the Internet hour after hour, and finding miraculous amounts of exactly the right information. Don't be fooled: there *are* mountains of information available via the Internet all right, but whether it is what you want or need is, in most cases, doubtful. Moreover, getting at it can be very much a hit-or-miss affair, unless you have had some training. So, although the computer can be a great help if used properly, it is still not the answer to all your information needs. Don't throw out the filing-cabinet – the paperless society is not here, and never will be!

Before establishing any guidelines about organizing information, it is a good idea to define exactly what is meant by the word itself. Broadly speaking, 'information' can refer to absolutely anything that comes to you in electronic, printed, or oral form, including these sorts of things:

Printed

- Letters from outside the office.
- Internal mail (e.g. reports, memoranda, requests for leave, sick notes).
- Circulated journals.
- Your daily newspaper.
- The contents of your filing-cabinet(s).
- Business cards.
- Desk diary.

Electronic

- The front screen of your PC.
- E-mail (internal and external).
- The contents of the office groupware files.
- Other networked material.
- Your private files.
- CD-ROMs.
- Floppies.

Oral

- What you are told in conversation or discussion.
- Conference papers given by speakers.
- What you overhear (accidentally or on purpose).
- Voice mails.
- Radio/television programmes.
- Anything else conveyed to you by voice rather than reading about it.

That last item may seem slightly ephemeral – and the spoken word is one of the most ephemeral ways of recording information possible, unless it is literally recorded (e.g. taped) at the same time. Nevertheless, it is a perfectly valid method for our purposes. Some of the most useful snippets of information are picked up when standing by the drinks machine, or lunching with colleagues or with people from other organizations.

Organizing all of these different types of information, and ensuring that they can be accessed in the quickest, most relevant, and most efficient manner throughout a whole organization is frequently referred to as 'knowledge management'. Your knowledge management is for your own office – or space, as is more likely in these open-plan days. There is a great deal that you can do to arrange things to suit yourself. But the advent of the computer means that there will also be a great deal arranged for you, including the method of accessing any network, the model and make of computer that you use, and the software that is loaded on it. Only the smallest businesses can afford the luxury of letting individuals have a choice in this area.

STARTING SOMEWHERE

The ideal time to set up a system for managing your information is when you move into a new office or office space. When you walk into your office for the first time, whether it is a new one, or one vacated by someone else, the first impression will be more or less the same. It will be empty and *tidy*. Maybe there are a few drawing pins left in the wall or notice board, or a scribble or two on the calendar, but that's all. The desk will be pristine – no overflowing trays (maybe no trays at all), pen tidy gaping open-mouthed back at you, computer (if it has been delivered) set neatly on the desktop, and a chair at the wrong height, as you discover when you sit down.

When all this neatness is imprinted on your memory, here is what you do: make a note on the wall calendar to look again in a month's time. Then switch on the computer and make an entry in the scheduler to the same effect (if you find you can actually do this, you will now know that the computer works as well). After the month has passed, you will see something very different. The trays will be there, but they will be buried under piles of paper. There will be dog-eared and outdated notices on the notice board, and the phone will be ringing somewhere under another pile of rubbish – sorry, information. The computer screen – should you have remembered to switch it on – will be showing yet another variation on a silly screensaver. Sounds familiar? I thought it might, but don't just nod despairingly and turn the page.

You can start with those trays. Are they labelled IN, OUT and PENDING? Is the largest pile always in PENDING? It needn't be. You could try and make a pact with yourself, and your secretary or PA, if you have one, to make the OUT tray contain the largest pile by the end of every day. It won't always be possible, but set it as a target, anyway. Leonard Woolf, when working in the Ceylon Civil Service, insisted that all letters received in his office should be answered *on the same day,* which is one of the best ways there can be of keeping the balance of contents right between these three trays. Another way of preventing the PENDING tray from becoming overloaded is simply to do away with it. You'll be surprised how much easier it is to deal with just two trays, instead of three.

USING THE COMPUTER

If you are using a computer, there won't be as much room on the desktop as there used to be, unless you have one of those L-shaped jobs, with the computer on an extension, and a chair that swivels. As I believe that paper and equipment, as a variation of Parkinson's Law, expands to fill the space available, I have always tried to avoid this arrangement of office furniture and equipment. Otherwise, you can quickly find yourself swivelling like some kind of manic robot between surface and surface, shuffling a few pages here, clicking a few keys there, until you are dizzy and totally confused. Far better just to sit at a desk, on a chair, screen and keyboard in front of you, and with a little space on either side of the latter on which to place a cup of coffee and a few notes. Naturally, everything will be ergonomically correct (i.e. at the right height for you), so as to prevent any aches and pains, and with the computer screen at the correct angle to the light source(s), both natural and artificial, if you have both. In case you are wondering what all this has to do with managing information, you will find it much easier to spend considerable periods working with any information which is available to you via the computer on the desk if you are comfortable while doing it. You will be able to concentrate and work faster and more effectively this way than if you are fidgeting around trying to get rid of the niggling ache between your shoulder blades, or trying to focus on a screen which is partly unreadable because of the light shining on it.

The two great advantages of the computer are:

1 The ease with which you can call up files from somewhere else.
2 The saving in the need for storage space in your own area/office.

Both factors only apply, of course, if you are 'computerate' (as in literate or numerate) yourself. Anyone who still believes that it is demeaning for them to do their own typing – or keyboarding, as it is now called – is so old-fashioned as to be risible. If you can't type, learn immediately. There are several software products available for those who prefer to learn in private. You do not have to reach touch-typing standard in order to make full use of a computer, but you do have to know where the different keys are and be able to find them quickly. I can't touch-type, but I go at about 45 wpm these days, which is more than adequate for my needs.

The contents of any computer files can be divided roughly thus:

● Information that you can obtain from the network.
● Information that you create and store yourself.

Let us now look at them both in more detail.

INFORMATION FROM THE NETWORK

Computer networks are often considered a raison d'être in themselves, especially by those sad people in the IT department. Well, a network, whether it is one that connects five computers in one room, or the Internet, is simply an enabler. Like the road, rail and canal (seriously) systems that connect everywhere in the country, plus the sea and air routes that connect us with the rest of the globe, the Internet allows you to move from point to point and computer to computer – *and that's all!* The Internet itself does not contain information; it is the computers it connects that store everything. The same is true of your internal network. This allows you access to information stored on other people's computers (if the files are not password-protected) and information in files kept centrally on the server. If there is a library or information centre in your organization, there may well be services from there straight to your desktop computer, too. The latest systems allow you to search for all this by using browsers (search software), just like the browsers that have been developed for the Internet. Those with a fondness for jargon have promptly christened this facility 'the Intranet' (sigh), but you do not have to be a tekkie to be able to use it to find the information that you want or need. Some offices now have a system that uses an outside service to acquire the latest news updates, which are downloaded to your own PC all ready for you every morning, such as the one offered as *Reuters Business Alert*. Fun though this can be, especially if you can select your own areas of interest ('store your profile'), try to be as selective as you can, or you will be spending the whole day reading the news that comes to you. It may look more like working than reading a newspaper ever could, but it is still wasting time, if you're honest. Broadly speaking, what you receive from the network comes from another computer, whether it's across the hall or in New York.

INFORMATION THAT YOU SET UP AND STORE YOURSELF

As well as looking at files from all over the world, you will need to set up your own files. There is not enough space to go into all the details in a single chapter but, briefly, the three main kinds of software that you use for this purpose will be:

- *A word processor* This is what you use to write letters, reports, memos and any other written work that you have to do in the course of the day. Each separate item is a document, and they will all need *unique* file-names if they are ever to be found again.
- *A spreadsheet* This is what you use to work out budgets, do simple calculations, and check that your salary slip is right every month. The average person needs practice to master spreadsheets, but if you work at it you'll get there. As with all software, the programmers are getting better at designing something that ordinary people can use.
- *A database* This is where you keep records of names and addresses, lists of machine parts, book catalogues, results of surveys, and so on. If you have any training in information management, you will quickly adapt to it. If not, think of a database as an electronic form of, say, your file of business cards, but easier to use and almost impossible to lose.

These three items are frequently part of a suite (group) of software. One of the best known is Microsoft Office, which contains all three, plus a tool to help you design and produce professional-looking presentations. It has all sorts of refinements to help you work, like spellcheckers, and the ability to import and export data between the different parts (e.g. spreadsheet table to word processor). It is a great advantage, when making presentations to other people, whether in the office or another organization, to use something like PowerPoint to share information with others.

There are two other functions for which you may use the computer to share information with others, although you will be the compiler. These are 55

E-mail, the facility which enables you to send messages to other people inside or outside the organization, and a scheduler (diary) which, run on a network, allows people to check who's available in the office and where they are if they're not in. Sometimes, when either of these are introduced into the organization, people feel some concern that their privacy is being invaded, but that is really not the case. You can choose who receives your messages, and who can check on your whereabouts; this information does not have to be available to anyone and everyone. Most schedulers have security devices: for example, to show that you are not available but without revealing what it is you are doing.

MAKING COPIES AND KEEPING THEM

It would be a mistake to think that using a computer for information management means that you can dispense with other storage media and forget about paper. Consider, for instance, what happens if there is a power cut? If you work in a highly computerized environment, the moment the electricity stops flowing, so will your work. It will also become eerily quiet momentarily, before the disadvantage of open-plan offices becomes apparent. The equipment that hums away all day acts like 'white noise': that is, it masks all the noise being made by other people, so that you don't hear it so clearly or loudly. When the machines stop, humanity intrudes with a vengeance.

Do not wait for this to happen before you realize that you must make and keep backup copies of everything you produce using the computer. Develop the habit of backing up important documents at least, by making a copy on floppy disk. Paper copies of correspondence are still best kept attached to the original correspondence. Despite the fact that most organizations make arrangements for archiving documents, whether by storing them off-site on tape, or even in paper form somewhere, do not rely on anyone but yourself to make copies of documents that you produce.

GOOD OLD PAPER

The previous paragraphs have already reminded you that paper is still a vital part of information management. Sometimes, it is just easier to write things down, or store something in printed format, rather than electronically. Business cards are a case in point: unless you are really obsessed with computers, or have contacts running into the thousands, it is simply not worth keying all the information on everyone's business card into a database. Far better to keep the cards in some kind of box file, or in one of those smart folders with plastic pockets that you sometimes receive as publicity from another organization. Just decide whether you are going to file by name or by organization, and stick to the rule you have made for yourself.

The same idea is true of items of information that come into the office as paper. A four-drawer filing cabinet is still one of the most useful pieces of office furniture ever invented. But you cannot just put it in the corner, shove paper into it, and forget about it. There are decisions to be made at the beginning about the order in which things are filed. Most commonly, people choose to file alphabetically by organization, then by date within each name – preferably with the latest date at the front of the file, where it is most easily accessible. Once the system is set up, each file or folder must be properly labelled, and filed in order. Label the front of each drawer, and use hanging files if possible. This keeps things neat. Above all, once the system is set up, make a note to weed the files regularly. This will ensure that you do not have several copies of the same thing (unnecessary) or ancient and dog-eared copies of abandoned contracts, correspondence, projects and so on. Naturally, contracts which are in force must be kept on file in a secure place, either in your office or, if such a system exists, in a central file elsewhere.

Most people keep collections of books and journals relating to their own specialism, plus a dictionary and other general reference works, in their office or space. Keeping these in order will help you to find them quickly, as well as keeping the work area looking tidy – and you looking organized and efficient. If there are no bookshelves in the office when you move in, order some at once, and don't rest until they arrive. Then place your collection up there on the shelves: general reference (dictionary, phone book) first, followed by other material in broad subject areas. No one expects to see a classified library in an office, but do divide books and papers into broad subjects, so that you can find them again. You can file books and journals in a single run if you like, but it is easier to keep journals in box files, or periodical boxes (those things that come folded flat and require you to push flaps over and under each other, until they stand up on their own), and file them by title separately, before or after the books.

USING THE LIBRARY OR INFORMATION CENTRE

Nobody can possibly keep all the information sources they are likely to need in one office, even with the advantage of having a computer to help you. Libraries, especially those set up by the organization in which you work, are there to help you find the information that you do not already have. If there is such a place in your organization, when did you last visit it? Many middle and senior managers claim to have no time to do so, little realizing what a useful place it can be. As well as its obvious function, a library can be a useful place to retire to if you need somewhere quiet to sit and think, or write, without constant interruptions. This assumes that the library is large enough to have room for a few desks and chairs, of course; some information centres are so small that there is barely enough room for the stock and the staff, let alone for people from other parts of the building! Thank goodness the need for information services is being recognized again, as the recession recedes. The existence, or otherwise, of information centres seems to be cyclical, according to whether there is a boom or a bust going on in the economy. Unfortunately, libraries tend to be closed down just when they are most needed: a period of struggle for survival is surely exactly the time when access to information is most needed, not the time to cut the service that gives you access to it.

It is a good idea to make yourself known to the librarian/information officer, or whatever title is used. He or she can be a valuable friend. Well-run units of this type keep profiles of all senior staff (at least), giving details of their interests and information needs. This helps them to feed you the right information as it arrives – another means of keeping you up to date with the latest developments. You will be a favourite if you pass on circulated journals as quickly as possible, and return borrowed material rapidly. The information staff will make an extra effort for you, and will do their best to provide the information you require as soon as they can. Remember, it is often possible to order material which is not available in your own organization via a national and international system of inter-library loans.

Of course, computers play a large part in the information profession nowadays, and most information staff are trained to use them. Tell them your needs and leave them to it, but be reasonable, and don't always expect immediate results. Looking for a specific item can take some time, especially when you have not been able to give full details of your request. If you can give a title, author, and date, plus (in the case of a journal article) some idea of the name of the journal, it will be found much more quickly than if you mutter vaguely about books with green covers that you saw last time you came in.

Other information resources and services available in your library will involve you using your own computer skills. Increasingly, CD-ROMs, containing vast amounts of information, are made available to users in the library. Most commonly, these contain company, financial and/or legal information, but machine parts catalogues, interactive educational titles, dictionaries, encyclopaedias and medical texts are also widely available. Catalogues of other libraries are issued on CD-ROM, in addition to the shared catalogues available via on-line systems – all there for you to use. It is likely that some kind of introduction to their use and content will be offered to library users: you are advised to take advantage of any training offered, in order to make the best use of such resources.

Many in-house libraries, especially in academic and research organizations, ask for copies of any papers, articles, or presentations that you may make during the course of your work. Budgets for information services tend to be on the mean side, so anything that you can pass over for addition to library stock will be appreciated. This does not include rubbish that you just want to dump on someone else, or items that are in very poor condition (unless they are unique). If you have particular expertise in a subject which is relevant to your organization, most information professionals will welcome your recommendations for additions to that area of the information service. If the librarian says that the budget will not stretch to it, don't blame the library – take it up with whoever decides how much should be available for spending on this service. (If it's you, perhaps you should be taking another look at the budget?)

CONCLUSION AND SUMMARY

Whatever kind of manager you are, you are an information user as well. While there will be someone who has the responsibility for making sure that the computer network and the central server work properly, and that those files are regularly sorted and archived, it is up to you to take the same care over the files on your hard disk. If you try to see everything there is on your subject, and also try to keep it forever, you will rapidly become an inefficient manager, who is being pushed out of your space by the mass of unsorted material lying around. You will also damage the efficiency of your colleagues and, eventually, of the whole organization.

If, on the other hand, you manage the information that comes to you by the methods outlined above, you should be more efficient, because you will have it all under control, most of the time (or vice versa). All you have to remember are the following points:

- Whatever else you do, ensure that you are computerate!
- You control the computer, not vice versa.
- The office network is for sharing files.
- Your own computer is for your own files.
- There is no such thing as an absolutely secure computer document.
- Always back up your files.
- The Internet is the infrastructure, not the information itself.
- There will never be a paperless office.
- Filing cabinets and bookshelves are vital equipment for managing information.
- Once you have decided on the filing arrangement, stick to it.
- Weed all files (paper and computer) regularly.
- Use the library and befriend the library staff.
- Information flows both ways.

FURTHER READING

Eager, B. W., *Information Payoff: Manager's concise guide to making PC-based communications work*, Prentice Hall, 1994.

Etzel, B. and Thomas P., *Personal Information Management: Tools and techniques for achieving professional effectiveness*, Macmillan, 1996.

Hamilton, F., *Corporate Information Strategy in Accountancy Firms*, Elan Publishing, 1996.

Martin, E. W. *et al.*, *Managing Information Technology: What managers need to know*, 2nd edn, Macmillan, 1994.

Norton, R., *Managing Information in a Week*, Headway, 1995.

Wang, C. B. and Rothkopf, D. J., *Techno Vision: Executive's survival guide to understanding and managing information technology*, McGraw-Hill, 1994.

Webb, S., *Creating an Information Service*, Aslib, 1994.

4 Information technology

Barbara Smolny-Kostrewski

In this chapter we will define information technology in the broadest sense to encompass all those tools which aim to facilitate the transactions and progress of modern business. Where appropriate I will point out variations in approach in relation to the different types of business carried out.

THE TYPEWRITER

The typewriter is one of the oldest aids, originally conceived as in-house printing for clarity of presentation of formal documents. While typewriters are still used in some instances, the semi-automatic word-processing variety is gaining popularity. Appreciate, however, that these machines are not computers with a wider range of task capabilities, but typewriters with an electronic capability for correction and document presentation.

THE TELEPHONE

The importance of this invention cannot be underestimated. Having become so accustomed to telephone communications, we now tend to forget that the telephone has revolutionized communications. Indeed, most modern telephone exchanges are computer controlled, allowing for rapid around-the-world contact, and mobile telephone technology based on radio-waves is also directed by computer technology.

However, with the large number of communication aids now becoming available, the role of the telephone has diminished, though it should in fact be reconsidered and given its proper place. The telephone allows for voice contact and hence it can convey a range of messages which go beyond the word itself: it can, for instance, convey persuasion and friendliness, sympathy and grief. Hence when a more direct contact is needed with an individual there is a clear role for the telephone. Nevertheless, the telephone should be used with discretion. Senior staff will make their own judgements, but within the office there should be guidelines for the use of the telephone, first, in relation to the type of business that can be transacted on the telephone, and secondly, regarding who is allowed to make external calls.

Guidelines should also be produced concerning internal calls. Obviously the making of calls during working hours should be contained, so the nature of these calls should be specified, though always allowing some flexibility for emergencies. An example is an accounts department in a busy international conglomerate that employs external consultants to whom payments by the accounts department has to be authorized by a specialist from another department with a signature on the appropriate form. Let us assume that the signature was omitted and the form was returned to source in the internal mail for signature, but by the time it was returned it was late for payment. In returning the form by internal mail rules were certainly adhered to, but this delayed payment. In this instance, therefore, a telephone call would have expedited the matter. If the person handling this case was in doubt, then contact with the supervisor would have resolved the issue. Hence while rules are important, they have to be applied intelligently and with flexibility to make work easier.

The answering machine is another telephone-related device which is now used extensively. For many, it is a boon, allowing the capture of potentially missed contacts, and in some cases it can be used as a screen or even as an automatic 'receptionist'. Whatever the nature of the business, however, the way in which the answering machine is used should be examined and rationalized. First, with the exception of emergencies or for strictly name-taking applications, answering machines should not be used during office hours. If such an emergency should arise, then the message on the machine should be welcoming, friendly and explanatory. The tone of voice is important, as is the quality of voice, which should be authoritative without being harsh or abrupt. In the case of mail order or catalogue distribution it may be more cost effective to ask the enquirer to leave his or her name and address on an answering machine. People accept this as reasonable provided that queries are unlikely. Furthermore, where enquiries or ordering from well-controlled lists of stock are concerned (e.g. a catalogue), then a touch phone system can guide the enquirer to the correct section or answer. An example of such a system is that implemented by IKEA concerning stock availability. However, where institutions relating to education, healthcare, the law and advice are concerned, including social services and consultancy, the answering machine is not well received by the enquirer, and if it has to be used in these contexts, then the caller should be asked to leave his or her name and number and the call must be returned promptly.

FAXES

The use of fax technology has revolutionized the speed of delivery of copies of papers and documents, but these, except in special circumstances, are not replacements for the original. The use of fax machines for the transmission of documents reduces the time taken for the delivery of the sense of the document itself, but the legal validity of faxed documents needs to be established. In the majority of cases the document proper has to follow through postal or courier services. Faxes are particularly useful:

1   When speed is of the essence.
2   When contact with the destination is complicated by difficult land services: for example, in developing countries.

COMPUTER-BASED TECHNOLOGY

Computer applications are now extensive and expanding daily. The application of computers ranges over such complex and challenging tasks as placing a man on the moon, the control of telephone systems, the monitoring of medical equipment, the control of artificial limbs, and, on the domestic front, programs controlling washing machines and ovens. This is only an indication of the diversity of applications. Underlying all these activities, however, is a rigorous step-by-step analysis to identify the components, the alternatives and the decisions to be taken at each step, given certain conditions. In the simplest form it is a zero/one situation, or yes/no, or off/on. A program is a set of instructions written specifically for solving a particular problem by a computer.

Originally, the installation of computer systems was a very costly and time-consuming affair. It is still quite costly but much less time consuming. The expense incurred in the installation of these systems means that the applications have to be accurately identified and the required functions precisely defined in computer terms. One of the main reasons for the time reduction is the use of available 'blocks' or suites of programs which are put together according to the client's requirements. Some individual tailoring may be needed and then special programs are written. The approach whereby systems installers utilize ready programs from their own 'libraries' is one of the main reasons for the reduction in the overall cost of computer installations.

WHEN TO INSTALL A COMPUTER SYSTEM

The computer can, in fact, be used as an extension of the human brain. Capable of performing at speeds and volumes which by far exceed the capacity of the brain, computers can be used to carry out repetitive tasks, which leaves people free to carry out more creative and responsible work. Good examples are modern billing systems like those issued by the service providers and commerce. The addition of modern peripherals extends the potential for computer applications to pictures and graphic representations as well as text. Always remember that the computer 'does as it is told': that is, it operates according to the way it has been instructed through a series of programs and is worked by the operators. 'The computer produced this' or 'The computer says so' are frequently heard expressions, with the implication that this must be right and hence conferring an element of infallibility on the tool. Nothing could be further from the truth, however, since the machine will only perform as instructed, and if something does go wrong it is certain that, mechanical or electrical failure apart, there has been a human error somewhere along the line, which, in turn, will necessitate extensive and expensive investigation and testing. Thus all systems must be subjected to rigorous testing *prior* to the 'real' run, a particularly critical requirement where applications relating to billing or legal notifications are concerned.

Computer services operate within a social context: that is, first, the population which they inform or serve, and secondly, the office within which they are implemented. Thus, though people will now accept computer-generated bill, bank or benefit statements, any response or query from the client regarding such statements must be handled with sensitivity. Because of the continuing tendency, mentioned earlier, to perceive the computer as infallible, many people may still feel threatened by it. We have heard, for example, of the problems caused by the mass arrival of final notices for payment prior to the receipt of the original bill. Much distress can be caused by such errors, with dire effects on the helpless and elderly. At present, little is understood about the social impact of computerization. Some research has been carried out, but there is still so much more to understand before we can begin to appreciate its full social impact. Nevertheless, the economic benefits of speed and volume are clear and, coupled with automated addressing, greatly reduce the clerical work involved.

COMPUTER TECHNOLOGY IN THE OFFICE

There is now an increasing trend towards installing dedicated computers in a department. A central machine may sometimes still be used, but this approach is now being overtaken by the dedicated approach.

For example, because of the ease with which computers perform 'number crunching' operations they are particularly applicable to accounts. An accounts department can operate on either method, but in the main it is more likely to have a dedicated machine. If there is dependence on a shared machine, then there will have to be an agreement as to the times and volume of usage. The rapid expansion of the storage capacity of PCs means that a good volume of data can be dealt with at any one time and also that the data is to hand and can be accessed as needed. This ease of access is an important reason for using dedicated computer systems.

Once the system is installed a period of intensive training will follow. It is important that all staff who are concerned with the use of computer technology are familiar with the procedures and the software packages used. The systems suppliers will provide manuals relating to the hardware (i.e. the equipment itself), and the software (i.e. the programs, which are the instructions for carrying out the defined tasks). The software will also have a set of manuals with instructions relating to the actual practical use of the system. Those who are concerned with the use of the computers must be fully familiar with the manuals and must be able to implement the instructions on the machines. The use of the computer systems does present a challenge that is both interesting and responsible, and which should therefore hold an appeal for staff. Following the installation of the system, there should also be an allocation of tasks to specific staff; this will make for a clearer demarcation of responsibility and a smoother running of the office.

In relation to the hardware itself the user will need to be guided to a considerable extent by the supplier. Since there is continual progress and expansion of storage capacity and since the requirement for computer space tends to increase once it is seen what computers can do, it would not be appropriate to make recommendations relating to storage volumes in a chapter such as this. However, consider the following:

1 The size of the record.
2 The 'lifespan' of the record.
3 The quantity of data to be stored.
4 Allowance for growth and expansion.

The size of the record and its complexity will be determined by the type of information. In the main, accounts-based records will tend to be simpler than text-based records; they will have fewer fields and a less complex method of retrieval. The problem of volume can be partly solved by storing only the most up-to-date records on the machine, while the 'old' data is stored in electronic form in a 'library' framework, with extra copies stored in a secure environment off the premises. Current work should also be backed up on a floppy disc and stored safely. In relation to the preparation of accounts, bills, lists and text, the backup process should be carried out throughout the complete work session. It is also a very good idea to keep safely copies of the software used, because in the event of loss of the software through accident or a disaster, that software would have to be repurchased at considerable expense.

The safe storage of the information is essential. The backup discs should be kept in a fireproof safe, while highly sensitive and confidential material may be stored in a bank vault. There are now business services which offer safe storage of computer discs and other materials.

The security of the information itself can be ensured by the use of encryption techniques. A commonly used encryption package is Pretty Good Privacy (PGP). It is available from computer software libraries and, once installed, it is easy to use and offers a high level of security. In this package, the code of the programs to which it is applied and the information being processed are convoluted to make absolute nonsense. The encryption can be reversed by the use of appropriate programs, but this presents an added problem for the perpetrator who wants to work at speed. Private Volume (PV) is another method of controlling security for sensitive data; the user has direct control over the placing of the files and can control access. Selective access to the information held on computers can also be controlled by the use of special passwords which will give clearance to access a certain level of information by automatically establishing the user's security level.

Security of the data as well as the hardware is very important. Bear in mind theft, industrial espionage, fire and other disasters which can be responsible for the collapse of an organization if the information is lost. Always remember that information is at the core of any endeavour – knowledge is power, but information is the lifeblood.

Another cause of software and data corruption is computer viruses. These are useless but damaging programs which become entangled with useful software. They are picked up when exchanging software, or even by downloading programs down the telephone lines. Sometimes viruses are let loose in a mischievous manner, causing extensive and expensive damage. (College computers are notorious for viruses as a form of student prank!) Computer viruses can also multiply and copy themselves. The problem can to a certain extent be solved by the use of anti-virus software which cleans up existing viruses and prevents infection. However, it can only deal with known viruses, and new viruses are being formed all the time. Computer users should therefore ensure that they are always up to date with the latest developments in the battle against viruses!

Other reasons for corruption or loss of data are loss of power supply and overheating by the machine. Here are possible solutions for both these problems:

1   An *uninterruptible power supply* (UPS) unit will smooth out the fluctuations in the electricity supply from the power grid. Cold spells and commercial breaks in popular television programmes are a known reason for drops in power. A UPS will also serve as a backup in the event of power failure. The UPS units vary in output and cost. There are some highly sensitive applications, where the computer power is entirely dependent on a UPS.
2   More powerful machines have a tendency to overheat and therefore require *coolers*. It is the chip which becomes overheated and can cause damage, with resulting loss of programs and data.
3   The use of a modem to connect with external services also carries risks of disconnection and destruction, in particular through lightning strikes over telephone lines with an upsurge in power which is beyond the capability of the machine, resulting in a burnout. A *line surge protector* (LSP) can be installed to help overcome this problem. BT wall sockets do contain a basic surge protector, but this is not sufficient to overcome a strong strike.

It is also worth considering insurance for both the hardware and the software, although whatever the extent of the insurance coverage, all other possible security precautions must be taken. It is worth remembering that in the   *65* case of computer theft, it is not only the hardware that is lost but also the programs and data, if these have been installed. The loss is therefore far in excess of the nominal value of the hardware and the software since it also represents work and business contacts and thus the potential loss of business, with severe consequences.

There is a market in secondhand electronic equipment, and it is therefore sensible to make it as difficult as possible for a thief to dispose of the equipment. For instance, mark the equipment thoroughly with an invisible marker, using unique symbols which are recorded and stored safely. Bolting down the equipment is another deterrent, but now there is a market for the chips alone, so a computer can be dismantled *in situ* and the chips removed! Also remember to dispose of the discarded packaging straightaway; when replaced in the original box, stolen equipment can give the appearance of bona fide stock.

SAFETY

Under the Health and Safety Act of 1974 employers are duty bound to safeguard the safety of their employees. The Employment Medical Advisory Service (EMAS) which is part of the Health and Safety Executive may be approached for advice by employers, doctors and trade unions. The computer is not a dangerous machine in the sense that heavy engineering equipment can be. However, there are still certain precautions that need to be observed:

1   The prolonged use of the VDU can result in eye strain, and guidelines have been issued by Health and Safety at Work for the duration of work involving VDUs. The time spent at the VDU should not be excessive and there should be regular breaks. There should be frequent sight tests for VDU operators, and if an operator wears spectacles, these should be adjusted for VDU work.
2   Prolonged use of most keyboards often results in cramped fingers. In touch-typing the fingertips are in constant use, which can place excessive strain on the finger joints. One solution is the use of a wrist support; this is a soft strip of foam or rubber upon which the wrist can be rested during typing.
3   Repetitive strain injury (RSI) has been in the news of late. Operatives at terminals claim that they have become afflicted with weakening of the joints through constant input into the computer. This is certainly an important consideration. There should therefore be frequent breaks for the operator and time spent at the computer terminal should not be excessive, particularly when inputting data.

DOCUMENT PREPARATION

Conventional typing has now been largely replaced by word-processing facilities. In addition, large volumes of text can be input using scanners. These are *optical character recognition* (OCR) devices which are able to 'read' the text electronically and input this into the computer. This is obviously a much faster and more efficient way to input ready text, and is an approach that could be used to create files of specialized information (e.g. research files and related publications). When the creation of new text is involved, then there are other methods involving word processing. There are a number of packages or suites of programs which have been written for the purpose of text input and storage in the computer in electronic form. These are commonly referred to as word-processing packages. The advantage of this technique, as opposed to the use of the typewriter, is the versatility of the method, the facility to correct mistakes on the screen, and the potential for manipulation and inclusion of graphics to produce professional-looking documents with relative ease. The keyboard and the arrangement of the characters in roman script is according to the QWERTY format, so that a person who is able to touch-type is also a potential keyboard operator.

Word processing also has a wider range of editing facilities: for example, the movement of words, sentences and paragraphs; the copying of blocks of text from one document to another; the changing of typefaces; and the inclusion of tables and diagrams. The layout of the text can also be preset, as margins, indentations and footnotes. There are different fonts (styles of typescript) and these can also be specified in different sizes (points). Text can also be underlined, and can be specified in bold or italic.

There are several word processing packages currently available, and it is best to choose that which is best suited to the chosen hardware and the requirements defined by the activity of the organization. Currently popular is software based on the WINDOWS approach developed by Microsoft, such as WORD.

There are a number of correction aids built into most word-processing packages. The most useful is the spellchecker, but do make sure that the spelling is appropriate to the culture (e.g. United States or United Kingdom). The usefulness of grammar checkers is more debatable. They can be quite good fun to play with, but the human being is much better than the computer in the use of language. Another useful device is a computerized thesaurus, which is rather like the printed version in that it suggests alternatives, and being computerized, it can be used in an integrated kind of way.

The more powerful the package, the more it will lend itself to *desktop publishing* (DTP). Such facilities are very useful and mean that a number of useful documents can be produced quickly. DTP software is an extension of word-processing software with greater potential for text manipulation (e.g. headings, columns, boxes, and so forth). Most packages can work with colour, but this will require a colour printer. Word-processing and DTP packages are frequently used together to give very professional-looking results.

MULTIMEDIA

Sometimes text is not sufficient to convey the entire message, and sound and video may also be needed. There are specially adapted computers which work on multimedia presentations. Obviously similar machines are required to read these presentations. The use of hypertext techniques is appropriate to multimedia applications. The idea is that there are 'hidden' pages which can be called up by the use of appropriate signs (e.g. highlighted words to call up a new set of related information). For example, in the case of stock control lists, the stock can be grouped according to the type of stock (e.g. screws) and then a 'hidden' list of types of screws by composition and size. Computer-based help systems for users are also based on the hypertext format. Another use for a hypertext format is the content of a book or a report subdividing chapter headings and section headings in the same way. Variations on these basic facilities are available on different computers and this may be one factor influencing choice of machine.

EXCHANGE OF INFORMATION

The simplest way to exchange information is to hand over to a colleague or an enquirer the requested information in an electronic medium such as a disc or tape. The problems of viruses should always be borne in mind. While most reputable institutions do all they can to deliver clean software, some corruption could take place *en route*, so that a sweep through for viruses is recommended.

There is an increasing trend towards the transfer of information in electronic format, and, in the case of programs, this is the easiest way. For example, a suite of programs was prepared for those who wished to submit applications for research grants to the EU in the AIM (Advanced Informatics in Medicine) programme. This was particularly useful because the information needed was clearly structured and, from the point of view of the evaluators, the information from all the applicants was presented in a standard format and was thus easily comparable.

Information can also be exchanged by computer networks, and there is now an increasing volume of networking. *Local area networks* (LAN) are limited to one site, while *wide area networks* (WAN) operate across distances and can, for example, be used to connect several sites within a company. The specialist services to which users can subscribe also operate on the WAN system. These are generally information providers for defined groups of users. Internet is also a WAN system, but this is open to anyone through a number of servers worldwide.

ELECTRONIC MAIL (E-MAIL)

Electronic mail passes information from computer to computer directly. There are two levels of E-mail: first, that which is based on a restricted LAN or WAN system for a specific group of users; and secondly, that which can be accessed from around the world. The advantage of this mode of communication is the speed and relative cheapness of the method, but a disadvantage is that it can be intercepted and this can have very serious consequences relating to security. An efficient way of overcoming this drawback is to encrypt the E-mail message.

INTERNET

Internet can be accessed by anyone. The connection is made via a telephone and a modem. A modem is a device which converts telephone signals into electronic form; nowadays, most modems are built into the computer. Some years ago the modem was a rather amusing coupling device where one inserted the receiver, having first dialled a computer and obtained a connection tone. When these devices are described to modern students, there is much hilarity! To use Internet it is first necessary to open an account with an Internet service provider. There is a charge for this connection with a monthly subscription. The other payments are dependent on the type of services offered by the provider. All act as gateways connecting the computer to Internet, while others also perform such services as 'letter-box' for E-mail.

A wide range of information is available on Internet. Some of this is specialized (e.g. stock market information), which is expensive to use, while other information is free and is based on the exchange of information between interested parties. There is highly specialized, professional information as well as debate, chat, gossip and fun. There are definite advantages to the use of Internet in a disciplined way, because there is news, technical and financial information as well as the facility to use it for E-mail around the world; there is also expert assistance on a range of computer-based issues. However, bear in mind that the interest created by using Internet, once discovered, could become too time consuming for the efficient running of a department. Therefore, some control has to be exercised.

The *bulletin board service* (BBS) is similar in concept to Internet. This system is adopted by some companies for their products and clients can access the service at any time to place their orders. The BBS has to be set up by the company, and the software for this is not expensive. The forerunners of Internet were systems which are still available today and were also based on the WAN concept: an example is Data Star based in Switzerland. These systems can be accessed for a variety of specialized databases via nodes which are local telephone numbers connected via modems to the network. The computers holding the information may be in another country but the relevant material is delivered electronically to the user. A fairly complicated query language is involved to structure and refine the information in complex subjects. There are also extensive terminological and subject models which need to be used by specialists to obtain the optimum retrieval from the database.

Computers have enormous potential. They have enabled us to make huge strides in the understanding of the world and also to make life easier for people, from medical applications to the working environment. Like all tools, they can go wrong, but precautions can be taken to minimize these possibilities. Thus people and computers should have a fruitful coexistence.

CHECK LIST: POINTS TO BE BORNE IN MIND WHEN USING IT

1   Ensure that the systems installed are compatible with other systems in the organization.
2   Documentation: all manuals relating to the system must be obtained and must be stored in a safe and accessible place.
3   Staff should be sent on courses initially to learn about the system, and also subsequently on refresher courses.
4   Safeguard health and safety by adherence to the HSE recommendations.
5   Ensure that there is a power backup to safeguard against power failure.
6   Always keep duplicates of all software.
7   Back up all work by copying on to disc and store in a safe place.
8   Keep a complete set of all data and software in safe storage off the premises.
9   Ensure security by the use of passwords.
10 Change the passwords at regular intervals.
11 Allow selective access to the information by different levels of security clearance; this facility would be password linked.
12 Give serious consideration to the use of E-mail, Internet and BBS, but controls should be exercised with respect to access.
13 Remember that the use of IT is intended to make work easier and contribute to greater efficiency; it can be fun, but it should not dominate.
14 Be aware that a small error can have far-reaching repercussions.

FURTHER READING

Health and Safety Executive, *Guidance on Regulations*, display screen equipment, HSE, 1992.

Health and Safety Executive, *Regulations*, display screen equipment, HSE, 1992.

Einstein, D., *PCs for Busy People*, Osborne/McGraw-Hill, 1996.

Gookin, D., *PCs for Dummies*, 4th edn, IDG Books, 1996.

Knorr, E. (ed.), *The PC Bible*, Peachpit Press, 1995.

O'Mara, M. and Routledge, G., *Using your PC*, 2nd edn, Que, 1996.

O'Reilly Associates Inc., *The Computer Users Survival Guide*, O'Reilly Associates Inc., 1995.

Information sheets on repetitive strain injury (RSI) are also available from:

> RSI Association
> Chapel House
> High Street
> Yiewsley
> West Drayton
> Middlesex UB7 7BE
>
> Tel: 01895-431134

5 Writing

Krystyna Weinstein

What is written without effort is rarely read with pleasure.

(Dr Johnson, 18th century)

To do our work well we all have to read a mass of papers. Nearly all of them are far too long. This wastes time, while energy has to be spent in looking for the essential points. (Winston Churchill, 20th century)

If men would only say in plain terms what they have to say, how much more eloquent they would be. (Samuel Coleridge, 19th century)

If language is not correct, then what is said is not what is meant. If what is said is not what is meant, then what ought to be done remains undone.

(Confucius, 5th century BC)

We should write one way to a strong man, another to a sluggard; one way to a green youth, another to an elder who has fulfilled his life; one way to a proud and successful man, another to a victim of adversity; one way to an enlightened literary scholar, another to one who can't grasp any high thoughts.

(Petrarch, 14th century)

Whatever you want to say, there is only one word that will express it; one verb to make it move; one adjective to qualify it. You must seek that word, that verb, and that adjective, and never be satisfied with approximations, never resort to tricks, even clever ones, or to verbal pirouettes to escape the difficulty.

(Gustave Flaubert to Guy de Maupassant, 19th century)

To fix something in the memory, it is of great value when we are reading to imprint on the memory the colour, shape, position or placement of [words].

(12th century reminder to manuscript writers)

These seven quotations, spanning many centuries, sum up most of what needs to be said about how to write well. They remind writers that their sole purpose in writing is to gain the attention of a reader, and make sure the text delivers to that reader what he or she needs or wants to know. We should not, as writers, be writing solely for ourselves.

Many people find writing difficult. Maybe because what is written down is saved and can be referred to later. Maybe because it appears to carry more weight than spoken words which disappear into the ether. Yet writing has a very positive side to it: it helps us organize our thoughts. As we write we often find ideas and insights emerging that we did not have before the act of writing. We also discover what we know and what we don't know – because it is impossible to write about something we are not clear about. Woolly thoughts emerge as woolly writing.

WRITING IS LIKE HAVING A CONVERSATION

Perhaps it is time to think of writing in a more positive way. For writing is really no different from having a conversation with someone. The only real difference is that you cannot see your reader: you cannot have a dialogue with him or her, or see where they do not understand you, or disagree. Your side of the relationship, however, is – or should be – as close to having a con-versation as possible. But because your listener/reader cannot respond instantly, and give you the chance to follow up or explain something you have said/written, you must do more thinking before you embark on a piece of writing (although hopefully, you also think before you have a conversation!).

Therefore, whether it is speaking or writing to people, the same rules apply: Who are you talking to, what is your intention, what outcome are you hoping for, and what will you need to say/write to achieve what you set out to do? None the less, writing is no substitute for a face-to-face conversation. So much of what we say is conveyed by body language and tone of voice, and both of these will, inevitably, be missing from a written text (although tone can be conveyed by the right choice of words, and by using short sentences). (See also Chapter 20 on 'Communication'.)

The aim in this chapter is to give readers – who are also writers – help and hints on more effective writing, and to pinpoint the pitfalls to avoid. To begin: one way to highlight the writing process may be to outline how this chapter itself was written.

WRITING THIS CHAPTER

Writing this chapter on writing was very like sitting down to write a letter, a memo or report, or any other document, no matter what its purpose. They are all texts that will be read by someone for a purpose. My first thought was to be clear who the chapter (and hence this book) is aimed at. Who would be reading it, for what purpose, and what would they hope to gain by reading it? Next, I thought about my own intentions, and what I considered would be helpful. What did I hope readers would be able to do differently after working through this chapter?

This process led me to begin to analyse what I wanted to 'say', what infor-mation I would present – and I began to jot down ideas on paper. Very soon, and before I had too many jottings, I began to think of the structure of the 73 chapter: how I would begin (beginnings are almost always the most difficult!) and how I would then move on – how my text would flow from point to point. It was at that stage that I conceived the idea of outlining how I approached the writing of the chapter. So, I then sat down and wrote it – but went on adding to the text in the course of writing.

It was after writing this section, and assembling my ideas in some coherent form, that I was able to create a structure for the chapter as a whole. The points began to fall into place. Luckily, with word-processors, one can write and then rearrange the text at will. Thus I was aware that I was not writing in a strictly linear fashion: that is, beginning at the beginning and ending up with a conclusion, for that is not necessarily the best, or only, way to write, although it may suit some people. I knew that I could begin by writing the parts that were the easiest, and then turn my mind to those points that I was still unclear about.

Once I began to write, I became aware of the language I was using, the words I was choosing, and how my sentences were forming. Sentences should be relatively short (after all we speak in short sentences), and I had to make sure that no one sentence conveyed too much information. What I was trying to do was to write in a way that resembled the way I speak, and I had continually to check that the text was easy to read.

After writing large passages I reread and edited what I had written (I don't stop too often, though, because that stops the 'creative' flow). I was checking for logical flow (structure), the content and sentence length; checking how my paragraphs were structured, and whether there was enough link and logical connection between the ideas I was trying to convey as I moved on to new sentences or paragraphs (this was not always the case, however, and I had to rewrite, add in, take out or move parts of the text). As I read – not quite aloud, but almost – I was 'listening' to see whether my language was straight-forward.

At this point I also started to put in headings and subheadings, making sure that both main headings and subheadings were all 'of a kind' (i.e. in the correct typeface and type size). At the same time I looked to see what parts of the text needed to be highlighted – for instance, by placing them in a 'box', or by creating lists – to emphasize the points I was making.

Once I felt the text had something approaching its final shape, I printed it out and read it. You cannot edit properly on screen. After incorporating all the corrections into the text, I once again printed it out, this time to proofread it – a stage that is so often missed out by writers.

Obviously there is more to writing than the process outlined above. The rest of this chapter will look in more detail at the various stages I mentioned. But before doing so, it would be useful for you, the reader, to do the exercise below. Since we are all readers, as well as writers, our own insight – as readers of other people's texts – helps us to see our own weaknesses!

Exercise Ask yourself: What annoys you, as a reader, in other people's texts?
Write down the points. You may, for instance, be bothered by spelling

mistakes, poor layout, and so on. When you have done this, then consider: Do your own texts contain any of the points you have listed? Many writers admit to finding in their own writing those points that annoy them in other people's texts.

THE SIX STAGES OF WRITING

When people sit down to write, one of several things may happen: the words may tumble out in a rush; or the writer suddenly feels paralysed, with nothing to say; or thoughts emerge in an incoherent mass, and will not fall into place logically. For the lucky few, writing is an easy exercise: beginning at the beginning, ending up where the writer intended and the finished piece is a pleasure to read.

Good writing results from the writer having worked through six specific stages: thinking, jotting, planning and structuring, writing, editing, and proofreading (see Figure 5.1). No matter what you write – for example, a short memo to your staff, a letter to a customer, an E-mail to someone in another department, a report for your boss, or a presentation for a meeting you have to attend – all the stages are important.

The stages do not have to be strictly sequential. You may prefer to start with writing, for only in that way do you gain enough of a feel for the subject to do more thinking. You may view structure in the same way: that you need to have thought out more of the content, before you can develop its structure.

We each work differently. There is no single optimum way of working. The

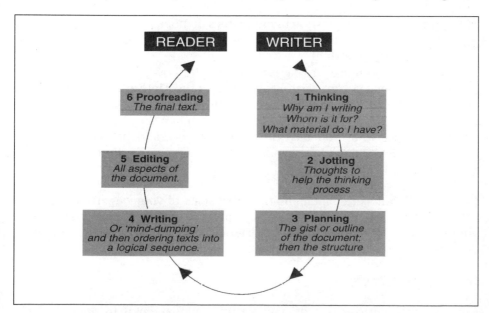

Figure 5.1   The writing cycle

important thing is to make sure that at some stage you pay attention to all six stages. You will discover for yourself which order suits you best.

Stage 1   Thinking

This is a stage that is so often missed out. You are asked to write something, and you just sit down and begin to write. In some cases, thoughts tumble out, ideas follow one another, incoherently and illogically; or else you feel threatened because you don't know what to say or how to say it. You sit and panic. Alternatively, you may write a brilliant text, but it will not serve the purpose for which you were supposedly writing, and it may not be what the reader needs or wants.

All these symptoms may occur if you have not first thought through the five Ws of writing (which every good journalist knows and uses):

- *Who* is your reader?
- *Why* are you writing?
- *What* will you write?
- *Where* and *When* will the piece you have written be read?

You also need to ask a sixth question:

- *How* can you best convey your text?

Who is your reader?

This, surprisingly, is a question many writers do not ask themselves. And yet, if you heed what Petrarch had to say 500 years ago (see above), who you are writing for is very important.

Knowing who you are writing for will tell you how much knowledge that person has of what you are writing about, what their interest in the subject is, and what language to use when writing. Even if your readers are your colleagues at work, you still have to consider how much they know, or what particular angle of what you have in mind they need to be told or will be interested in. If you don't know your readers, you can ask others, or do some research to find out.

Exercise: If you were explaining the intricacies of your department's work to, say, your managing director, or to someone outside the company, or to your husband/wife or girlfriend/boyfriend, how would your 'text' differ in each case: in detail, length, language, and 'angle'?

Why are you writing?

Knowing the purpose of why you write is fundamental to good writing. Without knowing that, you cannot really construct a coherent text; you will simply drift around the subject. Consider, therefore, which of the following is the purpose of the text you are about to create – maybe your next letter or E-mail:

- To pass on information.
- To instruct.
- To discuss and comment on ideas.
- To evaluate suggestions.
- To provide recommendations.
- To advocate a strategy or course of action.
- Anything else?

Whichever of these it is will, in turn, depend on two things: your own intention, and any request you may have had from the reader(s). Are you clear about either or both of these points?

Another way of looking at this question of 'Why?' is to ask yourself: 'What do I want my reader to be able to do or think after reading my document?' Once you have the answer, focus your text in such a way that your reader moves to that point. Thus, if you want your readers to take urgent action in a particular matter, you must tell them so clearly and concisely. When you come to structuring your text, you also need to state this requirement very early on in your text (see Front-loading, below).

Having decided on the 'why?', stop and consider for a moment: Is a written message – say, a memo or E-mail – the best way of achieving what you want? Would it be better to go and see the person or people concerned (if that is feasible)? Or, rather than write a report, would a verbal presentation be better?

One way to help you remember your original intention in writing, is to think in terms of three *colours*: red, green and blue.[1] Red means that you are simply giving information; green means that you are proposing ideas, giving suggestions, being inventive; and blue means that you are taking decisions, making choices, passing judgement. So, when you write – or are asked to write – ask yourself: Should I be in red, green, or blue? Do I need to make sure that all three are in my text, or is, say, staying in red sufficient? For instance, if you have been asked to recommend a course of action, remember to be strong on blue, but also bring in the red to back up your judgement.

What will you write?

This is not a question concerning the subject on which you will be writing – on which there may be no discussion – but about the approach to it. The 'What?' is to do with level, detail and angle, which will be determined largely by the answers to the previous two questions: who are you writing to, and why are you writing.

Exercise: Consider the following circumstances:

1 You are explaining changes in your working procedures: first, in a letter to a customer, client, or supplier; and secondly, in a memo to other departments in your own company. How will the angle, level of information, and detail differ in each case?

2 You are explaining the impact of new market opportunities that have opened up: first, to the production department, and secondly, to the personnel department. How will what you write differ between departments?

3 You have been asked to brief your boss on a subject for a meeting. Will he or she want just facts, or a particular argument with supporting data, or material to counter someone else's arguments? How do you know what angle to take?

Where and when the text will be read and/or used?

You must think about the 'Where?' and 'When?' before you launch into any writing. If the material is for a meeting, you will need to write reasonably short and 'accessible' notes, well laid out, because people at meetings do not have the time to scan many pages and hunt for detail. They need to see at a glance the relevant passages of text. They may, in fact, prefer bullet lists, key words emphasized, and lots of diagrams and other visual material, rather than a lengthy text.

How to present the text?

The 'How?' refers to four elements:

1 What is the most appropriate form for your text? Is it a memo or a more formal letter? Should it be a written report, or a presentation?

2 Is a written text the best option, or would visual material better convey your message?

3 What language should you be using? Jargon is fine if your readers know about the subject matter. If they don't, use plain English.

4 The presentation and layout of any document is important. What would make it easier to read and digest? Have you broken up each page so that it looks inviting to the reader? A page-long paragraph, for instance, will rarely be read.

As Winston Churchill pointed out (see above), we all have too much to read. We will therefore read either what is written in an easy-to-digest form, or what looks attractive. We are used to seeing highly professional visual layouts in brochures and magazines. We must incorporate those standards in our own writing.

Exercise: Look critically at a text that you wrote recently. How does it look? Is it something you would willingly pick up and read? Or would you push it to one side?

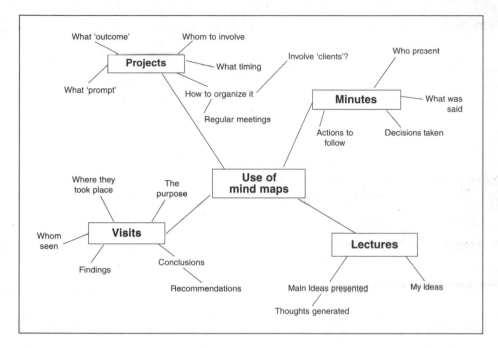

Figure 5.2   Mind maps

Stage 2   Jotting

As you are thinking through the five Ws you will probably already be jotting down some ideas. These jottings may be simply key words, headings, whole sentences, or ideas in note form. Whatever form your jottings take, however, you must make sure at this stage that you put all your ideas down on paper, so that you can then decide which are the most important and which are of less importance.

We are used to writing down ideas in a linear form by making a list down a page. This is certainly one way of jotting down points. However, there is another way which collects this information in a format that enables you to summon up a broader range of ideas. Known as a mind map[2] (see Figure 5.2), its value is that it engages both the right and left sides of the brain. Creating a linear list, down a page, uses primarily the left side of the brain, in which reside our logical, sequential abilities. In the right side of the brain reside the lateral, connecting and visualizing abilities. This means that when you create a mind map – which is a visual way of placing ideas – you are more likely (though not necessarily) to come up with more ideas and make unforeseen connections, than by simply making a list.

As you build up a mind map, you are creating a large amount of ideas and other material that is relevant to what you are planning to write, but not yet in a logical form.[3] For the purpose of writing, these ideas must be organized into a logical and sequential form.

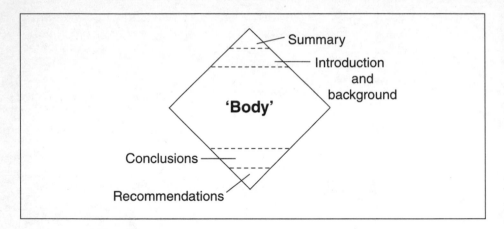

Figure 5.3   The diamond

Stage 3   Planning

Planning the structure of a text – letter, memo, longer report, or whatever – is often the most difficult part of the writing. It is not possible to list all the different structures and permutations available. In the end, a structure has to be worked out by the writer. Nevertheless, there are a few ideas that might help.

Prepared structures

Some texts follow prepared structures. For instance, visit reports often have a few headings that need simply to be completed (e.g. date of visit, who was

---

Summary
A brief text, giving the main points from each section of a longer document. It should be a document that can stand on its own, to give to people who either do not want or do not need to read the whole document.

Introduction
A brief text that tells the reader what the following document is about, and what it hopes to achieve. For example, an introduction might be just one paragraph at the beginning of a letter, or several paragraphs at the beginning of a report.

Conclusion
A text that pulls together the various points which emerge in the document. It sums up the ideas, facts, insights and judgements reached in the body of the document.

Recommendations
A text which moves on into the future, and, on the basis of the conclusions drawn in the document, suggests what action should be taken.

Figure 5.4   Elements of a report

seen, what was discussed, what conclusions were reached, what recommendations made, and so forth). Many other reports have a common, diamond-shaped format (see Figure 5.3).

This, however, merely tells you the order; it does not explain what goes into a section entitled 'Summary', 'Introduction', and so on. For what these sections normally contain, see Figure 5.4. It is not really possible to say what goes into the body of a particular report, for that will depend on the subject and the purpose. But we will now look at some ideas on how to structure that body, by using flow charts and other approaches.

Flow charts

If you do not have a prepared format – either for your entire document, or for the body of a report – you have to think it out for yourself. All texts need to be structured into a logical and coherent form to enable your reader to build up a picture of what you are saying – and not to have to work too hard while doing so.

One way of building up such a logical train of thought is to create a flow chart (see Figure 5.5). If you have created a mind map, use that and think through what would be a logical way of organizing this mass of material. Become a reader, as well as being the writer. What would you see as a useful progression? You could approach this in several ways:

1 *Working backwards* You might go back to the 'Why?' question, which provides you with what you want to achieve – in other words, you are working backwards. Let us take the example, shown in Figure 5.5. You have been asked to provide recommendations on how to develop specific skills among your staff. By working backwards:

   (a) You would have to end your piece by saying what these skills would be *after* the training.
   (b) The next step back would be to say how these skills would be acquired.
   (c) Stepping back again, you would find yourself pointing out that staff did not have these skills, and what problems this caused.
   (d) You might describe how the initiative to train the staff first came about. This last point would then become your introduction.

   At this stage, you would probably revert to the 'end', and add in a conclusion which points out what benefits will be achieved by this retraining. Alternatively, you could decide that such a section would be better placed near the beginning, after the introduction. And as you continue to look at the flow chart, you may have other thoughts that you can slot in at the appropriate spot.

2 *Working forwards* You might prefer instead to work forwards. Look at the ideas contained in your mind map, and decide what you think is the *81*

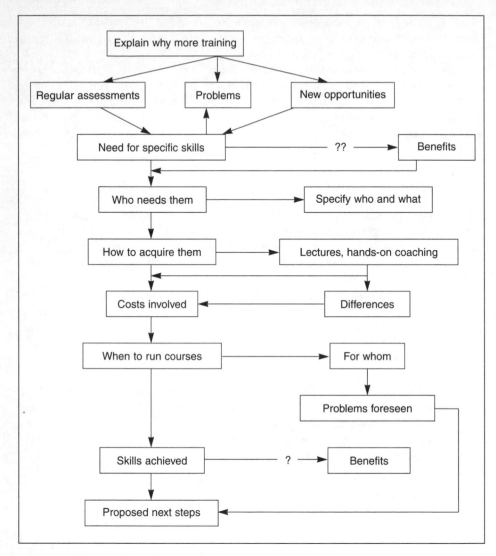

Figure 5.5   A flow chart

most logical way of structuring this information. You may gain some insights by going back to the 'Why?' of your writing. You may also find it useful to think of yourself as the reader, and ask yourself what order and what presentation of ideas you find most convincing and helpful.

3   *Front-loading*   This is a very useful structure for letters and memos. Instead of beginning your text with a historical outline of some event, and then leading up to the point you are trying to make, which means placing it at the end, reverse the order. Begin with the point you want to make, and then explain the background.

Thus, if you are writing because you want something to be done, say this in the first sentence. Don't force your reader to plough through the whole text before reaching the main point.

For example, if you are responsible for, say, a computer card procedure, and you find that people are not following it, what do you do? Do you write a text that tells them that a procedure exists, and why it was introduced, but unfortunately it isn't working, and so this is what needs to happen – and then list the procedures that have to be followed?

Or do you reverse this, and front-load your text? Why not begin with the fact that new procedures are required to carry out the work in hand. The existing procedures have been ignored recently, so you would welcome co-operation in ensuring that the new procedures are followed. Then list them.

What this front-loading is doing is reversing our usual way of writing. We are taught throughout our school days to write in such a way that we build up our ideas or evidence until we reach a point at which we can say, 'And so ...': that is, we reach a crescendo. This is a scientific, or inductive, way of writing, presenting all our evidence step by step until we reach a conclusion. In business, however, we often need to take the reverse action – what I call 'upside-down structuring' – and say at the very beginning what we have uncovered, discovered, want to do, or have done. We then go on to point out the benefits, followed by 'How I reached that discovery', 'Why I need that done', and so on. In other words, this way of structuring your writing is the opposite of the scientific/inductive approach (see Figure 5.6).

By front-loading, you are telling your readers directly what you are writing to them about. They don't have to wade through a mass of text while asking themselves all the while, 'Why have I been sent this? What am I meant to do with it?', and having to read through to the end to discover the main point. Remember Winston Churchill's exhortation (see above).

A letter of complaint written by a customer to a kitchen supplier exemplifies this 'front-loading' principle. She began with a description of everything that had gone wrong, and in the final paragraph she ended by saying, '... and I wish to be reimbursed'. Then it occurred to her that

	Scientific/inductive structuring	Upside-down/business structuring
1.	We uncovered ... and discovered ... and these are the benefits.	We discovered ... and the benefits are ... and here is how we arrived at this.
2.	Because so and so occurs, the result is ... and the benefits are ...	We have a result that offers the following benefits ... and this is how it came about.

Figure 5.6   Two different structures

the purpose of her letter was contained in the last paragraph. She was writing because she wanted a refund. She therefore reversed the order of her letter, beginning by saying that she wanted a refund, and then going on to explain why.

Exercise   Look at some of your own texts. Where, within them, is the main point you are trying to make? Is it in the first two or three sentences? In the first two or three paragraphs? Or at the end of your text?

Other options for structuring

1   You might create a structure by thinking through the five Ws (listed earlier) which every journalist uses when writing a story. But you still have to decide on the most logical order.
2   If you have been asked to prepare ideas or evaluate suggestions, then the format might be:

(a)   An introduction stating that this is what you have been asked to do – and to what purpose.
(b)   Then you list the ideas, one by one, and state the advantages and disadvantages of each.
(c)   Next, you may have to choose one and recommend it, stating why you have done so – and maybe adding what would happen if it was not chosen.

Stage 4   Writing

At last, the writing! What are the pitfalls to avoid, and what should you be aware of, as you start to write. You may have begun writing your text as you thought and planned. You may now be able to link up ideas or words. Or you may have waited until you were ready to write the whole text in one go (though this will rarely be the case if you are writing a long report).

Reports, in particular, worry many people. This probably has to do with the term itself, which hints at something long and complex. It may therefore help if you call it something else, to lessen the mental anxiety. Try thinking of it as 'My thoughts on ...' or 'My insights into ...'. On the same lines, if writing letters or memos worries you, it may help to think of them as conversations with the other person.

Even after working out a good logical way of structuring, you may still not know how to start writing. Here are two tips that may help to resolve the problem:

1   Start writing those passages that you feel will be the easiest for you – and that might even be the conclusion.
2   Or simply start writing ... literally anything. Even something like, 'I don't know where to start, the idea of having to put down my ideas worries

me, because ...'. This act of writing often loosens up the mind, and allows ideas to start flowing.

But even once ideas start flowing, the next barrier is the language that you, as a writer, use. The text sounds unnatural. It doesn't 'sound' like you, or recognizably written by you. Often this is because the language you are using is stilted and long-winded. You are using long words and complicated sentences, thinking that the written word has to be formal, that it has to impress. And yet by trying to impress, you cease to express what you have to say. You confuse and lose the reader, who in turn has to read such texts two or three times to grasp your meaning.

Exercise Do you recognize the way you write in the description above? Check with some texts you have recently written. What do they sound like if you read them out aloud? Are they you? Do they convey their meaning straightforwardly? Do the sentences in fact convey their real meaning? Remember what Confucius had to say (see above).

Write more like you speak

There is a place for formal yet expressive language, and there is also a place for natural language. The main 'hint' to help writers produce writing that flows, is easy to read, conveys its message straightforwardly, and yet has a sense of individuality about it, is: write more like you speak.

There is no reason why writing should not resemble speech. True, we often speak ungrammatically, but that can be remedied at the editing stage. And if we use everyday words where possible, in the text we are writing and for the intended reader, we need more formal words, these can also be substituted at the editing stage.

If you feel that your writing sounds stilted (and you will know by reading it out aloud and realizing it just is not you), then imagine, while you are writing, that you are talking to someone. 'Say' what it is you want to say and then write it down. It will be much simpler and more comprehensible – and your reader will be much happier. Inevitably, however, some managers will have rigid views on how things should be expressed, and will be unwilling to let their own, or others' writing be simplified and made more readable.

Writing sentences and paragraphs

The second main point to remember is not to write in long sentences. We speak in short sentences – because we have to take a breath. The same happens when readers read. They need to 'take a breath' in order to digest what has been written. Writing in short sentences gives them a tiny break before going on to the next point, in the next sentence. Ideally, sentences should have no more than 20 words in them, and each sentence should contain only one thought. If you have more to add to the thought already *85* expressed, start a new sentence. When you edit your piece at a later stage, you may decide that the two separate sentences would be better as one. Luckily, any such changes are easy on word processors.

Sentences must have a verb in them, and end with a full stop, exclamation or question mark. These points sound obvious, but it is surprising how often texts do not follow these grammatical rules. When writing, try also to put verbs into the active voice, rather than the passive. Instead of writing, 'It was decided by the committee that ...' write, 'The committee decided ...' It is grammatically correct and shorter – and it is what you would say! (The indication that a verb is in the passive voice is the word 'by'.)

Next, do not allow paragraphs to be too long either. On average, a paragraph should be made up of five or six sentences (i.e. about 100 words). Remember that a paragraph expresses and develops an idea. The first sentence will usually introduce it in some way, and the following sentences will develop that idea. When you start to talk of another idea, begin a new paragraph.

Headings help

Headings are a form of signposting which helps the reader, as well as the writer. They are a reminder to the writer of what he or she has announced will be in the following text. By returning to the heading a writer can check that he or she is still writing to the point. If there has been a change of subject, maybe a new heading is needed. And to ensure that even within individual paragraphs the writer keeps on track, an 'invisible' heading above that paragraph – that is, a heading that is not left in the final text – also helps to keep the writing focused.

For the writer, headings ensure that the logic of his or her text is being followed. In fact, writing out the headings of your text will show you where your logic may have gone astray. Headings may be suggested both by the flow chart and by the mind map.

For the reader, headings help in following the writer's train of thought. They are also a way of helping readers scan through a text to see what sections to read.

When using headings there are two points to remember. First, if they are to be helpful signposts, you must make sure that their style is consistent: that is, all main headings need to follow the same style (e.g. upper case, bold face), and similarly, all subheadings must also follow a consistent style.

Secondly, try to bring your headings alive by placing verbs in them. Instead of writing, for instance, 'Management commitment to changes', write 'Managers are committed to changes'. Headings with verbs have energy in them and entice readers. The same, of course, is true about titles of reports, and even memos. For instance, a title such as 'Computer procedures' is a 'dead head' which tells you nothing about the text beneath it. But 'How to follow the new computer procedures' instantly tells the reader what he or she will be reading about.

Above all, avoid headings and titles that consist of a string of four or five nouns. The reader will have difficulty trying to work out their relationship to one another.

Exercise How do you personally read texts? Do you read them word by word, or scan? And if you scan, how do you do that? Now look at your own texts. Would those texts enable you to read or scan them easily? If not, what is missing? Next, look at your headings. Do they convey sufficiently to a reader what follows in the text? Do you have many that are a string of nouns? Would more active headings and titles help?

Check your grammar and spelling

Bad spelling and grammatical mistakes detract from a text, no matter how good its content and structure. The reader may become so angered by both that he or she stops focusing on the content of the text and sees only the mistakes. Worse: he or she may begin to doubt the quality of the information in the text. If the writer, so they think, cannot take care about spelling and grammar, can you trust him or her to be careful about the content?

If you are unsure about elements of grammar, buy a book that will point them out to you; and if you are unsure about spelling, buy a dictionary (you cannot always rely on spellcheckers in word-processing packages). The other indispensable book any writer needs is a thesaurus: a listing of words with all their synonyms. A thesaurus enlarges the vocabulary you use – and the English language is a very rich language.

How does the text look?

How the text looks may be vital. Readers are more likely to read and appreciate a text that is well laid out and makes the reading easy. Leave some white space within the text: that is, don't pack the text too tightly. Remember also to highlight points you want to make. And use headings.

The text may also be improved – or made easier to understand – if you use visual material: diagrams, maps, charts (tables are difficult to read unless well thought out). You may find that using a diagram or other visual aid can eliminate many words. A picture speaks a thousand words, we're told.

Stage 5 Editing

This next stage is as important as the preceding four, but it is often omitted by writers. A reader, however, will recognize an unedited text instantly. It will have mistakes, inconsistencies, even illogical structuring, and will look messy.

Good editing can only be done on hard copy (i.e. on a text printed out on paper). You cannot edit effectively on a screen.

To be a good editor of your own text, try, if you can, to leave 24 hours   *87* between the writing and the editing. In that way you can begin to distance yourself from your own words (never easy at the best of times) and begin instead to see your text as a reader might. You might also ask someone else to read it for you.

There are several points to look out for when editing:

- Is the content right for the task you intended it for? (Go back to 'why' you are writing, and 'who for'.)
- is it well and logically structured? Do some parts of the text need to be moved?
- How does it read? Does it sound like you? Is the language stilted, or does it flow naturally? Is it in language that is comprehensible for the reader – or have you been trying to impress with long and complex words, or jargon?
- Are there any spelling and grammatical mistakes?
- Lastly, what does the text look like? How is it laid out? Is there enough 'white space'?

Make any necessary changes. But do remember that if you make any corrections to the text by adding or taking out text, that may well affect other sections of your document. Similarly, if you alter even just one sentence, read the preceding and following sentences. A small change may affect both of them.

Breaking down the editing of a text into the five elements listed above is a useful guide for anyone who is responsible for editing other people's texts, or for managers who are helping their staff learn to write better documents. It offers a way of pinpointing what may be wrong in a text. Hence, instead of saying to someone, 'This text is bad', a manager or editor can identify precisely what is wrong with it (e.g. the structure or the grammar), and can offer specific help to the writer. Unspecific feedback on a 'bad' text is less than helpful.

Stage 6   Proofreading

Once you have corrected your hard copy and transferred the corrections on to the screen, print out the final text and proofread it for any small errors you overlooked at the editing stage. Proofreading can only be done on paper – not on screen – and can only be done effectively by reading one line at a time. To do this, cover the text with a sheet of paper or ruler, and move it down, line by line, as you read. Read each word, slowly. If you read quickly, you will skip mistakes, because you will be reading what you think is there and not what is actually written. And remember to read all the headings. Mistakes frequently lurk there.

AFTERTHOUGHT

From an interview with Ernest Hemingway (20th century):

> HEMINGWAY: I rewrote the ending to *A Farewell to Arms*, the last page of it, thirty-nine times before I was satisfied.
> INTERVIEWER: Was there some technical problem there? What was it that stumped you?
> HEMINGWAY: Getting the words right.

NOTES

1 The book that discusses this idea in detail is J. Rhodes and S. Thame, *The Colours of Your Mind*, Fontana/Collins, 1988.
2 For a full account of how to create and work with mind maps, see Tony Buzan, *The Mind Map Book*, BBC Books, 1993 (rev. edn 1995).
3 Mind maps are also an excellent tool for planning and carrying out projects.

FURTHER READING

Barker, A., *The Right Report*, The Industrial Society, 1993.
Barrass, R., *Scientists Must Write*, Chapman & Hall, 1993.
Miller, C. and Swift, K., *Handbook of Non-Sexist Writing*, The Women's Press, 1981.
Staunton, N., *The Business of Communicating*, Pan, 1982.
Sweetman, S., *The Executive Memo*, Wiley, 1986.
Wainwright, G., *Successful Business Writing in a Week*, Hodder & Stoughton, 1993.
Weinstein, K., *Writing Works: A Manager's Alphabet*, Institute of Personnel and Development, 1995.

6 Speaking in public

Brian Sanders

We are all capable of speaking effectively to an audience large or small but many of us are woefully out of practice, some of us have never had any practice, and the vast majority have had no tuition in the skills involved.

In this chapter my aim is to provide a practical and basic introduction for the busy manager who has to talk to a group of people. The chapter is divided into four parts:

1 The spoken word.
2 How to make the best use of oneself.
3 How to prepare the material.
4 Extending the vocal range.

The word 'talk' has been used throughout and is intended to cover presentation, speech, address, lecture and synonymous expressions. The word 'audience' is used to include listeners, conference, meeting, assembly and similar expressions.

THE SPOKEN WORD

The art of speaking has been neglected in favour of writing. Few schools teach it. On a recent course a man of 45 said that the last time he spoke to an audience was at a primary school assembly!

Because of this neglect, confidence is lacking and the results may be disastrous. But with effort and practice much can be achieved. Preparation and practice are essential.

Effective speaking

The term 'effective speaking' has replaced the older 'public speaking'. The latter suggests a formal gathering with a platform and a large audience. Much work today is done in an informal situation and with an audience of only three or four.

But one must be effective. Do not underestimate the amount of effort required to talk to a small group. The world is full of mutterers. Do not be one of these. If you are to sound enthusiastic and convincing, vocal vitality is essential.

Whether you talk to 3, 30 or 300 the basic approach is the same. You require a conversational style. But both your physical self and your voice need enlarging and projecting to meet the needs of the larger audience.

Lord Curzon (1859–1925) was recognized as one of the finest orators of his time. He made a perceptive statement about talking to audiences. He said that the three most important things to remember, in their order of importance, are:

1 Who you are.
2 How you say it.
3 What you say.

At first sight the second and third statements may appear to be the wrong way round. But no matter how excellent your material, if you cannot present it in an interesting and entertaining way, if you cannot make it palatable, then you might as well not bother.

Who you are is your personality, relevant knowledge and experience. You must engage the whole of yourself – voice, eyes, face, hands, arms – the whole of your physical self to assist communication.

If you are extrovert, then discipline yourself as necessary; don't completely overwhelm the audience. If you are a quiet and shy person, use these attributes to draw your audience towards you. Shyness does not prevent voice projection or vitality.

Don't be over-modest. Use relevant experience whenever you can. Anecdotes always stick in the mind.

How you say it demands the best use of your voice, the best possible presentation of your whole self and of the material.

Every effort should be made to increase and enlarge the vocal range and to keep the voice in trim with constant exercising. (Refer to the final section 'Extending the vocal range'.)

You must create the right atmosphere. Jargon and technical terms must be avoided if they will not be understood.

What you say requires careful selection and ordering. Everything must be relevant to the particular occasion.

Personality

You will be effective only if you are willing to disclose your personality. The actor hides behind the character he portrays. You must be yourself. You must be prepared to put yourself at risk.

But the element of risk causes nervous tension which will inhibit your performance. Relaxation will prevent this. Until you are relaxed you will never give of your best.

To learn relaxation takes some weeks of practice. But it can be done. Once relaxed you will enjoy the experience of talking to audiences.

HOW TO MAKE THE BEST USE OF ONESELF

Speakers sometimes fancy that if they take refuge behind an overhead projector or some sophisticated aid their lack of skills or nervous tension will go unnoticed. It is not so. In fact, the more sophisticated the aids, the more the weaknesses of a poor speaker are highlighted. A multiple projector presentation has often been followed by a disastrous question time because the speaker was tense, looked desperate and mumbled the answers. And this is what the audience remembered.

Relaxation will solve all the problems caused by tension. Practice will improve the speaker's performance.

Nerves and tension

It is important to distinguish between nerves and tension. Nerves are essential to set the adrenalin flowing into the blood stream. This has a stimulating effect on the system and gives the necessary 'edge' to our performance.

Some think, quite incorrectly, that eventually a person 'grows out' of nerves with the benefit of experience. This is not so. The time to worry is when you don't feel nervous!

Watch actors pacing, coughing and fidgeting backstage before a first entrance. See the effect of the red light in a BBC radio studio on the most experienced actors. But they have learned to control their nerves and so prevent the assault of tension.

Tension is a wrecker. It constricts the voice, prevents breath control, and makes the speaker look anywhere but at the audience. Clinging to a lectern or a piece of furniture, swaying, fidgeting and other distracting mannerisms are further manifestations.

Controlling nerves and eliminating tension

Useful exercises practised for a few minutes each day will eventually enable a person to relax at will. It is simply a question of mind over matter. Once relaxation is achieved, speaking engagements become a positive pleasure. The speaker knows that self-control through relaxation will give an appearance of relaxed authority.

Some exercises for relaxation

1   On tiptoe, stretch arms upwards, fully extended; stretch fingers on hands. Stretch calves and thighs. Stretch the abdomen. Imagine yourself on a vertical rack with toes nailed to the floor and fingers pulled by unseen wires towards the ceiling.

   Feel the discomfort of it. Hold the position for a few moments and then relax. Feel the pleasure of relaxation. Repeat this exercise three times.

2   Tense the arms from shoulders to fingertips. Feel the discomfort. Relax and feel the pleasure of relaxation. Repeat three times.

3   Keeping the soles of the feet on the floor, stretch the legs from thighs to tips of toes. (Keep the arms relaxed during this exercise.) Feel the discomfort. Relax and feel the pleasure of relaxation. when you relax keep both knees braced but not rigid. Repeat three times.

4   Stretch arms and legs together (as in 2 and 3). Feel the discomfort. Relax and feel the pleasure of relaxation. Repeat three times.

   The shoulders and neck are most prone to tension. Breathing becomes difficult, the voice is stifled in the throat and the speaker is extraordinarily aware of hands and arms.

   The following exercises are designed to help remove tension from these vital areas.

5   Shake the fingers loose on limp wrists and try to throw them on to the floor. Next, shake the fingers and lower arms from the elbows. Finally, throw the arms from the shoulders. Feel all tension in the arms being flung out of the fingertips.

6   Roll the right shoulder forwards and then backwards several times in vigorous circles. Repeat with the left shoulder. Then exercise both shoulders together.

7   Relax the muscles in the neck and allow the head to fall forward. Roll the head round *slowly* three times, bending from the waist so that the weight of the head takes it round. Stop and rotate slowly in the opposite direction three times. Stop with the chin resting on the chest. Lift the head level. *Note:* This exercise must be undertaken slowly.

CREATING A FEELING OF CONFIDENCE

Standing or sitting well creates a feeling of confidence in both speaker and audience.

For the speaker it aids relaxation, enables ease of movement, assists breath control and helps to free the voice.

The audience see someone authoritative, knowledgeable, confident and delighted to talk to them.

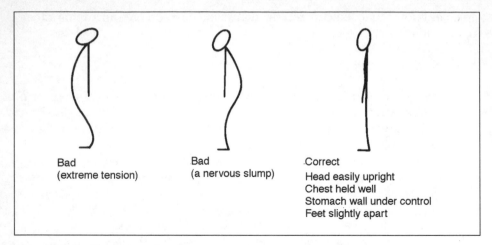

Bad
(extreme tension)

Bad
(a nervous slump)

Correct
Head easily upright
Chest held well
Stomach wall under control
Feet slightly apart

Figure 6.1   Posture: standing

If the audience exceeds 15 or 20 in number, it may be necessary to stand, however informal the occasion. If, when seated, you cannot see all the faces, they cannot see you.

Standing well

The feet should be slightly apart. This gives a good grip on the floor. Never stand with your feet together. Brace both knees firmly but without tension. Bring the stomach wall under control so that it is firmly held but not pulled in.

Hold the chest freely without pushing it forward and settle the shoulders on the chest with two or three easy movements up and down. They should be very slightly braced.

Look comfortably straight ahead. The position should be 'head in the air' and not 'nose (or chin) in the air'.

Have the weight of the body on the soles of the feet and not the heels. If you stand on your heels the blood flow is restricted and this will make you tense and tired. Stand in your footprints.

Keep the feet anchored and swing the trunk left to the back and then right to the back. This will prevent any stiffness creeping in. See Figure 6.1 for examples of correct and bad posture.

Sitting well

Choose a chair in which the seat and the back form a right angle. Place your bottom as far back as possible. When you sit up, the back of the chair supports you. You can sit both comfortably and in a position which allows maximum freedom for movement from the waist upwards. It also allows freedom for breath control and voice projection.

If you are condemned to a badly designed chair sit forward on the seat and lean very slightly forward as well. See Figure 6.2 for examples.

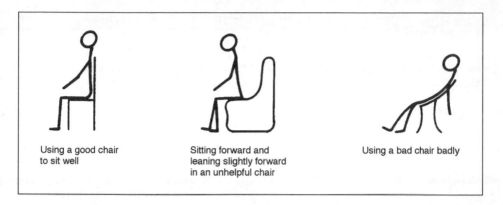

Using a good chair to sit well

Sitting forward and leaning slightly forward in an unhelpful chair

Using a bad chair badly

Figure 6.2   Posture: sitting

Eye contact

Standing or sitting well enables an ease of eye contact with the audience. The top half of the body can move freely and, so long as the neck muscles are relaxed, the head will turn freely in every direction.

Eye contact with a large group is easier than with a small one. When talking to an audience of less than 20 people, the speaker's eye must light occasionally on each person. But don't 'searchlight' the group from side to side. This can be very wearisome all round!

With a large group, the speaker should look for the most part about two-thirds of the way back. Occasional glances should be made to left and right of the front rows.

Gesture

Good gesture helps to underline what is said. All movement of the arm should be hinged at the shoulder and not the elbow.

The elbows give strength to gesture, the wrists enable precision and the hands contain power and control.

Bad gesture distracts. Twitches, fidgets and repetitious movements are fatal. The audience spots them and attention is diverted from what is said.

USING A MICROPHONE

There are times in a large hall or a room where acoustics are bad when a microphone becomes necessary. Neck microphones are preferable to stand microphones, particularly if your talk requires movement. The neck instrument remains at a uniform distance from the larynx and allows you the necessary freedom to move about.

There are many types of stand microphone. Rehearse well before the event to discover what the instrument will and will not do. Take the advice of a technician if one is available. But remember that even technology cannot provide all the answers.

You must bring vitality to the microphone. There must be something irresistible about your performance. If you project both subtlety and vitality, then the microphone will be most effective in transmitting them.

PREPARING THE MATERIAL

Pre-preparation

Before attempting notes or jottings for the talk ask yourself the following five questions. Answer each as thoroughly as possible. This will help you to concentrate on material relevant to the specific occasion, will ensure that you pitch the talk at the correct level, will prevent last minute panics, and will also save you time.

1   *What is my aim?* You may wish to inform, persuade, teach or stimulate. You will certainly always wish to entertain.

To entertain does not simply mean telling jokes. It is a combination of 'who you are' and 'how you say it', together with the eventual selection and ordering of your material. It also includes relevant jokes and anecdotes. But if you are no good at telling jokes, don't.

Remember too that you cannot talk on technical matters or specialized knowledge for long without giving your audience a chance to relax a little.

Within your general aims, consider your specific aim. What is it that you most wish your audience to remember, or what action do you wish them to take? This gives you a 'cutting edge'. It is worth noting now that your specific aim may change during the course of the preparation.

2   *Who am I talking to?* Find out all you can about the audience. Detailed research may be necessary but it is worth it in the long run. You must gear your talk as closely as possible to the listeners. Avoid jargon and technical terms if they will not be comprehensible. Find out what your audience wants to know, needs to know and does not need to know.

3   *Where am I giving the talk?* Know the size and shape of the room, the height of the ceiling, whether there are heavy curtains and a thick-piled carpet. The room may resemble a concrete box. These things will affect the acoustics. A microphone may be necessary, but don't use one unless you have to.

Decide where you will stand or sit. You must be seen easily by everyone. You should be in a dominating position, though almost certainly not on a platform unless the audience is very big.

The natural light should always come from the side of the room unless the artificial lighting is excellent. If you are using electrical apparatus, make sure that the sockets are conveniently placed.

Knowledge of these matters will help relaxation when the time comes.

4 *What time of day am I talking?* This may affect the arrangement of your material and will certainly shape your opening remarks.

After morning coffee is a good time to speak – probably the best. The audience are fully awake and ready for you.

After lunch – the siesta session – is a bad time. You will need to entertain to your utmost.

If it is an evening talk, discover how your audience have been occupied during the day.

This information will enable you to gear the talk correctly from the start of your preparation.

5 *How shall I organize the time available?* Forty-five minutes is the longest time one person can sustain. If you have over an hour, you must organize the time carefully. After your introduction you might divide the audience into groups. Each group would retire, appoint a leader/secretary, and discuss some particular point(s). After a given time the groups reassemble, each secretary reports back to the whole audience and a general discussion takes place. It would then be the speaker's task to pull the threads together, summarize and point the way ahead. All this takes a great deal of preparation.

Decide how you will organize question time. And consider whether visual aids will be helpful.

Even when refurbishing an old talk it is still essential to answer these five questions.

Preparation time and the shape of the talk

The ideal time for preparing a talk is two or three weeks. Many have only two or three days, or even hours. The notes on assembling and selecting the material have therefore been divided into sections according to the time available.

All talks should have an introduction, a main part and a conclusion. Where should you begin? The principal facts or arguments go into the main section and this should be your starting point in the preparation. This section will comprise all but four to eight minutes of the total talking time.

Assembling and selecting material for the main part

Two weeks or more to prepare   Write down on a large sheet of paper, notes, key words and headings. These may eventually form the basis of your notes. Don't write sentences, and don't worry about the order at this stage. Check dates, figures, statistics; do necessary research.

Work at this in bursts of 15 or 20 minutes and then turn to something else. Return a while later and do some more. Your subconscious will work for you during the break and thoughts and ideas will flow more freely. Work again for   *97* only a short time and return again later or on the next day.

After five or six days, perhaps sooner, you will have a sheet or more of paper filled with a mass of material. There will be far more than you can possibly use in one talk.

Analysis on audience retention carried out some years ago produced most interesting figures. In a series of 40-minute talks it was found that an intelligent audience (an audience knowledgeable about and interested in the subject) could remember seven facts. An average audience could remember three facts. These figures are not sacrosanct, but they are a positive guide.

Leave your jottings for a couple of days and allow your subconscious time to get to work again. Stored in your brain you have the answers to the five pre-preparation questions and all the rough headings and notes.

A burst of insight will tell you the theme you wish to pursue on this occasion because you are talking to that particular audience, in that place and at that time.

Now comes the vital moment of selection when you know what in your jottings is relevant and what is not. Strike out what is not relevant. Be ruthless. Take no matter you can dispense with. Better to say too little than too much.

Two days to prepare   Notes and headings concerning the subject should be jotted down on a large sheet of paper. Don't worry about the order. Check facts and figures. This work should be done in 'bursts' and should be completed in one day.

You will probably have too much material for one talk. Realize your specific aim for talking to this particular audience. Then remove any material not wholly relevant.

Two hours to prepare   Jot down all the headings which seem relevant. Leave the jottings for about half an hour. Return and delete irrelevant material. If you must add to the list, then do so.

Two or three minutes to prepare   Should you wish to speak at a meeting and without prior preparation, write down half a dozen key words on a sheet of paper. Then put them in a useful order. Speak for no more than three minutes and you may find yourself popular!

The main part of the talk

The skeleton of the main part is now to hand in what remains of your headings and jottings.

Put your headings in the correct order. If you are following a procedure or the way a piece of machinery works, then the order may be dictated by this. If there is no obvious order, then arrange your points in order of importance.

Suppose you have six main headings. Arrange these in order of merit: 1 is your least important; 6 is your most important. Follow the Greeks, who were masters of oratory. Begin your main section with point 5, your next-to-best; it will commend your whole case. Then proceed with 1, 2, 3, 4, and finish with 6.

You must work up towards a climax and not down. If you begin with your most important point ('They'll doze off after five or six minutes'), then subconsciously you will know you have made the vital statement and you will 'run down' whether you like it or not. And they will doze off! Always work up to the point of greatest interest or intensity.

Next you must put the flesh on the skeleton of your talk. Write each heading on a separate large sheet of paper. Jot down your thoughts on how you may illuminate or develop that section. When you have completed the section in note form, reshape your jottings to produce the right order. If you have stuck to notes and headings you will almost certainly find that the essential key words and phrases have emerged. Transfer these to the cards you will use for notes.

Pattern your notes in the way that suits you. Once you have found a satisfactory method of note making stick to it.

Having completed one section of your talk, work on the others in a similar fashion.

The conclusion

The conclusion forms a reiteration of the main points. Gather all the threads together and end on a conclusive or challenging note according to the purpose. Point the way ahead. Leave the audience with something to consider.

Introduction

The introduction is the last section to be prepared and falls into two parts: the general introduction and the introduction of the subject matter.

The general introduction   Both the audience and yourself must 'tune in' to each other. They may never have seen you before. If so, they will size you up visually before they are fully prepared to listen to you. If you begin with some vital matter, most of them will miss it.

If you are a stranger they need to be told who you are, your relevant experience and background. Your host may do this but it is often helpful to reserve some of this information for yourself.

If possible, compliment your audience. Find out something about their organization. Show that you are interested in them outside the specific subject matter. Make them feel you are delighted to talk to them. If this is sincerely done the effect will be positive and helpful.

This general introduction can be done without reference to notes. This enables you to make eye contact with everyone and allows you to hear your voice projected to the back rows. If you can manage a smile as well – so much the better!

You may be addressing the firm's board of management or colleagues at a weekly meeting. In these circumstances, much of the general introduction will be inappropriate. They may already know far too much about you! But an audience of colleagues still requires about a minute's 'settling time'. An appropriate observation or two will induce all eyes and ears in your direction.

Introduction of the subject matter   Your subject and objectives must be made abundantly clear. Avoid startling and striking openings. A clear, quietly stated opening is best. Tell them succinctly the ground you are about to cover and your aims.

NOTES

Cards (6″ × 4″) are best for making notes. Find a pattern for note making which suits you and stick to it. When these are completed, number each card in the top right-hand corner. Then punch a hole in the top left-hand corner and tag the cards together. This makes it easy to turn them over and, should you drop them, they will remain in the right order!

Always carry your notes with you. There is no one to prompt you if your mind goes suddenly blank. And it is easy to miss something out. Discipline yourself to glance at the notes from time to time even if you are familiar with the subject matter.

A GENERAL OBSERVATION

Remember that the people being addressed are receiving the information for the first time. Facts and ideas must be presented simply and logically. Precise English is essential.

Always proceed from the known to the unknown. Build bridges from one point to the next. Do not elaborate the obvious.

Support statements with examples and anecdotes; tell jokes if you can and if they are relevant. Keep to the point.

USING VISUAL AIDS

Visual aids are used to assist communication and to present information so that it will be quickly grasped. They convey what words cannot.

Always let the subject matter speak for itself. Words are not visual aids. If using words, keep them short and simple; make them forceful.

When showing a visual aid, keep quiet for a little to allow the audience time to take it in. It is difficult, if not impossible, to read and listen at the same time. Remove the visual aid when you have finished with it.

Do not lose eye contact with the audience by talking to the flip chart or screen. Use a pointer or pencil and talk to the audience. But don't be afraid to write or draw on a flip chart or blackboard and talk a little at the same time, provided of course that you are talking about the matter on the board. Project your voice a little more at the same time.

The projector is better than other means for maps, charts, graphs and diagrams.

Visual aids should never be used merely as a concentration break or as a cue for the speaker.

Never display all headings at once. Use an overlay and limit strictly what is being looked at – that is what is being talked about.

Take care with colours. Blue and green together appear the same to the partially colour blind. Some colours are weak when projected.

Do not use too many visual aids. This confuses the audience and often confounds the speaker.

Prepare carefully and rehearse assiduously. Check equipment and always carry spare bulbs and extension leads.

Know beforehand what you will do if for any reason you are unable to use your visual aids.

ANSWERING QUESTIONS

In most cases a question session is essential unless you are satisfied you have given a complete performance. It is a matter of getting nearer to the whole truth and of meeting the needs of the audience.

Unless the talk is 'in house' it may be necessary to have a short interval when you have finished your talk. An audience cannot go into reverse at once. Tell them that questions will follow in two or three minutes. This will give them time to consider.

Answer as briefly as you can. Having answered the question, don't go on answering it beyond the point of satisfaction.

If you do not know the answer, say so. Call on somebody in the audience or offer to find out and write. Or suggest sources. Never invent an answer.

If you should know the answer but don't, the fault is probably in your lack of preparation.

Rephrase a bad question before you answer it in order to avoid possible misunderstanding and embarrassment.

Repeat each question so that the back rows know what is being answered.

In the face of hostility remain courteous and keep your sense of humour. If a heckler persists and if there is no one in the chair to intervene, offer to discuss the matter at the end as time is short and others wish to be answered.

When time is running out say, 'There's just time for three more questions', and hope to finish on a high note.

EXTENDING THE VOCAL RANGE

The human voice is a unique instrument. Unless physically impaired, we each possess the necessary equipment and may do wonderful things with the

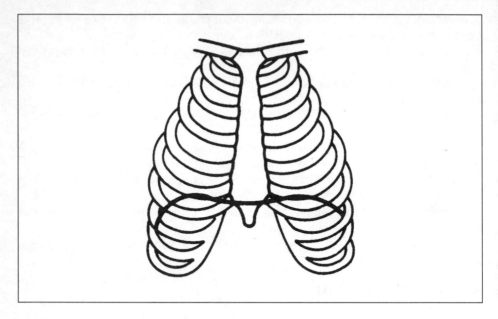

Note: The thick black line indicates the position of the diaphragm before inhalation.

Figure 6.3   The chest from the front

voice. But we must learn to use it properly and to realize its full range. Relaxation and good posture help to free the voice.

Breathing

Correct breathing assists projection, helps avoid strain, gives the voice the necessary vitality and helps the speaker to sound enthusiastic.

For any form of public speaking, we need to inhale quickly and deeply. In normal conversation we breathe through a slightly open mouth. This enables speedy and silent inhalation.

To breathe more deeply we must learn to expand the chest cavity. In normal breathing the rib cage moves upwards and outwards, and the diaphragm (a powerful muscle separating the chest from the abdomen) contracts and descends. These movements increase the volume of the chest cavity, a partial vacuum is created and air is sucked into the lungs (see Figure 6.3).

The more movement of the ribs and diaphragm, the more air is drawn into the lungs. The more air in the lungs, the better our voice control.

Exercises for expansion and control

These exercises are best done near an open window or in a room with plenty of fresh air. (Outside is best of all – if you dare!)

Spend only two or three minutes at a time on breathing exercises. Should you feel dizzy, then stop immediately. Overdoing things may result in hyperventilation.

1   Practise heavy sighs. This is a natural way of relieving tension. Sigh heavily and feel the rib cage collapse. Sigh several times. As you draw breath before the sigh feel the upward and outward expansion of the rib cage.

   Note that the shoulders play no part in breathing. They should be slightly braced (as for good stance), relaxed and still. On no account should they hunch at the time of inhalation.
2   Stand at one end of a large room. Inhale deeply and whisper 'One, two, three, four, five' using all the breath. Send the whisper on the stream of breath to the far end of the room.
3   Hum quietly. On the same note intone (or chant) 'One'.
4   Fill the lungs and intone 'One, two, three, four, five'. Repeat two or three times.
5   Once able to complete exercise 4 with ease and with 'five' fully projected, repeat the exercise to 'ten'.
6   When you can complete exercise 5 with ease, gradually extend the counting to 'fifteen'. The final number intoned should always sound as resonant as the first. When you run out of sufficient breath, then stop.

The exercises are to employ the rib cage and diaphragm so that they may

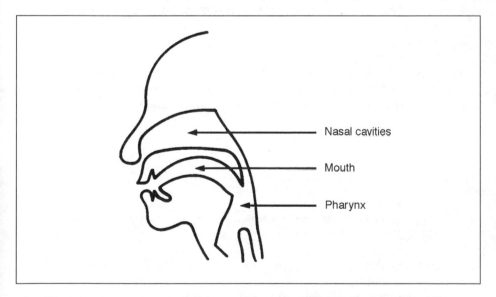

Note: The term 'nasal cavities' is intended to cover the nose and the various tubes and chambers associated with it.

Figure 6.4   Cross-section of the head showing the resonating chambers   *103*

work fully and easily; they are not voice exercises. Constant practice (a little at a time) will help to ensure an ease of deep breathing.

Resonance or the human amplification system

We should strive to make the best use of our vocal tone by ensuring that we are fully resonant.

All hollow chambers above the voice box (larynx) act as resonators. These are the pharynx (the back of the throat), the nose and all the cavities and chambers connected to it, and the mouth (see Figure 6.4).

The key exercise is humming:

1 Moisten the lips with the tongue and hum gently on an 'm' sound. The lips should be lightly together and the teeth slightly apart. When you hum a tingling sensation should be felt on the lips. If no sensation is felt, part the lips slightly and make a sound like a foghorn by blowing through them. Repeat this, but after three seconds bring the lips together for the hum. The tingling should resemble that when playing the comb and tissue paper. Quality of humming is more important than volume.
2 Hum, feel the tingle, open the mouth slowly and as wide as possible and sing 'ah'.
3 Intone 'Mary had a little lamb', feeling the tingle at the beginning and end of the line.
4 Speak this sentence with conviction, 'I must keep my voice in the front of my mouth'.
5 Do 3 and 4 together. Attempt to speak the words of 4 in the same place that you intoned 3.
6 Hum up and down the scale with a slow, smooth beat. Think and feel the sound on the mask of the face.
7 Hum any tune you know and keep the sound forward.

These exercises help to produce a forward voice and a well-balanced resonant tone.

Clarity

Good articulation helps to make speech clear and distinct. The key instruments are the tongue, the teeth and the lips:

1 Say 'Articulation is a form of gymnastics between the tip of the tongue, the teeth and the lips'.
2 Say 'the tip of the tongue, the teeth and the lips' three times as nimbly as you can but without gabbling. The letter 't' is made by the explosion of teeth and lips parting.
3 Say *ttt ttt ttt ttt* (don't say *tee tee tee*).

4 Practise '*t-say*', '*t-sow*', '*t-sigh*', and then try '*t-snake*' '*t-slave*' '*t-star*'.
5 Practise precision of consonants:

ppp ppp ppp ppp (lips)
bbb bbb bbb bbb (lips)
ttt ttt ttt ttt (teeth and tongue)
ddd ddd ddd ddd (teeth and tongue)
kkk kkk kkk kkk (body of tongue and soft palate)
ggg ggg ggg ggg (body of tongue and soft palate)

6 Practise tongue twisters.

Modulation

To modulate means to vary or to change. Vocal modulation helps to highlight important words and phrases and makes it easier for the listener to comprehend the meaning.

The communication of technical information is particularly dependent on a well-modulated voice.

Vocal modulation depends on inflexion (glides or kicks up or down on one word), changes of pitch (usually on a phrase), the use of pause, and pace (here defined as a slight speeding up or slowing down of the rate of speech in reaction to the matter). A voice that is not modulated is monotonous.

1 Use inflexion to change the meaning of the following words:
goodbye; hello; yes; what; please; fancy.
For example, goodbye:

● to a friend you will see tomorrow;
● exit in fury, slamming the door;
● Romeo/Juliet leaving Juliet/Romeo.

2 Vary the meaning of the following groups of words by changing pitch (steps up or down) and using inflexion:
what is that; if I must; why me; yes sir.
3 Using inflexion, pitch, pause and pace, how many ways can you say:
You are coming home with me tonight.

Phrasing

A phrase is a group of words which makes sense. Phrasing is the grouping of words in a way which is calculated to bring out the meaning. All words forming a phrase belong closely together and nothing should spoil or break this sequence. A phrase therefore should be spoken on one breath.

Exercise Practise reading aloud from good prose. Stories for children provide excellent material.

The voice

The voice is our main and easiest means of communication. It can also be the most effective. But we must learn how best to use it, and to keep it in trim.

Athletes, singers, boxers, golfers, rugby and tennis players and people in many other professions practise daily. So should we, if we have a professional approach.

KEY POINTS

1 Make the best of yourself:
   - control nerves and eliminate tension;
   - share your personality;
   - stand and sit to advantage;
   - make eye contact with your audience.

2 Prepare thoroughly:
   - realize your aim;
   - know your audience;
   - select and organize your material;
   - shape your talk.

3 Explore the full potential of your voice:
   - practise breath control;
   - achieve full resonance;
   - articulate;
   - modulate.

FURTHER READING

Cole, W., *Sound and Sense: A handbook on elocution*, Allen & Unwin, 14th impression 1976.

Gowers, Sir Ernest, *Complete Plain Words*, Penguin, revised by Sir Bruce Fraser, 1973.

Kapp, R. O., *The Presentation of Technical Information*, 2nd edn revised by Alan Isaacs, Constable, 1973.

Klien, R. L. and Ludin, I. S., *Stand and Deliver*, Gower, 1995.

Partridge, E., *Usage and Abusage*, Penguin, 1963.

7   Managing your health

Dr H. Beric Wright, MB, FRCS, MFOM

HEALTH AND WELLBEING

To the extent that management is about taking decisions concerned with the
allocation of resources and the settlement of priorities, an individual's health
– your health – can increasingly be viewed against a similar grid. Starting with
genetic inheritance and the degree to which one has learnt from experience,
health is, in my view, very much a reflection of general wellbeing and adjustment.

On the whole, well-adjusted people, enjoying what they have set out to do
and not being continually stretched beyond their capabilities, and involved in
good relationships, are unlikely to be ill. Illness is largely dis-ease, and well-
ness, as I have said, is a function of general wellbeing. As the World Health
Organization said shortly after the war, 'Health is a state of physical, mental
and social wellbeing'.

This somewhat pompous definition implies that to be well, one must be
reasonably in tune with the physical, mental (emotional) and social parameters of one's life. In other words, the avoidance of too much dis-ease in
one's lifestyle is likely to influence mortality and morbidity.

Lifestyle is very much a matter of choice and discipline. Diet, and more
particularly calorie intake, largely determines weight. Animal fat consumption against a genetic background determining metabolism (the way in which
the body deals with nutritional essentials) plays a part in coronary risk rating.
Smoking, drinking and exercise are well within the control of a reasonably
motivated and knowledgeable person.

As will become apparent, in the present state of our understanding of the
common killer diseases, lifestyle, which is very much open to choice, is a
significant determinant of disease risk. And conditions like coronary thrombosis (CHD), which still kills at least a fifth of all men in the United Kingdom, *107*

can be usefully 'risk rated'.

Such an assessment of the odds, which can be made from the results of a detailed health check, will give you the probability of suffering a coronary. It does not necessarily mean that you will suffer one, or even avoid one entirely, but it does measure the likelihood and you can make your own choice as to what you do about it.

To make such a choice, it is necessary first to understand the various risk factors and the causes and incidence of common diseases; also to know about yourself, your aspirations, attributes and a few other basic facts. For instance, you cannot know what your blood pressure is, or the balance of lipids (blood fats) in your blood unless these are measured periodically. We know that what becomes an overt disease, like CHD, is the end result of a process that in its early stages produces no symptoms, and that the process can often be halted and reversed if caught early enough and dealt with vigorously.

To give another example, breast cancer kills about one in every 13 women. Breast and lung cancer are the commonest cancers in women; the former is increasingly treatable if detected early and the latter is very much smoking-related. Thus it is sensible for a woman to attend a breast-screening clinic and practise regular self-examination to maximize the chances of early diagnosis and treatment by minimal surgery. Similarly anyone who chooses to smoke cigarettes must do so in the sure knowledge that they are reducing their life expectancy. This is then their free choice, based on the facts as they know them.

Management, as I have said, is about taking decisions in the light of the best information available to obtain a desired objective: in this case, optimum health and functional efficiency. As I hope to be able to explain, your life is largely in your hands because you *can* decide how you live and what your priorities in living are. Traditionally, doctors treat established disease. This doctor wants to keep you out of the hands of his colleagues!

Health is probably our most precious asset, and good managers are a company's least replaceable one. Thus, as I see it, there is both a joint responsibility and mutual benefit in contriving a situation in which both flourish. Some companies – which, in my view, are badly run – have a propensity to consume people by driving them too hard. Managers, on the other hand, can be bribed or seduced into becoming full-time workaholics to the neglect of their other relationships and the needs of a compensatingly reasonable physical and emotional 'other life'.

When I was counselling stressed and overwrought managers some ten years ago, the position then was, to quote the old aphorism, 'If you can't stand the heat, get out of the kitchen', to which was always added the reminder that 'Life is for living'. Now, sadly, feelings of insecurity and possible unemployment seem to limit one's choice, causing even greater concern and legitimate anxiety. Nevertheless, we all have to try to make a truly objective assessment of our health and future. After all, a wage earner struck down by coronary or breakdown has even more limited prospects.

Thus it requires bravery and imagination to 'take' early retirement or to make a radical change in one's career path, but it could be salvational and immensely beneficial to both health and wellbeing. Living successfully is very much a matter of facing realities and making the right choice. Therefore, in seeking alternative work, my first advice is not to be proud and expect automatically to stay at the same level of seniority and authority that you are leaving. Be prepared to 'start again' and take anything that is on offer and which you can do or train to do competently. Secondly, you might consider starting something on your own – being your own boss. Analyse your strengths and then look around – there *are* opportunities out there that you have never thought of. For example, offering a personal service, even if it is an everyday activity that potential customers do not have time to do themselves, can be satisfying – for you as well as the customer. It is always rewarding to be wanted.

Moreover, health will improve dramatically with regular hours, exercise, a proper diet, peace of mind and so forth. Although it is difficult to prove statistically because there are always exceptions in all things biological, reasonably fit people are on the whole more lively, more disciplined and more effective. They know what they are trying to do and they have their priorities right.

Also, do not be afraid of seeking specialist advice. Stress counselling in various forms is a growth industry, and it is an acceptable and often effective option to take. Enlightened employers are beginning to realize that they are in some instances driving too hard a bargain with their employees; indeed, some companies are starting to provide in-house advice on this front. Management and welfare consultants, trade unions, and other organizations can also advise – and so can Relaxation for Living, cited at the end of this chapter.

In summary, what I am trying to say is that health is very much a matter of choice and that the ground rules and assistance to enable you to make the right choices do exist.

As we tend to work in one group and live in a family unit, it is the 'climate' in these and the rules that are set up for them that largely determine our wellbeing. Exercising the right options and understanding the odds are what is critical, plus a willingness to change if the equations do not balance.

WHAT YOU HAVE TO SURVIVE

If management involves understanding and choosing priorities and backing probability, management of your health should follow a similar path. Although you may inherit good, long-lived genes or bad, short-lived ones, because of genetically determined diseases or predispositions, it is useful to know something about the more common hazards to your survival.

Two short examples will help to make this point. Coronary heart disease (CHD) still kills at least a fifth of all men in the United Kingdom before retiring age, and this amongst other things creates many widows. The incidence of CHD in developed countries increased rapidly after the war and has been rightly regarded as an epidemic. In America the incidence has fallen significantly over the last few years. In Scandinavia it is under control and falling, as it is also at last beginning to here. Most of the predisposing or 'risk factors' for CHD are lifestyle related: that is, they are well within an individual's or community's control and can thus be considered as a management problem.

Cigarette smoking, or the inhalation of tobacco smoke, increases the chances of a man suffering a coronary by three or four times. It is also the main cause of lung cancer, and through chronic bronchitis – often euphemistically disguised as 'smoker's cough' – is responsible for a great deal of lost time and serious disability during the working life, as well as seriously clouding the retirement years through breathlessness and a weak chest.

Similarly, breast and lung cancer are the commonest killers in middle-aged women. The latter can be avoided by not smoking and the former, to an increasing degree, mitigated by early diagnosis and early removal of small lesions by minimal surgery. This depends, as does the more acceptable cervical smear for cervical cancer (which has about one-quarter the incidence of breast cancer), on the woman's willingness to attend a specialized Well Woman clinic.

These, then, are some high-priority areas which are very much a matter for individual decisions, but decisions which significantly determine life expectancy.

Going back to probabilities, all this can be regarded as a relatively simple equation in which the overall odds are made up of the incidence and risk factors for various common diseases and the denominator provided by genetic inheritance and personality factors. Thus, if there is a family history of heart disease, it does not mean that all the sons of a coronary mother will be so afflicted, but it does make it more likely that they will be. It is therefore prudent for them, and indeed for all of us, to know what the odds are and then to proceed more wisely through life, to minimize the overall risks.

Equally, someone with long-lived parents can more safely risk being mildly overweight and perhaps eating more animal fats because they may well have a less vulnerable metabolic system. Obviously, in order to make such decisions the facts must be known: hence the prudence of regular health checks so that you know what your blood pressure is and how your lipid and blood fat levels are behaving. If you like, this personal data is as important to health management as is regular information about your company's cash flow and sales ledger.

What this means is that having your staff, yourself and your family regularly serviced should be seen in the same light and with the same priority as servicing your car, plant and machinery. These are serviced to minimize breakdown and it is, I suggest, merely a matter of wise asset protection and a legitimate and tax deductible cost for a company, to encourage health servicing of staff.

Another and sadder denominator, about which space precludes detailed consideration, is the factor of social class or occupation. Although the incidence of the common diseases has been falling in the professional and managerial classes over recent years, the gap between them and the semi-skilled and unskilled workers has been widening. Thus the incidence of CHD, hypertension (high blood pressure), and lung disease is several times higher in these groups. This is partly for socioeconomic reasons and partly because the 'lifestyle message' has not got through to these groups. Smoking, for instance, obesity, alcohol consumption and so on, have a higher incidence in social classes IV and V than in classes I and II. Sadly, this reflects a failure of the NHS to significantly improve the health of the nation, but it does provide management with a chance to improve the health of its own workforce.

Some years ago, the Electrical Contractors Association and the Electricians Trades Union broke new ground by controversially instigating a BUPA health check for blue-collar workers. Similarly, Marks & Spencer started to provide Well Woman screening at branch level. Since then, various forms of on-site screening have become widespread, and monitoring for known toxic hazards is obligatory under health and safety regulations. Facilities for this are available from several health-care organizations.

Incidence of common diseases

Figures 7.1 and 7.2 show the common causes of death in men and women. Figure 7.1 shows how death rates have fallen over the last 25 years. The main drop is in heart disease in men, but in general terms, except for lung cancer in

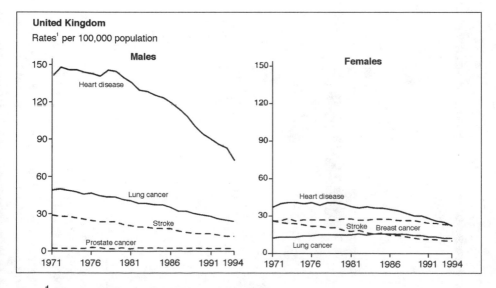

Note: [1] Age-standardized to the 1971 population level.

Figure 7.1 **Death rates for people aged under 65: by gender and selected cause of death. (*Source:* Office of Population Censuses and Surveys: General Register Office (Scotland); General Register Office (Northern Ireland).)**

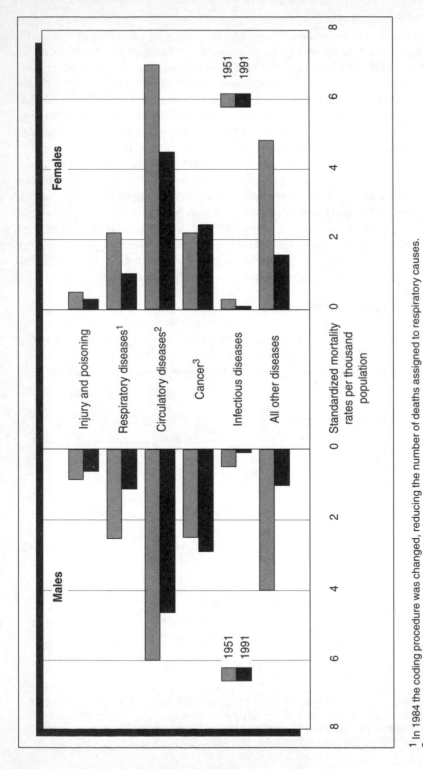

112

Figure 7.2 **Selected cause of death: by sex, 1951 and 1991** (*Source*: Office of Population and Census Surveys; General Register Office (Scotland); General Register Office (Northern Ireland))

1 In 1984 the coding procedure was changed, reducing the number of deaths assigned to respiratory causes.
2 Includes heart attacks and strokes.
3 The figures for neoplasms include both malignant and benign cancers.

women, there has been a significant drop in mortality and corresponding increase in life expectancy, which accounts for the now dramatic increase in the number of people over 70 years old. This demographic fact, although known for some time, is only just being recognized as possibly the biggest social problem of the next 25 years, in terms of finance, dependency and general care, particularly for women likely to be widows.

The fall in heart disease and cancer rates in men represents a triumph for changes in lifestyle and general health promotion. The rates for women were much lower to start with, but nevertheless the fall in those rates is less significant and the rise in lung cancer is a disgraceful reflection on postwar smoking rates. The drop in cardiovascular disease (coronaries and strokes) reflects better treatment, mostly in terms of hypertension, for strokes.

Figure 7.2 shows more graphically the main causes of death and the changes since 1951. The lower rates for women for all causes is of course a reflection of their longevity and preponderance in the older survivors. Figure 7.3 shows the dramatic increase in life expectancy over the last century. A man of 60 can now expect to live another 18 years and one of 80, of whom there are now many more, another 7 years. Women do even better and achieve either 81 or 90. All of which accounts for the 'old age bulge'. It also has to be noted that many of these conditions are related to social class, being significantly higher for classes IV and V. Arguments now range about

Years	1901	1931	1961	1991	1996	2001
Males						
At birth	45.5	58.4	67.9	73.2	74.0	74.5
At age:						
1 year	53.6	62.1	68.6	72.8	73.5	74.0
10 years	50.4	55.6	60.0	64.0	64.7	65.2
20 years	41.7	46.7	50.4	54.3	54.9	55.4
40 years	26.1	29.5	31.5	35.2	35.8	36.2
60 years	13.3	14.4	15.0	17.8	18.2	18.7
80 years	4.9	4.9	5.2	6.5	6.7	7.0
Females						
At birth	49.0	62.4	73.8	78.6	79.5	79.9
At age:						
1 year	55.8	65.1	74.2	78.1	78.9	79.3
10 years	52.7	58.6	65.6	69.3	70.1	70.5
20 years	44.1	49.6	55.7	59.4	60.2	60.6
40 years	28.3	32.4	36.5	39.9	40.6	41.0
60 years	14.6	16.4	19.0	21.8	22.4	22.7
80 years	5.3	5.4	6.3	8.1	8.6	8.8

Note: Figures show further number of years which a person might expect to live.

Figure 7.3   Expectation of life in the United Kingdom: by sex and age
(*Source:* Government Actuary's Department)

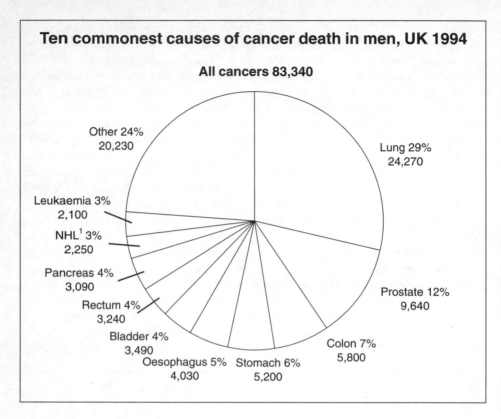

Ten commonest causes of cancer death in men, UK 1994

All cancers 83,340

- Other 24% 20,230
- Lung 29% 24,270
- Leukaemia 3% 2,100
- NHL[1] 3% 2,250
- Pancreas 4% 3,090
- Rectum 4% 3,240
- Bladder 4% 3,490
- Oesophagus 5% 4,030
- Stomach 6% 5,200
- Colon 7% 5,800
- Prostate 12% 9,640

[1] Non-Hodgkin's lymphoma.

Figure 7.4 Frequency of cancer deaths: men (*Source:* Cancer Research Campaign, 1996)

the influence of depression and unemployment on these figures, but the differences, although not shown here, are very real, especially for heart disease and lung cancer.

In general terms, cancer can be considered as a primary cause of death from middle life onwards (see Figures 7.4 and 7.5). Because of this factor, coupled to the general fear of dying of cancer, patients with related symptoms in the United Kingdom tend to delay seeking treatment. In this country, people talk about dying of cancer, whereas in the United States, they openly discuss their successful operations. UK attitudes to cancer and to dying in general are changing for the better, but they still have some way to go. Such change is necessary, however, as it leads to early treatment, which is the key to better survival rates. Some cancers have a genetic determination and others, such as lung cancer, are due to environmental factors (like pollution and smoking), radiation, and various toxic exposures.

Thus the keys to survival are, first, to have good genes, second, to be sensible about risk and exposure, third, to be a woman, and fourth, to be in social classes I and II, or even III.

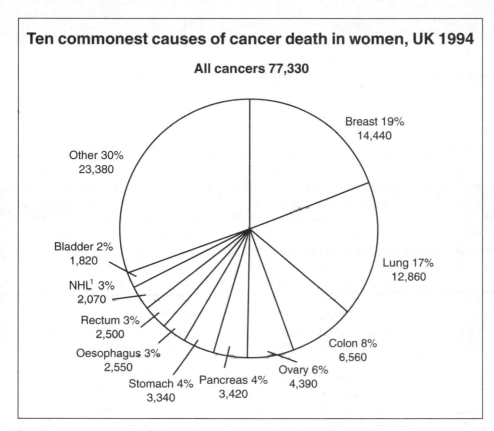

Ten commonest causes of cancer death in women, UK 1994

All cancers 77,330

Breast 19%
14,440

Other 30%
23,380

Lung 17%
12,860

Bladder 2%
1,820

NHL[1] 3%
2,070

Rectum 3%
2,500

Oesophagus 3%
2,550

Colon 8%
6,560

Stomach 4%
3,340

Pancreas 4%
3,420

Ovary 6%
4,390

[1] Non-Hodgkin's lymphoma.

Figure 7.5   Frequency of cancer deaths: women (*Source:* Cancer Research Campaign, 1996)

Coronary risk factors

As many of the keys to living sensibly, particularly for men, relate to avoiding CHD, it is worth describing briefly the factors which predispose to this still too prevalent killing disease.

Genetic factors

Reference has already been made to the fact that CHD can run in families. As will be apparent from the risk factors to be described, CHD is a multifactorial disease: that is, it has no single cause but results from an amalgam of factors which permutate differently in different people. Similarly, there is no single gene responsible for, say, blood pressure, lipid metabolism or personality. But we do know that a serious condition called hypercholesterolaemia, in which blood fats are raised, is genetically determined. And there is reason to believe that some aspects of the way in which the body deals with fats, either well or badly, lies within the genes. Thus it could be that in the years to come, genetic engineering will become a factor in coronary control. At the moment, however, this is highly speculative.

You will, I hope, remember that the genetic set-up, good or bad, is the main denominator of the coronary and other equations.

Blood fats – cholesterol

When I was first interested in the prevention of CHD in about 1960, it was becoming apparent that men with high cholesterol levels in their blood were at greater coronary risk. This started the interest in low cholesterol diets by reduction of animal fats, and established cholesterol as a risk factor. It did not explain, however, why some thin men with low cholesterols suffered from CHD and, conversely, why some fat men with high levels avoided it. We now know much more about the 'cholesterol package' and have refined ways of measuring its individual components. From this, it has been found that the two main factors are called *high* (HDL) and *low* (LDL) *density lipo-proteins*.

Very briefly, HDL is metabolically good and the main way in which usable fats, for energy, are transported round the body. LDL, on the other hand, is more unfriendly and is the substance that is deposited in the walls of blood vessels to narrow them and predispose to blockage. A coronary thrombosis is a blockage of the coronary arteries that supply the heart muscle, which if severe enough destroys the muscle itself and the heart's capacity to function as a co-ordinated pump. What we now know is that it is the ratio, within the cholesterol package, between HDL and LDL which largely sets the coronary governor: high HDL levels are much less important than raised LDL, which is mainly found in animal fats and dairy products.

Two factors seem to govern the way in which an individual deals with his or her cholesterol. The first is, fairly obviously, the amount and nature of the fats eaten, and the second is the genetically determined governor that deals with these fats. The latter is more important than the former, but a strict low-cholesterol diet will reduce cholesterol levels and bring the ratio back into better and less harmful balance. It will also remove at least some of the LDL out of the vessel walls.

Recently, and because of its importance in the causation of heart disease, research has led to the introduction of more effective cholesterol-lowering drugs, including a new group, the statins. Drug control of hypertension has also improved with newer drugs, so that combined treatment is becoming popular. But also, as both conditions relate back to obesity as a risk factor, general dietary supervision is essential (see below).

Diet

We are now, in developed countries, on the verge of a dietary revolution. There is a growing move away from a high protein, high animal fat diet, towards a more vegetarian – fruit, fibre, vegetable – one. Since the war the consumption of meat, dairy products and sugar has gone up significantly, and so has the incidence of CHD.

In America, Norway and Finland, careful long-term studies have shown that by changing diet not only do cholesterol levels alter for the better, but also the coronary rate falls. Obesity is said to be the commonest 'disease' in developed countries, particularly America and Germany. That thin people live longer than fat people has been known for years by life insurance companies. This is largely, but not entirely, through the relationship between weight and blood pressure, but there are other considerations as well.

Lack of exercise, as we will see later, is also a risk factor, and it is obviously more difficult for an overweight person to be physically active without putting undue and dangerous strain on bones, joints and muscles.

Obesity again is genetically determined through body build but essentially if you eat more calories (energy) than you need for daily living, these will be banked within your body as fat. A calorie overdraft is, in fact, starvation. Most of us eat far more than we need and hence have a podgy credit account. Sugar and fats are chiefly to blame, and their overconsumption has become a serious reflection of postwar life, which is only now being reversed by health re-education.

Eating is very much a culturally based habit pattern. We like what we are used to and have been brought up with. Being human, we resent change and are reluctant to experiment. This is very true of salt consumption. We eat salt in most prepared foods without knowing it is there, but we would miss it if the level was reduced. Some of us also add extra salt. High blood pressure is again a complicated multifactorial condition. It relates to arteriosclerosis, which is part of the coronary picture. Hypertensive people are more coronary prone but also suffer strokes, heart failure and blood vessel disease. Salt is very much one of the factors relating at least to some forms of hypertension. There are thus good grounds for reducing direct and indirect salt consumption, and at least demanding that food manufacturers state the salt content of their products.

Weight control is now internationally recognized as important because of the continued increase of obesity. It is now the subject of government exhortation as a target for national health improvement by the end of the century. Overweight people have a significantly increased incidence of cardiovascular disease. And now, because physical exercise, particularly for older people, is recognized as a critical anti-risk factor and as obesity is increasing worldwide, diet has become an important issue, starting with children and running right through the generations. Figure 7.6 shows the incidence of obesity, expressed as body mass, for men and women in this country. Only 40 per cent of men and 50 per cent of women approach ideal weight and consequently have the longest life expectancy. This incidence, as with smoking and drinking excesses, also relates to social class. Classes IV and V have significantly higher incidences and correspondingly higher death rates. The incidence in America and Germany is probably even higher because of the way they eat. *117*

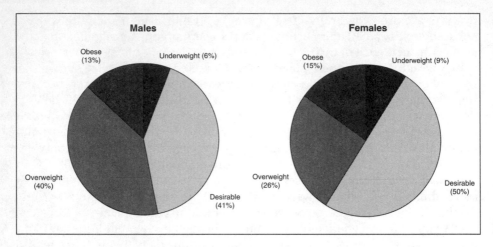

Note: [1] Body mass index of persons aged 16 to 64.

Figure 7.6   Obesity, as body mass (*Source:* Office of Population Censuses and Surveys)

But as has been said, diet and weight control is now an urgent social, personal and medical problem area.

It is also a problem that is beginning to be addressed by company personnel and medical departments. Moreover, weight plays a traditional and cogent part in risk assessment for life insurance, since weight control is very much a factor for which the individual can be held personally responsible.

Exercise

As has already been implied, exercise is now accepted as being a key factor in the maintenance of both health and wellbeing. Biological systems exist to be used and wither if neglected, muscles have to be regularly exercised, joints kept mobile and, perhaps surprisingly, bones also benefit from being 'used'. The motto is, 'Use it or lose it'.

Thin people live longer than fat ones, your heart is as flabby as you are, and obviously, the less there is of you to carry around, the easier it is so to do. This is why, because of the interrelationships of the risk factors, exercise is the kernel of the defence system. Interestingly, it puts up the HDL levels, while smoking lifts the dangerous LDL.

The value of exercise is now accepted as being greater in later life when other margins are diminished. Together with weight control – and allowing of course for genetic inheritance – exercise seems, in fact, to be a critical determinant of longevity. This is particularly important for women who suffer from osteoporosis (thinning bones) after the menopause, because of the hormone changes involved. It is now known that apart possibly from HRT (hormone replacement therapy), exercise best maintains bone strength. And, for instance, it is seen that rural women suffer fewer hip and other fractures than do urban ones, because of the inevitably more active lifestyle.

A reasonable amount of exercise, perhaps in the company gym, is thus of vital concern in matters of personal and family discipline.

Smoking

Inhaling tobacco smoke is an addiction which has a higher mortality and morbidity rate (death and disability) than all the other 'drugs' like alcohol, heroin, and so forth. Until very recently it was socially acceptable, and of course the government obtains a large slice of revenue from tobacco tax. Additionally, money spent on advertising and sponsorship oils many of the wheels of our social life.

Tobacco smoke is chemically complicated, but nicotine – a substance with a direct effect on the autonomic nervous system and a depressant or tranquil-lizing effect on mood – is the addictive element.

The tars in the smoke are irritant and the lungs, being an efficient filter, absorb substances from it which are both locally irritant and chemically harmful. Efficient inhalers, that is those with relatively undamaged lungs, can raise the level of carbon monoxide in their blood significantly above that allowed under industrial legislation. This carbon monoxide damages the lining of blood vessels, which in turn facilitates the deposition of cholesterol and the narrowing of the vessels, reducing blood flow and increasing the chances of blockage by thrombosis.

Smoking is also harmful because it raises the level of LDL and smokers are three or four times more likely to suffer a coronary thrombosis. As has been said, lung cancer is uncommon in non-smokers. Chronic bronchitis and emphysema, which can also be related to smoking, cause a great deal of respiratory disability and ultimate death.

The incidence of smoking has been declining significantly over the last ten years, so that in social classes I and II smokers are in a growing minority. The problem now is to reduce smoking in social classes IV and V and to stop youngsters becoming addicted at an early age.

It is never too late to stop and some of the benefits are immediate. Physically active smokers appear to be better off than their less athletic brethren, but are still a lot worse off than abstainers. Pipes and cigars, which are not inhaled, appear to be relatively safe.

Companies are now taking action to restrict smoking at work, because of fears about the dangers to non-smokers from 'passive smoking'. More than four out of five large companies impose restrictions on smoking, while total bans are becoming more common. Some companies too give preference in recruitment to non-smokers because of their lower absentee rate.

Up-to-date figures for the incidence of various cancers due to smoking sadly show that whereas the incidence for men has dropped significantly, it has rapidly increased for women and is now much the same as for breast cancer, which is beginning to show a downturn due to more active early diagnosis and other preventive measures. The delay in these figures coming through is due to the long lead time since more women took to smoking after the war. But this bodes evil for the future, with the current epidemic of smoking among children, particularly young girls.

Alcohol

Alcohol is not a direct coronary risk factor. Indeed, modest drinkers, particularly of wine, have a lower CHD rate. This may be because alcohol raises HDL. Nevertheless, alcohol, which is socially acceptable and encouraged – that is, a drink is offered at most social occasions – remains a dangerous addiction, with social and directly medical ill effects.

We do not really know why a few people become uncontrolled or truly dependent drinkers, but the probability is that there are both biochemical and personality-related factors which predispose. Individuals have to be careful about how much they drink because, unlike smoking, there is a tendency as tolerance develops to drink more, rather than to stay at the same level. Individuals and organizations thus have, in my view, a responsibility to set modest personal and corporate standards and to demonstrate appropriate examples.

Alcohol is a useful social lubricant and enjoyed by many people. It is now vital that we try to control consumption to avoid penal taxation and legislation. This is, I suggest, a legitimate area for management intervention by both setting standards and providing counselling and discipline for their staff who drink too much and perform badly.

Alcohol has two quite different harmful effects. The first is to damage the liver, which is responsible for most of its metabolism. This damage is called cirrhosis and unless caught early will lead to death from liver failure. This effect can be measured by blood tests done as part of a health check. As a result, it is possible to tell a patient that he is drinking more than his liver can deal with and that he ought to stop for three months and then proceed at a lower level.

The second effect is the behavioural decline of the alcohol dependent. This reduced performance disrupts families and will end either on Skid Row or with cirrhosis.

Experience has shown that what the Americans called 'job jeopardy' is the strongest weapon for dealing with an alcohol dependent employee, hence the value of a firm company policy. Everyone in the organization knows who the drinkers are and they must be seen to be discouraged.

Alcohol dependency, through habit and regular consumption, presents a difficult paradox insofar as, on the one hand, it is now established that controlled consumption is beneficial in limiting CHD, while on the other, too much is socially and medically dangerous. (Interesting arguments can be held on when 'how much', becomes 'too much'.) Children are drinking more and sooner, as do competitively stressed younger managers on the way up. There is also a social class difference, as well as more women drinking more from stress and so forth. The addictive nature of alcohol must therefore be recognized and controlled, and here, peer group and family pressure plays an important part and must be emphasized. Also, losing a driving licence is a social stigma that should be more widely publicized.

New hazards

Life today presents not only wider opportunities, but also new, possibly serious hazards that have to be faced objectively, and we could be criticized if there was no mention of these latest threats, particularly those that face the itinerant manager. Thus travel around the world requires a knowledge of the risks of local disease and adequate preventive cover: there are, for instance, still deaths every year from malaria because precautions are neglected. And if, on return, one experiences odd, perhaps febrile symptoms, it is wise to point out to the doctor where one has been. Diagnoses are often missed because they are thought of in purely local terms.

Companies and senior managers should ensure that staff are adequately covered and it may be sensible to have a medical adviser well up to date with the regulations. But one has to make the point that the greatest risk today is from HIV-related disease which, particularly in tropical countries, is very much hetero- as well as homosexually acquired.

Modern medicine too is not without its risks. Drugs are almost too clever and doctors are expected to produce miracle cures with them, but some such remedies may do as much harm as good. There is also a tendency for folk with possible fatal disease to look for miracles, possibly in America where therapeutic benefits tend to appear greater. Remedy- or doctor-induced disease is called iatrogenic, and in any difficult or uncertain situation it is wise, and legitimate, to seek a second opinion, perhaps from an older consultant.

Another contemporary trend is in complementary or alternative medicine, of which I am on the whole a strong supporter, and attempts are now being made for registration and control of its practitioners. Generally, it has the great advantage that, particularly with homeopathy, there is a long and analytic discussion, including details of lifestyle and stress, before the prescription is written. The danger with alternatives is that they may postpone legitimate and successful treatment of severe disease like cancer – so be just a little wary.

When we started the Institute of Directors Executive Health Clinic, which became the BUPA medical centre, apart from a sophisticated screening regime – now used more for the mature than the young – our work was based on a detailed holistic lifestyle (work, home and leisure) assessment. Such an assessment is now especially valuable to enable older managers to look at themselves in the mirror of life and perhaps change course and priorities, thus minimizing the chances of burnout and so on. The survival rate for big fish in small ponds is greater than vice versa.

Stress and relationships

Stress is discussed in detail in the next chapter, but as it is a variously inter-preted phrase, I must make my position on it clear. All living things, including humans, require challenge from the environment to keep them alert. Indeed, it is by meeting challenge in a variety of ways and at various levels that we gain most of our satisfactions in life. Conversely, failure or inability to cope causes conflict and frustration.

Stress is a term borrowed from engineering, where it implies an ability to withstand strain. If the strength of the substance is exceeded by the load, it will distort and collapse. Thus, in my definition, stress is *not* challenge, but is what happens to an individual when he or she cannot cope with the chal-lenge. It is a biological defence reaction to escape responsibility or avoid a conflict.

This may sound simple but in fact it is a very complicated and subcon-scious or 'automatic' reaction, without necessarily obvious relation to the cause of the stress. The reaction can be physical, in terms of pain, a skin erup-tion or a peptic ulcer, or purely behavioural in emotional or performance terms. Thus anxiety, insomnia, irritability, and so on, are just as much dis-eases as are more traditional physical disorders.

Another complication is that stress thresholds vary for different types of challenge and relate to personality and past experience. Calm, extroverted people react differently from tense, anxious, introverted ones. Moreover, stress can arise from too much challenge or conflict in any aspect of life. It can be work or home based or, to a degree, due to lack of alternative relaxational satisfactions balancing out the other pressures.

This concept of stress and its relationship to wellbeing is obviously the basis of the whole man or holistic approach to disease. Why someone is ill – or out of balance – is as important as what is actually wrong with them. Symptoms may be treatable by drugs but it is better to deal with the cause. This involves understanding and insight or objective knowledge about one-self.

In my very general terms, even busy people who are succeeding are not necessarily stressed but are managing to carry a heavy load of challenge. They may be tired but they are on top, particularly so if they have good relationships at home.

One of the skills of survival, then, is both to know your own aspirations and attributes and to pick, as far as possible, the right challenges for you. Each person has his or her particular strengths and no one person has all the skills. Underemployment or being without prospects in one's job is just as stressful as having too great a load.

Management must organize the enterprise so that unnecessary stress is minimized and energies directed in productive rather than frustrating direc-tions. Jobs must have a discernible end point within the skills and experience of the individual.

Across the biological spectrum, most of the challenge to living things comes from the physical environment: the need and competition for space, nutrition, warmth, water and so on. Species that live in social groups, like monkeys, elephants and many others, have evolved a series of harmless rituals to settle the problems of aggression and competition with minimal trauma to the participants. Very seldom does a species prey on its own members as humans do.

In developed countries, however, a reasonable physical environment is largely available and the majority of challenge – and stress – originates from the psychosocial and interpersonal environment. Our successes and failures tend to relate to people rather than things. It is our ability to deal, in bio-logical terms, with our own species at work, at home, in our social groups and then in the world as a whole, that provides the stress and the conflict. At personal, national and international levels, we do not seem to be very good at it.

A last point, in this brief overview of the stress field, is that there is nothing new about stress or being stressed. Each generation tends to claim that its life is more complicated and difficult, and therefore more stressful, than that of its ancestors. This is nonsense because, as I have said, challenge is central to our lives, and throughout time there have always been individuals and 'tribes' who cannot cope without that challenge. All that alters is the nature of the stress, and as we learn to cope in the here and now, so society evolves to throw up new problems.

It worries me at the moment that because of lack of understanding about the difference between stress and challenge, being stressed has become a bit of a status symbol. Busy people tend to think that they cannot be working hard unless they are stressed, but in fact if they are doing their job efficiently, then they are largely winning and coping well. In very general terms, stress is a manifestation of failure rather than success.

In the main, it is our ability or otherwise to deal with interpersonal relation-ships and to achieve positions in which our aspirations and attributes largely match, that determines our level of stress.

It may, in these terms, be better to change a job, a marriage partner or a place of residence, than to be perpetually torn by conflict which cannot be resolved. At work, particularly, interpersonal relations tend to be hierarchi-cal, so that it is difficult for an individual to deal with incompatibility from above, unless the organization is sensitively structured to allow such matters to be discussed openly and objectively. For most of us, however, it may be better to be brave enough to do our own thing in a smaller or different pond than to be continuously buffeted by an uncongenial system. But remember too that work is only one source of stress. Stress originates from all aspects of life and impinges on our whole personality and not just on one segment of us. Work, home and play do interrelate with the 'whole of us' to determine who we are and how we react.

MANAGING HEALTH

Two points should now be clear about the management of health. The first is that it is manageable and that the odds are both worth playing for and reasonably understood. The second is that in the medium and longer term there are considerable benefits, in terms of both survival and effectiveness, to be obtained from successful management.

To this I would add two further points. First, that in spite of the hazards I have listed, living prudently is in no way living miserably. Good or sensible habits are just as enjoyable as overindulgence. Prudence and survival are very much a matter of achieving a sensible habit pattern and maintaining it. The second is that in terms of at least the larger working groups, the management of health is also very much the joint responsibility of the individual and the organization. Their interests should be mutually devoted to health and survival.

Thus the individual should set him- or herself the right priorities and have the requisite understanding of the pitfalls. As part of management, particularly at a senior level, he or she should insist on providing a 'healthy' environment – not so much in physical as in psychosocial or dynamic terms.

Companies should be organized so that the challenges of individual jobs are appropriate, communications good, end products obvious and satisfying, and frustrations minimal. It is also sensible to create an atmosphere in which problems and frustrations can be brought into the open and discussed objectively. I think too that regular assessments of performance against defined targets are helpful, and so is the availability of counselling and career guidance, particularly on promotion. When an interpersonal problem or a failure becomes overt and may even lead to possible job loss, the individual may often complain that 'nobody ever told me about this weakness'.

It is assumed that because a person is deemed to be good enough for promotion, he or she will, *ipso facto*, be capable of doing a more demanding job without training or indoctrination. I often used to see rapidly promoted youngsters stressed by having to run to stand still. This is particularly true when a technically trained person, good at doing things as an individual, is promoted into a role where he or she has to work closely with people, ideas and hierarchies.

Neither individuals nor organizations themselves realize clearly enough that there are inevitably and necessarily management styles into which individuals have to fit. Within this framework there are senior people with whom subordinates have to be reasonably compatible if they are to flourish. Thus, in choosing a job or appointing a person, there must be a large degree of congruence between the individual and the overall climate, which means that individuals should be prepared to change their jobs, even to ones of lesser status and income, rather than be driven to a coronary by perpetual frustration or boredom. Doing one's own thing, even in a small way, may be more fulfilling than being a small cog in a vast but safe bureaucracy.

In these terms, then, management can shape and control the environment in which their staff can be healthier. I think that regular health checks are part of this because they provide both a database, an early warning and a counselling service. But at a more mundane but nevertheless useful level, should management actively discourage smoking at work? Many now do. Should they employ non-smokers, who are known to have a better health record, in preference to smokers? Should they take more interest in what their canteens serve? Do they have sensible standards about alcohol consumption both in-house and in relation to expense accounts? Along these lines the list is endless but the issues are important. The standards they set must feed back into both the individual's lifestyle and the company 'climate'.

In more positive terms, should management encourage staff to take exercise and even provide facilities for this? A number of companies are beginning to provide their own fitness centres. (Fitness for Industry, Riverview House, Beavor Lane, London W6 9AR, will advise on this.) Similarly, it is sensible to see that people take their holidays and do not overwork for prolonged periods, and to look out for signs of stress, like a fall-off in performance, irritability, increased drinking and work taken home but not done effectively.

It is also wise to monitor sickness records, because an individual who has previously had a good record and suddenly 'goes bad', must certainly have a lifestyle-related problem which needs resolving. If one group has a worse record than another, something could have gone wrong with the motivation and supervision within the group. The probability is that there are personality clashes or frustrations that require attention. Although it may be superficially expensive, attention to the welfare of staff and help with personal problems will raise morale and increase productivity.

What then for the individual? He or she has to appreciate the ground rules for their own health maintenance and be prepared to adopt the necessary disciplines. These are relatively simple and to a degree have their own reward. Smoking, drinking and weight must be controlled within reasonable limits. Diet should be sensible and 'modern', in terms of less animal and dairy products, and more fresh food and fibre. Regular exercise of any sort is a must and will promote a sense of fitness.

But most important is the matter of relationships, both at work and at home. In my view, couples still marry too young and without thinking through why they want to get married and what it will mean for both of them. Their aspirations will change with age and status and will need occasional renegotiation. The conflicts of career development and home life are considerable and unless faced and agreed lead to much unhappiness, particularly for the isolated wife. The needs, for instance, of job mobility and business travel can cause considerable conflict, and therefore merit open discussion. And nowadays there may well be the additional problem of career clash between husband and wife.

The vital requirement about dealing with relationships is to be honest and open enough to discuss the problems and differences, rather than to bury them as a smouldering grievance which may surface as total incompatibility years later. A relationship must at all times be satisfying for both partners. *125*

Children as they grow up must be established as independent adults and should not be expected to remain obedient and grateful dependants.

Relationships are difficult, complicated and require constant attention, but for most people they provide life's greatest single satisfaction. Nevertheless they need more work and attention than they receive in most instances, both at home and in the workplace.

I would suggest that periodically you examine three aspects of your life. First, ask yourself what you are like to work for, how you are perceived by your peers, and whether you are giving them a square deal in terms of delegation, supervision and encouragement. Second, ask yourself what job satisfaction you think that your spouse gains from being married to you. A useful extension of this would also be to try and assess yourself as an effective parent.

The third and more complicated point is to be brave enough, particularly in middle age, to review your self-image. Look at yourself, as it were, in the mirror and try to see yourself as others see you. Are you brisk, alert and reasonably well dressed? More important, are you reasonably happy and fulfilled or are you frustrated and miserable? If the latter, what are the options open to you and what are you going to do about them? Much stress and frustration stems from the feeling of being caught helplessly in some interpersonal trap. It is useful to try to analyse the situation by listing the matters that cause you anxiety and what you can do about them. It may be that you are caught and cannot move, in which case live with it, find other outlets and stop worrying.

If you are a tense, nervous and rather stressed person, it is also worth remembering that relaxation can be learnt and that there are techniques and teachers about. In a similar way, there are coping skills that can be acquired for dealing with stress from work or home, and by learning these you can reduce the size of the problem. But if at a moment in time that problem does become insurmountable, be brave enough to take radical action to resolve it. Life is for living rather than mere endurance. A smaller house on a lower income, and a simpler lifestyle, can be far more satisfying than endlessly commuting to a boring or uncongenial job.

What all this adds up to is that there are two keys to 'health'. The first is to know the main hazards to survival and how to avoid them. The second, and more important, is to understand that health is a reflection of general well-being which can be cultivated by understanding, insight and discipline. If you achieve this you should join the 80-year-old bulge, and this will present other problems! However, it is very important that you should maintain your well-being as long as you live. The more successful you are at this, the longer you *will* live.

KEY POINTS

Your life is in your hands

1 *Management* involves making informed decisions, based on hard data and defined objectives.
2 *Exercising personal responsibility* The same principles should be applied to decisions about personal and family health.
3 *Health* is synonymous with wellbeing, which is a function of the relationship between the individual (personality, skills and experience) and the environment (psychosocial and physical).
4 *Hard data on survival* comprise two main elements:

● Understanding the hazards to be avoided in terms of the incidence of the main killer diseases for men and women of specified ages and socio-economic class.
● Knowing the individual risk factors (e.g. diet, exercise, cholesterol, stress) which predispose against this background. After a detailed health check or 'medical servicing', a personal risk rating can be calculated. You need to know the facts about yourself.

Equipped with this knowledge, and with as much objectivity as you can muster about your strengths, weaknesses, aspirations and attributes, your wellbeing and health should be largely and beneficially controllable. Caring and successful managers should contribute to personal, family and company health in this way.

FURTHER READING

Wright, Dr H. B., *Ease and Dis-Ease*, Longman Professional, 1986.
Wright, Dr H. B., *Managing Your Health*, Industrial Society and Allied Dunbar, 1991.
Wright, Dr H. B. *et al., Allied Dunbar Retirement Planning Guide*, Longman Professional, 1985.

Advice on relaxation and coping can be obtained by post from the following organization:

Relaxation for Living
Foxhills
Shanklin
Isle of Wight
PO37 6LS

01783 866666

8 Coping with stress

Andrew M. Stewart

Stress, and the way it affects people at work, has been receiving a great deal of attention recently. There have been radio and television programmes about it, and there is a wide range of published work available. This work tends to be at one of two extremes. It is either academic and rather heavily research based, or it is popular and inspirational but based only loosely on fact. This chapter aims for the middle ground, and poses the following questions:

- What is stress?
- What does it cost?
- What causes it?
- What are the signs?
- What can the individual do about it?
- What can organizations do about it?

After reading this chapter you should have some answers to those questions.

This chapter concentrates on stress at work, but people are not divided up into watertight compartments. What happens to you at work will affect you at home, and vice versa. Because the home or leisure environment can affect your performance at work, this chapter will also look briefly at a few of the main domestic considerations. This is not a medical chapter, so clinical problems are mostly avoided. People who find themselves in difficulty at work are usually normal, healthy, sane individuals who find themselves for the time being in an environment which is, for them, abnormal, unhealthy or insane.

People sometimes use stress as an excuse for not performing as well as they should, or for failing to do what they said they would. It is true that many people do experience levels of stress which are too high, but others might be helped by increasing their level of stress. The aim should be to help people find the level of stress that is best for them in their particular circumstances, and to help them to maintain it and adjust it to change. This will sometimes mean increasing it rather than necessarily reducing it. Stress management is about *managing* stress, not about making people so relaxed that they forget to *do* anything.

WHAT IS STRESS?

You are likely to experience stress when you face a challenge or when you perceive a threat, and you see that there may be an imbalance between the demands being made on you and your resources. Stress arises, therefore, in a specific kind of interaction between you and your environment:

- You perceive a situation of challenge, threat, or harm.
- You consider the outcome important to your welfare.
- You are uncertain whether you will be able to meet the challenge successfully, or avoid the threat.

People vary enormously in the amount, intensity, type, and duration of stress that they can cope with.

You should realize that stress is not something strange and separate, unrelated to normal things that happen to normal people, but that it sits firmly on a continuum. This continuum runs from having too little to do, through normal healthy levels of activity, to rushing around trying to do too much too fast. Either too much or too little to do will trigger changes in your physiology. People are quite good at detecting some of these changes, but it is often more difficult to do anything about them.

The motivation connection

To understand stress you have to understand a little about motivation. Motivation is not a single-shot event, but a cyclical process. One of the more stressful aspects of managers' lives is that the task of motivating their subordinates is truly never-ending.

The cycle begins with a motive, drive, or need. You want to do something (motive). You do something as a result. If what you do takes you closer to your desired goal, then you will experience relief. If what you do is unsuccessful, then you will feel no relief, and there may be an increase in the drive or need. In either event, the cycle does not end, since you are now merely in a new motivational state, and ready to do the next thing on the way to attaining the next goal. Put briefly, people are never satisfied for long. This is an ample source of stress for managers, since it implies that they can never win.

It may be possible for managers to reduce the stress they put on themselves when thinking about how to motivate their staff. Perhaps it is not possible to motivate other people at all, at least in the sense of doing something to them directly which will make them 'motivated'. It may be possible, however, to create the conditions under which people are more likely to motivate themselves. This is both an easier task for the manager, and more likely to bear fruit.

There is an old-fashioned view about motivation which can be expressed as: the more you push people, the more they will do for you. This theory of motivation is wrong – or at least inadequate.

The truth is more complicated. Up to a point it is true that people will do more for you if you push them harder. After that point their performance will level off. If you try to start them on the upward path again after that, you are likely to achieve the opposite of what you want. You may actually impair their performance.

This curious state of affairs was first demonstrated by two psychologists called Yerkes and Dodson. In 1908 they found that motivation works in this way over a wide range of circumstances. They also found that it did not matter much whether the motivation was self-generated or created by someone else. Two factors will modify the picture, however. First, the *simpler* the task, the higher the level of motivation it can tolerate. Second, the *shorter* the task, the higher the level of motivation it can tolerate. Thus, if you are digging the garden and someone shouts that lunch is nearly ready, you can probably get that last row dug in double-quick time. It is a simple job and you know it will be over in three or four minutes. On the other hand, if you are sitting at your desk trying to work out next year's budget you are unlikely to respond well either to being shouted at or to being hurried up. That is a complicated job and needs unhurried consideration to make it more likely that you will get it right.

The relationship between motivation, performance and stress is shown in Figure 8.1, where it becomes clear that either too much or too little motivation can lead to stress-related behaviour. The most important point to note, however, is that for most people, stress is not something peculiar which

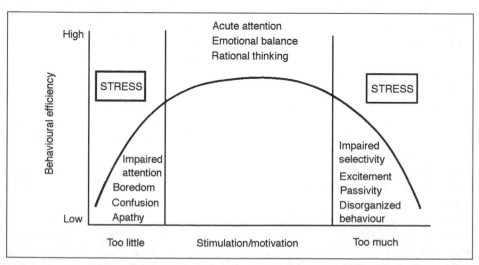

Figure 8.1   Motivation, performance and stress

means that they are losing control or actually ill. Stress is just what happens to motivation when there is a bad match between the person, what they are being asked to do, and the way they are being asked to do it. Stress is, if you like, motivation gone bad.

Fear and anxiety

Fear is a special kind of stress. Fear experienced during an event or, more usually, fear experienced before the event, will cause the same changes in your physiology as stress. Not many of us meet real fear very often, but most of us experience anxiety. Anxiety might be described as the fear of something which has not happened yet or which may never happen. You may experience fear half-way up a rock face, but your anxiety beforehand may prevent you from even starting the climb. Many outdoor development programmes have special techniques for helping people meet and cope with this sort of situation. The idea is that you are then better equipped to deal with less obvious sources of fear or anxiety at work.

Free-floating anxiety occurs when you have acquired the habit of being anxious, whether or not there is actually anything to be anxious about. If you cannot think of anything to worry about, you will worry about that! This kind of anxiety is quite difficult to deal with because there is no obvious or concrete source, so it can be hard to find anything to do to fix the problem. Because free-floating anxiety is often about things that may never happen, sufferers sometimes receive rough treatment – 'Pull yourself together. It's all in your imagination.' If you could pull yourself together, you would. The fact that it is irrational does not make it any less real for the sufferer.

Type A behaviour

In 1960, two American cardiologists, Friedman and Rosenman, began a study of over 3000 people – the Western Collaborative Group Study (WCGS). They found that those who showed one particular pattern of behaviour were more than twice as likely to experience coronary heart disease than others. They called the high-risk pattern Type A, and the low-risk Type B. The chief characteristics of Type A behaviour were said to be:

- insecurity about status;
- hyper-aggressiveness;
- free-floating hostility;
- sense of time urgency (hurry sickness); and
- drive to self-destruction.

Type As have a clearly identifiable response to stress. They are already highly vulnerable before the event because of their high expectations of themselves and others, combined with their physical hyper-reactivity. They live on the edge. The trigger for the stress episode can be anything and everything, since

131

Type As treat even minor obstacles as serious provocations. Their reaction to the event itself is usually out of proportion, since Type As have no brakes to dampen or slow down their response. All wars are nuclear wars! Arousal is too strong, takes too long, and may even interfere with efficient performance. Finally, people without the Type A behaviour pattern will take time after a stressful event to regroup, to review what happened, to replenish their energy, and to prepare for the next event. Type As do not take the time for any of that. Their idea of recuperation is to look immediately for the next battle until they are finally felled by exhaustion or ill health.

This presentation of Type As led to the conclusion that Type A behaviour was 'bad', and that stress management programmes should aim at encouraging the opposite – Type B. This was probably a mistake. Friedman and Rosenman did not suggest it in the first place. Second, the analysis is too simple.

It is possible to be a healthy and effective Type A. The Type A characteristics listed earlier are those of the ineffective, unhealthy, vulnerable Type A. In the original study, over 11 per cent of Type As experienced some form of coronary heart disease, as against less than 6 per cent of the more laid-back Type Bs. But that also means that over 88 per cent of Type As in the study did *not* experience problems. So it is entirely possible for a Type A to get it right. This is just as well, since organizations need effective Type As to make things happen fast and efficiently.

The ineffective Type As are too quick on the trigger, indiscriminate in the strength of their mobilization, and too slow to recover. As a result, they get the job done, but with a wastefully and unnecessarily high use of energy. The effective Type As are alert but not over-reactive, mobilize quickly to the level of response which they judge to meet the nature of the problem, and review the event afterwards, so that they can learn from any mistakes and store any successful solutions for future use. The job is done swiftly and with economy, with an eye to improving the response to anything similar.

Finally, the initial definition of the unhealthy Type A may have been too broad. The significant components appear to be hostility and cynicism, leading to what has been called 'joyless striving'. This kind of behaviour is both ineffective and a good predictor of coronary heart disease. Impatience and irritability are bad signs. There appears to be nothing wrong with vigorous achievement striving – indeed, it should be encouraged.

The physiology of stress

To understand and cope with stress, it is useful to know what is going on in your body when you experience fear, stress or anxiety. It all starts when you perceive some kind of threat. This could be a bump in the night, someone stepping out suddenly in front of your car, or a sharp comment from your boss. Whatever the source, as soon as the message reaches your brain and is perceived as actually or potentially threatening, a number of changes take place (shown in diagrammatic form in Figure 8.2).

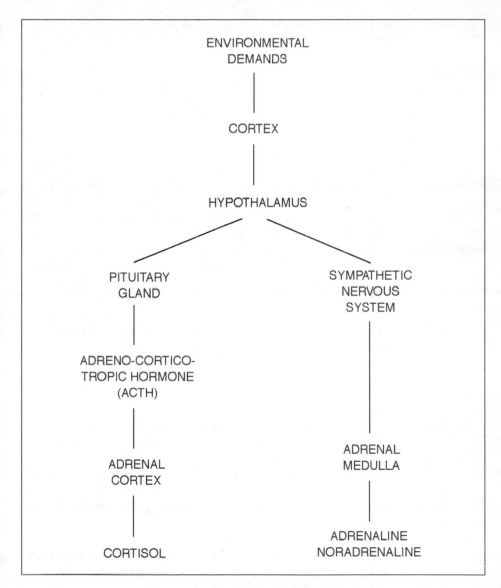

Figure 8.2 The physiology of the stress response

Information about external stressors will enter your system through one or more of your senses, and will be received in your cortex (grey cells, which make up the outer layers of your brain). Internal stressors, generated by your own memories, thoughts, and fantasies, are already there. In either event, signals now pass to your hypothalamus, a pea-sized organ in the middle of your brain, which triggers action via two separate routes.

The first route goes to the pituitary gland (about one inch in from the bridge of your nose) to stimulate the production of a hormone called the adreno-cortico-tropic hormone (ACTH), which is released into your blood stream to bring your adrenal cortex into play. Your adrenal glands sit like small hats in the small of your back, one over each kidney. The adrenal cortex (outer part) produces cortisol, which influences your immune system, counteracts inflammation, and affects the metabolism of carbohydrates, lipids, and proteins in all body tissues to produce energy.

The second route runs from the hypothalmus to your sympathetic nervous system, which is responsible for most of your normal automatic physical responses. The sympathetic nervous system in turn stimulates the adrenal medulla (middle part), which produces adrenalin and noradrenalin (also known as epinephrine and norepinephrine). Adrenalin increases your heart rate and re-directs your blood from inner organs to muscles. Noradrenalin causes blood pressure to rise by contracting your blood vessels. So far you will not have been aware of any changes, but from now on they become apparent.

The main changes are listed below, together with the reasons for them. None of these changes is without one main purpose: to help you survive.

- The pupils of your eyes will get larger. More light will enter your eyes so that you can see any potential source of danger earlier and better.
- Your hearing may become more acute, again so that you can detect danger further away and give yourself more time to think of something to do about it.
- You will breathe faster. This increases the amount of oxygen in the blood, which is your fuel for action.
- Your heart will pump faster and harder, so that the flow of fuel is speeded up, and also so that any waste products caused by the burning of the fuel are quickly carried away.
- You may go pale. This is because blood has been taken away from the outside of your body, so you will bleed less if wounded. Another agent ensures that your blood will clot quicker, reducing blood loss if you are cut.
- You may feel sick or have upset bowels. This is because blood has been removed from your digestive system as well, and, in extremes, you will empty yourself either by vomiting or diarrhoea. This is to rid yourself of surplus weight if you have to run fast.
- The fuel-rich blood is sent instead to the muscles you may need to use in a hurry if the threat is real.
- You may sweat more. This is because physical effort generates heat. You only work efficiently over a quite small internal temperature range, so your cooling system is switched on. You lose heat by evaporating fluids from the surface of your skin – sweating.
- You may shake or tremble. This is partly because your muscles have tensed up generally. It may also be to warm you up if the cooling system has come on but you have *not* done anything physical to actually generate any heat.

These changes are all normal, healthy and aimed at ensuring your survival in an emergency. They were extremely useful when we lived in caves. They can be a real nuisance in the office or at home.

What has happened is that your body has been prepared for *fight or flight*. You may be in no position to do either. Many of the problems of coping with stress have to do with finding some way of discharging all this potential energy in a harmless or constructive way. If the energy is not discharged it will eventually cause damage. You will find that you have been pushed over the top of the curve in Figure 8.1, and your performance will suffer. At home or at work the problems may become worse. An anxiety spiral has been started.

WHAT DOES STRESS COST?

Managers usually prefer to spend money in ways which show some measurable return. There is no point, commercially speaking, spending money managing stress unless it is costing more money to ignore it.

In the days when you had to have a certificate for any spell of absence from work through sickness of more than three days, it was easier to estimate the commercial damage caused by stress-related disease. Even then, the bulk of absences were not covered because they were for only half a day or a day, and therefore did not appear in the official figures. Even working on those reduced figures, the number of working days lost through psychosis, psycho-neurosis, nervousness, debility and headaches was well over double the days lost through industrial accidents. Other forms of sickness thought to have a psychological component, such as indigestion, skin complaints, muscular aches and pains, back problems, ulcers and heart disease, are *not* included in those figures. A fairly modest estimate of the working days lost through stress-related problems each year is around 120 million. That is expensive.

Worrying though that figure undoubtedly is, it still does not address the whole of the problem. There is no estimate of the cost of mistakes made by people who remain at work while under stress. The figure relates largely to losses at shop floor level, where you can measure losses in production, orders not sent on time, poor quality products and paperwork errors fairly easily. But how do you assess the cost of lost management days? It is even more difficult to assess the costs of wrong decisions, wasted time, over-long lunch hours, together with too much alcohol and tobacco, and poor or inaccurate monitoring of performance. Evidence of the cost of poor decision making is all around us.

Industrial unrest may well have some of its roots in stress. The boredom (under-motivation) of routine production line work probably contributes to the readiness of some production workers to strike, even if only to generate some variety! The girl working on the supermarket till who would much rather talk to her friend than serve you is quite likely to be thoroughly bored. Even worse, the only feedback she may get on her performance is the occasional and unpredictable ticking-off from her supervisor when she happens to   *135* be spotted doing something wrong. How often is she rewarded specifically for good customer work? Can she predict which actions will get her into trouble and those which will lead to some form of reward? If not, why should she bother?

At management and shop floor levels, stress in its various forms is squandering resources we can ill afford. The cost of cure is a very small fraction of the total bill. Prevention would be even better. The whole cost might even be recovered simply from reduced labour turnover costs.

WHAT CAUSES STRESS?

Different people react in different ways to the same situation. What you find merely stimulating might be uncomfortably heavy pressure to someone else. With that reservation in mind, some of the common causes of stress at work are now reviewed.

Physical causes

Noise is a source of stress for many people, and its occurrence is the most usual source. This has now been recognized in legislation about maximum noise levels. Many workers have now been persuaded to wear ear protection who might have scorned to do so before: tractor drivers, road drill operators, boilermakers and chain saw users, for example. Attention is also being turned to domestic noise generators, such as vacuum cleaners, washing machines, food processors and the nuisance of other people's radios. The damage that is being inflicted by discos is also well understood.

It is less well known that things can also be too quiet! British Rail met this problem when building new modern coaches. The level of soundproofing was originally so high that the quiet interior made it too easy to hear other people's conversations. It was necessary to reintroduce some noise to mask the distraction from other passengers, and to allow relatively undisturbed reading, conversation or thinking. The level of quiet in a jumbo jet is very near to this disturbance level.

Tiredness causes stress as your ability to perform decreases. Worse, at the early stages of tiredness, you may not know that your performance is declining, and therefore you may assume that all is well and go on to make expensive errors or omissions. On top of that, because you are tired, you will be less willing to hear warnings about your performance from anyone else. The ability to assess your own performance accurately is one of the first things to go when you are tired, coupled with your emotional resilience.

Shift work patterns sometimes allow or encourage people to do other jobs during their off-periods. Split-shift patterns for bus crews often lead to this problem. As a result, neither the official nor the side job is done well. In the case of drivers of any kind, this has immediate and obvious dangers. Few managers in the United Kingdom work shifts, but some of them put in very long hours. Not all those hours are productive because of fatigue. Midnight-oil burners can make bad mistakes. Frequent changes of shift pattern are also disruptive. It is better to have a long stint on nights, then a good break, followed by a long period on days, rather than changing every two weeks or so.

Jet lag is a special sort of tiredness, made worse by changing time zones and upset body rhythms. It is most unwise to make important decisions immediately after a long flight, especially if you have travelled from west to east. Few organizations seriously advise their people to rest for at least 24 hours before doing anything that matters, however.

Temperature and humidity also need to be controlled. Legislation lays down working limits, but greater extremes of temperature can be tolerated at lower levels of humidity. There are suggestions that increasing the level of negative ions in the air is beneficial, but this is quite hard to do on a large scale and the results are not yet certain.

Amount of work

Too much to do is a familiar idea, although it is often claimed before it is a fact. There are three different types of overload:

- the skill level demanded may be too high for the person;
- the speed may be too high for them;
- the volume may be too much;

or some combination of these.

Too little to do is also possible, but less often talked about. Again, there are three kinds of underload:

- the skill level may be too low (e.g. asking a graduate to do a school-leaver type of job);
- the speed may be too slow (e.g. when a meeting takes all day to decide something you could have done on your own in ten seconds);
- the volume can be too small (e.g. when a bright secretary is asked to do two letters and some filing in a whole day);

or some combination of these.

A sure sign of underloading at work is when the level of office politics starts to rise. People who have too little to do may fill the time with politics. The long-term unemployed have met the underload problem. They often find it difficult to get out of bed and go out at all. The level of stimulus in their environment has dropped to the point where they actually need help to get going again. This is not deliberate idling at all, but a genuine psychological problem induced by boredom, loneliness and a sense of defeat.

Nature of work

New or unfamiliar situations, such as your first day in a new job or organization, will be stressful because they are full of uncertainty.

Personal threat may be felt if your personal space is invaded by crowded conditions or by your boss standing too close when talking to you. If you feel that you are the victim of unreasonable control or arbitrary decisions about personal matters, such as going to the lavatory, your stress level will rise. Too little personal threat can also create problems. If nothing much happens when you fail to meet standards, then your standards of performance are likely to fall.

Pacing The inability to pace your own work is highly stressful, as many production line workers will tell you. Likewise, if you happen to work in an office where your colleagues, your manager or your customers make frequent and unpredictable claims on your time, your performance will suffer.

Ambiguity People vary a great deal in the amount of ambiguity or lack of clarity which they prefer. Some salespeople like very little uncertainty and prefer to work in the short term. They like to know at the end of each day how much they have sold and how much they have earned. On the other hand, a salesman dealing with large computing systems may have a long wait and a lot of work before he knows whether he has the order, and the nature of the installation may change during the course of implementation. It is much more difficult to establish a direct link between sale and reward; nor would that kind of salesman seek it. If you are a manager, the relationship between performance and reward can seem very indirect and uncertain indeed.

Feedback needs to be reliable and undistorted, frequent, and based on clear standards. Unclear standards and unreliable, distorted or non-existent feedback are the surest way to stress employees. They often lead to the use of some form of punishment as the only feedback offered, with no obvious connection to performance.

Fear of freedom

Most of us kick against rules and regulations. 'If only "they" would get off my back' is the frequent cry. When the restrictions are removed, the reaction often surprises. While it is a true liberation for some, for many it leads to great uncertainty, stress and even complete inability to act. We seem to need rules to react against. They provide a map which lets us know where we are and how to get somewhere else. If there are no rules and no map, many people simply feel lost and unable to move. Many managers, who have been excellent performers on their way up the organization, disappoint when they finally reach the top seat because they suddenly find that there is no one to tell them what to do and no one to react against. They are fine as subordinates, and their impatience to succeed may have driven them on well, but now they have 'made it' they are no longer sure what their target should be. Their reaction can be to sit very still and to do the bare minimum necessary to keep out of trouble.

Domestic troubles

Stressors are also found at home. Domestic troubles, ranging from bereavement to marital discord, often coupled with financial problems, can severely affect performance in all spheres of your life.

Communication is a common problem amongst married couples. Imagine you have come home after a bad or boring day. The last thing you want to do is talk about it. You have just lived it. You do not want to go over it all again. Your partner, on the other hand, has just spent the day in the company of your three-year-old offspring of apparently manic and suicidal bent, is desperate for someone adult to talk to, and wants to know what you are doing so that some sharing of your life is possible. You are both right. Here lie real problems which can lead to marital breakdown. Worse still is the case where both partners work and may wish to discharge some of their day's problems. A perfectly reasonable response might be. 'Don't tell me. You want to try my job!'

Relocation is an increasingly frequent source of difficulty for families. When one partner is promoted, or finds a new and better job which involves moving house, who has priority? The male? The higher earner? The one who stayed put last time? The children's education? Will 'weekending' offer any solution, or will that simply lead gently to total and permanent separation? Pressure on the family will be heavy, and the solution may well affect the career prospects of one or both partners, quite aside from any personal damage that may occur.

WHAT ARE THE SIGNS OF STRESS?

The signs become easier to detect if you recall the fight or flight reaction mentioned earlier in the chapter. Under short-term stress, the fight or flight nature of the reactions is quite clear. Under long-term stress, it is not always so obvious.

Short-term stress

The fight reaction when escape is possible is usually to have a short, sharp row on the spot with whomever is seen as causing the problem. The form of the row can vary from verbal abuse to a punch on the nose.

The fight reaction when escape is not possible, which is what most of us experience, is either to take it out on others or to punish yourself. If you take it out on others, then your staff may suffer because you have had a difficult meeting elsewhere. If you take it out on yourself, then you may spend the rest of the day sunk in gloom.

The flight reaction when escape is possible is to go sick, take long lunch breaks, resign, or retire early. The main point is to remove yourself from the situation.

The flight reaction when escape is not possible may involve slowing down, withdrawing commitment to the business, delaying, acting with extreme caution, withdrawing from involvement with the business, or simply sleeping a lot more than before.

Long-term stress

Psychosomatic illness may occur where there is no obvious physical cause for a physical ailment. It is arguable that ulcers, some heart attacks, strokes, indigestion, headaches, migraines, skin irritation, acne, over- and under-sleeping are all associated to some degree with stress.

Predisposition to illness can be caused by stress. You become vulnerable to illnesses that otherwise you would have brushed off, and your recovery is slower. The self-employed tend not to get colds!

Absenteeism may occur, ranging from lateness, through continuing small bouts of illness, to complete withdrawal by striking or leaving.

Indecision may increase to the point where it is difficult to get anything done at all without setting up a committee.

Capriciousness in decision making may appear. There is little hesitation, but there is equally little reason underlying the decisions. You may also see surprisingly light-hearted behaviour from the normally serious, or sexual promiscuity from the previously well behaved. You will find it increasingly hard to predict their behaviour.

Excessive consumption of food, drink and tobacco are fairly sure signs. No one should smoke anyway. Alcohol taken in more than moderation is damaging, and may be lethal if combined with driving. Too much food leads to obesity and all its associated health problems. It is also possible to consume material possessions to excess (cars, furs, jewels, and so forth). Excessive consumption of the opposite sex is often a sign of serious, unresolved stress.

140   *Theft* may increase under stress. When a factory is about to be closed,

security should be tightened because anything not actually bolted to the floor may be considered fair game. On a smaller and more day-to-day scale, stationery, personal phone calls on company time, over-long lunch breaks, and a decision not to return to the office after an appointment that ended at three o'clock, are all forms of theft. Theft of goods is readily detectable. Theft of time, which may be more costly, is harder to see and control.

Workaholism It is sometimes necessary to put in unusual hours to get a job done. If it becomes a habit, your job needs reorganizing or you are running away from something.

Displacement activity You find yourself doing all kinds of things except the really important one that is actually causing the problem.

Identification with the aggressor Your boss is difficult with you. You cope by being unpleasant with your staff. They pass it on down the line. Soon everyone is having a terrible time.

Over-reaction to normal events The phone rings and you leap out of your chair to answer it, rather than taking things in a more measured fashion. Your boss calls to say you are to meet at five o'clock. You assume that you are being fired, or promoted, instead of assuming that this is the only available time for a routine discussion of something.

Change is the key to detecting stress. Whatever your normal pattern of behaviour, any sudden change should be looked at briefly, in case it indicates some unsuitable level of stress. If someone you work with is always miserable, that may not be a sign of stress. That is just how they are. But if they suddenly become amazingly cheerful, something has obviously changed for them. It may well be perfectly pleasant and understandable. On the other hand, they may have decided to jump!

WHAT CAN THE INDIVIDUAL DO ABOUT STRESS?

There seem to be four main groups of techniques that can make long-lasting beneficial changes to your ability to manage stress.

Exercise Walk until you sweat slightly. Try swimming. Find something you can enjoy doing that makes your heart and lungs work a little harder than usual. Try to do it three times a week. *Warning:* if you have spent twenty-five years getting out of condition, do not try to fix it all in half an hour on the squash court. You could damage yourself seriously. Build gradually into physical exercise; do not slam into it.

Biofeedback teaches you how to control consciously some of the physical stress reactions that are normally automatic. By linking yourself to heart rate   *141* or skin resistance monitors, you can quickly see variations in the readings. Heart rate will rise and skin resistance will fall as you become more stressed. You can learn what you have to do to lower your heart rate or to increase your skin resistance, getting feedback on your success from the monitors. After a number of training sessions you will no longer need the monitors, but will be able to control a number of stress symptoms directly and consciously.

Cognitive techniques   Much of what we call stress we do to ourselves. You can be helped to recognize when a particular stress reaction started – usually an event when you were quite young. You can then review your actions at that time, and acknowledge that there was probably not much else you could have done about it at the time. You can then be guided to question whether the coping technique which was appropriate or necessary at, say, 6 years old is still appropriate or necessary now that you are, say, 36. Probably not. What else would you like to do if you were in that situation again, but as you are *now*? Gradually you are enabled to recall past events, recognize and evaluate realistically your reactions to them then, assess their suitability to present events, and think through new and more appropriate actions to replace the old reactions. This process has a strong appeal to the highly rational individual, but can be effective with a wide range of people.

Relaxation techniques   Breathing exercises and some forms of meditation have been shown to produce enduring physiological and psychological benefits for individuals. However, this is one set of techniques which needs careful introduction to Type As. If the purpose is clear, and the expectation is set that the Type A will emerge from the process more vigorous and alert, and better equipped to tackle whatever problems come their way, then they will accept relaxation techniques readily and obtain great benefit from them. If Type As gain the impression that these techniques are designed to slow them down and make them somehow dreamy and detached, then they will resist and may respond with increased stress levels.

In addition to the above four main groups of activities, you might want to see if any of the following techniques interests you enough to try them. They have all worked for someone.

Physiological and physical action

Control eating   Surplus is surplus. You do not need to consume it. You do not need to carry it around. It is a waste of time and energy.

Control alcohol intake   There is some medical evidence to suggest that a little wine may be positively beneficial, but treat alcohol with care. If you drink a bottle of brandy in one go it will probably kill you. Alcohol is high in calories and will allow your other food intake to go into store as fat.

Abolish smoking   Smoking kills about 100 000 people a year in the United Kingdom.

Control posture   Sit up so that your lungs can breathe properly and your digestive system has room to function. Walk as if your pelvis were a bowl full of water which you must not spill. Keep the spine stretched and head erect. Make sure you get up and move about during the day.

Control breathing   Sit somewhere comfortable. Take a normal breath. Hold it for a slow count of three. Let it out with a slight huff. You may find it helpful to have your eyes shut while you are doing this. Do this twice a day for three weeks. See how you feel.

By controlling your breathing in this way you are breaking into the alarm reaction that you read about earlier. When your system picks up that your breathing rate has dropped, it will assume that the threat has gone or at least lessened, and will automatically run down the rest of the alarm system. Do not try to interfere with this process. You have a perfectly effective automatic system for doing all this, which you can trigger with the pause breath. Over a period of three weeks you are likely to find that you have become generally calmer and more alert, as well as being better able to cope with stress when it occurs.

Aim for contrast   Whatever you do during the day, try to find something different to do in the evening or at weekends. Try to find ways of varying what you do during the day. Vary the pace. Vary the intensity. Vary the importance. Do some things alone and some with other people. We thrive on variety, provided we feel that it is of our choosing and under our control to some degree.

Action against stress at work

Recognize that you can be a victim of stress. You are not invulnerable. If a problem does occur for you, you can waste a lot of time denying that it exists when you should be getting on and fixing it.

Analyse the probable causes. Keep this simple. They are not usually hard to find. They may be harder to admit.

Can you leave the situation?   This is not a cop-out, but simply a quick check to establish whether you really do have to put up with the interview, training course, car journey, meeting, conversation or social gathering in which you find yourself. What is the price of leaving? What is the price of staying? Do your arithmetic. Then act.

Decide when to cut your losses   Make a date with yourself. By then, the situation will have changed, you will have resolved the situation, or you will take   *143* more emphatic action (leave, go over your boss's head, fire your subordinate, dump the customer, and so on). Once you have made this kind of deal with yourself, stick to it. If you break your word to yourself, you will never quite trust yourself again to do what you set out to do. This can be very destructive, so think over your bargain carefully before you commit yourself.

Control the pace   Good tennis players do not spend all their time at the net. Sometimes they need to get to the back of the court so they can see what is going on in time to plan what to do next. Someone may be firing questions at you very fast and hard. You do not have to let them control the speed of your response. Play it your way. They have no control over your choice in this matter. If things seem to be slipping away from you, make sure that, whatever your answer, your final sentence is a question. This puts you in control of the conversation. You can even induce stress in others by delaying your replies just a fraction longer than they are comfortable with.

Discharge   Make sure you have something explosive to do to wash out any unresolved anger or frustration at the end of the day. If you play a high-activity sport, that will help. If not, try digging a hole in the garden, thumping something inanimate, or just shouting loudly, once. Be careful who is around when you are doing any of these! Again, you are fooling your physiology into believing that the violent physical activity for which it has been preparing itself (fight or flight, again) has actually happened, and it can now relax.

Set your own objectives and life goals   Decide what you want to do, then go for it. This goes broader than merely work, and extends beyond retirement.

Medical aid   If you are in trouble, ask for help. This is not weak, but sensible self-management. Drugs will not solve your problem, but they can sometimes help you temporarily to a frame of mind in which you *can* solve your problem. Tell your doctor the moment you are not happy with what you feel the treatment is doing to you. There may be another way of dealing with the problem.

Review before relaxing after you have coped with the problem. Celebrate when you know *why* what you did worked. That way you know what to do if the problem ever occurs again.

Action against stress at home

Recognize that it can happen to you and yours. No household is immune.

Analyse the probable causes.

Discuss the problems openly and early, before they become too difficult to talk about.

Recognition mechanisms exist for most people. Offer the signs that you are getting upset to your partner. Accept their signs in return. This way you can both spot when trouble is looming before it gets too developed.

Share some planned time and activities together. Do not spend all your home time in retreat.

Communicate with your partner and family. They need information from you and you need information from them so that difficulties can be dealt with early and opportunities for pleasure and reward can be developed.

Financial information needs to be shared. Many wives have been blamed by their husbands for spending the family into debt, when their husbands had never let them know what was happening and how much money was on hand. There are large cultural differences within the United Kingdom on this point, so check your family's expectations before acting on financial matters.

Consult on domestic arrangements. It is not a good idea to bring three colleagues home from work unannounced on a Friday night for a meal. Similarly, it is not helpful to announce as your partner comes in the door that Uncle Joe and Auntie Ethel have moved into the spare bedroom and are here for a week, especially if you have known for some time that they were coming.

Territory Everyone needs somewhere that is their own. It need not be large. A desk; a dressing table; a small patch in the vegetable plot will often be enough. But that territory should be unique to the individual 'owning' it, and other people should only enter by invitation.

Solitude Even in the most affectionate families, people sometimes need to be alone. This should be respected. It is not rejection. It may even be a statement of confidence that the relationships are so good that it never occurs to the person concerned that it would be seen as rejection. It can be difficult to find a moment of quiet in a busy family, but it is important to have the freedom to try.

COPING AT THE TOP

Figure 8.3 represents a very simple picture of the essential differences between healthy and unhealthy coping.

The healthy Type A is active and satisfied. Adrenalin levels are raised, cortisol levels are lowered. High demand has combined with autonomy and influence, requiring the mobilization of considerable effort. But Type As enjoy working in this kind of situation. This is 'happy stress'. The unhealthy Type A is active and distressed. High demands are coupled with lack of control and influence, leading to both effort and discomfort. This state is associated with sharply increased adrenalin levels, combined with increased cortisol levels. *145*

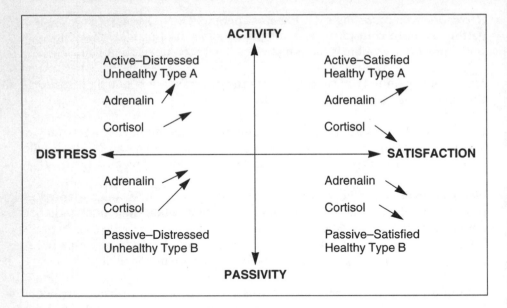

Figure 8.3   Healthy and unhealthy coping

Taken to extremes, the Type A will take refuge in learned helplessness, in which nothing is done but the frustration and anger levels soar.

The healthy Type B is passive and satisfied. Adrenalin and cortisol levels are both lowered. A pleasant and undemanding environment offers the Type B relaxation of both body and mind, with no feelings of either effort or distress. This does not mean that they do nothing, however. The healthy Type B can be creative and imaginative, or at least will do what needs to be done at a steady pace and without fuss and bother. An unhealthy Type B is passive and distressed. Adrenalin levels are slightly raised and cortisol levels are considerably raised. The unhealthy Type B exhibits distress without effort, appearing unwilling or unable to do anything about the situation. It is easy to confuse the learned helplessness of the unhealthy Type A with this passivity in a damaged Type B, but the Type B is unlikely to be angry about it.

A survey of a large number of Type A chief executives, from a wide range of industries and professions, yielded the following stress management techniques held in common. Note that they are all preventive, the very area into which individuals and organizations seem least willing to put effort.

- *Be intellectually curious.* Intellectual curiosity and education (formal or informal) expand a person's understanding of the world, providing perspective as well as knowledge for problem solving.
- *Be physically active.* People who are physically active dissipate stress-induced energy while at the same time developing a stronger and more efficient cardiovascular system.
- *Balance work with non-work.* People who balance work with non-work

activities place their work in a larger, broader context which gives perspective and reduces psychological dependence on work.
● *Seek social support.* Supportive relationships satisfy a variety of informational, evaluative and emotional needs essential to healthy functioning.
● *Create systemic change.* The people at the top need to be able to create a work environment that is challenging, productive, creative, and at the same time emotionally healthy.

WHAT CAN ORGANIZATIONS DO ABOUT STRESS?

Organizations, as such, can do nothing. If you are a manager, you may be able to, however. What you and your colleagues choose to do can be understood as the organization doing something.

Remedial action

A problem has occurred. You now have to try to cope.

Recognize that it has happened. Do not ignore it or hope it will go away by itself.

Removal   Does the person concerned have to stay in that situation? If not, move them. If so, plan with them how they can cope better.

Expert help   If the person has had a serious problem, and especially if they do not seem to be improving now that the apparent cause has been removed, get help. This is probably beyond you as a manager, and you possibly should not be spending that much time on it, even if you could do something about it. This is not your only subordinate. You could be adding significantly to the stress of others by overconcentration on this one problem.

Frequent feedback on performance will help restore confidence and ability. Give the person a lot of short-term tasks which are well within their capability. Make sure they know they have done them well. Gradually increase the difficulty and length of the tasks, giving positive feedback all the way, until they are back to strength again. Do not make a big deal if they fail on some of the tasks. Just go back a step and try again. Do not expect or seek thanks for your help. They need to feel that they are standing on their own feet, and acknowledging any kind of dependency may make this difficult for them. This is part of your job as a manager.

Preventive action

It is far better to stop undue stress occurring in the first place than it is to cure it once it has arrived. You may never know if your efforts have worked. That is   *147* why prevention is not popular. Cure is much more obvious and dramatic. There are some measures which you can take as a manager which are highly likely to pay off by leading to a better-managed organization anyway.

Recognize that stress can occur.

Collect stress related data   This includes labour turnover, absenteeism, lateness, pilferage, accidents, performance appraisal ratings, and employee attitude surveys. Be especially alert for sudden change.

Cut out deliberate stress   This includes lack of feedback and poor communications generally; sudden and unannounced moves of people and offices; and making people wait unnecessarily.

Working conditions may be at fault. Check lighting, heating, ventilation, humidity, noise, smoking, shift patterns, and the possibility of flexible hours at work.

Selection   There are few organizations that could not improve their initial selection methods. Having the wrong person in the wrong job is bound to cause problems.

Induction   Having introduced good people into the organization, make sure they know what they are supposed to do and help them form the connections and gather the information which will help them do it.

Training   We all need training and retraining to cope with the changing demands of work. The United Kingdom has a bad record of inadequate educational preparation for work, followed up by poor or non-existent training and development at work. You will become stressed if you are being blamed for poor performance but no one is helping you in any concrete way to do it better.

Potential assessment needs careful attention if you are to avoid appointing people to more senior posts who then fail to produce results. It is bad for them and bad for the organization to promote people to positions which they cannot cope with.

Feedback   Give frequent, reliable feedback on performance.

Performance appraisal   Check that the formal annual appraisal is doing what it is supposed to do. Has it become an administrative chore? Is it too formal or too complex?

Job design   How well matched are people's capacities and what they are being asked to do? Do they have too much or too little to do? Is it too fast or too slow for them? How much control do they have or want over what they do?

Face up to bad news early, and then take action before the problem gets out of hand.

Avoid indecision   You will hardly ever have all the information you would like to help you make your decision. Do not take rash risks, but do not hesitate overlong either. Do not create indecision in others by your own unwillingness to make decisions or to let them do so.

Use stress positively   Remember stress and motivation are part of the same continuum. There is a large healthy area under the middle of the curve in Figure 8.1. People can take a surprising amount without burning out if they know what is going on.

Counselling   Have a confidential counselling service available. People need someone to whom they can go to talk freely about their problems, of whatever scale. Companies which run such programmes claim that they make a considerable contribution to the health of the organization and the people within it, but the confidentiality must be absolute.

Medical/psychological help should be available at short notice. When you hit a crisis, or one of your employees does, you cannot wait three weeks for an appointment. Something needs doing *now.* You might want to consider routine health checks for all employees as part of your action to prevent stress building up in the first place.

You can manage stress – both your own and others'. Your objective should be to achieve that level of stress which best matches the person, what they are being asked to do, and the circumstances under which they are working. Sometimes this may mean increasing their stress level to help them achieve more, but never to the point of asking them to risk damaging themselves.

It might be as well to conclude with a warning. Do not overdo your concern with stress. Not every problem is stress related, and attempts at do-it-yourself psychiatry for trivial upsets are likely to be a waste of time, and may do more harm than good. But managing yourself and others to avoid inappropriate stress is a highly profitable venture.

CHECK LIST

1   *Take stock.* What is your physical state? What is your psychological state? How are things at work? How are things at home? How are you doing as a manager (if appropriate)?

2   *Do a gap analysis.* Where are you now in your stress management? Where do you want to be? Make the clearest list you can of achievable   *149*

changes, together with measures which will let you know that you have done what you set out to do.

3 *List the resources* you have available, or that you could obtain or create.

4 *List the limitations* on what you are trying to do.

5 *Create an action plan,* which says what you are going to do, by when, given your resources and limitations.

6 *Carry out your plan,* one item at a time. Make sure that you get accurate feedback on the results of your efforts, especially if you have to give it to yourself.

7 *Revise your targets,* and select new ones, in the light of your progress.

There is no end to this check list. It is a continuous process.

FURTHER READING

Booth, A. L., *Stressmanship,* Severn House Publishers, 1985.

British Medical Association, *The BMA Book of Executive Health,* Times Books, 1979.

Quick, J. C., Nelson, D. L. and Quick, I. D., *Stress and Challenge at the Top: The paradox of the successful executive,* Wiley, 1990.

Roskies, E., *Stress Management for the Healthy Type A: Theory and practice,* Guilford, 1987.

Rudinger, E., *Living with Stress,* Consumers Association, 1982.

Selye, H., *Stress without Distress,* Corgi, 1987.

Wood, C., *Living in Overdrive,* Fontana Paperbacks, 1984.

Part II
MANAGING OTHER PEOPLE

Introduction: understanding other people

Management involves getting things done through or by other people. Here is where most managers make their first mistake. 'It's quicker to do it myself,' they say. 'The only way to make sure something is done correctly is to do it yourself.' And so on. This is not what management is about.

If you insist on doing things yourself, instead of getting them done by or through other people, a number of things happen:

- You fill your days doing things that should be done by other people.
- You waste your organization's money: calculate the rate per hour your organization is paying you and the rate per hour for those subordinate to you who should be doing what you are insisting on doing yourself. Subtract the difference. That is what your organization is losing.
- You have less time available to do the things you are actually paid to do. This may be deliberate – you are too unsure of your ability to operate at the level you have been promoted to, so you spend your time doing things you know you *can* do.
- Your subordinates do not have enough work to do and have to find other things to do: for example, office politics, rumour mongering, industrial relations.
- Your subordinates do not have the opportunity to learn new skills.
- Morale and motivation drop.
- Your stress levels rise.

The answer, of course, is management through people: achieving *your* targets through *their* contribution, *their* work.

First, you need to be clear about what your targets are: what are you meant to achieve? Next, who are 'your' people? What are their skills, their strengths and weaknesses? A brief review of these points will provide a valuable basis *153* for assessing current performance and planning for the future.

But it does not touch upon the heart of the matter. How do you marry 'your' people and their skills with the tasks and targets you need to achieve? In this section, we cover a range of skills you may need to help you: the people skills you may find useful; listening; motivation; developing your people; dealing with problem staff; team building; influencing; performance appraisal and counselling; selection and interviewing; the skills of communication with staff, and making meetings work.

FURTHER READING

Handy, Charles B., *Understanding Organizations*, 3rd edn, Penguin, 1987. Detailed yet very readable introduction to organizations and the people who 'are' those organizations. An illuminating and useful overview of organizational theory, designed to be of practical use for the intelligent manager who wants to understand as well as manage.

9 Recruitment

John Courtis

People are a fundamental resource common to all organizations. Money is the other, and you need the people to obtain and use the money properly, even in a non-profit-making environment.

It follows that obtaining and using the people properly is also important. Most employees are 'obtained' by a process known as recruitment. This has parallels with the procurement process, in that you aim to get the right people in the right place, at the right time, and for the right price.

Purchasing (or buying or procurement) is generally done by professionals. Recruitment is generally done by amateurs, unprofessionally. There are parallels with child rearing. Most people only have their parents' example to guide them when they in turn try to raise the next generation. Previous faults are repeated. So it is with recruitment. Everyone believes they know something about recruitment because they have themselves been recruited. It is not wholly surprising that simple errors are repeated and even presented as good practice. This is bad news for the victims (and in these cases everyone is damaged by bad recruitment – the candidates, peers, bosses and the organization itself) but good news for anyone who is prepared to take a fresh look at recruitment policy and practice.

This chapter offers a menu for such a review. It cannot be encyclopaedic but it should make it possible for you to improve most aspects of the process. There is an added bonus. Recruitment divides naturally into seven stages and being only 10 per cent better at each stage multiplies up to an improvement approaching 95 per cent. If the 1990s have their fair share of skills shortages, such an improvement must give you a head start over the competition, that is, the 'unprofessionals'.

First, the seven stages from which we shall build our menu are as follows:

1   Is there really a vacancy and for what?

2 How are we to find the candidates?
3 How do we process the results through to interview?
4 Interviews (see Chapter 10).
5 The selection decision and relevant tools.
6 Offer and contract.
7 Induction.

All of these are important and in each phase it is well to remember a very old piece of advice: 'Do unto others as you would be done by'. Candidates are people. They are also potential customers. On both levels, good practice pays dividends.

Good practice, as in many areas, starts with the basic advice – read the instructions. This chapter is only part of the instructions. Other books and management media are worth attention too. Even the national daily and Sunday papers are printing some sound advice as part of their continuing efforts to enhance their credibility as recruitment media.

One thing the media may forget to tell you is that the comparison with the purchasing function is only part of the context. Good recruitment is also a marketing exercise. The employer is not allowed to turn the open door into an obstacle course or a high-security minimum disclosure ego trip. The best candidates will only be attracted by open and interesting advertisements, letters or other approaches – in short, a direct marketing programme. Helping your colleagues to think like this about recruitment may be one of the most helpful things anyone can do for them. Reminding them of the level of disclosure and attention they might welcome if they were in the job market may also help. Or asking 'How would you want your friends or family to be treated?' may be necessary if it becomes obvious that they are masochists about the obstacles.

Conditioning is paramount. There is little point in practising properly if your colleagues are dedicated to mediocrity or, worse but not unusual, are working against what you are trying to achieve. Nowhere is this more apparent than in the politics and practice of defining the vacancy and the candidate – the first phase of the seven.

IS THERE A JOB, AND WHAT IS THE CANDIDATE SPECIFICATION?

Whether or not there is a job is a very significant consideration. Busy managers tend to assume that resignations create vacancies; or that too much work implies a need for more employees. Neither is the correct starting point. In both cases the initial reaction should be to analyse the work involved and to ask:

- What are the tasks, objectives and benefits?
- Is the work really necessary'?

- Could we avoid, reduce, reallocate, mechanize or subcontract it?
- What would happen if we did not do it?

The same ruthless attitude should be applied to defining the minimum candidate. Not the ideal, the minimum. Both are important but the ideal is a luxury, whereas the minimum is the more realistic yardstick, particularly if someone is looking for a clone of the departed job-holder or for someone who has done the job before somewhere else.

In the former case, it is necessary to point out that even if the lost paragon was good, he or she came into the job with much less experience, and it may be correct to go back to their entry standards as the baseline. Equally, good people who have done the job before seldom want to do a replica of it, unless there is something new and exciting about the environment or the problems. Specify again, from a clean sheet of paper. Accountants love zero-based budgeting. Make them practise zero-based candidate specifications, or all the marginal jobs in the accounts department will be filled by qualified accountants and, elsewhere, jobs that A-level entrants could do will be filled by graduates. If they are so filled, it will not be for long. The best people will realize they are underemployed. Only the mediocre will stay.

The worst political problem is usually the manager who needs support staff to support his or her (usually his) ego. Empire building is common. Fortunately, most managers are assessed on financial and headcount budgets. Reminding the culprits of the performance benefits of running a tight ship should be an adequate counterargument. If a new job is involved, the nuisance of getting budget approval should be an adequate deterrent. If a replacement, the reflected glory of making 'headcount savings' may be an adequate carrot unless the culprit is very backward, in which case, a different headcount saving may be worth considering.

HOW DO WE FIND THE RIGHT PEOPLE?

The sourcing decision is not just about the sources you choose. It also concerns timing. Proper attention to the questions posed in the previous phase should have identified that the performance of the job will increase revenues, reduce costs or otherwise pay for itself, preferably several times over. If this is not so, have another think about the rationale for recruiting.

If the job is worth doing, it is worth doing *now,* unless your people planning is so good that you are recruiting at leisure for a forecast future need. It follows that the choice of source(s) must recognize a degree of urgency. 'Saving' money by choosing a cheap, slow or unreliable sourcing programme will actually cost money because the job is not being done fully or at all.

We have to remember this point as we review the sources, some of which cost thousands of pounds, some of which are free. These include:

- People you already know, including ex-employees and past applicants.
- Direct advertising, supported by a sound advertising agency.

- Employment agencies and registers.
- Selection consultants, plus advertising.
- Search consultants (headhunters).
- DIY search, using your own network.
- Contact with local or specialist redundancy situations, direct or via out-placement consultancies.

The first one is seldom mentioned, but is often a significant ingredient, particularly if there is a policy of retaining past applications – and if there is not, start one. Do not be afraid to talk to past employees who have the massive advantage that you know their merits better than any interview and many tests can show.

With direct advertising, DIY headhunting and trawls of redundancies, you remain in control of the programme. The key question is whether the chances of a successful appointment justify sticking to these sources. In many cases, unless you are looking for scarce skills, you can avoid agency and consultancy fees, but probably not some advertising costs.

Advertising, properly written and placed in the right medium, on the advice of a competent agency, can be successful and cost-effective. The difficulty is to ensure that the professional route is followed without amateur interference. In brief, the advertising copy should achieve a high level of disclosure about the organization, the job, rewards, problems, opportunities, location and reply method sought. Non-disclosure, tricky copy, poor typography, wasted space, verbiage and onerous reply instructions all erode response. Poor disclosure of the candidate requirement and rewards also ensures a high level of junk replies, and a reduced level of good ones – or none at all.

The only problem with advertising agencies is that they are paid by the media, in the form of a discount on the space cost, so there is a tendency for them to write longer copy than is strictly necessary and to use more space in more expensive media. Good agencies do not fall into this trap, because they know that in the long run the client does notice the balance between costs and results. If you want to eliminate the temptation you could negotiate a fee-based reward system, with all the media discount credited to the organization and a further incentive for reducing average costs per hiring.

The use of agencies and consultants is more complicated. They exist because they satisfy employers' needs and you have to decide for yourselves which of the many firms satisfy yours. The services on offer can be summarized crudely as follows:

- No-sale, no-fee access to a database of relevant candidates.
- Genuine consulting advice on all aspects of the job and related variables, plus advertising support.
- Search competence.
- Selection competence, that is, an ability to relieve you of most of the processing burden and deliver a short list which has been objectively assembled as well as you could do it, or better.

- The time to concentrate on the recruitment task as a priority.
- Test administration, reference checking, and so on.
- And, of course, a mixture of any or all of the above.

Other things being equal, the quality of the service will vary with the quality of your organization's input. Proper disclosure by the client company is a key factor in getting results out of the agent.

PROCESSING THE RESULTS

The same principles apply whether you are reviewing the results of an advertising campaign, a bundle of CVs from an agency or more informal data from the other possible sources. From the moment you establish contact with the potential employee, you are involved in a marketing exercise in parallel with the selection process. As indicated above, the same applies to your contacts with consultants and agencies. Bad behaviour by your staff will be noticed and cost you goodwill, service, good candidates and money in the future. It can also make your organization a laughing stock or drag you to an industrial tribunal. This applies to everything from discourtesy, through incompetence, to accidental or deliberate discrimination against minority groups.

The IPD Recruitment Code is an excellent starting point on this front. It is too long to reproduce here but single copies are obtainable direct from the IPD (see Further Reading for details).

The recruitment trade association, FRES, also produces a pragmatic leaflet entitled *Opportunities For All* which makes the commercial case for avoiding discrimination and is therefore a useful tool for convincing colleagues who do not care much about good practice or the niceties of employment law.

Good practice is good marketing, and vice versa. The quality of ad replies and their relevance will increase in direct proportion to the level of disclosure you achieve and the quality of the reply instructions. The warmth and practicality of those instructions also help. Make the process easier and people are more likely to think well of you. People with rare skills are often the most demanding of candidates. Good practice can solve skills shortages, providing much more than the modest 10 per cent improvement suggested earlier if the rare bird is attracted to your presentation and rejects the competition.

The effect will be enhanced if you generate enough information to permit interview decisions without the necessity for candidates to complete application forms. Sending candidates a brief about the organization, job and candidate specification also helps retain their interest and lets them help you in the selection process in that if there is no real match they can cry off without a meeting.

The same applies to flexibility over interview timing, which can make you look more professional and more sympathetic. And there is another side to the coin. If you achieve high standards in the pre-interview process, you are in a better position to look at the candidates' actions and decide whether they   *159* meet your standards. If you have been unhelpful or cavalier in your corporate behaviour, it is not a fair test to expect impeccable reactions, whereas poor reactions to good behaviour are in some ways a work sample – and one to beware of.

Finally, the other under-recognized area in the pre-interview process is the difficulty of comparing the different results from the various sources. A CV prepared by a candidate may be less overwritten than one prepared by an agency, but more so than a report from a good consultant. Similarly, the limited amount of data volunteered by a search target or someone whom you have found through your network may do less than justice to the individual. And the ex-employees' records may be on a warts-and-all basis. It is vital to allow for these differences, or you may end up with an interview programme which is totally unbalanced, toward the incorrigible optimists. And people are seldom better than their track records, provided that you have the full record!

Interviews

Interviewing is covered in detail in Chapter 10, but there is one point about attitudes which must be applied by everyone in the interview programme. It is simple. Interviews are designed to help you gather information, so that you can determine how well the candidates would perform in your environment, usually in a specific job. They are not supposed to lead only to the first (subjective) reason why the candidate will not fit. If your colleagues interview on the latter basis, they will not accumulate enough data to make an intelligent comparison between candidates at the later stage when you find that between you you have vetoed *all* the candidates and must think again!

As a minimum discipline I would now recommend that all notes of interviews indicate clearly the extent to which each candidate meets or approaches the specification, with objective reasons for rejection. If the interviewers cannot understand this instruction, perhaps they should not be interviewing. One useful guide is to insist that all interviewers have agreed the candidate specification before the start of the exercise and that later rejections relate to matters covered by the specification. Introducing new criteria later is not on.

DECISIONS, DECISIONS

Well, you have done the interviews and perhaps the tests, reviewed the track records and taken up those references which can be sought without damaging the candidates' current employment or position in his or her incestuous little world. If you have not covered all these points you are not yet in a position to make a valid comparison between the candidates, not least because the interview has a poor record as a predictor of work performance. It can be made better if properly structured, but formal tests are significantly better. So are work samples and, if referees are given the right context and questions,

so are informal references (face-to-face or by telephone, pl...
reference is usually just a parlour game about euphemisms)...

There is no space here to explore the shades of grey whic...
be compared in making the selection decision (e.g. too ma...
weighting and no way of knowing how your colleagues thi...
some of the guidelines above may help. It will also help if someone ᴴᵁ...
firmed that each candidate is actively interested and has gained some idea of
what the organization has to do to attract each of them. There is no point in
choosing the one whom you cannot afford, or cannot interest.

ACCEPTANCE

This section is about reaching a contractual acceptance. This word is
stressed because the objective is that the parties make an agreement which
they can keep. The offer is only a part of that process and, although important, should not be considered in isolation. In particular, there is a dangerous
temptation to produce an offer which is acceptable and is therefore accepted,
thus distracting attention from the need to produce documents which satisfy
the statutory requirement for contracts of service. Two different aspects of
good practice clash here. The warm, welcoming offer letter is important, so is
the formal contract. It is very difficult to merge the two, but some effort must
be applied to making the contract simple and intelligible so that it does not
destroy the effect of the upbeat offer by its length, legality or petty content.

Also, following the direct marketing theme, create an opening for the candidate to query anything anomalous. Ideally, the offer should not be a *fait
accompli*, but the result of a discussion about the likely content of the package, which could even lead to the question, 'If we were to construct an offer
along these lines, would it be acceptable to you?' This preliminary spade-
work, plus an indication in the letter that the candidate must feel free to telephone you about anything which needs clarification (this must be carefully
worded – do not accidentally invite bargaining!) should produce an acceptance or a convertible response. If it does not, you should have left the door
open with the runners-up so that they are not affronted by the delay.
In this context, telling them earlier that you all like him or her, but that there
is one other candidate who is slightly closer to the technical or functional
specification (usually true), is a useful insurance. Leaving them in the dark for
weeks is not a valid alternative.

INDUCTION

Induction is a crucial part of the process. Errors and omissions in the induction process cost time and money, both if you lose the candidates and if you
brief them incorrectly.

Inadequate induction demotivates people, increases staff and labour
turnover, causes disputes, makes work for industrial tribunals and/or generates litigation, damages corporate reputations and, in extreme cases, injures

kills people. Hence good induction pays for itself. It is just as important to have a formal induction plan at senior level as at blue-collar level. Employees at every level are entitled to be properly briefed, and in the absence of positive information, people may make assumptions or ask the wrong person and receive information which is at best incomplete and at worst totally wrong.

This message is not just for personnel staff. Everyone involved in recruiting and settling in a new employee should be aware of the principles and the organization's practice.

Create an induction check list, or adapt the Recruitment Society's standard example, which is slightly too long to be repeated here. Constructive points which are often missed in a traditional induction programme include:

- Use the telephone reference check for guidance on how to get the best out of the employee. This has two advantages. It sounds and is constructive and it also encourages disclosure of weak points.
- Make sure new employees hear about events in the organization before they read about it in the papers. Perhaps put them, temporarily, on the PR department mailing list?
- Keep in touch during long notice periods to make people feel wanted. The more important they are, the longer the notice to be worked out at the previous place and they can be diverted in many ways. Don't let them be!
- Make sure you honour all promises on time or early! This applies to everything from removing the previous incumbent, through car availability, to review dates for rewards packages.
- The above also involves recording all the promises made or implied at interview. In other words, the induction process starts at the beginning of the first interview, a point which needs to be registered with every interviewer.
- Make time to talk about first impressions, by appointment, after the first week or so. This exchange can eliminate a lot of misunderstandings.

Finally, remember that the effort applied to the induction process needs to be continued *ad infinitum*. Keeping good people is almost invariably better than having to hire new ones, and it is cheaper, too. Good practice means good hunting and you can then practise the 'finders keepers' principle!

RECRUITMENT CHECK LIST

See Figure 9.1 shown opposite for a recuitment check list.

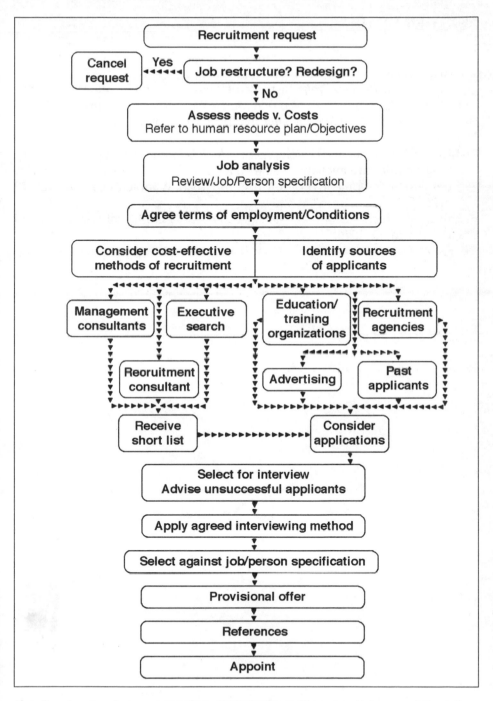

Note: Examine at each stage, areas where discrimination could occur and take preventative action.

Figure 9.1   Recruitment check list (*Source:* Reproduced courtesy of the Institute of Personnel and Development)

FURTHER READING

Courtis, J., *Interviews: Skills and strategy,* Institute of Personnel and Development, 1989.

Courtis, J., *Recruiting for Profit,* Institute of Personnel and Development, 1990.

Davey, D. Mackenzie, *How to be a Good Judge of Character,* Kogan Page, 1989.

Higham, M., *The ABC of Interviewing,* Institute of Personnel and Development, 1979.

Institute of Personnel and Development, *The IPD Recruitment Code,* IPD, 1995. Single copies are available free with an SAE from The Institute of Personnel and Development, IPD House, Camp Road, Wimbledon, London SW19 4UX.

Plumbley, P., *Recruitment and Selection,* 2nd edn, Institute of Personnel and Development, 1976.

10 Interviewing

John Courtis

For most managers, interviewing implies recruitment and selection interviewing but the same rules apply in other applications, such as appraisal, counselling and fact finding. The subject is massive and is therefore treated here on an exception basis, with pointers to additional sources of specialist texts and advice.

We start from the premise that most interviews are unsatisfactory in some way, a premise supported by independent research over many years. Many interviews are abortive or unnecessary.

OBJECTIVES

It may seem trite to mention that you should be certain about your objectives before starting or even planning an interview, but the point is often forgotten or taken for granted. For example, in hiring, few people stop to consider whether they are involved in a selection interview or just a recruitment ratification. Selection involves a qualitative filtering process in which you choose the best – or none – from a number of people interviewed. Recruitment, on the other hand, implies that you choose the first person who matches up to the minimum criteria, or perhaps all those who meet them.

There are secondary objectives which, although peripheral in many cases, are none the less important; for instance:

- your time management objectives;
- the public relations aspect of each meeting;
- house advertising, as an investment for the future;
- product and service advertising;
- research; and
- counselling (during internal selection processes).

If you do not identify your objectives clearly, you cannot plan to achieve them. You may also emerge from the interview without enough data to enable you to meet the objectives when you later realize what they are.

ABORT THE ABORTIVE

Several of the objectives outlined above demand that you do not run interviews which, in retrospect, prove to have been abortive. If you know they are abortive, your interviewee probably does too, in which case, not only have you wasted your time and the victim's, you have also damaged your own and your organization's reputation.

Better communication is the key. If there is an adequate exchange of information beforehand, some interviews will prove to be unnecessary. Others can be modified in content or objective to make them worthwhile. The simplest example is the person who is being interviewed for an inappropriate job, because details of the individual or the job have not reached employer and candidate respectively in a form which permits qualitative judgements by either or both. The defence which both sides usually offer for partial or non-disclosure is that they are afraid of 'putting off' the other side. This is at best shortsighted. It does not impress busy employers or busy candidates (usually the best ones) to find that time has been wasted for this reason. Worse, the chance to have a correctly planned interview which related more accurately to the individual and his or her potential within the organization has almost certainly been missed.

Even at 'recruitment' interviews it is still discourteous to interview people who do not fit the candidate specification or know that they could not or would not do the job as finally described to them. There is a tendency to dismiss this sort of error with the thought that 'It's only half an hour', conveniently ignoring the candidate's travel time, inconvenience, disappointment, and loss of earnings at a level where pride, money, time – and, sometimes, self-confidence – may all be in short supply. Your moral obligation to do the right thing is actually greater the wider the gap in seniority between interviewer and candidate.

TIME FLIES

Given the preceding fairly discouraging introduction, you may be wondering how it is possible to perform a good or worthwhile interview in the time normally allotted. The quick answer is that you cannot! Even in the sort of interview which is planned to take several hours (rather than simply dragging out to that length by the incompetence of the interviewer or the loquacity of the 'victim'), it is entirely possible that the results will be incomplete, misleading, or just plain bad.

The secret is discipline: discipline about the conduct of the meeting and discipline about preparation. I have a theory that much of management consists of the avoidance of error, rather than dramatic flights of flair, fancy or invention. Nowhere is this more true than in interviewing. Proper research and preparation before the interview will make all the difference. Part of the selection process, for example, can be conducted on the telephone. Five minutes per candidate is enough to form a preliminary opinion about their merits, without the need to proceed further (except for a gracious written rejection later if both sides have not agreed that there is no point in going further).

PREPARATION

The environment may be the most important ingredient in the interview preparation. Certainly the difference between good and bad can change an interviewee's chance of communicating well quite considerably. A stress-free room – free of interruptions, threatening layout (e.g. large desk, uncomfortable guest chair), sun in eyes, draughts, excessive heat and noise nuisance – is firmly indicated.

Getting them there

We should not need to labour this point. However, you will have colleagues who are not prepared to be flexible about interview timing, either in respect of the time of day or the day of the week. They may also be thoughtless about the lead time necessary for someone in a worthwhile and demanding job to plan absences. (Where selection and recruitment is concerned, the following is worth considering: other things being equal, the best people are those who are still trying to honour their contracts with their present employers. Excluding the idiots who play hard to get on principle, the elusive are likely to be better than the all-too-available.)

As a final preparation you should:

- read their paperwork again;
- read again what you have sent them;
- smile;
- go out and greet them;
- tell them who you are; and
- make sure they are who you think they are.

Tell them what you want to achieve during the meeting. (Call it a meeting, not an interview.) Make sure they are there for the purpose you think they are. Tell them the structure of the meeting. Now go ahead.

THE INTERVIEW PROPER

Reasonable readers might assume that this heading highlights a distinction between the main body of the interview and the peripheral matters previously covered. Not so. The alternative in mind is the interview *improper*, which is unfortunately the norm in many organizations.

The caring interviewer – especially the recruiter – when approaching an interview, must remember that the interviewee has almost certainly been conditioned badly for the interview, in one of three ways:

- Lack of experience.
- Guidance from friend or counsellor who considers the candidate's objectives without regard to those of the recruiter/interviewer.
- Lots of experience with bad interviewers (the interview improper).

According to the *Oxford English Dictionary,* the primary meanings of 'improper' are 'inaccurate, wrong, not properly so called'. 'Wrong' will do for our purposes. The ways in which other interviews are wrong and yours can be right are varied, but they all come back to the questions of objectives and control. The interviewer must run the meeting and concentrate on matters relevant to the objectives outlined earlier.

The alternative is anarchy and a wasted hour or more. For example, the sort of interview where the candidate takes charge and launches into a biography that duplicates the written material already exchanged (or is necessary because adequate written material has not been exchanged in advance) is wholly unproductive, except to demonstrate the candidate's poor grasp of the objective. Given that he or she has been badly conditioned, it may be unfair to make an adverse judgement on this basis. The effective interviewer, by controlling and setting guidelines for the conduct of the meeting, does both sides a service.

This is less stressful for the candidate, who desperately wants to recite a biography, if the objectives are clearly specified. Something like this may be appropriate:

> I want to achieve three things during this meeting. First, to clear up any queries arising out of the paperwork we sent you, so that you can clearly understand the job and the company environment. Second, a brief review of your track record so that I can make sure that I have understood its relevance to the job. Third, I want to give you a chance to mention any experience or evidence of excellence that is not brought out in your CV.

It is useful at this stage to enquire whether the candidate has any timing constraints and to mention your own, if any. There are few things more damaging to an interview than one of the parties being under pressure on time, while the other is relaxed and could go on all day. Communication can be even worse when both have time problems and neither has disclosed them.

However, all interviews suffer from time pressures because no two people have the same idea of the right amount of time to allocate. The solution is for the interviewer to make it very clear that the exchanges are on an exception-reporting basis: that is, it must not duplicate matters already covered in writing. If this is done, the candidate is forced to discipline the use of time and is also reminded that this is not going to be the sloppy norm experienced in other places. If he or she does not react to the message, you have learned something else about them.

This economy of effort creates one trap. The quality and brevity of the information exchanges may improve, but the staccato rhythm is seductive and may tempt you, as interviewer, not to probe too deeply when an answer is superficially acceptable. This is exceptionally dangerous, because the most important things in an interview, apart perhaps from body language, are the answers to supplementary questions.

Information volunteered by candidates may well be useful but is of their choice. Answers to your questions are more important because, if you are doing your work correctly, they are more relevant to your objectives. Supplementary questions are crucial because they refine or highlight key matters arising out of the other two.

For instance, there are many questions to which a candidate can give a stock answer which is largely under his or her control and is no more informative than the carefully polished words on a CV. Getting behind that stock answer, to the unplanned spontaneous reaction, can be much more informative.

'Why did you leave the So and So Co.?' is a classic and deeply boring question which usually attracts a well-polished reply like, 'There was a promotion bottleneck. My boss was only two years older and unlikely to move.'

You can tackle this in one of two ways. Either change the primary question, so that you are asking questions which previous interviewers have not asked and which therefore demand thought and unique answers, or use the probing supplementary.

In the case quoted, the alternative question might be, 'Why did you leave the So and So Co. so quickly, when you appear to have been well paid and gaining new experience?' This is quite shrewd, because there are at least two and possibly three implied criticisms which the interviewee must consider and rebut. Listen extremely carefully at this point because most people will omit to answer you on one or two of these. Note them. Come back to them, either by way of supplementary questions or a later approach from another angle. Anyone who actually covers all three points without getting tied in knots is probably quite bright.

You may want to try several possible supplementaries, arising from the earlier conduct of the interview. The obvious one is, 'Why didn't you consider this when you joined them?' Because it is obvious it may be less informative than something more open-ended like, 'Does that mean your priorities have changed since you joined them?' This gives you a chance to ask later what the priorities are now, which is quite important if you are trying to weed out job-hoppers. Open-ended questions are almost invariably better than those requiring yes/no answers, except when you are trying to pin down a candidate of suspect credibility.

Questions of all kinds, as implied above, are more important than statements from either side. Even the nature of the candidates' questions can be more informative than their answers to bad questions. A pattern should emerge which will tell you whether the candidate is obsessed with detail, or is a 'broadbrush' operator, that is, paints a big, simple picture. Again, you must listen to and analyse these questions very carefully.

Apart from the set-piece question, there are some very useful interjections which can be as useful as the formal question. For example:

- For instance?
- For example?
- How?
- Why was that?
- What, exactly?
- Can you be more specific?
- Tell me more.
- Can you explain that?
- I don't quite follow.

You probably have your own favourites. All are designed to provoke clarification or a fuller picture without interrupting the flow too much. Even 'Yes?' is both encouragement and reinforcement of this kind.

This is not the place for a detailed listing of all the possible 'good' questions. Instead, the general principle needs to be stressed. Questions are more important than statements, in both directions. The answers are even more important. If you think back over horrible interviews you have attended, it is almost certain that you have experienced the 'improper' interviewer who has devoted massive effort to the construction and issue of a very good question and sinks back exhausted and deaf the moment he asks it. Do not be like the 'improper' interviewer. Listen – listen to their answers, and to their questions. Both are informative. Also, if you do not listen to their questions carefully you may respond with your slightly irrelevant stock answer. The second-rate candidates will not notice or, if they notice, may not mind. The good ones will notice and mind. Even if you decide they are worth offering the job to, they will not accept because they have formed an unfavourable impression. This is so even if they will not be reporting to you in the job, but doubly true if you are the potential boss.

If you are surrounded by 'improper' interviewers who are very obviously unaware of these problems, there are three or four aids which may effect or influence a cure. Tape-recording the meeting, overtly to permit later assessment, may aid self-awareness. Video-taping and playback does the same thing more forcefully. A proprietary video training package by Melrose Films called *Listen* is very helpful on this point. So too is the old Video Arts film, *Manhunt*, about the interview process as a whole. Finally, D. Mackenzie Davey wrote an excellent booklet for the Institute of Management called *How to Interview*.

Tape-recording your own sessions can also help. You will probably be unpleasantly surprised at first, both by your performance and by the number of *non sequiturs* and other communication failures evident in the first few tapes, but this is the only way to learn discreetly, from self-example.

Replaying taped interviews will show you that abortive interviews are signalled very early in most cases. The candidate who comes to a meeting uncertain whether he or she is right for the job and vice versa is usually giving out warning signs, either in the nature of loaded questions, the absence of any questions, or a desire to hurry parts which should normally be taken seriously and slowly. For this reason, I nowadays go immediately to the question of the candidate's interest in the job, without spending time on the candidate's relevance.

Other things being equal, unless you have a wide variety of jobs to fill, there is no point in interviewing in depth a candidate who is going to reject the job as soon as the nature of it is made clear. If this rejection can be identified early, both sides can save time and self-respect. The time saved can then, if appropriate, be devoted to exploring what the candidate can do which might be relevant to the organization's short-term management development plans. Or you can both go home earlier.

BODY LANGUAGE

Reading a good book on body language is doubly important. There are several. Two are called *Body Language*: one by J. Fast (Pan Books, 1972) and the other by A. Pease (Sheldon Press, 1984). Desmond Morris's books, *The Naked Ape* and *Manwatching*, also have relevant content.

You need this background for two reasons. First, it can help you interpret what the interviewee is thinking, if what they are saying or not saying is not the whole truth. Second, you can use the positions and signals described in the books to demonstrate sympathetic interest, or anything else you feel like, at times when you feel far from sympathetic or interested, but the good conduct of the interview demands that you be supportive. Conversely, if you want to get rid of a verbose candidate, body signals can help to reinforce other messages, without overt rudeness.

THE CLOSE

Closing the interview on time is a tempting objective in some circumstances, but it must not be allowed to interfere with the correct disciplines for shutting down the meeting.

You must both know what you have agreed and what comes next. Your next action must be mentioned, with a time forecast. If the interviewee has to send you something, remind him or her and agree how soon it is needed. If you are not sure where they stand about the job, for heaven's sake ask them.

If you are uncertain about a job candidate's relevance, tell them why, so that they have a chance to agree or clear the air. Even if it is disappointing for them, this is better than having them feel hard done by when an unexplained rejection arrives later. You may also find that some candidates drag themselves back into the running, on merit, at this point. Finally, ask them if they would accept the job if offered (also ask if there is anything else coming to the boil elsewhere). This gives a clearer picture than general interest queries. It also clarifies your lead time, if any.

INTERVIEWS AND THE LAW

This section covers some of the legal pitfalls which can occur in the badly run interview. The first, of course, is the possibility that someone inadvertently makes a verbal job offer at interview, which is then accepted. This is extremely rare and, unless the candidate is litigious and armed with a tape recorder, this is not a financial problem, just a goodwill and time waster.

The second, much more common, is that the interviewer asks questions or makes statements which are or could be misunderstood to be discriminatory. Given the nature of current equal opportunities legislation it is important, as pointed out earlier, that interviewers are briefed on what not to ask, or say, and that for every interview they make adequate notes which indicate clearly the reasons why the candidates meet or fall short of the organization's criteria. It is just as important that you record the reasons why Fred got the job as the reasons why Fiona did not. Tape recordings may help here in the training process. Even the most well-intentioned manager can use words or phrases which in the mouth of someone with a desire to see the worst in everything can suggest a pattern of prejudice. If, for example, the use of photographs on application forms became discriminatory here as it is in at least one other country, interviewers who care about remembering which candidate was which would have to revert to a pen portrait of the candidate. When you have a spare hour, try writing such a description of a few strangers in a way that will permit instant recall without any potentially sexist or racist connotations. It is not easy.

THE SECONDARY OBJECTIVES

Interviews as PR

Using interviews as public relations is not as blatant as it may sound. Public relations in the better sense refers to your corporate communication with various audiences in and around the organization. Potential employees could be a significant part of several audiences. They may be, or may become, employees, shareholders, suppliers, customers, enemies or even advisers. The quality of your treatment of candidates, whether or not you know they are more than just members of the general public, can be very important to the organization's future, even in small ways. To take an extreme example, a candidate who has first-hand experience of being properly treated and well briefed about the organization is likely to be a powerful ally in any distant discussion arising from press misquotation. If the distant discussion includes a thoughtful MP who is going to vote about you the next day, he or she is very likely to prefer a first-hand opinion to that of the press. All MPs know how the media misquote!

Interviews as advertising

Interviews often result from recruitment advertising. They can also replace future recruitment advertising, or product advertising. The warm interview with a good candidate who is of the right calibre for the organization but not quite right for the current vacancy should leave the door open for either side to renew contact in the future. If the briefing has conveyed a sense of excitement about the products and services of the organization, the candidates, their households and their present employers may be influenced as potential customers. Most sales staff would give much to have the attention of a prospect for an hour, half of which was to be spent discussing the excellence of the product. Good interviewing can be very effective marketing.

Interviews as sources

Reference to industrial espionage or illicit head hunting is not intended here, although, if the situation is tactlessly handled, either might be suspected. In brief, if an interview goes well but both sides decide that there is not a match between them, there is a special professional bond between candidate and interviewer for a short while which sometimes makes it natural for the recruiter to ask if the candidate has ever worked with anyone who could and should do the job. It has to be left to the candidate to decide if there are any ethical constraints about passing such a contact to the interviewer, but in most cases the new nominee will be a past colleague rather than a current one or, if current, is known to be disaffected.

This also raises the question of the tow rope. It is not generally realized how many people move in groups rather than solo from company to company. Much publicized migrations, as in stockbrokers' specialist departments, are not significant by comparison with the key functional managers who pull one or more of their team along to the next outfit. Sometimes the initiative comes from above, sometimes from below, because the old place isn't fun any more without Fiona or Fred. Quite often, senior functional managers, perceiving other weaknesses in the new organization, will also recommend members of their peer group or even their ex-bosses. Much more of this happens than is evident from the appointments column. The tow rope is very powerful. Do not ignore the potential of this when team building.

Finally, when exploring referees other than the conventional ones, do ask about their personal merits and their relationship with the candidate. This is not for head-hunting purposes – you need this information to evaluate the later reference properly – but there may occasionally be a by-product, such as future sources of trade information, which can be used without any twinge of conscience. The other bonus is that you find out how candidates talk about people close to them and can differentiate between the constructive and the negative attitudes. It is a useful part of your qualitative filter. (All appraisals tell you more about the author than the subject of the appraisal.)

OTHER KINDS OF INTERVIEW

Although we have concentrated on recruitment interviewing for examples so far, the other types are very important.

These include appraisal, counselling, fact finding, termination and warning (in the statutory context). Some are easier for the interviewing manager, some more difficult, but the basic disciplines remain the same. (Chapters 14 and 16 deal with appraisal and counselling in detail.) It is up to the individual manager to identify the extent to which each example differs from the norm and the need for special techniques or preparation.

The general rules which remain the same are as follows:

- Remembering that the 'victim' always feels nervous, sometimes even threatened, although he may outrank you.
- Allowing for the difference in context between the different types of interview. This does not just refer to the objectives of each participant, but includes timing, the extent to which the meeting is voluntary, the desire for communication, the threat (as above), ignorance about the reasons for the meeting (very prevalent, even when the alleged agenda has been declared in advance), suspicion about the motives of the interviewer or the organization (not quite the same as the threat problem), and the extent to which the interviewer is dreading the meeting as much as or more than the victim!
- The need for preparation and for putting certain things in writing if they are to be remembered afterwards. This does not mean in typescript. It can be very effective to do a spontaneous handwritten note during the meeting to which the interviewee feels he or she has contributed. Indeed, the content may well evolve naturally during the meeting. A photocopy for the interviewer and the original for the 'victim' (always this way – more courteous and more natural) suffices as an official but informal way of recording key points, whether one is explaining redundancy pay or listing points for personal improvement. In the latter case, the use of the 'victim's' own words is appreciably more comforting.
- The need for communication, remembering always that communication is supposed to be a two-way process. Any alleged communication which is structured to flow only in one direction deprives the originator of a discriminating response. The feedback can amend or eliminate the need for the rest of the meeting. Always keep listening. Watch for non-verbal signals.

Appraisal

In an appraisal, the key problem is to decide in advance the extent to which the objective of the meeting is compatible with the total disclosure that is sometimes mistakenly assumed to be implicit in the process. There are some highly dangerous appraisal processes in which the corporate system requires that a document containing virtually all the victim's weaknesses is discussed with each subject. This is inimical to the achievement of the objective, in that it destroys or demotivates. The preferred position for appraisal disclosure (unless appraisal has to be combined with a statutory dismissal warning) is to concentrate on the curable and ignore the incurable. This raises a secondary problem – that of deciding what is and is not curable – which must be addressed. The knack here is to find a way of discussing the marginal points, which you may suspect are incurable, as if they were open to improvement, but without making it sound like the end of the world if they are not cured. The precise technique can only be decided in relation to specific faults in a specific context, but, for example, suggesting that they are important for future career opportunities rather than crucial to current survival may impart the message without damage and with some chance that even an apparently insensitive employee may be interested in self-improvement.

A final thought on appraisal – people's job performance does not suddenly worsen without good reason. If someone who was competent last year is substandard this year, a change has taken place at work or at home which is creating problems. The appraisal meeting which ignores this is wholly wasted.

Counselling

Counselling is often, but not always, a by-product of an appraisal system. It is less widespread than appraisal and rather more difficult. Ideally, it should only be undertaken by someone with formal training. If this is not possible, someone relevant and sympathetic should be chosen. Allowing an untrained and even antagonistic boss to do it is not best practice. As with the pre-departure meeting, the choice of interviewer is the most important aspect of the preparation. The second aspect of the choice is that the interviewer must be given enough authority to help as a result of the counselling, which is seldom wholly one-sided. A good counselling interview will uncover faults in the organization, not just review the employee's past failings.

This point applies of course to all appraisal meetings and should be tattooed on all interviewers. Listen, record, react, keep promises.

Compulsory interviews

There is one outstanding respect in which most non-recruitment interviews differ from recruitment interviews. Most are compulsory for one side or other. This makes the climate quite sensitive. By comparison, a recruitment interview is easier because, although one or both participants may be nervous (actually, in a sample of all interviews everywhere, *most* participants are probably nervous – and if they are not, they ought to be), in the recruitment interview one party actively wants a job and the other actively wants to hire someone. This predicates a better climate than one could forecast for many other meetings.

The compulsory interviews do of course include appraisal, but there are different degrees of compulsion about the fact-finding meeting, which may be research, fact gathering from a departing employee, or just formalized data collection in normal operations. All require discipline but they are relatively non-threatening, and goodwill plus a willing and sensitive ear makes them effective. Only the pre-departure meeting is tricky, because there may be an immense amount to be learned and the employee does not necessarily see any valid reason for total disclosure. Equally, the interviewer, if too close to the problems, may not want to hear too much. Choice of a neutral and sympathetic interviewer is more important than trying to add technique to an unreceptive boss, who may well be the cause of the trouble anyway.

Firing people comes into the compulsory category, but need not always do so if the rule about listening is observed. If the organization has been communicating properly with its people, the meeting itself may be compulsory but the firing may not. In a substantial minority of cases the meeting may evolve into a resignation, request for redundancy, philosophical debate about how things are not working out, or even an announcement of an impending event whose imminence (undisclosed) has been a factor in the performance failures which were causing the rift. The lovelorn can be transformed both by engagements *and* by the departure of an unsatisfactory partner. Better still, they sometimes want to change employers as part of the therapy.

When all else fails, listen – and keep quiet.

WHAT WE HAVE LEARNED

This chapter has not been an encyclopaedic dissertation on every facet of every possible interview situation. Instead, you have a series of concepts, principles, thought-starters and horrid examples which should enable you to formulate your own policy and practice in the light of your unique knowledge of your own organization and, indeed, your own personal style.

There is no one right method of handling interviews or their preparation. What feels right for you is better than something which feels so alien that it impairs your performance, provided that you satisfy the basic guidelines given. You must satisfy them. Interview rules, especially in recruitment, are not made to be broken. If you want to break a rule, you must create an alternative discipline which satisfies the original objective. The best test has not yet been mentioned. It is very simple. If you were the candidate, would you be satisfied with what you and your colleagues are doing and not doing with each recruitment exercise? Even if you have not been a candidate for some time, it should be possible to answer this.

STRUCTURED INTERVIEWING

Good recruitment interviews involve much discipline but can still be wrong. Some of the ideas in this chapter can improve discipline and therefore
results. However, there is another route to better results: that is, structured

interviewing, offered by several proprietary sources, and perhaps best exemplified by the Gallup 'SRI' practice.

In brief, this involves researching certain personal characteristics already shared by existing good performers and not displayed fully or at all by the average or below average. When these are known, one can interview almost by algorithm to see if new recruits, internal or external, display the same signs. Most of us already recruit by characteristics believed to be desirable or essential for proper performance. These are seldom researched or validated. You and Gallup can improve on this.

There is a catch. Structured interviewing involves research and application work which appears superficially to be costly not only in time and effort, but also, therefore, in cash.

However, consider the costs of:

- recruiting delays;
- failures due to not recruiting, later firings, or keeping poor recruits; and
- doing everything twice.

The net benefits accruing from structured interviewing then justify most reasonable spending on this system.

CHECK LIST OF KEY POINTS

1   Why are you doing this: that is, what are your aims, desired results, possible 'product'?
2   When are you doing it?
3   Have you allocated enough time – soon enough, flexibly enough?
4   Have the others to be involved?
5   Who is responsible for the programme?
6   Where will you interview?
7   Is it an acceptable environment?
8   How will you do it?
9   Have you planned:

- adequate exchange of data beforehand?
- avoiding unnecessary meetings?
- essential questions?
- common post-interview report format?
- quality control (could you meet BS 5750 . . . !)?
- post-interview action and follow-up?
- criteria by which selection is to be made?

10 Is everyone involved aware that interviews are like computers: garbage in, garbage out?

FURTHER READING

Courtis, J., *Interviews: Skills and strategy*, Institute of Personnel and Development, 1989.

Davey, D. Mackenzie, *How to Interview,* Professional Publishing, 1986.

Melrose Films, *Listen,* video training package.

Morris D., *Manwatching*, Pan, 1978.

Morris, D., *The Naked Ape,* Pan, 1981.

Video Arts, *Manhunt*, video training film.

11 Listening

Meribeth Bunch

No matter how good the communication, if no one listens all is lost.
(Max DuPree)

Some managers perceive communication skills to mean talking, others writing, and yet others using the media or computing. The most human, and least
mentioned, of the communication skills is listening.

The working day of the modern manager is filled with meetings and discussions that require hours of listening, yet precious little time is devoted to
learning how. In many situations managers can spend less than an hour a day
at their desks. The amount of information and processing that is needed on a
daily basis is remarkable, and can lead to information overload, frustration,
confusion and stress.

It is said that by remaining quiet and listening almost all of our questions
will be answered. Yet in our haste to make quick progress, we rush in with
comments and questions, hardly waiting for the end of a sentence. No wonder
so many 'clarification' meetings are necessary.

When in doubt, listen! Listen with an open, accepting and uncritical mind,
and with no expectations. Leave the internal questions and analysis for later.
Those who know how to do this enable others to be themselves and to communicate comfortably and confidently. Hearing this way encourages an
atmosphere of trust and acceptance in which discussions and issues can be
pursued in a rational and logical manner.

The art involved is inner silence and quietude each time we listen; the skill
is in achieving this state. Have you ever tried talking to a radio? It seems like a
ridiculous question because everyone knows that it is impossible. Yet that is
what we are doing much of the time. Most people are busy holding an internal
conversation rather than listening. That inner conversation can consist of a
number of facets: an occurrence at home; an analysis of the other person or

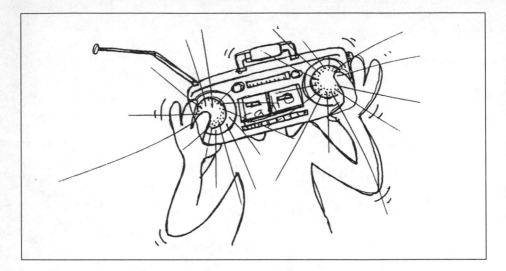

Figure 11.1 Have you ever tried to talk to a radio?

what he or she is saying; going off on a tangent because of something that was said; mentally interspersing personal beliefs, interpretations, judgements and values into the dialogue; and so on. All of this is equivalent to having a radio going full blast (see Figure 11.1).

In the busy, often hectic, day-to-day world in which we live, how is it possible to switch off that internal radio? What follows are some suggestions and tools for achieving a modicum of quiet and a maximum of listening.

BECOME CENTRED AND STILL

First, become physically still. Twitching and shifting about is the outward manifestation of a busy circuit board – your brain. Firmly place both feet on the floor and place your hands on something flat like a desk or your thighs. If you tend to be a 'twitcher', this may be difficult. However, persist with this exercise because it becomes a valuable tool for centring in a variety of situations. When you can do this easily, place your hands in a more natural position but leave your feet firmly on the floor. Your connection with the ground is important.

A technique for becoming still

1 Sit in a chair with your bottom firmly in the seat and your head moving upwards so that your body has a sense of stretch.
2 Place both feet firmly on the floor with the toes long and relaxed.
3 Place your hands, with fingers relaxed and long, on something flat like a desk or table, or on the tops of your legs.
4 Breathe easily and naturally.

5 Remain still and quiet for one minute. This means no twitching or the moving of any toe or fingers.

I WANT TO BE HERE

Once you have become grounded and centred, you are on your way to becoming present – that is, being in the moment, rather than mentally racing off somewhere. The most important aspect of any communication can be summed up in one sentence: 'I want to be here.' You have to want to be where you are at each moment in time, otherwise your mind is distracted and not available for what is happening directly in front of you. Wishing you were somewhere else helps neither you nor the person to whom you are speaking. Furthermore, where you are right now is the only place you can be.

How often have you sat at a meeting and thought about everything you could be doing, rather than concentrating fully on what was happening then and there? The result of meetings full of people with this same problem is that nothing is accomplished. It is easy to behave like this and it is extremely inconsiderate to those around us.

Have you ever been guilty of mentally planning or rehearsing what you were going to say next, only to have someone say it before you, thus leaving you speechless because you were unsure of what else had been stated while you were practising? We all do that at some point in time. In these circumstances, we are left with no opportunity for spontaneity, creativity or intuition, and every likelihood of missing the point entirely. To avoid this situation, one has to trust that the mind will respond – and it will if you are fully present. You will have an appropriate response.

Being fully present allows you to have a sense of what is happening, and encourages other people to talk comfortably in the knowledge that they are being heard. It invites openness on both sides. Some tangible characteristics of people who are 'present' include: eyes that see the other person in the context of whole picture rather than a very uncomfortable glaring 'eye contact', an open, responsive face, a physical body that looks centred and energetic at the same time, a response to what the speaker is saying rather than turning the conversation to suit him- or herself, and asking supportive questions that evoke information rather than suppressing it.

USE 180 DEGREE VISION

Eye contact is rarely explained, so people are left to their own devices to use it – sometimes in a most uncomfortable manner. Glaring straight into someone's eyes makes it difficult to have a decent conversation. The intensity creates such a feeling of self-consciousness and discomfort that it is sometimes hard for the speaker to think of what to say next. Basically, there is no space.

Seeing simply means having a person or group within our range of sight – not staring or glaring. Our eyes are capable of almost 180 degrees of   *181* peripheral vision. When we see people by using peripheral vision, we are see-ing them as part of the whole picture. This gives the eyes a soft look and makes us much more aware of what is happening around us. People who are included in that width of vision will feel included by you even when you are not looking at them directly. Those who use their eyes this way seem more open and receptive.

A technique for practising 180 degree vision

1 Place your hands together with your arms straight in front of you.
2 With your eyes straight ahead, move your arms apart until you cannot see your hands. You will find this is close to 180 degrees.

'BLANK YOUR SCREEN' MOMENTARILY

We tend to become so focused that we forget to see the whole picture. The more we see the whole, the more aware we become and the more information we absorb. This is seeing without thinking and is analogous to blanking a computer screen to write on it.

Think of yourself as a computer. You have information and knowledge stored on your hard disc. To put new information in your computer you need a blank screen. There is no need to analyse or judge the information as you write it down. The computer will do this later. You are then in a position to edit, use what is appropriate and mentally delete what is not. Your brain oper-ates in this way when it is quiet. While this defocused approach may seem contrary to your perception of trying to 'focus' in order to listen, experiment with it for a week and you will see and feel a difference.

LEAVE YOUR INTERNAL CRITIC OUT OF THE CONVERSATION

To 'blank the screen' or turn off the mental radio it is necessary to disable the internal critic during communication. The internal critic is the hyperactive child of the self-critic and uses much of the same language (Figure 11.2). Who needs earplugs when you can have a noisy family of critics stopping all sound from entering. It is worthwhile to have a brief look at the development of this family of critics.

Development usually begins with a traditional vocabulary which all of us have heard from family, teachers, mentors and friends. A list of six words in particular is imbedded firmly in our culture. The first two are *right* and *wrong*. The thought of having to get something right releases considerable anxiety and tension. Observe for yourself the reaction of others when told to 'get it right'. Do you see a smile? Or does apprehension cross their faces? When people think or are told they are wrong, the colour visibly drains from their faces. Is this a way to facilitate co-operation in the workplace?

In another situation, there may be a problem. However, that problem is with the action or behaviour, not the person. Telling someone they are wrong

Figure 11.2   The self-critic

will not solve the problem. But by listening carefully with 'new ears', a solution will present itself and will be helpful to all parties concerned.

The second set of words follow naturally from the first. When we use vocabulary such as right and wrong, the next step is to proclaim *should* and *ought* – a kind of internal or external finger-pointing. These words are the result of not being right or of being wrong. We develop the habit of self-righteously chastising ourselves and others.

Then, to keep ourselves from getting into the above situations where we are uncomfortable because of perceived shortcomings, we feel we must *control* the situation or *hold on* to keep it from worsening. Controlling or holding on to something inhibits the dynamic aspects of the situation and therefore prevents any possibility of spontaneity, creativity or intuition – all the qualities that are needed most for open, honest information and good communication skills. Therefore, not only does this family of critics prevent us from listening, it also prevents us from learning.

Exercises for taming the self-critic

1 Look through any recent directives you have issued and change the six words that follow to more positive and encouraging terms: right–wrong, should–ought and control–hold. How do the directives sound and feel now?

2 Compose positive sentences, both oral and written, without using the 'critic-feeding' words.

STOP ANALYSING EVERYTHING THAT IS BEING SAID TO YOU

Trust your mind and your knowledge. You did not get where you are in business because you are stupid. Your knowledge is not going to go away for the short time you are listening to someone else. Trying to analyse what the other person is saying and to listen at the same time is another form of internal sabotage. Such analysis is simply a kind of inner conversation. It is a great temptation to hold on to our own knowledge while at the same time trying to understand the information we are receiving. Remember the computer analogy (see Figure 11.3). Trust that your own knowledge is safely there inside you.

One way to ensure that you are listening is to offer a brief summary of what you have heard. In summarizing, you reiterate the information for yourself and test the accuracy of your concentration, while, at the same time, giving the other person a chance to hear what they have said and the possibility of changing anything that is not accurate.

Rather than directing the conversation towards yourself, focus on drawing information from the other person. Ask open questions like: 'Tell me what you liked best about this project?'; 'What was most difficult for you or your team in reaching your goal?', 'Tell me what you need from me?' Such questions can be followed by asking for more detailed and specific information.

These same techniques hold true for social conversations and listening.

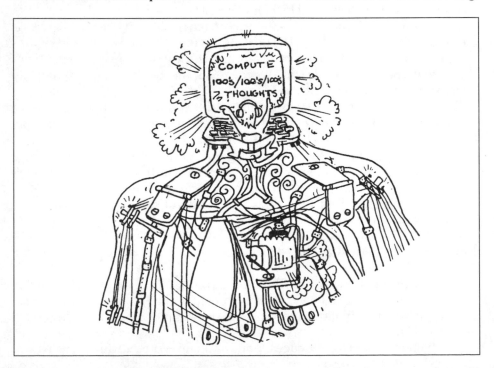

Figure 11.3   Computer with full screen

Ask questions to discover more about the other person's interests. Some examples are: 'What was your favourite part of the movie?'; 'If you could have any car (dress, kitchen, dog, house, and so on) you wanted, what would it be?'; 'What is it you especially like about it?'

Exercises for focusing on what the other person is saying

1 Repeat or pick up key words in their conversation (which may include gentle interruptions).
2 Summarize frequently to make sure you have heard correctly and to let them know they have been heard. Do not interpret what has been stated but repeat it as accurately as possible, using their vocabulary. 'Let me see if I have heard you correctly. You said ...'

A SPECIAL NOTE ABOUT LISTENING TO CRITICISM

Listening to criticism is difficult for us because we usually want to justify ourselves. Such justification only serves to prolong or create an argument. We should acknowledge that there is a problem – because there is when the other person is not satisfied – but in no way do we have to accept the blame, unless we wish to. The point is to direct the conversation towards correcting the problem. A good listener will hear the other person out without interrupting, ask questions which will elicit specific answers that can be acted upon, and will first determine what the other person's concerns are before offering solutions or opinions.

ACCEPT WHAT YOU ARE HEARING

Always listen to a person as if you are just meeting them for the first time and have no past record on which to base any opinions. Act in this way even when you have reason to doubt the other person's accuracy. By giving them a chance to hear themselves, you will allow them space to be far more open or to acknowledge what they do not know. A non-threatening environment is the best place for discussion of controversial subjects. When the object of the discussion is accurate information rather than one-upmanship, two people can work together to sort out the problem or issue.

Accept initially that everything the other person tells you is the truth as they see it. They are giving you information as best they know how according to the situation. By remaining quiet inside, you are better able to sort out the sense and viability of what is being said. It is possible then to respond from the vantage point of logic, knowledge, experience, and – with luck – wisdom.

Exercise

1 Talk to everyone you know or meet as if it is the first time you have ever seen them.

2   When meeting someone new to you, display the natural curiosity and courtesy you would show in your own home.

ALLOW THE OTHER PERSON TO BE HIM/HERSELF

Every person needs to be acknowledged as another human being – no matter what else is happening. We do this quite naturally when someone comes to visit us, but sometimes we forget to do it in situations where we see the same people every day.

The least that is required is to 'see' the person. Listening with your head down is disconcerting and basically rude. Visual clues are important in any conversation and we miss them when we do not see. This is where 180 degree vision is extremely useful.

By accepting the other person we acknowledge their existence. Listening in this way encourages reciprocal action and leads to honest person-to-person communication.

SUMMARY

Be fully present, acknowledge the other person, listen with great curiosity and treat them as if they were in your home, and you will be a wonderful listener.

SKILLS CHECK LIST

1   Prepare to listen by quieting your mind and body. Remember: 'listen' and 'silent' contain the same letters.
2   Momentarily suspend all judgement and analysis.
3   Be fully there for the other person – accept *their* truth.
4   Listen fully to criticism without feeling the need to defend yourself or to apportion blame.
5   Summarize what you have heard when it is appropriate.
6   Be a good host/ess; after all, your personal presence is your home.

FURTHER READING

Covey, S. R., *The Seven Habits of Highly Effective People*, Simon & Schuster, 1992.
DuPree, M., *Leadership is an Art*, Doubleday, 1989.

Cartoons by Jay Obrecht.

12 Helping people learn
Norman Gealy

You are a manager not a teacher. Why should you bother to help your staff learn? You should help them because *you* stand to benefit. If your staff can learn to do their jobs better, then you will benefit:

- by having less to put right (because they will make fewer errors);
- by having less to do (because you can give more to them);
- by having more time to spend on the more demanding parts of your job (because you have less to put right and less to do);
- by improving your own reputation (because you have enough time to do the more demanding parts of your job properly);
- by being given more important work (because your reputation is so good); and
- by making progress in your career.

Your staff will benefit in turn:

- by making fewer mistakes (and nobody likes to have to do work again);
- by taking on more responsible work earlier (and everybody likes to exceed expectations); and
- by making progress in their careers (just like you).

You might reply: 'This is too good to be true. If the staff do get promoted, then I will have to start again with a new lot, and I will have to turn down the more important work, and I will end up spending all my time training, and I will stay where I am for ever. Far better for me to keep them in the dark, concentrate on my own work, and spend as little time on them as possible. Forget idealism. Concentrating on me is the real way to get on.'

We may all choose to believe what we want to believe. As author of this   *187* chapter, I believe in the benefits. Moreover, I see disbenefits in failing to help your staff to learn. First, you will have less choice of staff because no one will want to work for you. Second, the ones you have to choose from will be those whom no one else wants. Third, they will not see any point in working hard and well for you because you don't care. Fourth, they will be looking for jobs elsewhere all the time (and when they find them, you will have to start training their replacements whether you like it or not).

So why not look on the bright side?

WHAT SHOULD YOU HELP WITH?

You should help with whatever will benefit you, and whatever will benefit your staff.

Generally, you will benefit if you can help your staff to learn: how to carry out their present work more quickly and more efficiently; and how to carry out the less demanding parts of your work so that you can delegate more to them. This will also benefit your staff. But in addition, it will provide even more benefit for them, first, if you can accelerate their careers by helping them learn how to do whatever it might be which is looked on as a sign of readiness for promotion. And secondly, if you can anticipate and help them to learn how to take on future roles after promotion.

All these factors should accord with the needs of the business. You should be contributing to the business. Therefore, if your staff can help you more, then they should also be helping the business. The business should promote people on the basis of the contributions which they are likely to make. Thus, if you help an individual gain promotion, then you should be adding to the capabilities of the business. The individual's future roles after promotion will contribute to the business, and if you can help the individual to take on these roles, then you should be strengthening the business.

But it may not be so. The business might not be so rational. Even then, you should continue to help your staff to learn as much as you can.

No organization is ideal. Not all individuals within an organization work only for the common good. Somewhere along the way – from the organization's mission to the behaviour of individuals – other factors come into play. Promotion may not always be awarded solely on an individual's likely future contribution in the new role. The performance of future roles after promotion may include much that has less to do with making a contribution and more to do with being seen to act in particular ways.

Even if learning how to help you and how to advance their own careers do not match the needs of the organization, these are still the areas in which you should try to help your staff. This learning will bring benefits, as described above. Trying to help your staff learn to do what you think the organization needs, but others do not recognize as such, is pointless. Look at it from your staff's point of view. Why should they bother? Your efforts are likely to be ineffectual, and you could become bitter about training and probably about the attitudes of your staff.

Of course, you should try to align your work and the way in which contributions are viewed with the needs of the organization. But these are management issues. Your argument should be with other managers, possibly at the highest levels in the organization. If you can change their views, then the changes in what your staff need to learn will follow. Changes in organizational outlook and culture come from the top, not from the bottom. Do not confuse helping the organization to learn with helping your staff to learn.

SHOULD YOU SET TARGETS?

Yes. You should set targets, but only so far as they help.

If you and your staff share a common understanding about what they are trying to learn, all of you will find it easier to direct your efforts and to monitor their effects. It helps to establish a common understanding by writing down what is agreed, and by making copies available to all concerned for reference. Hence recording targets is a good idea.

The targets should describe what you and your staff agree should be the desirable outcomes of their learning. The targets should describe what, as a result of their learning, your staff should be able to do that they cannot do now. Ideally, they will also provide indicators of how well your staff will be able to carry out these activities. The indicators might be in the form of criteria which the staff will meet, or descriptions which will allow their performances to be appraised.

However, the very act of writing down targets can be daunting in itself.

For some activities it may prove easy, with obvious indicators of success. For example, if you agree that someone should learn to drive, you could set a target of passing the driving test. The indicator of success forms the target: it is passing the test.

But for other activities, writing down targets is difficult and the indicators of success can be extremely hard to identify. You may be able to recognize successful performance when you see it, but still be unable to specify the defining characteristics of that success. For example, if you agree that someone needs to improve his or her facilitation skills with small groups, you might take that as the basis of the target, yet still find it very difficult to identify indicators of success. Could you describe the identifying characteristics that you or others would be able to recognize as evidence of high-level facilitation skills? Probably, if you were able to think about it long enough – but how long do you have?

Write targets quickly – just do the best you can straight away. Otherwise, if it takes too long, it may need to be put off and that can delay learning. Do not feel that you have to write perfectly detailed and accurate targets, because that is the kind of task which lies at the bottom of the in-tray forever, and which eventually provides a (feeble) excuse for doing nothing at all.

Write targets, first by describing what it is your staff intend learning to do; and secondly, by describing the indicators which you and they can use to confirm their success.

First, discuss with your staff what they do in their current roles and what they might need to do in the future. Review performance and identify areas of strength and weakness. Use these analyses to identify the areas in which they need to develop their abilities, and agree what those abilities are. Write them down, defining them by describing what it is each individual should try to learn to do (the first part of the targets). Be as specific as you can: for example, 'write project reports', 'make presentations to small groups', 'word-process letters and memoranda', 'handle customer complaints', 'develop marketing strategies', 'prepare departmental budgets'.

Secondly, see if you can add indicators of success – straightaway, if possible. For example, 'word-process letters and memoranda in house style, without errors, and file according to house rules'. But if you cannot add indicators of success straightaway, then leave this section blank. You and your staff will have to think a lot more about the activity while your staff learn how to carry it out. You will be able to work out how to judge the success of their learning eventually, even if you cannot do so now. Whatever you do, do not put off training because you cannot yet write the perfect target.

During this stage, you may find published materials a help. In particular, the standards of competence written for relevant National Vocational Qualifications (and Scottish Vocational Qualifications) provide lists of activities and lists of performance criteria. These national standards can be traced through the Qualifications and Curriculum Authority (and the Scottish Qualifications Authority).

WHAT SHOULD YOU DO TO HELP?

'Give a damn!'

This will help most.

If you want to help your staff learn, then you and they together should be able to work out how you can do so. Drawing on established training and development practices will help, and these are the subject of much of this chapter. Nevertheless, they are secondary.

I have argued above that it is in your interests to help your staff learn. In addition, most people derive considerable reward just from seeing colleagues develop their abilities.

Concentrate on individual needs

Do not waste your time, or their time. Try to provide the help that they need, but no more.

This is far harder to do than it sounds, because it is very difficult to determine exactly what help any individual will need. Everyone is different. People differ in background, and hence in what they know already and in the ways in which they prefer to learn. Ideally, you would provide help to individuals only in the areas where they need help, and in ways which match each individual's preferred styles of learning. Realistically, though, you will not be able to do so. You are almost bound to cover ground where the individuals do not need help and miss areas where they do. And your styles of provision will suit some more than others.

Do try to match the individual's needs. Life is not perfect, but we can bring about some improvement if we at least attempt to address the issues. Talk to your staff about what they need to learn and about how they would prefer to do so. Then act accordingly.

Above all, do not fall into the temptation of telling them what *you* know, regardless of what *they* need to know. All of us are liable to do this. What better confirmation of our own success than admiring staff sitting at our feet and listening while we recount past exploits and lessons learnt. However, this process is not for your gratification: it is for their development. Do it their way.

Encourage self-study

Self-study will probably be your cheapest option, taking up the least of your time and the least of your budget. Also it may absorb less of your staff's time if they are used to studying on their own; and it may use their time more efficiently if they can timetable their study around other tasks.

Yet it is obviously not the whole answer. Learning, it has been suggested, requires an individual to be able to remember, to understand, and then to be able to do what is required. Self-study is in the main limited to the first two of these requirements. Of course there are exceptions, and these are discussed below. In most cases, however, self-study will only provide the information, methods and ideas which your staff need to apply. It will not be sufficient to enable them to develop competence.

The exceptions are where the study media are sufficiently realistic to present practice tasks that resemble what your staff will eventually have to do. For example, textbooks which present accounting problems, audio tapes which present foreign pronunciations, video tapes which show action sequences, computer-based typing tutors which respond to the keyboard, and interactive media which present problems and respond appropriately to the students' attempts to find solutions.

Such study media, when available, can take your staff further than plain descriptive materials. Use them if they are available and if you can afford them. Use them particularly where their fidelity is high (that is, their resemblance to the real activity). Also use them to make best use of your time when you are trying to help several members of staff rather than just one individual. Do not view them, though, as a total solution. The most sophisticated learning aids are biological, and you are one of them. You will still need to relate your staff's experience, built up through working with these media, to the requirements of their own working environments.

Don't send people on courses

Unless you can establish that the benefits of the courses outweigh their direct costs and their opportunity costs, don't send your staff on courses.

That may seem a tall order. On reflection, it is probably impossible to be so precise. But at least approach the question of whether to send your staff on a particular course in this frame of mind: only buy if you will get value for money, just as though you were buying something more tangible.

Why would you do otherwise? Well, because most of us do.

Two factors make it hard to spend wisely on courses. First, there can be pressure just to spend the money rather than to achieve benefits. Second, it can be very difficult to find the effective courses hidden amongst the plethora of courses on offer.

The pressure to spend money ad lib on training rather than specifically to achieve benefits comes from a need to be seen to train. Organizations can want to be seen to train because this attracts staff, impresses governmental and regulatory agencies, and improves the organizations' reputations. At the same time, managers at the same organizations can view the actual process of training as an unnecessary distraction from their real work (not having accepted or even considered the benefits of more capable staff which were outlined above). As a result, these organizations in effect take action to be seen to train, and in effect view the direct and opportunity costs of such action as necessary overheads. They send staff on courses and worry less about the content or quality of the courses than the costs. The costs have to be sufficiently high to give the appearance that the organization is taking its responsibilities seriously. Hence the pressure to spend rather than to achieve.

It *is* possible to find effective courses. They do exist. Try to find them by asking colleagues or even competitors for recommendations. Take up references from the course providers. Ask about their practical experience of the subjects which they are teaching. Ask separately about their experience as trainers. Ask how many participants will be allowed to attend the courses. Study the course outlines and ask how the topics of principal interest to your staff will be treated. Finally, send one member of staff to the most likely course, to report back. Even then, do not be too optimistic. If you have found the perfect course, rejoice and tell everyone. Encourage others to send their staff to keep the course viable.

It is easy for experienced trainers to run poor courses. If the course has been sold, for example, because its title encapsulates your needs and you did not research any further, then an experienced trainer can run it, regardless of whether he or she knows anything about the subject. For some trainers, it is a point of pride.

The process for a maverick trainer is as follows: read a few books on the subject; review a few learning exercises previously used in the subject area (which may be commercially available or which may be passed from trainer to trainer); assemble a programme which is cohesive and which varies activities to maintain interest; include sufficient work to keep the participants too busy to think about anything else (such as, why am I doing this?) during the course; run the programme using personal charisma to win over the participants; and finally, evaluate the programme by distributing a questionnaire when the participants are euphoric at being allowed to go home early on the Friday, and by distributing another questionnaire by post a few weeks later when the participants are too embarrassed to admit that they were wasting their time. Above all, keep the course moving too fast to allow participants to think about the topics in such depth that they might expose the superficiality of their teacher's knowledge.

You have to distinguish the good courses from the bad. There are excellent courses – often those where the trainer is the first person who thought of the course and has not handed over delivery. There are also dreadful courses, with less expert trainers who lack even charisma. Be careful out there!

Organize courses in-house

If you have enough staff to justify a course (possibly by joining with colleagues) and if you have identified a course provider in whom you have confidence (possibly through sending a member of staff on one of the provider's open courses), then consider organizing the course to run in-house. This should give you more control.

You can insist that the person who takes your brief and who will deliver your course is the same person whom your colleague saw on the open course. You can direct that person to tailor the course to the needs of your staff, rather than delivering the usual general course designed to appeal to everyone. You can supply examples of materials from your own organization to make practice exercises more realistic. During the course, you (and/or your staff) can provide feedback so that topics addressed too superficially can be revisited, and so that the most appropriate options are taken throughout. If there are to be future courses, you can revise your own aims and your recommendations to the provider in the light of the first course.

As an additional benefit, you will probably pay less for your own in-house course, as the economics of open and in-house courses differ.

Nevertheless, even the best courses are only courses. Like the alternative of self-study, they will deliver information, methods and ideas. They may also include practice to develop competence, but the exercises are seldom real and the logistics of course design usually mean that the extent of practice is quite limited. Courses are a preparatory step, not the whole answer to learning how to perform and how to make progress at work.

Provide tuition

Accept that you will have to provide tuition. Self-study materials are limited in their application. Even the best courses run by others will not exactly match the requirements of your working environment.

193

Your tuition should be purposeful. Agree with your staff what it is that they are going to learn to do, and record those targets. Try to be efficient in your tuition. Limit non-productive effort – both by yourself and by your staff to the minimum.

Help your staff do it right first time – and second time, and the third time. Try to prevent them from making mistakes even when they are just starting out. To do this, first make them prepare so that they understand what they will be doing and how they will be attempting to do it. Then, when they come to practise, provide feedback in real time to prevent them from repeating and compounding errors. Their first attempts will be slow and will involve you heavily. Their second attempts will be faster and they will make fewer mistakes, so your own involvement will be less. Their third attempts will be faster still and involve you less again. And so on, until you are not needed.

This approach has a primary benefit. All your efforts – both your own and your staff's – are directed towards their learning to carry out the task properly. Left to practise unsupervised at the start, your staff are likely to carry out the task wrongly. They will be bound to make mistakes and, as they practise, those mistakes will become habitual. When you eventually provide feedback, you will be faced by two tasks instead of one. You will have to help them unlearn their mistakes, as well as having to teach them how to carry out the task properly. Helping them get it right first time will eventually save you and them unnecessary aggravation and effort.

There is also a secondary benefit. Because the practice activities will be carried out well (if slowly), you may be able to use real work rather than artificial exercises. This will improve the relevance of the training and give some immediate business reward for the effort involved.

The process of providing tuition using this approach can more formally be broken down into the following stages:

- demonstration;
- confirmation;
- practice;
- repetition; and
- mastery.

You should start by demonstrating the activity if possible. This advice does not just apply to manual tasks. For example, if you need to help your staff learn small group facilitation skills you should arrange for them to be present when you will be working with a small group. Before the demonstration, you should explain what you will be trying to achieve, why you will use the methods which you propose, and how you will carry out these methods. During the demonstration – or if this is not possible, immediately afterwards – you should draw attention to key points which were critical to the success of the exercise.

Before you allow your staff to practise, you should obtain confirmation that they understand what they will be doing and how they will try to do it. Having agreed the practice exercise, you should ask them to describe what they will be trying to achieve, why they propose to use particular methods, and how they will carry out these methods. This stage is often ignored but it is very important for it enables you to ensure that they are ready to practise. There is no point in anyone practising anything without knowing why.

When they practise, you should not help, which will be extremely difficult for you. It is very frustrating to watch someone else struggle when you could so easily take over. But don't. Sit on your hands. Bite your tongue. In this situation, doing nothing is constructive. They can only find out whether they can carry out the activity if you let them try. You can only find out their capabilities if you let them try. So, try they must, and you have to let them. When they do make a mistake – preferably, just before they are obviously going to do so – or when they are genuinely stuck, give support, give guidance, gain confirmation that they now understand what they should be trying to do, and then withdraw once again. Suffer in silence.

You cannot predetermine the number of repetitions of the activity that any individual will require. It will depend on the activity and on the individual. You should carry on monitoring and correcting until you are sure that you are no longer necessary. Your staff have mastered their brief.

A final point on providing tuition. From your staff's point of view, individual tuition will usually be best. However, from your point of view, you may assume that it will save your time to deal with your staff as a group. This may or may not be true. For example, if you deal with your staff as a group, you will usually be less able to provide the individuals with immediate correction. They may then develop bad habits. The additional time which would have been required to provide individual tuition may be less than the additional time which will be required to overcome these bad habits. Therefore, do consider the option of providing individual tuition. Contrary to accepted wisdom, in at least one area it has been found that individual tuition makes more effective use of both tutor's and trainees' time.

Provide experience

People learn through experience.

The processes described above – self-study, courses, tuition – will prepare your staff to benefit from real experience, but they are not equivalent to real experience. If your staff are to learn to cope not just in theory, but also in reality, then you will have to ensure that they gain experience. Special efforts on your part will probably be required in order to make that experience sufficiently varied and sufficiently challenging. This will also provide other benefits. It will make an important contribution to your staff's job-satisfaction, and ultimately to their willingness to remain with the organization.

Look at your own work first. Does it include activities which could provide experience to help your staff develop their abilities? Could you take on other work which would increase the opportunities open to your staff? (Do think about the potential for staff development in any new work which you might be   *195* considering.) If you can identify activities that would provide suitable experience, can the activities be delegated? If not, why not? If it is because your staff are not ready, then go back to self-study, courses and tuition to help them prepare. Then delegate.

Look next at work in other departments. Might they be able to provide the experience your staff need? Would other managers be willing to use your staff? Could you use their staff in a reciprocal agreement? Try not to hold on to your own staff too tightly. If you are not providing sufficiently varied experience, they will leave you anyway.

When you delegate to give your staff experience, do not leave them to cope on their own. Certainly delegate the task and leave it to them to do without unnecessary interference, but do not abdicate responsibility. It should still be up to you to ensure that the task is done well, and if it is not done well, the blame should still rest with you. Without taking the task back into your own hands, provide your staff with advice when it is requested and correction when it is needed. Also give praise when it is merited – that always helps. You should take responsibility for managing the interface between your staff and others. Credit for a job well done should go to your staff (because they will have done the job): blame for a job done poorly should go to you (because you should have managed your staff better).

Delegation is not always easy. But if you are a manager, it is your job.

HOW WILL YOU KNOW THAT WHAT YOU DID HELPED?

You will need to determine whether:

- the targets were appropriate for your staff;
- the activities undertaken provided effective tools to help your staff to learn.

The targets will probably not be perfect. It is difficult to capture in words what you intend, before you develop the learning strategy. The process is iterative not sequential. Also circumstances, your needs and your staff's needs will change over time, so that what you originally intended to do may cease to be appropriate. The targets should be reviewed and updated periodically with your staff as required, but do not spend too long on this. Develop the targets only as a tool to inform future decisions, and not as works of art in themselves.

The various activities used to help a member of staff learn should be evaluated with regard both to their own terms of reference and to the larger picture. For example, one of your staff might have read a book to learn about double-entry bookkeeping, with a view to entering accounts onto a computerized system. You should evaluate the activity in relation to its own terms of reference, which would mean determining whether as a result of reading the book the individual understood the concept of double-entry bookkeeping. You should evaluate the activity bearing in mind the larger picture, which would mean determining whether the individual's new understanding of double-entry bookkeeping did help in using the accounting software.

All learning activities can be evaluated in these two ways: Do they meet their own objectives? Does meeting those objectives contribute to meeting the more fundamental needs of the members of staff?

To decide if the activity met its own objectives, you need to 'test' the member of staff. Self-study materials and courses might have internal assessments which you can review, but even so, you should set your own external test that will provide an independent measure. Set the individual a task or a series of tasks which will require demonstration of the abilities they set out to develop. This is a serious business, but it need not be threatening. You have to know whether you are wasting time and money, and your staff should understand that aspect. Otherwise, you might as well just say 'How did you get on at the course?' and bury your head in the sand.

Establishing whether the internal objectives of specific provision contribute to meeting the more fundamental needs of the individual is a less straightforward exercise. It is partly a matter of logic and partly a matter of experience. You and your staff should be able to work out the logic together. Do the abilities represented in the objectives of the provision need to be applied in carrying out the activities which your staff are trying to learn? This question can be more difficult than it seems. None of us really knows how competent practitioners think through complex tasks, but we can make a reasoned guess. The experience is your staff's. Having mastered the objectives of a self-study or tutored course, do they find their work easier? Disappointingly, the answer can be 'no', which will force you and them to revisit the logic of what is required. Eventually, when your staff have attained their targets, they should be able to advise you which provision was most useful and which was least useful. At least this will help their successors.

All this may seem impersonal. Were the targets right? Was the provision well chosen? But trying to help your colleagues is indeed a very human activity, in which you are likely to become deeply and personally involved. What of that? Did the fact that it was you make a difference? If you are the first manager your staff have had, even they will not know. They will have no one to compare you with. My first manager was an inspiration and I assumed that all managers were like that. Perhaps in twenty years' time you will see in a handbook a chapter written by one of your ex-members of staff, and in that chapter you will read the words 'Thank you', but it is unlikely.

SUMMARY OF RECOMMENDATIONS

1   Help your staff to learn because it will benefit you as well as them.
2   Concentrate on what will help your work and their careers.
3   Agree with them the activities they will learn to carry out and record these targets.
4   Try to match the support you provide to the ways in which they prefer to learn.

5 Choose your provision from:

    (a)   self-study materials;
    (b)   attendance at courses (possibly in-house);
    (c)   tuition (possibly one-to-one);
    (d)   enhanced experience.

6 When you provide tuition, use the sequence:

    (a)   demonstration;
    (b)   confirmation;
    (c)   practice;
    (d)   repetition;
    (e)   mastery.

7 Review and update the learning targets periodically.
8 Evaluate each part of your provision with regard to:

    (a)   its own objectives;
    (b)   how it contributes to your staff's targets.

9 Don't expect thanks.

FURTHER READING

Downs, S., *Learning at Work*, Kogan Page, 1995.

Holyfield, J. and Moloney, K., *Using National Standards to Improve Performance*, Kogan Page, 1996.

13 People skills

Peter Honey

People come in all sorts of shapes and sizes, which is another way of saying that people are complex and infinitely variable. Remarkably, however, there are some fundamental skills for handling people that are not dauntingly complex. In this chapter, I shall introduce you to those fundamentals and give sufficient practical advice to help you become even more skilful with people.

The chapter is written on the assumption that you have already acquired some people skills through an ad hoc process of learning from experience. There will undoubtedly be things you already do well, that no longer require any conscious effort on your part. The problem is that, quite understandably, we all tend to stick to the tried and tested and therefore repeat over and over again the same skills. In effect, therefore, we stop acquiring any new skills and this may mean we risk having too narrow a repertoire of skills to equip us adequately for the variety of people situations we are likely to encounter. This chapter will encourage you to experiment and broaden your repertoire of people skills.

WHAT ARE PEOPLE SKILLS?

People skills are behaviours, used face to face, that succeed in helping progress towards a useful outcome. Let us separate these ingredients and examine them more carefully. *Behaviours* are everything you say and do. As we shall see, they are important because they are so immediately apparent to everyone you come face to face with and therefore have a direct effect on other people. *Face to face* covers a whole multitude of different interactions between people. It might be an informal chat with someone or it might be a formal meeting with a group of people. The point is that it is only during face-to-face encounters that your behaviour is totally evident. During phone calls, by contrast, only what you *say* counts. Written communications are different

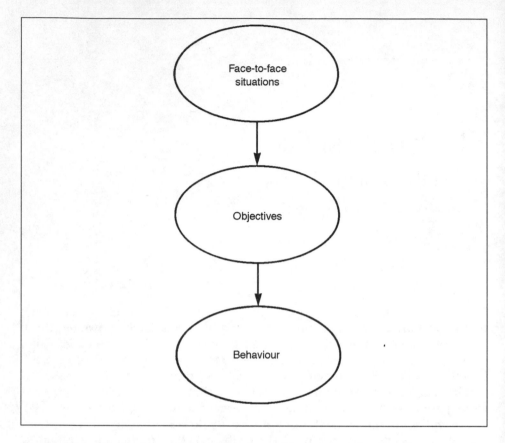

Figure 13.1   Behaviour is the means to achieving your objectives in face-to-face situations

because while what you write represents your behaviour even though you are not present, it is not happening 'in flight' as is the case with face-to-face behaviours. A *useful outcome* is the third ingredient, for what would be the point of skills that led you to a useless outcome? The proof of the pudding is in the eating and the proof of people skills is that they make it as likely as possible that we achieve our objectives with people.

The trick is to make all three ingredients come together in a smooth and easy symmetry. Face-to-face situations provide the context, objectives spell out the desirable end, and behaviours are the means (see Figure 13.1).

WHY THE EMPHASIS ON BEHAVIOUR?

Quite simply because your behaviour is the only part of you that other people can observe. So far as other people are concerned, you are your behaviour for they cannot observe your underlying thoughts, motives, attitudes or feelings (see Figure 13.2). It follows, therefore, that your behaviour influences:

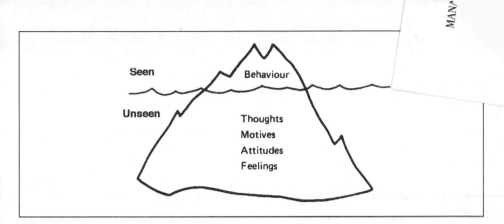

Figure 13.2 Your behaviour is the only part of you that other people can observe

- other people's perceptions of you (i.e. whether they like or dislike you, trust or mistrust you, and so on); and
- other people's reactions to you (i.e. whether they behave helpfully or unhelpfully towards you).

The only people skills that matter, therefore, are encapsulated in the things you say and do when face to face with other people: in a word, your *behaviour*.

WHAT ARE THE ADVANTAGES OF IMPROVED PEOPLE SKILLS?

Improving your people skills by extending your repertoire of behaviours is not easy. As with the acquisition of any skill it requires conscious effort as each skill is practised to the point where it becomes effortless. Since an investment of time and effort is required, it is important to be sure that it will all be worthwhile. Some of the advantages of improved people skills are that you will be better at the following functions:

- Assessing and understanding face to face situations. You will thus benefit from fewer misunderstandings.
- Setting specific and realistic objectives for face-to-face encounters with people. You will thus benefit from being clear about what you are aiming at and successfully achieving it more often than not.
- Choosing and using behaviours that complement the circumstances and are appropriate to the objective. You will thus benefit by having an easier, and pleasanter, interaction en route to achieving your objective.
- Being aware of other people's behaviour and influencing it. You will thus benefit from being able to use your own behaviour as a powerful influence.

201

ᴛhese are just some of the potential benefits of enhanced people skills. There are others which will emerge as the chapter pinpoints the skills more precisely.

CAN PEOPLE SKILLS BE IMPROVED?

The answer is 'yes', of course they can. You learned to behave the way you do now and there is nothing to stop you learning new behaviours. The secret of success is to learn from experience by:

- experimenting with new and different ways of behaving;
- reviewing what happened;
- concluding from the experience; and
- planning what to do next (i.e. continue with the experiment, modify it to make it more successful, or try something quite different).

Unfortunately, people are often reluctant to embark on this learning process. There are all sorts of excuses to stay exactly the way you are now. 'You can't teach an old dog new tricks', 'leave well alone', 'a leopard cannot change its spots', and so on. Pessimism abounds. There is, however, nothing to prevent you from improving your people skills except yourself. If you do not want to enhance your skills, then no one or anything can force you to do so. The door to development is locked with the key on the inside. Other people can hammer on the door, imploring you to open it; they can even entice you with attractive learning opportunities; but you and you alone hold the key. The choice is yours.

WHAT ARE THE FUNDAMENTAL PEOPLE SKILLS?

The fundamental skills are those which give us a process that is equally applicable in all situations. This is preferable to having a 'shopping list' of skills where the items on the list will inevitably vary in importance depending upon the situation. If, for example, you were in a foreign country where the water is suspect, then bottled water would be high on your shopping list. It would not, however, feature as a necessity on a shopping list in the United Kingdom. It is the same with people skills. If you are discussing how to solve a problem with a person who has more experience than you, then listening would be high on your list. If, on the other hand, you knew much more about what had to be done to solve the problem than the other person, then communicating clearly and testing the other person's understanding would be higher priorities.

We avoid this 'it all depends' qualification if we have a few fundamental skills on our list that apply in *all* situations. Just six are sufficient:

1 Analysing the situation.
2 Establishing a realistic objective.

3   Selecting appropriate ways of behaving.
4   Controlling our behaviour.
5   Shaping other people's behaviour.
6   Monitoring our own and others' behaviour.

The first three skills are essentially about thinking; the last three are about doing. It is the combination of both that is vital, for there is no point in thinking without doing, nor in doing without thinking.

Notice also how these skills provide us with a timeless wisdom, applicable to all 'people situations' anywhere. Analysing the situation helps us to detect the circumstances that need to be heeded when setting a realistic objective. The objective, in turn, provides a backcloth against which to make choices about how best to behave. Each thinking skill cascades into the next and the three combined help us to be aware of the situation and to work out what to do about it. By consciously controlling our behaviour we are more likely to do the things that need to be done to achieve the objective. In so doing, we influence other people's behaviour in the only way possible, via our own behaviour. And all the while we monitor, to keep a careful watch on what is happening and to receive the feedback we need to make in-flight adjustments.

Let us look more carefully at each of these skills.

How to analyse situations

Remember that in the context of people skills we are concerned only with face-to-face situations. There are six key questions to ask of any situation you encounter:

1   Is the task/problem/subject matter to be discussed complex or routine?
2   On balance, who has the most know-how, you or the other people involved in the face-to-face discussion?
3   Is time very tight (as in a crisis), or is there sufficient time to discuss all aspects thoroughly before reaching a decision?
4   Is commitment from everyone essential or merely desirable?
5   Are the risks of making a mistake unacceptably high (financially and/or physically and/or from a credibility point of view), or are the risks within acceptable limits?
6   How many people will be present at the face-to-face discussion: just one other person, or a small group of, say, 6–8, or a medium sized group of 9–15, or a large group of 15 plus?

The answers to these key questions produce enough data to move you on to the next skill.

How to set objectives for face-to-face interactions

An objective (for any activity, not just for face-to-face interactions) is a   *203* forecast of what you want to achieve at some point in the future. It might be a long-term, medium-term, or short-term objective.

An immediate objective forecasts what you want to achieve by the end of the interaction.

Here is a recommended procedure for setting an immediate objective. First, set yourself an *end result*. Do this by answering the question, 'What do I want to achieve by the end of the interaction?' Second, work out some *indicators of success*. Do this by answering the question, 'How shall I know that I have successfully achieved my end result?' As an example of an objective set this way, imagine that you are going to meet someone (let's call him Bill) for the first time, and you want to make a good initial impression on him.

End result

By the end of the meeting I will have established rapport with Bill.

Indicators of success

- Bill has asked at least six questions about me/my work.
- Bill has 'opened up' to me about a significant current problem.
- Bill has relaxed sufficiently to volunteer at least a couple of personal details (about outside interests, family, and so forth).
- We have booked a date, time and place for our next meeting.
- Bill has specifically asked me to provide some additional data for our next meeting.

All achieved within $1\frac{1}{2}$ hours (longer than Bill originally scheduled, i.e. he was 'happy' to overrun).

How to select appropriate behaviour

The secret is to limit the choices so that the vast spectrum of different behaviours is reduced to something manageable. It is best to think of your behaviour as a mixture of verbal (i.e. the things you say) and visual (i.e. the non-verbal things you do such as facial expressions, gestures with hands and arms, and so on). Both verbal and visual aspects need attention. Let us look at verbal behaviour first.

Verbal behaviour

Limit yourself, at least initially until you become practised at using this method, to nine alternative behaviours:

1 *Seeking ideas*   Asking other people for their ideas.
2 *Proposing*   Putting forward ideas (possible courses of action) as statements.

3 *Suggesting*   Putting forward ideas as questions (i.e. 'How about doing so and so?').
4 *Building*   Developing someone else's idea.
5 *Disagreeing*   Explicitly disagreeing with something someone else has said.
6 *Supporting*   Agreeing with something someone else has said.
7 *Difficulty stating*   Pointing out the snags or difficulties with something someone else has said.
8 *Seeking clarification/information*   Asking other people for further clarification or information.
9 *Clarifying/explaining/informing*   Giving information, opinions and explanations.

These nine behaviours are not an exhaustive list but you will find that they give you adequate scope. When it comes to selecting the most appropriate behavioural recipe, think of the behaviours as offering you a series of alternatives in the following way.

In a face-to-face interaction you could either:

seek ideas	or	give ideas (proposing or suggesting)
build	or	disagree
support	or	state difficulty
seek clarification/ information	or	give clarification/ explanation or information

You will quickly see that the left-hand side is a recipe for being participative and supportive towards other people. By contrast the right-hand side is a recipe for being more directive and challenging towards other people. In the case of meeting Bill for the first time (see page 204) with the objective of establishing rapport with him, clearly the left-hand behaviours are going to be more appropriate than the right-hand ones. This will not always be so. With a different objective, an alternative mix of behaviours would be necessary. This illustrates the importance of, first, being clear about the objective, and second, thinking about which behaviours are appropriate to achieve it. As the objective alters, so will the recipe of appropriate behaviours.

Visual behaviour

Visual or non-verbal behaviour covers a wide range of different aspects including:

- facial expressions;
- eyes;
- hand movements;

- gestures with hands and arms;
- leg movements;
- body posture; and
- spatial distance and orientation.

In addition, there are some fringe areas such as clothes, physique and general appearance.

There is overwhelming evidence that visual behaviours play a larger part in communications between people than is usually supposed.

It seems that, without necessarily being able to describe how they do it, people make judgements and form impressions based on the visual behaviours they see other people using. Perhaps the most dramatic example of this is when people meet for the first time. Within seconds, visual behaviours are sending signals which create a favourable or an unfavourable impression. Initial judgements are formed about whether the other person is friendly or unfriendly, confident or timid, trustworthy or untrustworthy, nice or nasty. Sometimes these first impressions are so strong that they linger stubbornly and defy revision, even when different signals are being transmitted by subsequent visual behaviours.

Clearly the great advantage of thinking about your visual as well as your verbal behaviour is that you can choose visual behaviours that help rather than hinder progress towards your objective. You may be in the habit of using some visual behaviours that run the risk of giving the other person a poor impression of you. The secret of success is to concentrate on some simple combinations. If you do just one thing in isolation it probably will not have the desired effect because people gain a general, overall impression from a combination of:

- your facial expression and head movements;
- gestures with your hands and arms; and
- the rest of your body including your legs.

All three aspects need to be practised so that they all come together to give the right impression.

Some combinations of visual behaviours are set out in Figure 13.3. Practise doing less of the left-hand ones and more of the right-hand ones.

How to control your behaviour

Obviously there is little point in using the first three skills (analysing the situation, setting objectives and selecting appropriate behaviours) if, come the important face-to-face interaction, you fail to keep your behaviour under control. The whole point of controlling your behaviour is to avoid doing things that will be detrimental to achieving your objective and to force yourself to do sufficiently the things that will aid and abet its achievement. The word 'force' is used deliberately since you will undoubtedly find that, initially at

Defensive

People will tend to see you as **defensive** if you:

Face and head
- Don't look at the other person.
- Avoid eye contact or immediately look away when it happens.

Hands and arms
- Clench your hands.
- Cross your arms.
- Constantly rub an eye, nose or ear.

Body
- Lean away from the other person.
- Cross your legs.
- Swivel your feet towards the door.

Anxious

People will tend to see you as **anxious** if you:

Face and head
- Blink your eyes frequently.
- Lick your lips.
- Keep clearing your throat.

Hands and arms
- Open and close your hands frequently.
- Put your hand over your mouth while speaking.
- Tug at an ear.

Body
- Fidget in your chair.
- Jig your feet up and down.

Overbearing/aggressive

People will tend to see you as **overbearing** and **aggressive** if you:

Face and head
- Stare at the other person.
- Have a wry 'I've heard it all before' type smile.
- Raise your eyebrows in exaggerated amazement or disbelief.
- Look over the top of spectacles.

Hands and arms
- Point your finger at the other person.
- Thump your fist on the table.
- Rub the back of your neck.

Body
- Stand while the other person remains seated.
- Stride around.
- If seated, lean right back with both hands behind your head and legs splayed.

Friendly/cooperative

If you want to come across as **friendly** and cooperative adopt the following combinations:

Face and head
- Look at the other person's face.
- Smile.
- Nod your head as the other person is talking.

Hands and arms
- Have open hands.
- Hand to face occasionally.
- Uncross arms.

Body
- Uncross legs.
- Lean forward slightly.
- Move closer to the other person.

Confident

If you want to appear **confident** adopt the following combinations:

Face and head
- Look into the other person's eyes.
- Don't blink your eyes.
- Thrust your chin forward.

Hands and arms
- Keep hands away from your face.
- 'Steeple' your finger tips together.
- If standing, have hands together behind you in an 'at ease' position.

Body
- If seated, lean back with legs out in front of you.
- If standing, keep straight.
- Stay still, no sudden movements, no wriggling.

Thoughtful

If you want to appear **thoughtful** try the following combinations:

Face and head
- When listening, look at the other person for about three-quarters of the time.
- Tilt your head to one side slightly.

Hands and arms
- Hand to cheek.
- Slowly stroke your chin or pinch the bridge of your nose. If you wear spectacles, take them off and put an earframe in your mouth.

Body
- Lean forward to speak.
- Lean back to listen.
- Keep your legs still (no jiggling).

Figure 13.3   Combinations of visual behaviour

any rate, you will need to stick consciously to a behaviour plan. You are more likely to be able to do this if your plan is:

- specific in spelling out precisely which verbal and visual behaviours to use; and
- realistic in pinpointing a few key behaviours to use or avoid, rather than being overambitious by listing too much.

The other important aid to good control is to be selective about when you will consciously practise using your people skills. At first, it may be sensible to choose face-to-face interactions where the risks of making mistakes or being more hesitant than usual are not too great. It also helps to practise on people who are likely to be supportive of your efforts rather than apathetic or hostile.

How to shape other people's behaviour

This is the key to the whole business. Clearly, if your behaviour made no difference to the reactions of the people you dealt with, then people skills would be of no consequence and this chapter would never have been included in this *Handbook*. The plain fact is, however, that the way you behave has a considerable influence on the way other people behave in face-to-face situations. The precise effects of the verbal behaviours have been more thoroughly investigated than those of the visual behaviours. Let us look at each behaviour in turn and see their shaping abilities.

Seeking ideas is a powerful behaviour. Nine times out of ten it is successful in provoking some ideas from the other person (Figure 13.4). It is a helpful behaviour to use whenever you need to pick someone else's brains.

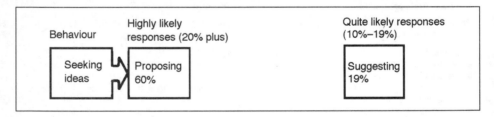

Figure 13.4   Responses to seeking ideas

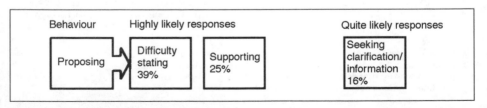

Figure 13.5   Responses to proposing

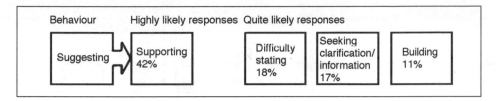

Figure 13.6   Responses to suggesting

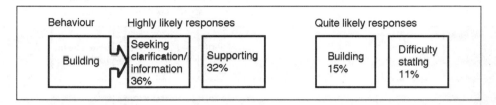

Figure 13.7   Responses to building

Proposing ideas unfortunately provokes difficulties or objections more often than it wins support (Figure 13.5). If you want to 'flush out' people's reservations, then proposing is a good behaviour to use. If, on the other hand, you want to make it more likely that there will be agreement to your idea, then the next behaviour is a safer bet.

Suggesting ideas is a more effective way of gaining agreement than proposing ideas (Figure 13.6). There are, of course, no guarantees that it will succeed because your idea may be such a rotten one that even though it is suggested it runs into difficulties. The actual statistics reveal that four times out of ten a suggestion is followed by an agreement, and that is not a bad rate.

Building on someone else's idea is a powerful way to get their whole-hearted support. Despite this, building is a fairly rare behaviour. It seems that people find it easier to find fault with ideas than to build them up into something better (Figure 13.7). This is a good example of having a choice. People who think about their behaviour are more likely to try building than people who are in the habit of immediately criticizing ideas. The fact that seeking clarification is so prevalent reminds us what a potentially confusing behaviour building can be. The lesson is to 'flag' building so that people are in no doubt, and then supporting and more building are the most likely reactions.

Disagreeing on seven out of ten occasions triggers a defensive reaction or even further disagreements (Figure 13.8). It is interesting how often people

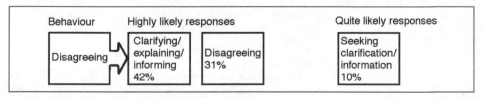

Figure 13.8   Responses to disagreeing

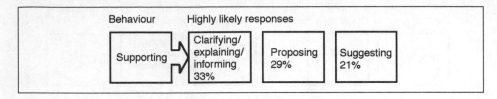

Figure 13.9   Responses to supporting behaviour

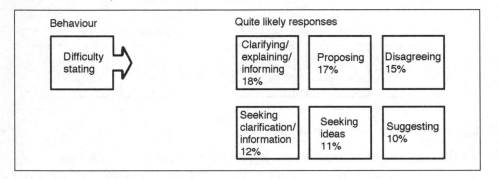

Figure 13.10   Responses to difficulty stating

get locked into a disagreeing 'spiral' where one disagreement breeds another that, in turn, breeds another, and so on. Disagreeing is very much a last resort. It is best to try some of the more constructive options first.

Agreeing with something someone else has said is a powerful way to encourage them to go on and say more. Eight times out of ten this will be the effect (Figure 13.9). Agreeing is therefore a useful behaviour if you want to gain more information from the other person. It is not an appropriate behaviour if you want them to shut up.

Pointing out difficulties is a very common behaviour, but it is one of the riskier ones because research shows that it is far from certain how people will take it (Figure 13.10). Marginally, the most likely reaction is to offer some clarification or explanation. However, people often take umbrage and start disagreeing or, if you persist with difficulties, they may give up and go and find someone more positive to talk to. You need to watch carefully to see whether pointing out difficulties is hindering or helping the proceedings.

No surprises with the next category (Figure 13.11). If you ask for clarifica-

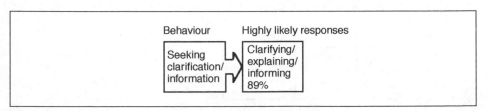

Figure 13.11   Responses to seeking clarification/information

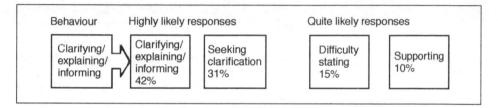

Figure 13.12 Responses to clarifying/explaining/informing

tion then nine times out of ten you will get it. Seeking clarification is a frequent behaviour that exerts a powerful influence over the behaviour of the other person. This is very useful behaviour when trying to resolve a problem and when you need to draw information out of the other person.

Informing is the behaviour that happens more often than any other in conversation between people. This is not surprising, of course, since the overall purpose of talking with someone is to impart information of some kind. The most interesting aspect is how informing breeds informing that breeds informing and so on in what can be a time-consuming loop (Figure 13.12). Sometimes this is appropriate and necessary. At other times the loop amounts to going round in circles and making very slow progress.

The reason why people often prolong the informing loop is because it is a relatively 'safe' way to pass the time. When you offer a piece of information, you do not commit yourself in quite the same way that you do when you propose or suggest an idea.

The lesson from all this? Simply that the behaviours you use have known shaping effects on the behaviours you experience in return from other people. The data underline the fact that you are more likely to succeed with people if you think about your behaviour, and select and use behaviours that help rather than hinder progress towards your objective. This process is enhanced still further if you adopt visual behaviours that reinforce what you are saying. It is the combination of verbal and visual that has the desired effect.

How to monitor your own and others' behaviour

This is purely a matter of practice. Since all behaviour, whether verbal or visual, is observable in a straightforward way there is no reason why you should not develop your powers of observation. When you next attend a 'boring' meeting where some of the agenda items do not directly involve you, try monitoring the behaviour of the participants. See if you can spot the differences between proposing and suggesting, disagreeing and difficulty stating. Count how many times clarification is sought and given. Study people's attempts to build on one another's ideas. Scrutinize each person in turn to see what non-verbal characteristics they display when they are speaking as opposed to when they are listening. Watch to see when people lean forward in their chairs and when they lean back. Monitor who speaks to *211* whom. Are any patterns that emerge associated with where people are seated round the table? There is no end to it, and certainly there is no excuse for being bored at a meeting ever again! Another obvious source of practice is when watching television, especially debating programmes such as *Question Time*. To study visual behaviour, just turn the sound down.

The whole idea of gaining practice in these ways is so that monitoring behaviour becomes second nature. When you yourself are a busy participant in an interaction it is best to monitor behaviour on an exception basis rather than try to cope with everything. So, for example, concentrate on the un-expected behaviours. If you were hoping that someone would be positive and develop your ideas, be especially alert to their disagreeing and difficulty stating, and think hard about how best to respond in order to nudge their behaviour towards building and supporting. (Do this by being careful to suggest rather than propose, and by seeking ideas from them and proceeding to build on them yourself. There are always hopeful things you can do *if* you use your people skills.)

ARE THERE ALTERNATIVE PEOPLE SKILLS?

That concludes our examination of the six fundamental people skills. Acquiring them is not easy, but the advantages of doing so are considerable and the skills are both sensible and pragmatic.

There are, of course, many different ways of describing people skills. We have focused purely on verbal and visual behaviours. Once you have mastered the fundamentals, what other skills could you practise? For the sake of brevity we will finish the chapter by looking at three interesting possibilities.

Management styles

You might find it useful to think about your characteristic style of management, when it is appropriate and when it is not, and when to adopt consciously a different style from your usual one. One of the simplest ways to classify alternative management styles is shown in Figure 13.13.

Since most managers seem to find it easier to be *directive* than to use the other styles it is good advice to:

1 Think *delegative* first.
2 If delegative is inappropriate in the circumstances, then next think *collaborative*.
3 If collaborative is inappropriate in the circumstances, then next think *consultative*.
4 If consultative is inappropriate, then go ahead and be *directive*.

This plan ensures that you consider all the alternatives. All four styles are appropriate at some time. The skills we looked at earlier of analysing situations and establishing objectives are the key to deciding when to use which management style.

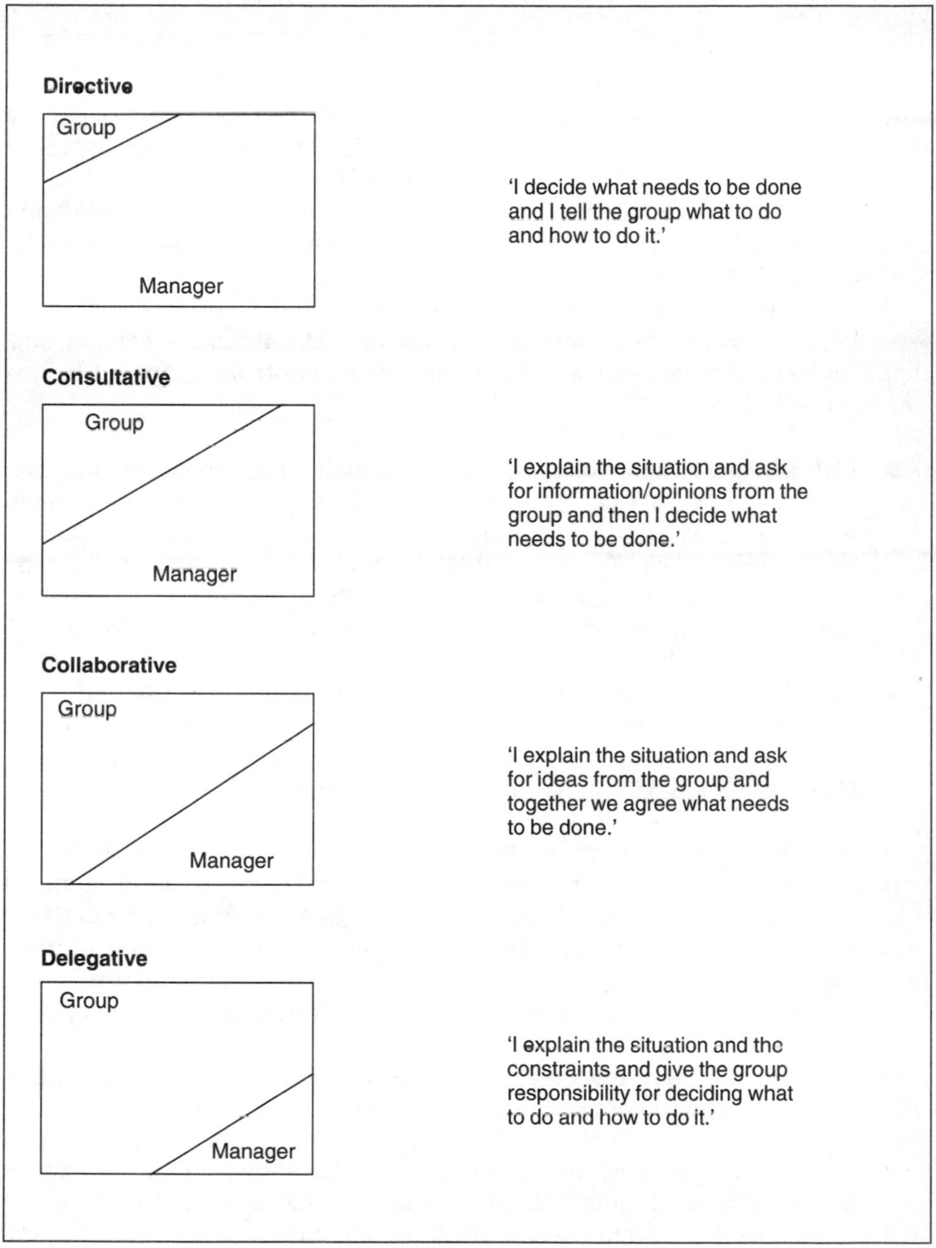

Directive

Group

Manager

'I decide what needs to be done and I tell the group what to do and how to do it.'

Consultative

Group

Manager

'I explain the situation and ask for information/opinions from the group and then I decide what needs to be done.'

Collaborative

Group

Manager

'I explain the situation and ask for ideas from the group and together we agree what needs to be done.'

Delegative

Group

Manager

'I explain the situation and the constraints and give the group responsibility for deciding what to do and how to do it.'

Figure 13.13   Alternative management styles

Ego states

You might have come across an approach to people skills called transactional analysis (TA). It originated from the bestseller *Games People Play* (André Deutsch, 1966) by Dr Eric Berne. A core concept in transactional analysis is a framework for describing three different ways of behaving.

The three behaviour categories, or ego states, are called Parent, Adult and Child. In TA they are distinguished from *real* parents, adults and children by the use of capital letters.

Parent behaviour stems from feelings about what is proper, right and wrong. This provides discipline and protection. The Parent speaks in dogmatic, autocratic terms with a heavy emphasis on controlling. Parent behaviour is subdivided into:

- *Critical Parent* behaviour: critical, prejudicial, moralizing or punitive. Typical non-verbal clues are the pointed finger, shaking head, handwringing, arms folded, foot tapping, wrinkled brow, sighing, impatient snorts and grunts. Typical verbal clues are 'always', 'never', 'remember', 'you ought to know better', 'you should do better', 'don't do that', 'you should never do that', 'that's wrong', 'stupid', 'ridiculous', 'absurd', 'how dare you'.
- *Nurturing Parent* behaviour: nurturing, protective, sympathetic and comforting. Non-verbal examples are: a comforting touch, patting a person on the shoulder, consoling sounds. Verbal examples are: 'there, there', 'you poor thing', 'try again', 'don't worry'.

Adult behaviour involves gathering information, evaluating it and using it to make, and implement decisions. The Adult has the capacity to monitor and, if necessary, update Parent and Child tapes. Adult behaviour stems from thinking rather than feeling. Non-verbal examples are: postures indicating interest, listening, thinking and generally being attentive. Verbal examples are: 'why', 'what', 'where', 'when', 'who', 'how', 'alternatives', 'possible', 'probably', 'relatively', 'practical', 'feasible'.

Child behaviour stems from feelings, either of joy or of sorrow, and, therefore, tends to be spontaneous. Child behaviour is subdivided into:

- *Natural Child* (NC) behaviour is entirely dictated by feelings; it includes being impulsive, inquisitive, curious, affectionate and playful. NC is also fearful, self-indulgent, self-centred, rebellious and aggressive. Non-verbal examples are: tears, temper tantrums, no answer, biting lower lip, downcast eyes, shoulder shrugging. Verbal examples are: 'look at me!', 'nobody loves me', 'that's mine', 'can't', 'won't', 'that's fun', 'I love you', 'whoopee!'
- *Adapted Child* behaviour is a toned-down version of Natural Child: it is literally an adaptation of completely natural impulses so that they are more acceptable to other people. Non-verbal examples are: giggling,

teasing, flirting, pouting and whining. Verbal examples are: 'please', 'thank you', 'I wish', 'I'll try', 'please help me', 'I don't care', 'I don't know'.

The whole idea of this classification system is to have a practical method of monitoring different modes of behaviour in ourselves and in others we encounter. A main tenet in transactional analysis is to practise using our Adult ego states to weigh up situations and decide whether Parent, Child or Adult behaviour would best suit. In other words, the Adult is encouraged to use the six basic skills that we examined earlier in this chapter. Many people have found the ego states a helpful way of looking at behaviour and bringing it under conscious control.

Assertiveness

Finally, you might find the assertiveness approach a useful way to enhance your people skills. This approach tends to specialize in behaviour in tricky situations where your needs are in conflict with the needs of other people. Such situations are made worse or better depending on how you handle them. Broadly, you have three choices: you can be assertive, submissive, or aggressive.

Assertive behaviour involves standing up for your own rights in such a way that you do not violate another person's rights and expressing thoughts, feelings and beliefs in direct, honest and appropriate ways. For example, if someone keeps disagreeing with your ideas, an assertive response would be:

> I appreciate that you want to see improvements as much as I do, and yet you keep finding fault with my ideas. What can I suggest that would be more acceptable to you?

So assertiveness is based on the beliefs that we have needs to be met, others have needs to be met; we have something to contribute, others have something to contribute. It is characterized by statements that value ourselves and also value others.

Submissive behaviour. You are being submissive when you:

- fail to stand up for your rights or do so in such a way that others can easily disregard them;
- express your thoughts, feelings and beliefs in apologetic, diffident or self-effacing ways; or
- fail to express honest thoughts, feelings or beliefs.

For example, if someone keeps disagreeing with your ideas, a submissive response would be:

> Well, I suppose you've got a point. My ideas probably wouldn't have worked out in practice.

HINDERING BEHAVIOURS	HELPING BEHAVIOURS
Lean away with hands clenched, arms crossed and legs crossed.	Lean forward with hands open, arms uncrossed and legs uncrossed.
Look at the other person for less than 50% of the time.	Look at the other person for approximately 60% of the time.
Listen silently with no continuity noises and/or interrupt before the other person has had their say.	When listening nod and make 'I'm listening' noises such as 'um', 'yes', 'really'.
Have a blank expression.	Smile.
Sit opposite the other person.	Sit beside the other person, or if this isn't possible, at a 90° angle to them.
Don't use the other person's name or use it artificially so that it jars.	Use the other person's name early on in the transaction.
Don't ask questions or ask closed questions.	Ask the other person open questions.
Offer no summaries and don't check your understanding.	Summarize back to the other person what you think they have said.
Stick rigidly to saying things that are routine and standard.	Say things that refer back to what the other person has said.
Don't acknowledge the other person's expressed feelings or point of view.	Show empathy by saying you understand how the other person feels and can see things from their point of view.
Acquiesce or never explicitly agree with the other person.	When in agreement with the other person, openly say so and say why.
Pick holes in the other person's ideas.	Build on the other person's ideas.
Criticize the other person.	Be non-judgemental towards the other person.
Disagree first, then say why.	If you have to disagree with the other person, give the reason first, then say you disagree.
Be defensive and never admit to any inadequacy.	Admit it when you don't know the answer or have made a mistake.
Be secretive and withhold information from the other person, even though it affects them.	Openly explain what you are doing, or intending to do, for the other person.
Have visual and verbal behaviours out of step with each other.	Be genuine, with visual and verbal behaviours telling the same story.
Remain aloof and don't touch the other person.	Whenever possible, touch the other person.
Don't give the other person anything.	Give the other person something, even if it is only a name card or a piece of paper with notes on it.

216   **Figure 13.14   Check list: hindering and helping behaviours**

So submission is based on the belief that our own needs and wants are less important than those of other people. It is characterized by long, justifying explanations, often putting ourselves down while accommodating others.

Aggressive behaviour. You are being aggressive when you:

- stand up for your own rights in such a way that you violate the rights of another person; or
- express thoughts, feelings and beliefs which may be honest or dishonest, but in inappropriate ways.

For example, if someone keeps disagreeing with your ideas, an aggressive response would be:

> To hell with all your objections. Just listen to me and I'll spell out what I want to happen.

So aggression enhances ourselves at other people's expense; it puts the other person down. It is based on a belief that our opinions are more important than other people's. It is characterized by blaming other people, blaming outside factors, by showing contempt, by being hostile/attacking, and by being patronizing.

The assertiveness approach urges us, when faced with a conflict situation, to hang on to assertive behaviour rather than succumbing to our emotions and either being submissive or aggressive. Once again this is only possible if we think about our behaviour vis-à-vis the situation we are in and the objectives we wish to achieve.

CONCLUSION AND CHECK LIST

Here, finally, is a check list (Figure 13.14) of behaviours that hinder and behaviours that help. It is not an exhaustive list but you will find more than enough to start you off. To succeed, practise doing less of the hindering behaviours and more of the helpful behaviours.

Remember, the choice is yours and, so far as other people are concerned, *you are your behaviour.*

FURTHER READING

Back, K. and Back, K., *Assertiveness at Work: A practical guide*, McGraw-Hill, 1982.

Honey, P,. *Face to Face: A Practical guide to Interactive Skills*, 2nd edn, Gower, 1988.

Morrison, J. H. and Hearne, J. J., *Practical Transactional Analysis in Management*, Addison-Wesley, 1977.

Video Arts, *If Looks Could Kill: The power of behaviour*, booklet accompanying training video, Video Arts, 1986.

14 Performance appraisal
Tim Russell

In some organizations, the appraisal interview is known as the 'annual amnesty'. For an hour each year you are allowed to say what you dare about the boss and the company and then, for the rest of the year, you keep quiet. In other companies appraisal runs in a four-year cycle. The first year, a new human resources (HR) director arrives and sets up a new scheme. After much threatening and cajoling, managers complete the appropriate forms and return them to the central HR department. Overwhelmed by the sheer volume of paper and swamped with requests for training courses well in excess of ten years' training budget, the HR people take little action other than to file away the forms. The second year, not so many managers complete the scheme and the human resources department is hesitant to push them to do so. The third year, no one bothers with appraisal. In the fourth year, a new human resources director arrives and ...

Most people would agree that appraisal is a hugely important part of the organization. Run properly, it enables plans to be agreed and monitored; it helps everyone to know what they are supposed to be doing; and it provides a structure for many other aspects of management. Unfortunately, the presentation of many appraisal approaches does not always fulfil the promise. Sometimes this is because there is an overemphasis on a 'system'. Sometimes the commitment or the skills of the managers are lacking. Sometimes it is a confusion of purpose. Appraisal has, to an extent, fallen into disrepute.

This chapter explains the purposes of appraisal, the confusions to be avoided, and how to plan, conduct and follow up the appraisal meeting. It includes a section on giving and receiving feedback, and concludes with check lists which also serve as a summary of the key points.

THE PURPOSES OF APPRAISAL

The reason why appraisal has had problems in some organizations is that the purpose of the whole concept has become rather blurred and a confusion has arisen between the three important and worthy functions: performance, potential and pay.

Performance

The most common reason for implementing an appraisal scheme is so that there is a regular, once or twice a year, review of a person's work progress. This is usually conducted between the individual and their immediate manager, though 360° is becoming popular now, involving the views of other people with whom the individual has work contact. These might include colleagues, subordinates and even customers and suppliers.

The performance appraisal offers the following four benefits:

1   It can be likened to an annual car service, a dental check-up or a review of personal finances in that it enables the person's work to be monitored on an overall, rather than day-to-day basis. The whole pattern of that person's work can be discussed and put into context. Normal, more frequent, work reviews will focus more on the specific tasks currently being performed.
2   It is an opportunity for everyone concerned to discuss problems that have been happening and to make adjustments for even better performance in future. The changes could be related to the organization of the department, the procedures or policies. By taking stock from the overall position, decisions can be made which are untainted by the urgency of immediate tasks in hand.
3   Training needs are often identified at the appraisal as, when the individual takes stock of their performance, an underlying cause for any problems might be realized to be a deficiency in certain knowledge or skills.
4   The appraisal is a chance for all parties to give and receive feedback on their performance, what they are doing well, what is not so good and what might need to be changed. The feedback aspect is very motivating for most people, even if there are complaints about parts of the standard of their work. Research studies have shown conclusively that it is more motivating to be reproved occasionally than to be ignored.

Potential

A second common reason for appraisal is to assess potential. This enables the person being appraised to discuss their career aspirations and to compare these with the future direction and the manpower and succession plans of the company. The appraisee can review their personal strengths and weaknesses, likes and dislikes, and consider in what direction they might want   *219* their career to go, be that a promotion within the same work function or a transfer to gain experience of other areas. Development of the individual can then be arranged through on- or off-the-job training, or through a variety of other methods including task rotation, coaching, projects and action learning. To say that a person has 'potential' is, of course, an incomplete sentence as it does not specify what that person has potential for. It means implicitly potential for promotion, but this is too vague an idea, as different jobs at a more senior level are conducted in quite different ways and the person might have the capability and aptitude to perform one promotional job but not another.

Pay

The third reason for an appraisal scheme is that it is sometimes linked to salary reviews and merit increases. The advantage of this is to show that there is a systematic method of deciding pay rises, and that those people who are appraised as having contributed most towards the success of the enterprise are those who receive the highest reward.

THE CONFUSIONS

If any two, or worse, three of these functions are combined, there is likely to be a confusion which will contaminate the effectiveness of the whole scheme.

Confusing performance with potential

If the appraisal system confuses performance with potential, it can cause the company to make the mistake of promoting someone into a managerial position because of their effectiveness in a non-managerial position. This leads to the old adage about losing the best operator or clerk and ending up with the worst supervisor. With some jobs, there is almost an inverse correlation between technical competence and managerial competence, as is witnessed by some dreadful sales managers who would much rather be securing the sales themselves than trying to coach their staff to do it. Clearly, people who have performed well should be rewarded. Promotion, however, should be seen as occupying a different job; in itself, it is not a reward. Indeed, with the associated stress and distancing from previous colleagues, it is sometimes a punishment. If the promoted individual turns out to be less than competent in the new post, the dilemma now arises of whether or not they should be demoted, or left in the new post, performing below par. Obviously, most people will appreciate the increased money that goes with a promotion, but they may be more concerned with the promotion itself.

Confusing potential with pay

In some instances, an organization is likely to pay staff not for what they do now, but for what it is hoped they will achieve in the future. Many graduate

training schemes fall into this trap. To encourage the graduates to join
stay with the business, an attractive salary is offered. The training scheme
could last for around two years, during which time the graduates do little
other than move from one department to another trying to learn the procedures. Their self-esteem is not too high as they know that they are still
learning rather than contributing, and their relationships with colleagues
often suffer since non-graduate staff, who are actually teaching the graduates,
are paid less than their charges.

Confusing performance with pay

The real problem area is confusion of performance with pay. Clearly, those
who contribute the most and put in the most effort should be rewarded with
the highest merit increases. However, if the appraisal becomes a negotiation
over pay, rather than a review of performance and improvements, the discussion may not be too open. A person will find it difficult to admit that they have
a training need if that admission could cost them £1000 because it highlights a
deficiency that perhaps only they knew about.

THE PERFORMANCE APPRAISAL SYSTEM

It is sometimes said that the best appraisal form is a blank piece of paper.
This can be rather formidable for some managers, though, and over the years,
in an attempt to help simplify the process, HR departments have provided
headings and these headings have evolved into forms. Unfortunately, in some
cases, this has overcomplicated matters, with the implication that the whole
process is for the benefit of the HR department, rather than for the benefit of
the managers and their staff as it should be.

The best forms for performance appraisal, rather than for any other purpose, operate on a rolling basis and attempt to be objective and specific. The
form should be a working document that records the goals agreed between
the manager and the staff member for the next year. It should be referred to
frequently to monitor progress and to alert to any problems that are
adversely affecting the achievement of the objectives, and it should then be
used at the end-of-year appraisal to ascertain whether or not the goals have
been met. This is also the time when goals for the following year should be
agreed.

So that the goals set are easy for all parties to understand and easy to
measure, they should be written in the SMART format as follows:

S   Specific (e.g. to increase sales of vacuum cleaners).
M   Measurable (e.g. by 13% over last year's sales).
A   Agreed (e.g. all parties should commit to these goals).
R   Realistic and reachable (e.g. and should be set after a feasibility
    study).
T   Time bound (e.g. by 31 December).

For most staff it is unlikely that they will have more than six or eight major goals for the year. Of these, most will be 'maintenance goals' aimed at continuing the way they are currently working. The one or two 'development goals' will be for new work that is being planned.

It the staff member is involved in setting these objectives, there is a far greater chance that they will be committed to their achievement. For the same reason, the staff member should keep a copy of the completed forms.

At the meeting to review last year's performance and to plan next year's, a discussion should be held to consider any problems that affected the achievement last year which might also negatively affect next year. These problems might lead, for example, to a change in the way the products, policies and procedures operate, a change to how the individual or their manager do their work, or to some coaching or more formal training in specific knowledge or skills.

Some appraisal forms ask the manager to rate the staff member on various scales and on various characteristics. The global one which asks for an overall assessment of performance on a scale of 1 to 5, or 'First Class' to 'Inadequate', is purely for the purpose of pay, as it is from this score that percentage pay rises are calculated. It has no place in the discussion of the goals and only serves to distract the appraisee from the interview. If the score is given at the beginning of the interview, the appraisee tends not to listen to much of the following discussion as they are either relieved or are trying to bargain for a higher rating. If the score is withheld until the end of the interview, they are trying to anticipate what it is going to be. The discussion of the achievement of the *goals* is not served well by an assessment rating of the *individual*.

In some cases, a more refined assessment of the characteristics of the appraisee is required. This also hinders the performance review and contaminates the findings. If a manager is asked to rate, on a scale of 1 to 10, how, say, 'reliable' the staff member is, it is a reflection of the manager's definition of 'reliable' that is recorded. A 'reliable' person could be someone who is 'accurate', 'trustworthy' or 'can work with minimum supervision'. These are three quite different interpretations of the same word, and so it is likely that the appraisee would be rated very differently by different managers with different definitions. For this type of appraisal, it is true that the appraisal says more about the appraiser than it does about the appraisee. For such an appraisal to have any place at all, it could only be in an assessment of the person's potential for another job.

THE APPRAISAL OF POTENTIAL

The appraisal of potential is the opportunity for the individual to discuss their career aspirations and ambitions and to compare these with the future plans of the company. In the days of the hierarchical organization, this would almost certainly mean a discussion about promotion. In the flatter businesses of today, vertical ladders are being replaced with horizontal career paths. In some companies, any idea of a career is left entirely for individuals to plan for themselves. However it works, it is unlikely that the person's immediate manager will have the breadth of knowledge of the whole enterprise to be able to see what possibilities might exist. They will probably not know all the manpower and succession plans for other departments and may not see how a production person could ever make a beneficial move to marketing.

If potential did mean a vertical move within the same department, the individual would probably be seeking to take the job of their direct manager. It would be a brave manager, indeed, who recommended that a staff member took away their own job, unless they knew that they were also currently the subject of an impending move.

For all these reasons, therefore, it is probably best that the appraisal of potential be carried out by someone more neutral and with a broader vision. This is likely to be a professional from the HR department. HR personnel will also have access to the latest psychological instruments and assessment centres that can add some scientific basis to the review of potential and ambition.

Some people are extremely happy and very competent at the work they are currently doing and have no reason to want to change. They have no desire to manage people, or to learn different areas of work other than to keep up to date within their own region of expertise. It is invidious, therefore, to impose an annual appraisal of potential on such people, some of whom may have no potential. Any potential review should be initiated by the individual with the HR department at any time that the person wants to discuss their future. It should not be just an annual opportunity, nor should it be initiated by the line manager.

CONDUCTING THE PERFORMANCE APPRAISAL INTERVIEW

The interview should be rather like a celebration, when the line manager and staff member can reflect upon the successes of the past year and plan for next year's exciting objectives. It should not produce any surprises, as any specific problems should have been identified earlier and plans put in progress to deal with them.

In advance

To gain the most from the interview some planning needs to be done.

Both parties should have the time to prepare for the meeting, to gather their thoughts and any documents and information that might be helpful, and to talk to any other people who might usefully make an input. At least a week's notice should be given. This also enables everyone to clear a sufficiently long space in their diary so that the interview will not be interrupted or have to be curtailed. It is common for appraisal interviews to last over one hour and sometimes two.

The location should be conducive to open discussion. Although it has been known for some managers to conduct appraisals in the pub, this may not fit in with the company image. Nevertheless, a hotel lounge or somewhere else off-site is not a bad idea. The familiar reminders of normal daily discussions will be avoided if the meeting takes place away from the manager's office. Comfortable chairs will enable people to relax and encourage them to stay to discuss the ideas rather than rush off because they cannot remain seated. Obviously all interruptions should be avoided and mobile telephones switched off. Depending upon the normal practices of the company, it might be best if the meeting were held towards the end of the day, so that there is no reason to have a specific deadline. In other companies it might be best to start early in the morning, so that there is plenty of time available.

At the time

The staff member should be put at ease by offering them tea or coffee, and by reminding them of the reason for the appraisal and the way that the meeting will be conducted. They should be invited to join in the conversation from the outset by asking them what they want to achieve from the meeting and if they have any view as to how the meeting should be conducted. The manager should keep notes to record the points coming up and to emphasize the importance of them. The staff member should be invited to comment on the content of the notes as they are written, as the manager is effectively writing them as a summarizer of the meeting.

The centrepiece for the discussion will probably be the appraisal form with the list of last year's goals. The manager and the staff member will discuss the extent to which these goals have been met and, if they have not, will decide what caused the problems. The staff member will be closer to the actual work than the manager, and should therefore be able to give valuable input to the discussion. Between them, the manager and staff member will decide if these same problems will be relevant next year and, if so, will decide what to do about them.

If the goals have not been met, it could be that they were, with hindsight, a little overambitious. The manager will also learn a great deal during the discussion about the management of staff and about goal setting.

After the interview

After the interview, any notes from the meeting should be distributed to the relevant people, one of whom will certainly be the staff member appraised. It might be helpful for the HR department to have a copy so that it can be kept on the employee's file and used by other managers who might be working with that staff member at a later date. It might also be useful for HR personnel who will conduct any review of potential, should the individual request one.

The notes and the list of the goals for the coming year will be used by the staff member and the manager to monitor progress towards those goals during the year, and will form the basis of the next year's performance appraisal.

GIVING AND RECEIVING FEEDBACK

The appraisal interview is a chance for both parties to give and to receive feedback about the work that they do and the way that they do it. Feedback is a skill that calls for practice and sensitivity.

How to give feedback

It is best to avoid the traditional 'praise–criticize–praise' sandwich of giving feedback as it is too obvious and just makes the recipient doubt the sincerity of the other person. Better would be the use of the 'feedback formula', where they know what they did, what the effect was and what they need to do differently to change. The 'feedback formula' is in three parts, as follows:

1 *Tell the person what they did (or show them if that is easier)*. Be as specific as possible so that there is no misunderstanding about it. The SMART formula provides a good foundation for this.
2 *Tell them the effect of their action (or show them)*. Again be as specific as possible. If they cannot see the reason for the feedback, they are unlikely to want to change.
3 *Agree with them how to make a change*. This 'agreement' can range from the manager telling the appraisees what to do differently, through to them suggesting a change for themselves. Again, if they are part of this process they are more likely to want to see a change happen. They will also come up with ideas that are within their ability to influence.

Parts 1, 2 and 3 are used for pointing out what was done wrong and for criticizing people. Parts 1 and 2 only are used for praising. Clearly, it is more efficient, as well as more pleasant, to 'catch people doing something right' rather than catching them doing it wrong.

The appraisal interview could last well over an hour, and during that time, the appraisee will probably only be able to accept three or four pieces of criticism before becoming defensive. We all have a threshold for how much criticism we can take. When pointing out problem areas, the appraiser should be selective and only highlight those few points that will have a significant impact on performance. Any other criticisms should have been dealt with at previous regular review meetings anyway, or could be left to subsequent ones. In cases where the appraisee has done things well half the time and not so well the other half, the appraiser should praise for what was done well so that the previous three or four criticisms can be saved for other feedback.

How to receive feedback

During the interview the manager should also be receiving feedback from the appraisee about what might be done to improve their management. It is not always easy for staff to criticize their managers and the way it is expressed may not always be the way that it is intended. The feedback given will be for the benefit of the manager and the organization, however, and so should be received in that spirit. If the manager can help the staff member to focus on particular incidents rather than generalized criticisms, it will be easier for the manager to understand what the comments are about. In some cases, it will be necessary for the manager to ask for clarification and for the staff member to give some examples. When the manager is sure what the feedback is, the following three stages should be followed:

1 Summarize in one sentence the feedback that is being given.
2 Accept the feedback (but don't necessarily agree).
3 Thank the giver.

CHECK LIST 1: PREPARING FOR THE PERFORMANCE APPRAISAL INTERVIEW

To gain the most from the interview for yourself and the staff member, it is advisable to carry out some preparation. This will include the following:

- Deciding what the purpose of the meeting is (performance, potential or pay).
- Doing your preparation and research.
- Warning the staff member a week in advance so that they can be doing some thinking as well as preparing their materials.
- Referring to previous appraisal forms, work review sheets, job descriptions and other information that might be of help.
- Perhaps discussing the staff member's performance with other managers with whom they may have had contact.
- Allowing plenty of time for the meeting. It will probably take at least an hour, and should be left open-ended if possible.
- Finding a relaxed location, possibly away from your usual office.
- Arranging for there to be no interruptions and for mobile telephones to be switched off.

CHECK LIST 2: CONDUCTING THE PERFORMANCE APPRAISAL INTERVIEW

Appraising the work of a member of staff is one of the hardest tasks a manager ever has to undertake, yet in some ways one of the most important. It is generally assumed that the value of a fully trained person is three times their annual salary, so the purpose of the performance appraisal is to give a regular check-up or service to that most valuable of resources. The following tips should help the process be more effective:

- Try to put the subordinate at ease by discussing in an informal manner.
- Offer tea and coffee.

- Have relaxing chairs.
- Explain what the meeting is about and how it is to proceed.
- Be as objective as possible in your feedback, trying to quote actual examples. Avoid opinions and generalizations.
- Discuss issues as mutual problems to be solved. Do not read your views out as if statements of absolute fact, and then expect the staff member to want to discuss them.
- Ask for the staff member's views and listen to them. If people can solve their own problems, they are more likely to be committed to the solutions and these are more likely to be within their capabilities.
- Listen to their perceptions of the problems. These may be different to yours and you might learn something, too.
- Be prepared to take criticism yourself. If you are going to criticize them, they have the right to criticize you. Think of it as a compliment if they feel able to do so to your face! Don't be afraid to criticize. They will not believe the good points if there are no bad ones.
- Take one issue at a time to prevent confusion and circular discussion.
- Having solved one issue, agree on action and write it down, together with standards and timescales.

CHECK LIST 3: AFTER THE PERFORMANCE APPRAISAL INTERVIEW

To maximize the return from the interview for yourself and the staff member, it is important to ensure that points are followed up, as follows:

- Distribute notes from the meeting to all concerned, especially the appraisee.
- Send a copy to the HR department, together with any requests for their involvement with training needs.
- Encourage HR to use the information for discussions with the individual at reviews of potential.
- Use the newly set goals at regular review meetings to ensure that possible problems are spotted early.
- Use the form again next year when reviewing this year's performance and planning next year's.

FURTHER READING

Armstrong, M., *Performance Management*, Kogan Page, 1994.
Fisher, M,. *Performance Appraisals*, Kogan Page, 1996.
Industrial Society, *Performance Management*, Industrial Society, 1994.
Lockett, J., *Effective Performance Management*, Kogan Page, 1993.
Neale, F. (ed), *The Handbook of Performance Management*, Institute of Personnel and Development, 1991.

15 Dealing with problem staff

John Rogers

This chapter considers the management of problem staff. The role of the manager in 'getting the best out of people' is introduced together with some typical staff problems. Establishing the gap between actual and expected performance and conduct is discussed in terms of the *unacceptable gap* and the *opportunity gap*. Eight categories of problems and problem staff are considered: performance problems, interpersonal skills problems, knowledge/understanding problems, legal issues, skills problems, contractual problems, personal issues and management induced problems.

The legal framework within which companies have developed disciplinary and other procedures to deal fairly with problem staff are considered. Moving from problems to solutions in terms of approaches involving positive discipline, managed coaching and counselling are developed and discussed.

THE ROLE OF MANAGEMENT

A manager's job is to achieve results through other people, and to be successful in this, staff must be carefully recruited and selected for jobs, inducted properly, managed so that they demonstrate strong performance, and rewarded sensibly. However, this idealism does not match the real world. Things do go wrong with staff – and with managers, too – and they can 'become problems'.

The word 'problem' is used here deliberately, although it has become unfashionable to refer to problems in many organizations: the word 'opportunity' is often preferred as it has a more resonant and positive quality. Problems are real, nevertheless. Indeed, a crucial difference is that problems require solutions, whereas opportunities do not. Sometimes, resolving a staff problem can create opportunities, but it is the problem and its resolution that remains the focus of attention.

Some examples of typical problem situations are as follows:

- Helen had been instructed by the manager to clear a backlog of work which had built up earlier in the year, in addition to her normal duties. Helen had failed to clear the backlog and has been called to a meeting with the manager.
- Daniel has had four bouts of self-certified sickness totalling twelve days so far this year – and it is only April. Daniel has been called to a meeting with the manager immediately on return from his latest illness.
- Colin is an average worker, adequate at the most. Unfortunately, he appears to think he is a really good performer, and disrupts the unit with his arrogant and dismissive behaviour. Colin has been called to a meeting with the manager.
- Barry has been with the company for 20 years and seen all this change many times before. Barry can do his current job in his sleep, and the job is unlikely to change significantly in the near future. By now he is a confirmed cynic, and although he works well, he can be disruptive. The manager calls Barry into the office.
- Gail passed her nursing training with distinctions and is looked upon as the ward expert – junior doctors have been known to ask her advice! Gail's bedside manner leaves much to be desired, however, and complaints from patients are becoming more serious. The manager invites Gail into the office following the latest incident.

WHAT IS A STAFF PROBLEM ?

Resolving staff problems becomes more manageable for all parties when the problem can be defined as objectively as possible. An excellent way of achieving this is through an understanding of the performance or conduct gap: that is, by defining precisely the problem to be addressed. Figure 15.1 defines this gap as the difference between effective and actual performance.

Effective and actual performance

The criteria for effective performance should be defined and clearly communicated to staff; involving staff in defining performance standards can be effective where the environment is supportive and individual commitment levels high. Everyone at work is supposed to have a contract of employment summarizing the main duties and conditions of employment; these can quickly become out of date and the manager needs to communicate any changes to the staff. Training opportunities, either away from or at the workplace, need to be understood by the manager, so that the best strategy for improvement can be developed.

Actual performance should again be defined and measured accurately. Comparisons with people doing similar work can be useful. Also, many conduct-related problems can be measured by reviewing customer responses

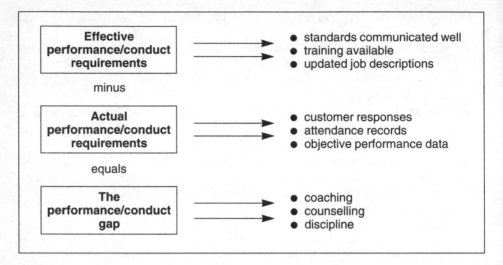

Figure 15.1   Diagram indicating a practical definition of the problem, namely, the performance/conduct gap

and personnel files for details of attendance records, earlier performance figures and so on.

The unacceptable gap and the opportunity gap

Managers must understand the nature of the individual problem before meeting with the employee and deciding upon solutions. Figure 15.2 indicates a spectrum of performance and conduct from poor to standard (the *unacceptable gap*), and from standard to superior (the *opportunity gap*). The unacceptable gap indicates that the problem is not acceptable and something has to be done about it. Three main approaches are recommended, as follows:

1   *Positive discipline*, in which approaches to correcting performance rather than merely punishing people is appropriate at the early stages, probably using informal approaches rather than company procedures. Serious breaches of conduct may well require more immediate action such as formal warnings, suspension and disciplinary hearings.

2   *Managed coaching*, where a form of coaching is applied but with more control by the manager than usual. The approach works on the basis of giving the employee every opportunity to change, and treating them as able to take some responsibility for ensuring the defined changes take place.

3   *Internal and external counselling*, particularly where there are emotional and personal issues involved in causing or affecting the problems. Managers are advised to learn basic counselling skills such as listening and empathy, but may often need to call in expertise or other help if they get out of their depth.

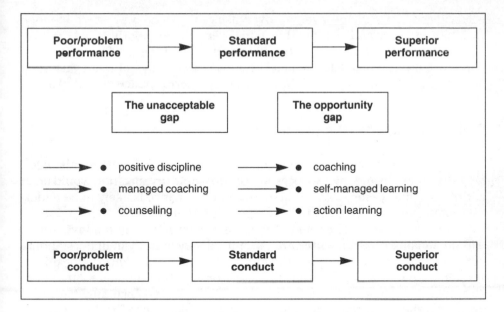

Note: The manager takes more responsibility for change where current performance and conduct is poor rather than standard.

Figure 15.2   Diagram showing the different approaches to performance and conduct improvement

EIGHT CATEGORIES OF PROBLEM STAFF

The eight categories of problem staff discussed below are not presented in any order of priority. Most problems that managers need to deal with in this context are likely to be a 'complex and dynamic mixture of causes and effects'. The way the elements of the problem work together is more important to understand than the elements themselves.

Approaches may well be influenced by whether the problem is temporary or permanent. Temporary performance problems are typified by someone having a cold, or access to the computer network breaking down so that the job search clerk cannot access the job database for clients. An example of a permanent problem – or at least ongoing for a considerable time – could be someone on the production line desperately awaiting early retirement next year and distracting others from their work with incessant casual chatter.

1 Performance problems

Managers quite rightly expect staff to achieve acceptable performance levels at work. A danger can be that expected performance is not clearly defined in the first instance. Performance standards can be straightforward to define: for example, to visit 25 customers in a week with 60 per cent sales; to produce

500 widgets per shift on average over a month; to answer the telephone within three rings; and no more than two till errors per month.

In many professions such as teaching and accounting, performance standards are more difficult to define. The most useful ways of managing such problems are to agree with or inform staff of the performance expected at the outset.

2 Interpersonal skills problems

Relationships with others in the company can cause problems. A mismatch between a person and their work group or the whole organization would need addressing. If a person does not fit in, their performance is likely to be underestimated and they are likely to have a poor internal image.

Clashes of personality should always be recognized early on. Inventories and personality questionnaires are often used successfully in understanding personal and interactive styles; the Myers Briggs Type Inventory, for understanding the different preferred styles of working, the Thomas Kilman Conflict Style Inventory and the Belbin Team Role Types Assessment can be useful. All these approaches build upon valuing differences and diversity in working teams as a competitive advantage – certainly better from a business standpoint than managing a harmonious and homogeneous group of clones.

The manager's role is to ensure that the problem employee understands the effect of their behaviour on others, and can change or manage the interface in new ways that ensure improved performance.

3 Knowledge/understanding problems

Shorter product/services life cycles, the increased use of technology and the mere speed of working today can cause problems. Many employees will struggle along, not admitting their ignorance, rather than ask for help or information. In the meantime, performance is dropping off; the manager notices this, but not the employee.

Hands are thrown up in horror as people exclaim that 'anything they touch falls apart' or that 'they have always been useless with numbers'. The manager can help by ensuring staff are sufficiently confident to raise queries about what they need to know and understand in order to succeed in their jobs.

4 Legal issues

External legislation can influence how managers approach many of the conduct problems at work. Health and safety legislation includes the responsibilities of managers and staff in workplaces, including offices. Moreover, discrimination legislation in terms of gender, disability and race legislation has evolved in recent years.

If the manager dismisses a problem employee, then that employee may take their case up through an industrial tribunal. The manager and other company representatives will need to persuade a panel that the dismissal was fair, using the facts of the matter. Indeed 'constructive dismissal' can be claimed where an employee resigns on the basis that the way they have been treated left them 'with no choice but to leave' or, in effect, 'dismiss themselves'.

The legal circumstances can be a confusing area for managers, particularly where interpretations are made from the way the popular press portrays the juicier cases. Where possible, managers are advised to attend short introductory courses on employment law and its implications, but they also need expert advice available in-house or externally.

5 Skills problems

Many jobs require far more and greater skills than they used to. Relating well to customers has become important as competition has increased. Learning by careful questioning to understand customer requirements and sell to these requirements is a demanding skill to develop. Some managers believe that you can only learn such skills by actually doing them, and to a certain extent they are right. However, managers can act as role models for skills and encourage people to watch and learn from those who perform the skill particularly well.

Managers may well need to be patient with progress in this area of skills. Behaviour change is not easy and there has to be strong motivation to achieve and permanently stabilize skill changes. Consider public-speaking skills, for example; many managers have a morbid fear of standing up and speaking to an audience that they never in fact conquer. In the end it may well be that the skills cannot be developed to standard levels and an alternative job more aligned to the person's skill-set will be advisable.

6 Contractual problems

Conduct problems can often be caused by the attitudes and behaviours that staff bring to their work. Regular absence needs addressing, especially if it is for the odd days at short notice or if it means hiring a temporary worker. Most managers can be realistic and fair about absence, but problems occur when the employee plays the absence card to the limit by regarding absence as extra holiday entitlement. Conversely, managers who have 'never had a day off in twenty years' should consider themselves lucky rather than a role model for everyone else to emulate.

Flexibility is important. Increasingly, staff have external responsibilities towards children or ageing parents and public transport is often unreliable. The more flexibility that can be built into jobs, the lower absence levels are likely to become. Good recording and analysis systems can help the manager resolve absence problems.

7 Personal issues

Many personal issues which interfere with or influence poor work performance are caused by external factors affecting the employee that are outside the company's control. These can be most difficult to deal with, as negative attitudes and cynicisms can be developed towards the company which affect work performance. Domestic circumstances, ranging from dual-career families where one person needs to relocate and family break-ups to a programme of dental treatment, can affect performance. Stress at work through being unable to cope with the pressures around can impair work performance.

Managers can often support with practical solutions and by arranging external counselling to resolve problems, particularly where the problem is of relatively short duration. Deciding for how long personal problems should be allowed to interfere with work can be an important decision for the manager to make.

8 Management-induced problems

Managers need to be aware of their own styles and prejudices when dealing with problem staff. If any of the above categories of problem are apparent they will not be resolved satisfactorily if the quality of management and processes are poor. Work needs to be distributed evenly and fairly, with appropriate materials and resources available. The right staff have to be selected and recruited, induction programmes well managed and performance review and rewards handled well.

Large companies can introduce sophisticated approaches towards ensuring that management creates the right environment to support acceptable and superior performance. One company, for example, is described as follows:

> a key feature of our approach is that individuals are aligned with the business, are clear about their roles, where they fit in and what they contribute. Clarifying strategic business objectives from which functional and departmental objectives and individual targets are defined has been critical to this task. Its success depends on it not being just a top-down, one way flow, but an interactive one involving a realistic degree of shared discussion and feedback.
>
> The importance of involving individuals in the setting of objectives, targets and developmental goals cannot be overemphasized in terms of gaining their commitment to achieving them.

THE LEGAL FRAMEWORK

Internal company policies, procedures and practices

Most companies have written rules concerning their contractual obligations to employees. In large companies these are likely to be collected together in imposing staff manuals, while in small companies they are probably more informally held and often communicated by word of mouth. Most companies – large or small – that are worth working with have the key rights and responsibilities available and in writing. In dealing with problem staff, the policies, procedures and practices that are most likely to be important are:

- *Terms and conditions of employment*, including contract of employment issues, discipline and grievance procedures, notice periods and professional integrity.
- *Personnel policies*, including equal opportunities, job evaluation schemes, and policies concerned with smoking, drugs and alcohol.
- *Remuneration and other staff benefits*, including grading structures, performance management, salary/wages scales, progression and allowances for overtime, shift working, expenses, and so on.
- *Attendance and holidays*, including special leave and any family friendly policies such as parental leave and career breaks.
- *Health, safety and welfare*, including staff responsibilities and counselling support.
- *Education, training and qualifications* support.

Disciplinary procedures

The Advisory, Conciliation and Arbitration Service (ACAS) state that: 'the main purpose of the disciplinary procedure is to encourage an employee whose standard of work is unsatisfactory to improve.' In other words, the procedure is about correcting behaviour – not about getting rid of unwanted staff. In addition, the ACAS advisory booklet *Discipline at Work* details the characteristics of disciplinary procedures. Specifically, they should:

- be in writing;
- specify to whom they apply;
- provide for matters to be dealt with quickly;
- indicate the disciplinary actions which may be taken;
- specify the levels of management which have the authority to take the various forms of disciplinary action;
- provide for individuals to be informed of the complaints made against them, and to be given the opportunity to state their case before decisions are reached;
- give individuals the right to be accompanied by a trade union representative or by a fellow employee;
- ensure that, except for gross misconduct, no employees are dismissed for a first breach of discipline;
- ensure that disciplinary action is not taken until the case has been carefully investigated;
- ensure that individuals are given an explanation for any penalty imposed; and
- provide a right of appeal and specify the procedure to be followed.

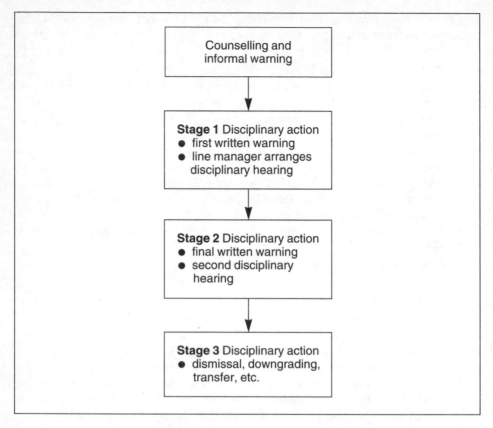

Figure 15.3   Summary of a typical staged disciplinary procedure in a large company

As a result of these guidelines, most companies who really do believe that their 'greatest asset is their staff' have introduced disciplinary procedures to deal with problem staff where all positive attempts to change work performance or conduct have failed. A summary of a typical procedure is shown in Figure 15.3..

Most situations should be resolved in the early counselling/informal warning phase. Indeed, a measure of the health of employee relationships is the relatively low number of disciplinary cases, with a very high proportion (over 95 per cent) resolved before the formal stages are reached.

Discrimination legislation

People are not a problem because they are women, black, religious or disabled; the legal framework around discrimination at work has been developed over the last twenty or so years and so should be well understood by managers. Problem staff demonstrate poor performance or conduct, and linking the problem with discrimination issues is strictly illegal in nearly all situations.

The 1995 Disability Discrimination Act, for example, is quite specific in stating that it is unlawful for employers with twenty or more people to treat disabled people less favourably than they do able-bodied people – unless they can justify the differing treatment. When a disabled person applies for a job, or indeed even enquires about a job, the employer must not discriminate:

- in the selection process; or
- in the terms on which that person is offered a job.

If the disabled person is already in employment in the company, the employer must not discriminate:

- in the terms of that person's employment;
- in the opportunities provided for promotion, transfer, training or other benefits; or
- by dismissing the person because of their disability.

The whole area of discrimination can be complex for managers to under-stand. Where one aspect of a problem could possibly involve accusations about discrimination, you are likely to need expert advice.

Minor, serious and gross misconduct

The relative seriousness of staff problems can vary between companies as a result of the company attitude to the offence, because of any particular circumstances prevalent at the time of the offence, and on account of any relevant clauses in the employment contract. For first offences in many situations, the following guidelines may apply:

- *Minor misconduct:* poor time keeping, poor attendance, failure to submit a medical certificate, most failures to follow company procedures where health and safety or other very serious repercussions are not involved, poor work performance when other efforts have failed, and so on.
- *Serious misconduct:* threatening behaviour towards others (but depending on circumstances), smoking in many non-smoking areas, and so on.
- *Gross misconduct:* unauthorized possession of an employee's property, violence to a customer, breaches of confidential business information for personal gain, conviction of possessing and using drugs at work, and so on.

Bear in mind that the sanctions for most staff problems requiring discipline are not clear-cut. Consistency of interpretation is important, as is publishing the rules and usual consequences applicable to problems like fighting at work, swearing, bullying and sexual harassment.

MANAGING: FROM PROBLEMS TO SOLUTIONS

Earlier sections have discussed what causes the problems to occur in the first instance. The manager's responsibility is to resolve these problems. This section considers approaches that involve discipline, coaching and counselling.

The formal disciplinary/grievance paths

When managers decide that a problem has reached a level where something just has to be done about it:

- Be fair and reasonable in handling the situation and not driven by motives of revenge or by their own obsessional behaviours.
- Handle the matter promptly by ensuring that the problem is not left until it has escalated widely: that is, 'nip the problem in the bud'.
- Ensure the facts are investigated and collected so that new facts relevant to the situation do not become apparent later at interviews.
- Judge cases on their own particular merit and ensure that the influence of 'personalities' is not overexaggerated.
- Remain calm and be firm.
- Decide if formal disciplinary action is needed and follow procedures if necessary.
- Try to find ways of encouraging improvement; after all, people do not appear to be born as 'walking problem-makers'.

When an employee has a concern with the employer it is termed a grievance: that is, a grievance can be seen as a situation where an employee wishes 'to discipline the employer'. Many aspects of the ways in which grievances and discipline are managed in large companies are similar. There is likely to be a procedure, and managers will be encouraged to resolve grievances before they escalate to other staff and develop into a collective dispute. Many grievances can be resolved by both sides fully exploring the circumstances and focusing on business and other proper reasons, rather than simply preferences.

Skills in managing discipline and grievance issues

Understanding the legal and company framework within which to manage discipline and grievance issues is important. Demonstrating the skills in real situations is equally important and should not be overlooked. Five key skills are as follows.

1   *Establishing the facts and preparing to meet with the employee* involves fact finding to separate facts from opinions, and developing a realistic interpretation of these facts in dealing with the problem. Remember to consider the wider implications of decisions for the other interested parties; these include other managers, other staff and any employee

representation. While there is a general need to address the problems as early as possible, it should not be to the detriment of good preparation; writing from experience, there is nothing more demoralizing in preparing an argument than new facts being unearthed that should have been found much earlier.

2   *Problem solving* moves us from the facts into what can and needs to be done. A danger can be that the thinking about solutions is too narrow; as a manager it pays to think more laterally at this stage, and especially to talk with peers about how they have resolved similar problems. The manager will now have a much wider choice of strategies to select from.

3   *Being aware of and managing the reasonable expectations* of all parties is vital. Skills in avoiding entrenched positions where the company and both parties are in 'lose – lose' positions are important; keep aiming for 'win – win' and demonstrate flexibility in trying to achieve workable compromises.

4   *General meeting and interviewing skills* are relevant, but particularly in the areas of listening, understanding, influencing and persuading. The manager needs to gain the employee's willingness to change, and this is best achieved in an agreed manner rather than relying upon vague threats and upon disinterest in the actual causes of the poor performance or conduct. Summarizing skills are needed to ensure clarification can be made during the meeting, and also in stating unambiguously the actions required by the employee following the meeting.

5   *Understanding procedural aspects*, using the appropriate procedures if necessary, and documenting outcomes are important in case the problem develops along more formal lines. Although the meeting may not at this stage be part of a formal procedure, an understanding of the possible implications if matters do escalate will enable the manager to approach the problem with much more confidence.

The coaching and counselling paths

Structured plans to improve poor performance have recently become popular in both coaching and disciplinary situations. Companies need to encourage staff to perform to high standards and use their abilities fully. Coaching is an effective way of achieving this. Companies also need to manage and support staff with poor performance and conduct difficulties by enabling them to achieve satisfactory standards.

These plans are particularly useful in monitoring the path to improvement following poor performance appraisals. They recognize that improvement seldom occurs overnight, and requires a managed mechanism for clarifying in detail the manager's 'objective expectations of measurable change over a specified period of time'. Typically, timescales for improvement are four to twelve weeks, with review meetings with the manager every two weeks.

The areas of the job or conduct needing improvement are listed in the plan document. Clearly, there will be some areas where performance is   *239* satisfactory or excellent, and although these are not included on the plan, it is recommended that they are considered in balancing the overall process of improvement. Within these areas of work there will be specific aspects that need addressing and a statement of the required standards. The final two columns of the plan should address what the manager/company agree to do to support achievement of the standards, and the actions the employee has committed to. Signatures and dating by manager and employee indicate a serious commitment to change, with the whole document underpinning the regular progress meetings.

Performance management systems

Large companies tend to have elaborate performance management systems. The systems are characterized by employees:

- knowing precisely what is expected of them;
- understanding the importance of their contribution in achieving business success;
- being appraised on how the organization rates their performance; and
- receiving practical support in delivering agreed objectives and high performance.

Typically, all staff are appraised annually with several interim reviews, which results in poor performance and conduct being quickly identified and recorded. Often, personnel specialists decide the strategic approach in discussion with line management, and then monitor the implementation and effectiveness of such schemes to support managers.

Many smaller companies have no such personnel expertise and are more vulnerable to implementing the wrong solutions with problem staff. There tends to be a more laissez-faire approach, as small companies need more adaptive employees and often have less time and resources to investigate matters fully. Thus elaborate and integrated performance management systems are less relevant in small companies, but the general principles of defining performance and developing plans for change are still relevant.

Employee assistance programmes

The more confidential and personal matters affecting employees' performance are increasingly being addressed by employee assistance or support programmes. External and/or internal counselling may be involved with legal, specialist and financial experts available to advise. The British Association of Counselling (BAC) have published a code of ethics for such programmes. It is important that the quality of counselling is excellent and that the manager's responsibility for staff is not undermined.

In answering the question, 'What kind of problems are dealt with?' in employee assistance programmes, one large company offers the following:

An opportunity to talk to someone trained and impartial may help to put things into perspective. A trained adviser may suggest avenues of support or action you could take to help you deal with these worries. These worries can be about work, relationships, family problems, bereavement, health, harassment, general anxiety, financial commitments and more...

SUMMARY OF KEY POINTS

Even in well-run companies there are problems with staff and managers that need dealing with from time to time. As a manager you must recognize that you are responsible for the performance of your staff, and that problems have to be recognized and resolved as soon as possible.

A check list of key points for managers to consider when dealing with problem staff is as follows:

1 Define the gap between actual and expected performance and conduct.
2 Recognize which of the eight main categories of problems you are dealing with.
3 Decide whether the resolution of the problem is best achieved through disciplinary, coaching or counselling-type paths.
4 Develop the interpersonal skills required to manage the interaction.
5 Recognize when an expert may need to be called in to support.
6 Understand the impact of any decision on other staff.

FURTHER READING

Advisory, Conciliation and Arbitration Service, *Discipline at Work*, ACAS advisory booklet, 1995.

Armstrong, M., *Performance Management*, Kogan Page, 1994.

Gennard, J. and Judge, J., *Employee Relations*, Institute of Personnel and Development, 1997.

Kennedy, G., *Managing Negotiations: How to get a better deal*, Business Books, 1987.

Macdonald, L., *Hired, Fired or Sick and Tired?*, Nicholas Brealey Publishing, 1995.

Stewart, V. and Stewart A., *Managing the Poor Performer*, Gower, 1982.

16 Counselling

Mike Megranahan

The use of counselling and counselling skills in an employment context is growing as companies become increasingly aware of the benefits that can be gained, by both employee and employer, from these interactions. A trained employee represents a valuable asset which should be protected in the same way as plant and machinery. Counselling is one way of providing the company, as a whole, with the means of alleviating different problems which, if not identified, discussed and resolved, could erode the effectiveness of the person, not only as an asset in the organization, but as an individual.

Every person at one time or another is likely to experience a personal or job-related problem. Most people are unable to package problems neatly and confine them to specific areas and thereby avoid the effect that one may have on the other (e.g. home or work). If the employee perceives his or her manager or supervisor as potentially sympathetic and approachable, the opportunity to discuss the problem may be sufficient to help him or her see how it can be resolved. Managers would be expected in the course of their jobs to undertake a number of formal and informal (or ad hoc) interactions with employees. The use of appropriate interactive skills in these situations should enable these contacts to be constructive, improve communication, and encourage trust.

This chapter sets out the differences between counselling and the use of counselling skills. This increases awareness of the respective uses of counselling and counselling skills: that is, which should be used, when, how and by whom.

WHAT IS COUNSELLING?

Counselling may simply be described as a form of communication between
two people. The person in the role of counsellor should be trained in

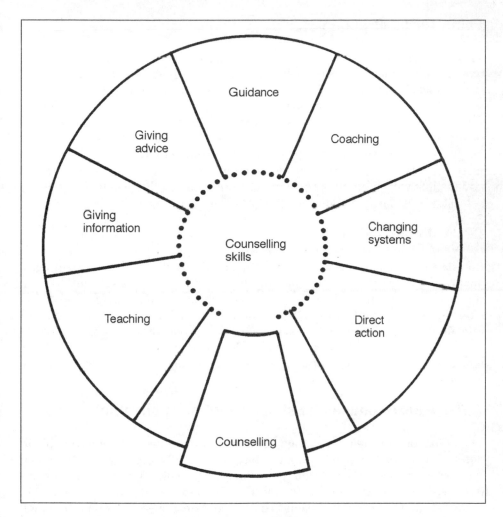

Figure 16.1   Helping interventions (*Source:* M. S. Megranahan 'Counselling at work', *Journal of General Management*, 11 (1), 1985)

counselling techniques; the person seeking counselling may need assistance with a particular area of concern. These elements set counselling apart as a form of communication. In addition, a number of important themes arising from different counselling strategies make counselling distinct from other forms of helping. For instance, counselling essentially adopts the premise that the person is the expert on their problem and the process of counselling therefore has two functions:

1   To help the person talk about, explore and understand his or her thoughts and feelings, and work out what he or she might do before taking action.
2   To help the person decide on his or her own solutions.

Other forms of helping

The need for counselling depends on the circumstances at the time; alternative strategies may be more appropriate and these may be enhanced through the application of counselling skills. The other forms of help which may be available to a person are summarized in Figure 16.1. We can readily identify with these forms of interaction since we have all been in a position of giving or receiving most of them. In all these forms of assistance, the source has to be perceived by the person as possessing sufficient relevant expertise to justify contact. Where a person simply needs some information, for instance, counselling would be inappropriate, although counselling skills may help to establish and clarify the need for the information.

COUNSELLING SKILLS

Counselling skills may be applied in a variety of situations, forming an integral part of the manager's one-to-one interaction with employees. In addition to the use of the actual techniques of counselling skills, the manager must consider other important aspects. For instance, the manager needs to be consistent in the use of counselling skills across a range of formal and informal interactions with employees. He or she also needs to assess which situations merit the use of these skills; some situations may require more directive action.

Areas where counselling skills would be applicable

The manager, through knowledge of his or her employees, should be able to determine when counselling skills may be usefully employed and would therefore form a useful addition to the 'kit bag' of skills. Further, the organization provides the manager with the 'inbuilt' opportunity for him or her to demonstrate his or her approach to employees on a one-to-one basis through formal contacts. For instance:

- disciplinary interviews;
- appraisal interviews;
- coaching an employee;
- redundancy;
- pre-retirement; and
- career development interviews.

Once employees become aware of a manager's style of interaction – for example, enabling employees to communicate fully and in confidence, with a tangible end result – informal interactions may develop. These could include work- or home-related aspects which, if confronted jointly by the manager and the employee at an early stage, may avoid later deterioration of relationships and work performance. This mutual objective could help to identify ways in which the particular concern could be alleviated and may involve referral to a counselling resource. Examples of informal contacts are:

- ill health at home;
- mounting debt; and
- feelings of isolation from work colleagues.

The employee may or may not be keen to volunteer thoughts, feelings or other information which he may perceive as potentially damaging to his or her situation if revealed to the manager. Therefore, if suspicion exists between a manager and an employee, communication is likely to be limited and interaction poor. Directive action in this case may lead the employee to further suppress and withhold information. This cycle could also develop between the manager and other employees, resulting in poor working relationships and repercussions on aspects such as morale, attendance, and so forth. Counselling skills, if used appropriately, could avoid this downward spiral.

What are counselling skills?

For counselling skills to be effective, the manager needs to have an awareness of his or her existing style of interaction and its subsequent impact on employees. Once this awareness has been developed, the manager may consciously make use of counselling skills to improve or refine interactions and therefore communication with others.

Appropriate verbal responses associated with counselling skills are insufficient if used in isolation. Consequently, the following guidelines need to be drawn upon to identify and utilize those facets necessary to a positive outcome. The guidelines are applicable to many formal and informal contacts and are as important as the person's ability to use spoken techniques effectively.

PRELIMINARY PHASE

The physical setting for the interaction needs to be comfortable for both parties. Consider seating arrangements: for example, do not have the employee facing direct sunlight, the room should be sound-proof, there should be no interruptions and the employee should have the sole attention of the manager. If background information is available or applicable, then this should have been read and digested well in advance of the meeting.

INTRODUCTORY PHASE

The manager should attempt to establish an open atmosphere for the meeting. The initial contact with the employee is important – rapport needs to be established quickly since this can set the tone for the whole interaction. It   *245* may take longer to establish this aspect with some employees, but it remains an essential element of future progress.

If defensive attitudes are detected in the employee, then attempts should be made to overcome these, by, for example, explaining the purpose, structure and objectives of the meeting.

WORKING PHASE

The discussion with the employee should be conducted without the use of unfamiliar jargon or technical terms. Confidence and trust have to be developed as a result of the interaction.

Effective listening is very important and the employee must be able to recognize that this is taking place. This requires 'reading' beyond the actual words that are spoken: that is, attending to what is *not* said.

There should be empathic understanding of the employee's difficulty. This requires an understanding of the situation from the employee's point of view, namely, to see and appreciate the feelings the employee has in his or her situation as he or she experiences it. Non-critical acceptance of the employee's difficulty is important.

Interruptions to the employee's flow of dialogue should be avoided. Be prepared for periods of silence and therefore avoid feelings of awkwardness. Opportunity should be given to the employee to express feelings and emotions – and as far as possible, these should be reflected.

PLANNING PHASE

At the conclusion of the interaction, what was said and decided should be summarized and agreed upon, as follows:

- Define the action he or she wants/needs to take.
- Express this in concrete attainable goals.
- Identify the strengths and resources he or she possesses.
- Identify what resources and skills he or she may need to acquire.
- Make provision to provide support and encouragement.

APPROACHES TO INTERACTION

Appropriate interview techniques and question style

The introductory, working and planning phases of the meeting need to be supported by an awareness of the use of both verbal and non-verbal responses by the manager. The employee has to be encouraged to consider and express his or her concern fully. He or she will also be very conscious of the way in which the manager is responding, an aspect which needs to be remembered. Various techniques may be usefully applied during the interview to assist both the manager and employee to ensure that important

TECHNIQUE	PURPOSE	QUESTION STYLE
Paraphrasing	This involves rephrasing what the person is saying in order to interpret and clarify factual information for both parties.	'As I understand it, ...?' 'So what you're saying is ...?'
Reflecting feelings	This requires careful listening to detect feelings, accurate interpretation to put them into words, and suitable responses. It is very useful for exploring attitudes and opinions in detail. Empathy is important for this technique to be used effectively.	'You feel that ...?' 'It seems to you that ...?'
Confrontation	This enables the person to identify inconsistencies, logical sequences, etc.	'What would happen if ...?'
Silence	This indicates to the person that more is expected and it should be accompanied by various non-verbal signals.	e.g. 'Hmm?' 'Ah?' 'Oh?' 'Uhh?'
Supportive statements	Used to encourage the person to continue talking. Non-directive in form.	'I see' 'That's interesting'
Mirror questions	An effective technique if used carefully. Simple rephrasing of the question tells the person that you would like to know more.	'I don't like the job' 'You don't like the job?' 'No, it is too boring' 'It's boring?'
Identification questions	These can be used effectively to isolate specific facts and information	'When did you first notice the pains?'
Extension questions	If further clarification or explanation of a subject is needed, then a fuller answer should be encouraged.	'How do you mean?' 'How can you be sure?' 'How do you know?'

Figure 16.2 **Examples of positive measures during a face-to-face interaction**

aspects are covered. Some of the main techniques and associated question styles are shown in Figures 16.2 and 16.3. In particular, the question styles require careful forethought, since the types of questions asked will either block or elicit responses from the employee. In addition, the nature and form of the questions must be supported by the non-verbal actions of the manager (discussed later).

Non-verbal communication – an area for caution

If what every person said could be relied upon to be a true expression of their thoughts and feelings, then the above would suffice. However, this is rarely the case, and the person conducting the interview needs to be aware during *247*

TECHNIQUE	PURPOSE OR OUTCOME	QUESTION STYLE
Multiple questions	This tends to lead to a confused response from the person. He or she is still trying to take in the questions, order the answers, and recall the next question asked.	'Does your wife work?' 'Can't you budget?' 'Do you drive?' 'Is it true that you're on holiday soon?'
Trick questions	These may be used on the wrongful assumption that they may reveal some underlying aspects which have not yet emerged.	'Do you drink?' 'When did you last see your doctor?'
Leading questions	This type of question is suggestive in that it puts forward the right answer that the questioner expects from the person. Leading questions can take many forms.	'You don't believe that ...?' 'Isn't it true that ...?'
Ambiguous questions	These tend to leave the person confused and the answer therefore of little value, plus they interrupt the flow of interaction and make the person suspicious.	'What are you like with people?' 'What about working with men?
'Why' questions	These should be avoided as far as possible since they may be perceived as threatening. They may also invoke justifications which prevent the actual causes being obtained.	'Why did you do that?' 'Why have you asked to see me?'

Figure 16.3   Examples of negative measures during a face-to-face interaction

the interaction of other indicators that may be contrary to the verbal communication.

Equally, the person conducting the interview will be projecting a range of non-verbal communications to the employee and it is essential that these support the type of questions asked. Very little could be achieved by inviting an employee to talk about their problem in a loud demanding voice and an aggressive posture.

Figure 16.4 illustrates the range of non-verbal communications which may encourage (or discourage) an employee to speak openly and freely.

Review

It would be beneficial to consider the use and outcome of the positive and negative aspects which may occur in a manager–employee interaction. Two approaches are described below. The first is directive in form and tends to disregard the principles of counselling skills. The second approach is non-directive and utilizes counselling skills. The position adopted by the person conducting the discussion determines which approach is used. The outcome for the individual is markedly different.

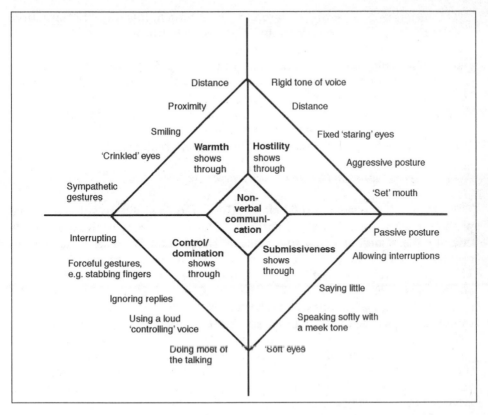

Note: Non-verbal communication can, during the course of face-to-face interaction, provide valuable or detrimental projections which will be perceived by the employee.

Figure 16.4   Non-verbal communication (*Source:* Adapted from I. Mackay, *A Guide to Asking Questions,* IPD, 1980)

A directive approach to the person's problem

In this approach the pattern of interaction between the manager in the helping role and the person seeking help begins after a statement of the problem by either the directive manager or the person. The former controls the discussion. The manager may be seen to encourage the person, to offer solutions to his or her problem by directing a series of leading questions. An example of this would be an employee whose difficulty is one of poor time keeping. The directive manager, after condemning the behaviour, may ask why the employee has this problem. This will often result in a non-committal reply. The next stage may be for the manager to use a number of leading questions (e.g. Do you oversleep? Have you been ill? Is your car not starting? Is it the children? and so on).

Not only does this process seldom lead to the discovery of the real problem, but it also suggests to the employee possible excuses which the supervisor–subordinate may find acceptable.

The main forms of remedy offered to the person in this directive situation, once a problem has been determined, are advice, warning, praise, and reassurance. All these actions emphasize the superior position of the person in the helping role and the dependent one of the employee. The manager assumes full understanding of the basic nature of the problem and both determines and attempts to introduce changes in attitude or behaviour which will remedy the conflict. An alternative action from the directive manager will be to make use of praise and reassurance in order to encourage the employee to overcome problems, or to realize that no problem really exists.

A non-directive approach to the person's problem

This approach is based on the belief in the person's ability to solve personal problems with the aid of a sympathetic listener. The role of the manager is one of understanding rather than passing judgement. There is no attempt to create a superior–subordinate relationship, positions are more or less equal. The non-directive manager assumes that the person is in the best position to know and understand the problem. An appropriate atmosphere has to be created through a permissive and friendly presentation by the person in the counselling role, with actions and statements which exhibit continuing interest but not judgement. Silence may be used as an invitation for the employee to speak further. Attention is given both to the words spoken and the feelings behind the words. The intention is that, as the employee talks about the problem, the situation will become clearer and a truer picture will emerge of what lies behind the difficulty.

Once the employee has gained greater awareness, new plans, actions or attitudes may be developed. At this stage the counsellor may assist the employee to check that as many alternatives as possible (and their consequences) have been considered. At no time must an exploration of this kind expose any bias towards any of the alternatives. A review of the actions taken at a later time may be useful for some people, but that choice remains with the employee.

Summary

These approaches to interaction with an employee give different outcomes. The non-directive approach can take longer and create more demands on the manager. However, the end result is that of an employee determining his or her own plan of action through a realization that they have the resources to confront and resolve the problem facing them. Since the plan is self-determined it is more likely to be carried out. The manager should never attempt to take over the employee's problem.

Directive action may discourage an open, honest and frank discussion of an employee's problem, and advice offered (with the best of intentions) may not be adopted and acted upon. This aspect alone may eventually give rise to further conflict and anxiety between the employee and manager if the problem recurs.

There may be occasions when the two approaches merge, and not every problem requires the depth that the non-directive approach offers. It is important to consider which features either prevent or assist the employee to express his or her thoughts and feelings about different areas of concern and to ascertain as complete a picture as possible before deciding a future course of action.

IDENTIFYING PROBLEMS

The early identification of an employee's area of concern may save both the person and the company from the loss of considerable time, effort and resources. There are usually a number of indicators of underlying problems, and it is the early detection of these which, if explored with caution and sensitivity, may provide an insight to more serious problem areas. Indicators of any kind will always need to be checked with the person concerned; a judgement on the basis of subjective assessment may be totally inaccurate and would not lead to the resolution of any problem that did exist.

How, then, can a manager begin to identify an employee with potential problems? A number of factors arising from the employee's behaviour, and manifested in inconsistent or poor work performance, irregular time keeping, scruffy dress, constant daydreaming, and so on, may have been observed by the manager, prompting him to initiate contact with the employee to investigate. Alternatively, the employee may not display any overt activity that may alert the manager to underlying problems. One example would be of an employee who regularly seeks information, perhaps not unusual in itself, but in practice it may be an attempt to initiate and sustain conversation. This type of behaviour is less likely to alert a manager to the potential difficulties being experienced by the employee, which in this instance take the form, first, of establishing contact, and second, of direct expression of the problem.

There may be a range of actions taken by an employee in order to 'sound you out' or to build up the courage to broach the area of concern. Personal experience and awareness of different employees should enable this form of activity to be recognized as potentially indicating a problem area. Registering these flagging signals and thereby keeping communication open is not easy. However, to actively seek out flagging signals or potential indicators may lead to the misinterpretation of employee behaviour.

Examples of the range of indicators that may be observed by a manager and the types of underlying problems which may be their cause can be a useful guide. If any of the categories listed in Figure 16.5 are noted by a manager or supervisor over a period of time, then these should be recorded and the employee invited to discuss these aspects in the context of employment-related issues: that is, informally (as a work colleague) or formally (e.g. in a disciplinary interview). Where specific problem areas emerge concerning out-of-work issues or other serious aspects (e.g. alcoholism), or where it is reasonable for the manager to suspect that other problems underlie the employee's behaviour, although the employee declines to reveal information

Cause	Indicator
● Marital separation, or threatened separation	● Lack of concentration
	● Irritability
● Enforced change of residence	● Indecisiveness
● Loss (e.g. bereavement, material)	● Poor memory
● Financial difficulties	● Verbal attacks
● Reduced social contact	● Panic attacks
● Role ambiguity at work	● Slow in thinking/speech
● Work overload/underload	● Feeling tired
● Poor work relationships	● Lack of energy/apathy
● Family illness	● Poor judgement in work
● Problems with children	● Irregular attendance
● Problems with parents	● Inadequate time keeping
● Alcohol/drug-related problems	● Unacceptable appearance

Note: There are no direct correlations between one list and its opposite; indeed, one cause may result in several different indicators. Furthermore, another individual may not display the same indicators, even where the cause is similar. No order of priority is intended in either list, nor is either list exhaustive.

Figure 16.5   Potential indicators and their causes

supporting such concern, it may be beneficial for the manager and/or employee to have access to professional counselling resources. For the manager, this would allow professional guidance on how to proceed with the employee, and for the employee, recourse to an external help agency. Whether or not an employee takes up contact with these resources remains the employee's decision.

SHOULD MANAGERS COUNSEL?

Managers can make effective use of counselling skills to identify, through discussion with an employee, potential areas of concern in a more sensitive and thorough manner, and this may enable the employee to find solutions. However, it is necessary for the manager to be trained in the professional use of counselling if he intends to take interaction with an employee further and therefore confront adequately the types of areas mentioned above. In both circumstances it is necessary for the person in the counselling role, first, to recognize, and second, to work to specific key factors:

- The counsellor needs to be aware of the limitations in his or her own personal areas of competence and experience. Attempts to go beyond such areas may have adverse affects on the outcome of manager–employee interaction.
- Unrealistic or unchangeable expectations on the part of the employee may give rise to problems (particularly if the counsellor is perceived to be part of the employing organization, since this may encourage the employees to seek solutions through the manager rather than through their own efforts and insight).

- The counsellor needs to avoid encouraging feelings of dependency on the employee's part, the aim being that the employee should be independent.
- The ability to establish appropriate boundaries at the start of a counselling relationship is an important element (e.g. time spent in discussion, personal relationship boss v counsellor, and so on).
- The counsellor needs to be able to call upon a range of resources available for referral purposes and know at what stage these are appropriate, who to contact, what the fees are, and so forth.
- There should be precise guidelines concerning confidentiality. The employee must be certain that information revealed during an interview will not be divulged, and if it is considered necessary or beneficial to the employee to break confidentiality, then this should occur with the person's knowledge and, where possible, approval. The person should also be encouraged to bring the matter out into the open. Managers may experience problems of dual loyalty.

While suitably trained managers would be able to handle the range of potential difficulties that arise in the course of a person's life to the depth required in counselling, they may find it difficult to be totally effective due to role conflict problems originating from organizational factors (e.g. role ambiguity, dual loyalty, time, and so on). Added to which, the employee's perception of a manager in the counselling role may not be conducive to the openness and honesty required before solutions can be sought. Managers not directly responsible for the employee, or for staff roles such as personnel or welfare, would also be subject to these difficulties, although possibly to a lesser extent.

INDEPENDENT COUNSELLING RESOURCES

An independent counselling resource would potentially overcome many of the problems originating from organizational factors. It could remain totally independent; meet the employee's expectations of total confidentiality, and not threaten future career progression or job security; achieve a non-judgemental environment; provide counselling for the potential range of employee's concerns, including work-related problems; and it would be able to assess and develop a range of suitable referral resources.

The negative aspects from an employee's perspective might be that the counsellor would have little or no authority to institute organizational changes. Communication goes from the employee to the counsellor, but external action comes from the manager to employee; therefore the value of the counselling resource depends on its ability to help an employee understand his or her own emotional problems and work out an effective solution to them, rather than implement changes on behalf of the employee. Employee-initiated solutions would be more likely to be adhered to and therefore enable them again to be fully productive not only in the workplace, but also at home.

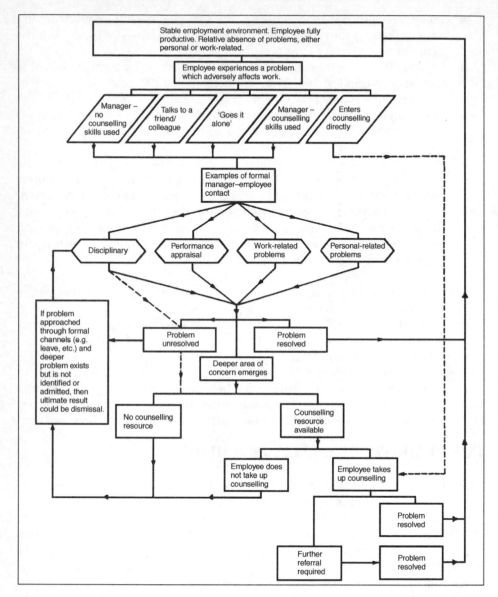

Figure 16.6   Interrelationship of counselling skills and counselling

Functions external to a counselling resource (e.g. line managers, personnel, trade unions, and so on) may draw upon its expertise in recognizing the extent of their limitations, and also that common objectives are shared: that is, those of a healthy, productive and happier employee and, consequently, organization.

One type of external counselling service which is increasingly being accepted is the Employee Assistance Programme (EAP). The EAP originated in the United Kingdom with the Employee Advisory Resource (EAR) in 1981. Since that time, several other programmes have emerged.

The EAP provides every employee (and member of their family) within an organization with access to counselling 24 hours a day every day of the year. In this way, the EAP is added to the benefits package and the employee can self-refer when they feel they want help and assistance.

THE OVERLAP BETWEEN COUNSELLING AND COUNSELLING SKILLS

We have discussed the use of counselling skills and the point at which counselling is more appropriate. The interrelationship of these aspects needs to be clarified to take into account the various permutations that may arise if an employee, for whatever reason, is not performing to the extent of his or her expected abilities. Figure 16.6 attempts to clarify these aspects and is based on the belief that work or personal-related problems may eventually affect a person's ability to maintain a fully productive position at work (or at home).

Once an employee becomes concerned about a particular area, there are a number of ways in which the person may respond. The type of response depends on the person's own coping mechanisms (vis-à-vis the type of problem) and the knowledge of suitable and available resources. The resources reflected in Figure 16.6 are taken to be: managers who are able to use counselling skills appropriately to facilitate the emergence, identification and potential resolution of the problem; an independent counselling resource which may be in-house or external, referred to by the manager or contacted directly by the employee; a sympathetic friend or colleague who can provide a shoulder to lean on; the person himself, who may be able to cope alone without any form of support; and lastly, the manager who does not employ counselling skills, becomes aware of declining work performance, and initiates directive action such as suggesting leave, proposing training, or even implementing disciplinary action which, if followed to its conclusion, could result in dismissal.

In other areas of concern, counselling may combine effectively with the range of other helping strategies to resolve difficulties. Redundancy is an example where the loss of a job may have repercussions which require a variety of coping mechanisms to be supported by different helping strategies as shown in Figure 16.7.

CONCLUSION

The benefits of counselling and counselling skills cannot be easily translated into neat, tangible ratios. Many of the benefits are preventive, which may appear in aspects such as reduced turnover (and associated recruitment costs) and absenteeism, and improved communication. These factors in turn

Coping mechanisms	Helping strategies
Financial planning Pension questions Statutory benefits }	Information giving and advice
CV compilation Application form filling }	Teaching and guidance
Interview training Job search activities }	Coaching
Personal problems Personal stress and anxiety }	Counselling

Figure 16.7 Coping mechanisms and helping strategies in a redundancy situation

Counselling is	Counselling is not
● Counselling is thinking with another person.	● Counselling is not thinking for another person.
● Counselling is a process for solving problems.	● Counselling is not speaking adages or cliches about what someone else ought to do.
● Counselling is accepting another person's feelings as relevant data bearing on the problem at hand.	● Counselling is not simply being sympathetic towards another's feelings.
● Counselling is understanding human nature and realizing that people are alike in some ways and unique in others.	● Counselling is not merely the application of techniques.
● Counselling is assisting in changing things and developing confidence.	● Counselling is not an ego trip for the counsellor.
● Counselling is building self-reliance by aiding someone else in making decisions and fulfilling commitments.	● Counselling is not being arbitrary or manipulative.
	● Counselling is not just talking things over.

Figure 16.8 What counselling is and is not

would be reflected in improved productivity and quality, plus better morale and job satisfaction. The contribution of counselling to the working environment and employee wellbeing is an aspect which may be 'felt' by the whole organization, but is not easily measured. Counselling, it must be remembered, is distinct from counselling skills, and the two should not be confused.

CHECK LIST

The use of counselling skills and counselling share a number of basic principles. Both can be used with good effect to resolve conflicts, implement changes, and facilitate decision making. There are clear guidelines for what counselling is and what it is not, as set out in Figure 16.8.

FURTHER READING

de Board, R., *Counselling People at Work,* Gower, 1983.
Kennedy, E., *Crisis Counselling: The essential guide for non-professional counsellors,* Gill & Macmillan, 1981.
MacLennan, N., *Counselling for Managers*, Gower, 1996.
Megranahan, M. S., *Counselling: A practical guide for employers,* IPD, 1989.
Nelson-Jones, R., *Practical Counselling Skills,* Holt, Rinehart & Winston, 1983.
Palmer, S., Dainow, S. and Milner, P. (eds), *Counselling: The BAC counselling reader,* Sage, 1996.
Reddy, M., *The Manager's Guide to Counselling at Work,* British Psychological Society, 1987.

The Counselling at Work Division of the British Association for Counselling provides an information and support network for people who use counselling or counselling skills in work or work-related settings. For further information please contact:

John Whapham
Secretary CAWD
6a Emmanuel Avenue
Acton
London W3 6JII
Tel: 0181 992 9094

17 Motivation

Jessica Levant

Without a workforce motivated to actively help the business survive, organizations slip (or freefall) into decay. Global competition demands constant creativity, innovation, attention to market trends and customer needs, and all that requires a committed workforce. In today's slimmed-down organizations – frequently staffed with people who have experienced their co-workers being cut from the payroll, and who may still fear that 'they are next' – employees are expected to do more work to tighter deadlines at higher quality than ever before. The task of motivating these 'survivors' to focus their energy and commitment into keeping the organization successful is not easy – but it is very important. And the manager who masters the ability to motivate people, even in the aftermath of staff cuts, is exhibiting the one attribute that sets apart a truly excellent manager from the rest.

There is no magic in it. With some thought and the will to get it right, any manager can develop the skills of motivation.

WHAT DOES MOTIVATION REALLY MEAN?

In its simplest terms, motivation may be defined as: *an internal state which initiates or drives some kind of human behaviour.* Not very helpful, perhaps, but the definition does highlight two fundamental considerations:

1　Motivation is an 'internal state': you cannot 'do' it to someone else.
2　There is desirable and nondesirable behaviour.

What managers have to do is to structure the situation – manage themselves and the environment – in such a way as to elicit the type of behaviour they want to see in their workers.

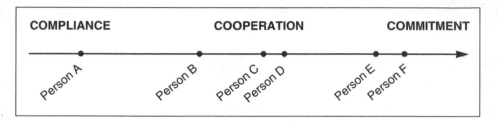

Figure 17.1   Compliance-commitment scale

DOES EVERYONE NEED 'MOTIVATING'?

Some people just seem to exude enthusiasm for everything they do, while others plod along apparently not caring. The issue for managers in the first case is to channel the enthusiasm to achieve the *right* outputs. With the 'plodder', more exploration is necessary.

A useful way of thinking about this is to plot a line from compliance to commitment (see Figure 17.1). At the left side of the scale the person does the minimum required. At the right, there is initiative, enthusiasm and creativity. Managers can choose either to assign work according to where people are on the continuum, or to employ skills to move people along towards the right-hand side.

Later in this chapter we shall look at how the manager does this. First, it will be helpful to examine how motivation works within the person.

WHAT THE RESEARCH SHOWS

The 'hierarchy of needs' theory developed by Abraham Maslow, an American psychologist and university professor, claims that the 'internal state' is determined by the individual's current perceived need, and that there are five levels of needs which drive behaviour (see Figure 17.2). The most basic need is physiological (e.g. hunger, cold, pain), and when that need is evident, the motivated behaviour will be focused on satisfying it. The next level of need is for security, which will motivate the individual to do those things which make him or her feel safe. After security comes a need for social interaction – a sense of belonging – which encourages people to do those things that make them feel 'accepted'. The fourth level is 'esteem' – the desire to have a positive self-image, self-esteem and esteem from others. The need for esteem will motivate people to try to 'shine', to be noticed, to go beyond the expected limit. Once all of these needs are satisfied, Maslow says, the highest level of need, for 'self-actualization', becomes apparent. Self-actualization – or the need for personal growth – causes individuals to do those things that develop their fullest potential.

While this theory makes perfect sense, and is useful for understanding why an individual staff member may be behaving in a particular way, it does not offer much help to the manager in raising the level of needs-driven behaviour.   *259*

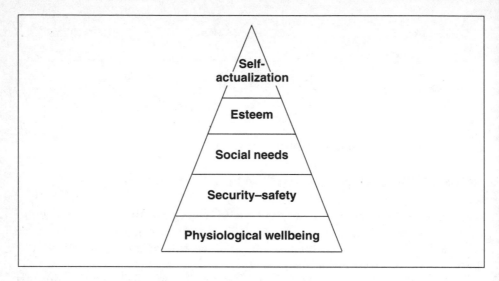

Figure 17.2   Abraham Maslow's 'hierarchy of needs'

Another frequently cited model of motivation comes from Frederick Herzberg, also an American psychologist and university professor. His theory, based on extensive research on job attitudes across many countries, defines two types of factors: one which motivates, and the other which merely satisfies, but does not drive behaviour (see Figure 17.3).

He found that certain factors previously thought to motivate were simply contributors to job satisfaction. The lack of these factors causes dissatisfaction, but their presence did not cause motivation. Herzberg labelled these 'hygiene factors', and they include: company policy and administration, supervision, relationships, working conditions, wages and fringe benefits, status, personal life and security.

Hygiene factors	Motivating factors
Factors on the job that lead to dissatisfaction	*Factors on the job that lead to motivation*
• Company policy and administration • Supervision • Work relationships • Working conditions • Salary • Personal life • Status • Security	• Achievement • Recognition of achievement • The work itself • Responsibility • Advancement • Potential for growth

Figure 17.3   Frederick Herzberg's research findings

A distinctly separate set of factors are called 'motivators', and they comprise achievement, recognition for achievement, the work itself, responsibility, advancement and the potential for growth. The implications of this theory are that to motivate people, the job must be 'enriched' and the organization must have the right processes in place in order to provide these motivating factors.

While not refuting any of the above concepts, the third and last theory to be presented here is much more practical from the point of view of the manager. First conceived by Victor Vroom of Yale University, it is called 'expectancy theory' and focuses firmly on behaviour.

Human behaviour, Vroom explains, is a function of two factors:

1 The perceived *value of the reward* that certain behaviour yields.
2 The expectation in the individual that *certain behaviour actually will yield that reward.*

Hence, the term 'expectancy'. Thus, in choosing between alternative behaviours, people will choose the behaviour that will result in their achieving the more valuable output or reward, *provided that they see the reward as attainable.* If they suspect the reward they most value involves a longshot or a significant risk, they will opt for an action or make a decision involving lesser value but greater expectation of success.

WHAT IT MEANS FOR THE MANAGER

To follow expectancy theory, there are five key steps the manager can engage in with an employee to ensure that the desired performance will be rewarded and that the reward will be valued by the individual:

1 *Define the expectations* In order for the 'reward' to seem attainable, the manager must ensure that people are quite clear about how to achieve it. Take the time to describe the necessary steps, any interim outcomes and deadlines, and the required final output. Clarify what the employee is expected to do individually and what areas, if any, will be collaborative. Do not assume that the employee understands your meaning. Check for comprehension and gain agreement as to how the work should proceed, and ensure that the employee knows how to obtain any relevant information needed to complete the job.
2 *Make the work valuable to the individual* People work to achieve personal goals, whether the goal is money, recognition, achievement, challenge or satisfaction of social needs. When employees believe that working toward organizational goals will help them attain personally valuable goals, their commitment to achieving what the organization values is greater. Because people's goals vary, the manager has to know what each person values. The more you can tailor the work to the employee's own drives and preferences, the better results you can expect.

3   *Make the work achievable*   Especially in times of heavy workloads, work assignments must be accompanied by exploration of whether the person is able to do the job. Fear of not being able to do a job successfully is often demotivating. Make sure the employee has the skills or the support to do the job, and if necessary, help the worker develop the needed confidence. Where there is concern, monitor progress.

4   *Give regular feedback*   Feedback is a reward in itself. Given well, it shows people that what they do is important enough to be commented on. It should not be limited to performance appraisal time! Give critical feedback as quickly after the action as possible. Be very specific, but avoid long lists and past grievances. Stick to descriptions – not labels – of behaviour. Make it a habit to let employees know when you think they are doing well, and again, be specific, so that they know what is especially valued about their behaviour.

5   *Reward employees when they meet expectations*   While people do give themselves internal rewards, the external rewards a manager can give will reinforce the more powerful internal ones. Be creative about rewarding: individualize the reward to suit the person. While money may be appreciated in the short term, people may attach more meaning to a write-up in the local newsletter, recommendation for a special project, increased responsibility, attendance at a conference, or, on the personal side, dinner at a special restaurant or a case of wine. One UK supermarket chain rewards high performance with a month's use of the company Jaguar!

In addition, relating back to Herzberg's findings, there are other actions managers can take to increase motivational levels:

1   *Make your staff feel valued*   Feeling valued comes from two sources: the work and the people.

- Ensure that each individual understands why their work matters to the larger organizational picture.
- Promote feelings of camaraderie both among your employees and between you and them. Treating them as 'people', not 'workers', will go a long way here. The 'team spirit' that results creates a personal commitment not to let fellow workers down.

2   *Job design*   Look at the job itself, perhaps jointly with employees, and 'redesign' it to add enrichment: for example, enlarge the scope, include more challenge for the employee, link it with development opportunities, enhance the relationship structure or opportunity to work with new colleagues, add variety, devolve decision making. In other words, introduce whatever will make the job itself more interesting or exciting to the particular employee and, at the same time, produce the desired output.

REQUIRED MANAGEMENT SKILLS

'Behind' the steps outlined above are key management skills that not only enable employees to perceive the manager as fair, supportive and worthy of their trust, but also help the manager to 'know' the individual employees.

Being perceived as fair means that managers have to make a special effort to deliver what they promise – or, indeed, not to promise what they cannot deliver. They must also treat employees equally in terms of difficulty of assignments, value of rewards, granting of favours, and attention paid to their wellbeing.

Building trust and being supportive are the results of well-developed inter-personal skills. Trust happens when there is a degree of interpersonal disclosure creating a personal bond. Where there is an atmosphere of personal trust, employees are not fearful of sharing their more personal dreams and concerns. The manager must be able to draw out information about what is most important to the employee as well as what the current concerns are. This means employing excellent listening skills, withholding judgemental comments, demonstrating empathy and expressing a sincere concern for the individual. Remember that trust builds up over time but can be broken instantly.

Supportiveness includes making time to explore problems, using good coaching skills to assist the employee explore solutions, offering or arranging for help, and making resources available for development when indicated. Again, showing genuine interest in the lives of employees reinforces the perception of the manager's commitment to support.

Moreover, the manager has to be a role model. Where deadlines are considered crucial for the employee, then the manager must be seen to meet them also. When quality is demanded from employees, it must be seen to be valued by the manager as well. If the manager is merely a conduit for the organizational values, but is perceived not to care about them personally, employees will not be motivated to work to those values.

HOW TO FIND OUT WHAT MOTIVATES PARTICULAR INDIVIDUALS

There are no short cuts. Managers must speak face to face and at length with each staff member in order to understand what they value. And this type of exploration may take more than one meeting, since trust must be built up before people will feel comfortable disclosing what is really important to them.

If you have not done this before, let people know you will be conducting goal exploration sessions with them, and do not be afraid to be honest about the reasons. People respond well to interest in them, but only when it is clear why it is being exhibited. Be forthright about needing their commitment. The point of the discussion is to work out together how to achieve this. If you have established a climate where employees respect and trust you, they will want to help you meet 'your need' if they possibly can.

Cover all types of goals – day-to-day, long-term, problem-solving, personal and so on. Use your listening skills to penetrate behind the surface comments. Move into joint problem-solving mode if you are met with 'It's just a job' or 'I just want to do a day's work for a fair day's pay'. Remember that *your* goal is to learn what the employee values, and how you can link that to reward, whether the reward is to be proffered upon task completion or is inherent in the job itself.

Goal exploration need not be limited to goal-setting sessions, however. Opportunities arise daily for managers to gain more information. In discussing individual work assignments, during a feedback discussion, walking back from a meeting, over a sandwich or coffee, during any social activities, and so on, managers should always keep their 'antennae' tuned for information.

WHAT ABOUT MONEY?

Time after time studies have shown that money – following obediently from Herzberg's original research – does not motivate workers to perform better. In research at business schools, on the shop floor, in management training programmes and in surveys of readers of various daily newspapers, it is the job challenge, involvement, recognition and the like that ranks higher than money as a motivating force. Money does sometimes provide short-term rises in motivation, and given the right match between a particular employee's personal goals and the possibility of a monetary reward, it may provide a short-term boost to productivity, but financial inducement should be used with caution. The reward value quickly wears thin. The only exception to the 'don't throw money at the problem' rule is with commission-based salespeople. For others, whatever their level in the organization, and despite the current preponderance of performance-related pay schemes, the evidence is clear: money does not motivate and more money does not motivate more.

HOW DO YOU MOTIVATE OFF-SITE STAFF?

A very current issue is that managers often do not have physical proximity to their workers. A 1996 study showed that there are at least 150 000 home-based teleworkers in Britain. A different study claims that over 7 per cent of UK employers use teleworkers. If some staff are working from home or are in the field more than the office, how do the motivational activities above apply?

Basically, all the same steps must be taken. The difference is that the manager will have to work harder to make them happen. Even if the home-workers are chosen from those with high levels of self-reliance, it is foolhardy to 'just let them get on with it'. Because the 'observation' component that comes into play with on-site staff will be missing, keeping in regular contact with off-site staff is very important. Frequent notes, E-mails, telephone calls, and making the effort to meet the employee off-site on occasion, will all enable plenty of interactions to occur. Feedback should be frequent – to praise, to give constructive developmental comments, and to let the off-site worker know that their work is noticed and valued. Consider a weekly (or some other reasonable timescale) contact in order to go over what has been accomplished, what the period ahead will look like, and how the staff member is finding the work. Allow time for questions, enquire about the person's well-being, and pay attention to any changes.

WHAT GOES WRONG?

The guidelines set out above are not new, nor are they complicated. Yet many managers continue to complain that they cannot 'motivate' their people. The main reasons are often because the manager is not 'finding' the time to deal with people issues or has not developed the required inter-personal skills.

With a typical manager now being responsible for a larger workforce, while, at the same time, probably serving on task groups, running special projects and being expected to come up with new ideas, it is easy to ignore the 'people' side of management. A conscious effort *must* be made to organize the day so that this does not happen.

Today, many managers have achieved their present positions by being good at the technical side of their jobs, and have never been encouraged to work on developing their interpersonal skills. Yet the one-to-one relationship between manager and employee is based on these skills. Most organizations now offer development opportunities to improve feedback, coaching, and influencing skills. Having the chance to role-play staff discussions will build both skill and confidence.

Finally, because they are only human, some managers are fearful that if employees outshine them, their own position will be placed in jeopardy. The result can be lack of attention to the employee, resulting in lowered motivation and reduced output. Ironically, however, from the organizational point of view, it is the manager who is seen as not doing well because he or she is not getting the best out of their team.

In sum, before putting the 'problem' down to poor employee morale, the manager would do well to engage in some self-assessment and soul-searching. The benefits of being at the helm of a high-performing team are far reaching and extend beyond the workplace.

CHECK LIST

The following questions can help you decide where you focus your own energy in developing your motivational skills.

Look inside

● Do you harbour resentment toward any of your staff?

If so, can you discuss it with a third party, possibly a 'disinterested' person?
Try to explore the reality of the 'threat' and look for some common ground on which to base a dialogue.

● Do you believe people can be inspired?

Read Ricardo Semler, *Maverick* (see below).

Skills check

Do you need to improve your:

Look into training possibilities and:

● listening skills?   See Chapter 12
● feedback skills   See Chapter 14
● coaching skills?   See Chapter 13
● time management?   See Chapter 2

Actions

● Do you model the behaviour that you require in others?

Take stock and be stern with yourself!

● Have you set up periodic meetings with each employee?

If the problem is time, make the planning a joint effort with your staff, your boss or your secretary.

Processes

● Do you know something unique about each one of your staff members?

Keep a notebook handy – even on the train. Try to imagine what makes each person 'tick'. Then check it out when you meet.

● Have you set up a 'goals section' in each employee file to keep track of their particular 'motivators'?

If not, do so – or some other system that works for you.

● Do you let your employees know you as a person, and not just as a manager?

Share lunches, sport or social activities. Do not be afraid to disclose some personal information – what you like, your own goals, what worries you, and so on.

FURTHER READING

There are multitudes of books on motivation or 'how to manage people' lining the management shelves of bookshops or even obtainable at airports. Those I have chosen to list are a personal selection of particularly 'good reads' that will inspire or provide a very practical base for the busy manager.

Bardwick, J. M., *Danger in the Comfort Zone*, Amacom, 1995. A template to help you decide how to deal with staff according to the cultural climate and individual reactions.

Byham, C. B. and Cox, J., *Heroz: Empower yourself, your coworkers, your company*, Harmony Books, 1994. A fantasy about the value of empowerment.

Herzberg, F., Mausner, B. and Synderman, B. B., *The Motivation to Work*, Chapman & Hall, 1959.

Maslow, A., *Motivation and Personality*, 3rd edn, Harper & Row, 1987.

Semler, R., *Maverick*, Arrow, 1994. The fascinating tale of a Brazilian conglomerate that was rescued from failure by unorthodox management practices.

Vroom, V. H., *Work and Motivation*, Wiley, 1964.

Waterman, R., *Frontiers of Excellence: Learning from companies that put people first*, Nicholas Brealey Publishing, 1994. Lessons about involving workers and creative rewards from several successful companies.

18 Team building

Alan Cook

Team building is the process of helping a team to become more effective in the way it operates, and to assist it in achieving more. A group of people working together can do more collectively than individually and separately, as their range of skills and experience together create accomplishments with a greater potential than the sum of those individuals on their own. But to be this effective requires a pulling together and focusing of complementary abilities, finding and establishing productive and efficient methods of working on tasks together, and the development of excellent working relationships. This does not happen immediately upon the formation of a team, but conscious attention to the known processes that make teams work well can accelerate progress. That is one reason for spending time and money on team building or development. The second reason is that people are complicated, changeable and emotional beings and this directly affects what happens within working groups and teams. Tensions, confrontations, personality clashes, unhealthy alliances, and power struggles always occur in groups that work, or live, together for any length of time. Effort spent on understanding and finding ways to deal with and resolve these problems helps a team remain focused and productive.

Teams vary hugely – any group of people trying to achieve something together is a team. Within this definition there can be huge variations: the number and types of people, aims of the group, circumstances, available resources, timescales of operation, environment, and external support are some of the most obvious. All of these will affect how a team operates and need to be considered when deciding how to build or develop a particular team. There are many techniques/exercises available for developing teams, ranging from self-managed activities (including some excellent and reasonably priced commercial packages) to highly developed programmes requiring expert facilitation. These also span in-house discussions to complex and lengthy outdoor events. All of them have their place but should be selected wisely. To decide exactly what to do with a particular team, and how, is often hard for managers. Too many managers opt for an obvious – or even the first – possibility, without thinking through what is really required and will work best. In this chapter I shall set out a process that will help you decide this, followed by some suggestions for activities that you could organize yourself. After commenting briefly on team dynamics, I shall conclude with a check list and suggestions for further ideas and reading.

THE PROCESS OF TEAM BUILDING

Any team-building or development activity is only as effective as the accuracy and depth of analysis carried out in setting it up and selecting the activities utilized. Most managers do not spend enough time working out what should or needs to be tackled and ensuring that the methods selected are relevant and helpful. Deciding a few weeks before where to hold the activity and who is going to run it is not good enough – although very typical, in my experience. In these circumstances, a day out together at the seaside, or an evening at bingo, would probably achieve more for the team! Below I describe the process that I follow, and encourage others to, when designing and preparing for any team-building or development process.

Define aims/objectives

The first stage is briefly to consider the aims or outputs required of the team development: that is, what the team should be doing differently as a result of team-building or development activities. Write a statement that summarizes the behaviours that an outsider experiencing the team would see as a result of changes and improvements. Do not spend too long on this exercise. More time will be spent later on analysing this aspect, and this step is just to start you off.

Assess the team's current state

Review the team's current ways of working and summarize the main features that best describe it. Think through the history of the team – you may find it helpful to draw a 'lifeline' of its history until now, which would probably include when and how the team started, significant and positive achievements, negative experiences, and important changes. (Note: this is an activity that can be done by members of a team in small groups or together to find out how the past is affecting present team operations.) Work out what are the current strengths and potential of the team, and then focus on its limitations and the difficulties it faces. Consider whether any recent circumstances are affecting or influencing team members, and ask yourself why you are contemplating team development at this point in time: for example, perhaps because of a recent precipitating event. Other techniques that can help you at this *269* stage are drawing a 'spidergram' – a picture of how you see the team – which can give you an overview of what is going on and crystallize in your mind what the real issues are. Discussing these issues or concerns with someone else can also help to clarify them.

Define the team competency gap

At this stage you should think about the differences between what the team is currently doing and what it should or needs to be doing. You know the timescales on which the team operates: for example, it may be a project team operating over a few months, or an established team dealing with longer-term policy matters, or something vastly different such as a production or sales team. Start, therefore, by looking ahead, and try to define what the team should be doing at some specific date in the future, and in particular – and in as much detail as possible – what will need to change in order for it to be working superbly well on that date. Under the section 'Areas of team effectiveness' below, you will find further detailed ideas about how to analyse the functioning of a team.

Define your aims and objectives

From the above analysis you can now write the specific objectives for team building or development. Try to write these in behavioural terms: that is, describing in detail the improved behaviour that you will experience as a result of the team development activity. In light of your analysis, review the statement you wrote initially about the behaviours expected as a result of changes and improvements, and amend it accordingly. Note: so far I have written in terms of a manager carrying out all of the setting-up activity. It could, however, be done by or with the team, which would create involvement and actually start the process of development through encouraging participation and ownership. I would encourage this, and recommend at least some discussions with your team before activities commence, otherwise they will feel that any team development is being done *to* them rather than *for* them.

Select methods/activities and devise the programme

Activities in team building/development generally follow the classic change procedure for human systems: unfreezing, moving and changing, and refreezing. Good team-building processes start with learning about how effective teams operate. Knowledge about team dynamics, team-working processes, and the stages of team development provide people with a framework for assessing their own team's performance. Such analysis creates awareness and insight so that teams can begin to identify their own strengths and weaknesses. For some teams, this may be sufficient to 'unfreeze' them and allow them to move forward without special action. Other teams may need to plan and implement activities which will enable the development of full team capability.

Practical issues should be reviewed: for example, time availability, financial resources for paying for facilitation, accommodation, materials and sustenance. The venue should be carefully considered; on-site is not a good idea as, despite best intentions, there are always interruptions and distractions. You may also choose to build something into work activities on a regular basis rather than setting up a specific event.

The actual methods to use, or activities to select, will depend on the aims and objectives defined. In the section below ('Some activities') you may find exactly what you need. If not, there are many manuals available (see 'Further reading' for some suggestions). You will need to work through the objectives, finding or devising activities that will help the team achieve each one, and then construct the list of activities into a cohesive programme. Do not forget to allow time for reflection, discussion and breaks. Do not try to achieve too much in one session. And remember that time for listening to each other is the most important of all.

Running the event

There are two options here: self-help or using a facilitator from outside the team. Of course, even if help is sought this can be specific and targeted, and can be integrated within a largely self-managed process. Criteria for the choice may include:

- The stage of development the team seems to be at.
- The nature and degree of problems it is facing.
- The urgency with which the team needs to reach full capability.
- The resources available to assist the team's development.

These criteria will help to identify the particular type of external help that may be needed: for example, problems of cooperation among team members will benefit from a skilled facilitator in interpersonal behaviour; problems in boundary management may be tackled by the team identifying a new strategy and action plan to deal with the particular weaknesses.

Practical considerations include sensible starting/finishing times that respect the dependence needs and travel arrangements of team members, and reasonable time allowed for meal and refreshment breaks.

Evaluate afterwards

Always evaluate the effectiveness of any team development event by assessing the following two dimensions:

1 *Initially:* Was the event itself enjoyable and useful? Did the team members find it both challenging and helpful? Did it move the team forward?   *271*

2   *Some months later:* Have there been lasting changes in the team? How has the team progressed? Is it still continuing to develop? And finally – back to the start of the process – what are the needs now?

AREAS OF TEAM EFFECTIVENESS

There are many ways of considering and defining the ingredients of effective teams. A survey of the most widely read books on team development shows the following areas to be important, and anyone trying to develop a team should consider to what extent that team is successful in each of them. In addition to those listed below, the team developer should consider whether there are other areas of competence that the team in question needs: for example, specialist project management skills.

Task management activities

An effective team uses systematic and adaptable work practices and decision-making disciplines, while considering other possible alternatives. It also uses delegation, monitors progress, and ensures that the team fully achieves its purpose.

Interpersonal processes

A well-developed team is distinguished by the quality of the relationships between team members. First, they are positive to one another, sharing information and feelings, and they listen, collaborate and confront constructively. Second, they value and support one another and put effort into maintaining excellent working relationships.

Personnel

A high-performing team has in it the right people, who know how to complement each other. They are clear about their own and others' jobs and competencies, and they use different team roles to contribute to the purpose and aims of the team. Individual strengths are utilized, while limitations are acknowledged and coped with.

Development

An accomplished team tends to its own development. It does this in two ways. First, it has a capacity to review experiences, with individual team members altering behaviour and practices to enhance individual and group performance. Secondly, it actively develops its capacity to meet new challenges and demands through anticipating needs for new and increased competency levels, and specifically obtaining or developing these.

Purpose

In an excellent team, the members have a shared and clear view of their goals and main objectives, and they adopt an action-oriented approach towards achievement. The main purpose(s) influences all decision making and activity – progress and completion is celebrated and discussed.

Leadership

Good teams require good leaders, who stimulate high performance focused on the team's purpose. Leaders must be responsive to the task and individual/group needs, and will support and reward team members. Leadership can reside in one person or be shared; either way it will operate flexibly.

External focus

Superb teams know that they work within a context – often a larger organization. They scan the working, commercial, political and social environments around them and carry out the following two activities:

1 Identify trends, ideas, opportunities and forces affecting their purpose, and deal with these or use them.
2 Actively promote the team's purpose and achievements.

At all times, external relationships are prized and worked at.

STAGES OF TEAM DEVELOPMENT

Like individual people, teams go through stages of development. Much has been researched and written about this, and a typical process of growth is described below. We also know that high-performing teams can regress in the face of great difficulties or unanticipated changes, and that unmanaged destructive interpersonal relationships can destroy effectiveness (refer to the next section for more on this).

Stage 1 'Start-up'

This is the beginning, when the team is newly formed, and is characterized by uncertainty and lack of clarity. Not much is known about each other, or the tasks required, and communication is superficial.

Stage 2 'Trying-out'

At this stage the team is experimenting with different ways of operating and relating, with much excitement and energy. However, this energy can be unfocused, and there is often a great deal of conflict and anger as well. Leadership is often challenged or ignored at this stage.

273

Stage 3 'Advancing'

The advancing team is one that is beginning to forge strong working relation-ships, and starting to focus more readily on achieving results, while minimiz-ing destructive patterns of behaviour. Leadership is beginning to settle down and exert positive control and influence.

Stage 4 'Reaping benefits'

The team has, by this stage, learned to operate effectively, while still recog-nizing the need to attend to team dynamics and processes.

Note: many researchers consider a further stage, when the team ends, splits up or is fundamentally changed. To be successful at this stage, a team will show concern and support for all members, and recognize the change processes that are occurring. Time will be allotted to working through the effects of these processes and appropriate methods of disengaging and refocusing will be utilized.

TEAM DYNAMICS

A dimension that can substantially affect team productivity is the quality of relationships and the behaviours occurring between people. If things are not going well, or there are difficult blocks, a deeper look may be needed at these areas. It is well known that the way we relate to others and behave in teams is profoundly affected by our own needs and desires, as well as being driven by the motivation to achieve new tasks. These personal dimensions can some-times impinge on team activities, creating tensions. For example, one per-son's need to be in a powerful and influential position all the time may clash with another's acknowledged position as an expert. If members are not used to acknowledging and holding strong feelings, pressure on the team may bring 'acting out' in the form of angry or hostile comments or unhelpful defen-siveness. It is not my intention to discuss this subject in depth, other than to point out this potential problem and to suggest that it be considered when developing a team. If it appears to be increasingly important, and cannot be discussed openly, then expert external advice or facilitation may be required to resolve the difficulties.

A SELECTION OF TEAM-BUILDING ACTIVITIES

In this section, possible activities that will help to build and develop the team are detailed under the same headings used above for describing the areas of team effectiveness. There are many manuals of team development activities available; if necessary for reference, select one that includes material which helps to explore the area of need you have identified.

Task management activities

- Use case-study or simulation as a vehicle for exploring and testing different task management processes.
- Learn about and explore the consequences of using different decision-making methods.
- Facilitate exercises in problem solving and decision making (e.g. consensus decision making).
- Use outdoor, task-focused, learning activities and experiences.

Interpersonal processes

- Share and assess team behaviours that help or hinder the team working well together – then agree together the changes required.
- Give and receive constructive feedback about each other's behaviour, strengths and limitations.
- Use video recordings of team meetings to analyse the team's dynamics – again, agree together the changes needed.
- Use a facilitator to observe, analyse and give feedback on the team's interpersonal behaviour.
- Facilitate practice of interpersonal skills and processes.
- Use 'time out' together (e.g. social outings or outdoor development).

Personnel

- Learn about and use various team role analyses (e.g. Belbin's team roles or the Margerison/McCann team wheel).
- Individuals share their potential and desired contribution to the team's work.
- Explore job/role expectations – and negotiate and agree meaningful roles in the team.
- Encourage team members to act in new or different roles, or rotate team roles around the team members, reviewing regularly the results.

Development

- Undertake regular reviews of how the team is performing and of outcomes achieved, and consider how improvements can be made.
- Consider any gaps in team skills and invite in external experts to help the team.
- Learn about, understand and consider the relevance for your team of the different stages of development of teams.
- Analyse individual learning styles of team members and assess the implications for learning together as a team.
- Involve team members in individual and collective performance appraisal processes.

Purpose

- Share perceptions of the team purpose, develop a united team mission, and identify team aims linked to it.
- Analyse values – of the team members and those central to the team's mission.
- Define the team's success criteria.
- Draw up a team manifesto setting out the product definition, outlining standards to be achieved.

Leadership

- Identify the team's leadership needs, analyse the leadership style of members and assess how to achieve congruency between the two.
- Use outdoor and other team exercises especially dependent on competent leadership.
- External adviser coaching and facilitating the team leader.

External focus

- Consider together how the team's creativity and competency is seen by outsiders.
- Develop a strategy for scanning the environment in which the team operates, noting where the team needs to market itself or achieve external influence.
- Identify a network of people who can help the team or who need to be influenced by the team.
- Use organizational surveys and assessment instalments.
- Use inter-team exercise (e.g. negotiation roleplays dependent on inter-group cooperation for a satisfactory result).

You may also wish to carry out some activities that help the team to an overview of how it is operating. The following may help:

- Draw a picture/write a description of the team and how it operates (artistry definitely *not* needed here!), as seen by individual team members, and compare and discuss the results (this can also be done in small groups).
- Do the above, but depicting/describing how members would like the team to be in the future.
- Each team member writes a list of ten words that describe the team – compare and discuss.
- Consider the areas of team effectiveness listed above and discuss how the team fares in each area, and how it could improve. Devise an action plan to take this forward.

CONCLUDING CHECK LIST

To start off, or to review team progress so far, consider the following questions:

- Why does the team need developing?
- What events and history of the team are affecting it now?
- Who are the people in the team, and how do they relate to each other?
- What stage of development is the team at?
- Do all team members have an effective role in the team, and if not, why not, and what can you do about it?
- What are the resources available to help the team develop?
- What are the practical constraints?
- Can the team help itself, or does it need external facilitation?
- How does the team fare in each described area of team effectiveness?
- What are the relationships like between the team and the other people/ teams it has to work with?
- What are the essential development needs, and over what timescale must they be dealt with?

FURTHER READING

Belbin, R. M., *Management Teams: Why they succeed or fail*, 2nd edn, Butterworth-Heinemann, 1996.

Buchholz, S. and Roth, T., *Creating the High Performance Team*, Wiley, 1987.

Hardingham, A. and Royal, J., *Pulling Together*, Institute of Personnel and Development, 1994.

Hastings, C., Bixby, P. and Chaudry-Lawton, L., *Superteams: A blueprint for organizational success*, Fontana/Ashridge Management College, 1986.

Larson, C. E. and Lafasto, F. M. J., *Team work*, Sage, 1989.

Leigh, A. and Maynard, M., *Leading Your Team*, Nicholas Brealey Publishing, 1995.

Margerison, C. and McCann, D., *How to Lead a Winning Team*, MCB University Press, 1985.

Woodcock, M., *Team Development Manual*, 2nd edn, Gower, 1988.

Woodcock, M., *50 Activities for Teambuilding*, Gower, 1989.

Woodcock, M. and Francis, D., *Organization Development through Teambuilding*, Gower, 1981.

19 Influencing
Richard Storey

Managers often believe that their communications with others are designed to inform rather than persuade. However, communicating information will always include the aim that the receiver should accept and believe what we have told them. When the American Management Association surveyed 2800 executives, asking, 'What is the number one need for success in business today?', the overwhelming response was: '*To persuade others of my value and the value of my ideas.*'

The chances are that like most managers you have to bring your influence to bear several times every day. Objectives to be kept in mind whenever you influence others may include:

- Wishing to maintain an existing relationship.
- Aiming to gain commitment to your proposition.
- Making certain that your message is passed on to other people.

Although you are in a position of authority over others, this in itself is not enough to ensure lasting commitment from those you influence. Inevitably, all influence gains some sort of reaction. On a scale of 1 to 5, these are the most likely responses you will receive:

1 *Total unswerving commitment* 'Brilliant idea. Can't wait to start.'
2 *General agreement* 'I like your idea but I have one or two reservations.'
3 *Compliance* 'OK, if that's what you want, I'll do it. You're the boss.'
4 *Overt disagreement* 'There are three good reasons why this won't work.'
5 *Covert sabotage* 'I may have agreed but I'm still not going to do it.'

Your eventual outcome should always be 'willing and cheerful compliance' or, at the very least, broad agreement.

Which of these areas of influence is of particular concern to you?

- Helping others to reach your conclusions, with integrity.
- Having some influence over an outcome.
- Convincing others that your suggestions are of benefit.
- Making people change their minds.
- Making convincing presentations.
- Negotiating successfully.
- Changing perceptions and beliefs.
- Convincing internal and external customers.
- Managing performance.
- Managing a project.
- Influencing senior groups.

Figure 19.1   Areas of influence

Increasingly, the successful manager is measured by his or her ability to influence others at work. With jobs at a premium and more people becoming self-employed, we all need to master the skills of influencing others in order to make the most of opportunities which present themselves. Unfortunately, there is no clear prescription for a 'best' approach to influence. This chapter presents a number of skills, strategies, tactics and techniques for you to over-lay on specific concerns that you may have (see Figure 19.1).

TEN KEY CHARACTERISTICS OF SUCCESSFUL INFLUENCERS

Studies have shown that successful influencers share attitudes and behaviours which ensure consistent success. These include:

- Maintaining a positive attitude and belief in what they are doing.
- Creating goals and realistic outcomes.
- Being flexible about how they achieve their outcomes.
- Using sensory acuity to help them 'read' people from body language signals and other subconscious behaviours.
- Building and maintaining rapport to create strong interpersonal relationships with a large network of people.
- Treating others as potential allies rather than enemies.
- Demonstrating integrity: that is, behaving in ways true to their own beliefs and feelings.
- Showing concern for the outcomes of others.
- Behaving 'as if' they will succeed.
- Having the reputation of a successful influencer.
- Being a good listener.

How do you match up? Which of these key behaviours would you like to demonstrate more consistently? Decide now on a personal action plan to develop your own powers of influence in all these areas.

SETTING YOUR INFLUENCING GOALS

Effective influencers operate in terms of the outcome of their influence, rather than set activities or processes. They focus not on *how* they will achieve influence, but on the *actual achievement* of their goal. This approach shifts the emphasis away from the processes, allowing greater flexibility of operation. An example of a process-bound goal statement might be: 'By the end of the meeting I will have convinced the board members to renew the contract for a further five years.' What is the goal – to achieve this *by the end of the meeting* or to renew the contract? If the board members do not agree by the end of the meeting, then you will have failed.

Outcome statements take the following format:

- Formally describe specific end results.
- Declare in positive terms what will be achieved.
- Include an awareness of the sensory evidence of achievement (what you will see, hear or feel when the goal is achieved).

Equally important to your success as an influencer is to understand the outcomes(s) of the person(s) you wish to influence. Influencers often fail to take into account the outcomes of others, which may be in direct opposition to their own desired outcome. The successful influencer will match or dovetail his or her own outcomes with others in order to produce a 'win–win' solution. Both parties will now achieve some or all of what they want, cementing their joint commitment to the proposal.

NETWORKING FOR GREATER SUCCESS

> Two thirds of all European business deals worth more than £6.5 million are agreed over a game of golf.
>
> (*Kapital*, German economics magazine)

Management can often appear a lonely occupation. Although you are an integral part of the organization you are probably attached to it in ways different from other managers Networking offers you a structured way of ensuring that your ideas and information are effectively exchanged with others. It also helps you to know colleagues, customers and others as individuals and to discover their values and beliefs, needs and wants.

Think of ways in which you can get to know your team, other managers, customers, senior figures in your company and outside agencies (such as suppliers, government bodies and so on). Join, for example, a management association, the Rotary or Round Table, business luncheon clubs, your local

Chamber of Commerce. Organize team events outside working hours – your team versus another in your organization (or play opposite a group of customers). Be seen at functions, offer to assist whenever you can, make yourself known; don't stand on the perimeter – dive in and become a familiar face. Never be afraid to ask advice or to seek opinions: this is a certain way to discover other people's basic motivation. Ask how things are done and why. Offer your advice and help, and make certain that you are available for others when they need you.

You could even take up golf.

UNDERSTANDING HUMAN MOTIVATIONS

To sell John Brown what John Brown buys, you have to see through John Brown's eyes.

Understanding and empathizing with others is the first step towards rapport – and rapport is the foundation of lasting influence. In order to influence others it is vitally important to understand as much as you can about their motivations. By doing this you can emphasize with precision the benefits and advantages you are 'selling'.

Many managers make the mistake of assuming that personal motivations are universal. 'What motivates me must surely motivate others.' Nothing could be further from the truth. Values, beliefs, needs and wants are far more complex than we tend to think. Most of us are driven by those matters we regard as important in our lives (see Figure 19.2). These might include: a house of our own; a healthy bank balance; a loving relationship; praise and

☺	Recognition	☺	Self-approval
☺	Security	☺	Culture
☺	Convenience	☺	Fashion
☺	Saving	☺	Religion
☺	Profit	☺	Love/affection
☺	Health	☺	Compassion
☺	Appetite	☺	Enjoyment
☺	Education	☺	Comfort
☹	Greed*	☹	Vanity*
☹	Fear*	☺	Sex*

Note:
*These needs can also be weaknesses. It is questionable to exploit these in others for the sake of influencing change – unless of course you can convince yourself that the change brought about is seen to have a positive outcome or that these needs are in themselves positive motivators.

Figure 19.2   Twenty basic human motivations

appreciation from those we look up to. But others may as easily be driven by negative motivations, such as greed, fear and envy; although negative, these drives can be every bit as powerful as the more positive motivators.

Some people are very skilled at observing behaviours and identifying motivations. It is common to base some judgements on 'gut feeling' which can often prove unreliable. There are three simple ways to understand what motivates other people:

1 Observe for yourself, conclude and verify your conclusions.
2 Ask the other person what motivates them (not as naive as it sounds). Observe what they tell you and verify its truth.
3 Ask a third party – someone who knows the individual concerned and has plenty of reference experiences on which to base a reliable judgement. Once again, observe and verify.

RAPPORT

Rapport is the bedrock of successful and sustained influence. Rapport can be defined as a harmonious relationship in which you feel naturally comfortable. Good personal rapport oils the wheels of most of the communications we have with other human beings (see Figure 19.3). Without rapport to smooth the interface of our daily communication, many potential opportunities to influence others can be lost. It is remarkably easy to develop early and lasting rapport with others with very little effort. You have excellent rapport with a variety of friends, relations and colleagues. You are already an expert. Therefore, your only requirement is to understand exactly what you do now that makes some of these relationships so successful, and then transfer the natural skills you use into all your working relationships.

People like people who are like themselves. Most problems concerning rapport lie in the fact that we are not like one another. Human beings are unique individuals. Try looking at matters from the following different points of view: your own; the other person's; and imagine how an outsider might view the situation.

In order to have empathy – that is, understanding how others see the world – it is not always necessary to agree with them or even to sympathize. Empathy is putting yourself in their shoes; sympathy is walking off in them. Making frequent contact with others and being prepared to self-disclose will help you to discover what you have in common.

It is easier to influence others if:

● You are able to form strong, long-lasting relationships quickly and easily.
● You understand how your personality dovetails with others.
● You can read and use elementary non-verbal communication.

Figure 19.3   Good rapport

	DOMINANT	
EXTROVERT	**Dominant extroverts** like to be allowed to make up their own minds, which they generally do quite rapidly. Do not try to butter up this type – they hate it. They would far rather hear your opinion expressed assertively.	**Dominant introverts** like time to think things through. They also want facts, figures and plenty of proof. They are often slow to self-reveal, so take time to get to know them. As they are seldom talkative people, choose your questions with care to get the best from them.
	Submissive extroverts are often jolly people, impulsive and eager to please. They have creative minds and appreciate innovative suggestions. This type can avoid making decisions in order to maintain a relationship.	**Submissive introverts** are definitely not impulsive. They are slow to trust and require plenty of careful nurturing support from you. Because they are themselves careful people they will expect care and thought from you.
	SUBMISSIVE	

Figure 19.4   Four types of personality

Overcoming a personality clash

By understanding whether a person is dominant or submissive, extrovert or introvert it is possible to see where your own personality matches (or clashes) with theirs.

The simple model in Figure 19.4 looks at personality from four angles. Notice which 'type' you prefer to deal with and why. Think what behavioural changes you may need to make in order to deal more effectively with those people with whom you presently have difficulty.

Using body language and behaving 'as if' you will succeed

The meaning of your communication is the response it elicits from others. If you notice that the reaction is not the one you want, change what you are doing or saying until you achieve the appropriate response. It is surprisingly easy to betray your own doubts and fears through verbal and non-verbal signals. Weak influencers pepper their sentences with negative words called 'weak modifiers' (see Figure 19.5), which signal concern that the outcome will be negative.

Use your voice tone to endorse your message and by stripping these negative words and phrases from your language you will strengthen your influence. Think, too, about what non-verbal signals you want to convey. Your posture, gestures, eye contact and even clothing all provide clues to other people about the strength of your intent. Your body language supports (or conflicts with) the words you use. The non-verbal components of your communication play a critical role and outweigh the verbal in both accuracy and

---

Weak modifiers include, for example:

● Possibly	● Might	● May
● Could	● Sorry	● Not usually
● Maybe	● Er ... umm ...	● I don't suppose

Figure 19.5   Weak modifiers

validity. Think how you want to look and how you would like your voice to sound to others. Imagine what effect your non-verbal communication is having. Does it support your message, or corrupt it? Read as much as you can on the subject (there are plenty of good books available) and begin to notice body language as a separate component of communication. Study the postures and gestures of successful and not so successful influencers, and notice how their non-verbal communication affects the message.

STYLES OF INFLUENCE

Different influencers achieve different results, and different personalities respond differently to influence. Depending on your outcome (and that of the person you wish to influence), the amount of commitment you seek, and how important the ongoing relationship is, you will need to choose the approach style most suitable and follow it through. There is no magic formula – you must have the flexibility to vary your approach as circumstances dictate.

The directive, push approach

The directive approach works best when it is accompanied and supported by power, authority, status or age. It can be a fast and efficient way of influencing and persuading others, since it is unlikely that there will be many serious objections to overcome. The process will probably take the form of a monologue rather than a dialogue. You will issue commands and receive little or no resistance.

The overuse of autocracy has its downside, however, as it is a one-way road. Others have little or no opportunity to 'buy in' to your ideas because those ideas will have been presented as a *fait accompli* with the expectation of full commitment. This approach often leaves others feeling 'You won, I lost.' Autocracy is a high-risk strategy. Therefore, only use your autocratic power when:

- you need a quick response;
- you seek only short-term commitment; or
- you are prepared to check that your suggestions are being followed correctly.

The collaborative, pull approach

The joy of the collaborative approach is that it works successfully without having to be backed with any power or authority on your part. By including others in the decision process, your proposals will attract a high level of commitment. This approach is most effective for developing and maintaining long-term influence, is low risk, and usually needs little or no enforcement.

Democratic collaboration is, however, a slower road to travel. The truly democratic approach to influence means handing over the entire decision process to others. Who is to say that they will arrive at the solution or answer you seek? It is likely that you will need to think things through carefully before inviting others to make decisions. Questions which you may want to consider could include:

- How long can I afford to wait for a decision?
- How many people can I usefully involve?
- Who should I involve?

The more democratic choices you can offer the more commitment you will gain. Try to avoid imposing too many parameters and conditions on the democratic influence process, as people find this frustrating. Democracy takes time – be certain to allow it that time.

The logical approach

Many people favour a logical explanation before reaching a decision. Although for some managers a demand for proof, detail, and supporting evidence can be tiresome, the logical approach to influence can offer very positive rewards.

No amount of optimistic enthusiasm will make someone who possesses a detailed, logical, linear way of thinking agree readily to your suggestions. The only way you can be certain of a sympathetic ear is by doing your homework. Leave nothing to chance – no guesswork, no exaggeration – just straightforward unassailable facts. And the more facts, the better – they are fascinating and convincing to the logical thinker. Naturally, the logical approach will take time: that is, time to prepare your argument, time to explain it carefully, and time while you wait for a reaction.

The emotional approach

Appealing to the emotions of others can be dangerous. Emotional decisions are often made on impulse. Perhaps sympathy, sorrow or even anger has been harnessed in order to influence an outcome, which can leave others with a sense of frustration and annoyance if they feel duped or emotionally blackmailed.

However, having checked the integrity of your objectives and motives, you *285* are quite in order to use charm or enthusiasm as a means of influence. Making other people feel part of an exciting project or idea is an extension of your own feelings. Enthusiasm has been defined as 'knowledge on fire', and it is fun to fire the imagination of others. This approach to influence works well with those people who are emotional or impulsive by nature, and who are swept up by the charm, charisma or sheer enthusiasm of your influence. By appealing to the long-term effects of your suggestions you will reinforce the continuing value of your ideas.

Advertising is a form of influence that frequently uses emotive words and phrases which can be incorporated successfully in conversation, presentations, meetings and written proposals or reports. So-called power words might include: *pleasure*; *happiness*; *love*; *security*; *admiration*; *appreciation*; and *satisfaction*.

Influencing through emotional appeal carries with it a risk. Check your motives carefully and remember that although this approach can be successful it can also leave a nasty taste in the mouths of those you persuade. Painful memories linger long –they will be out for revenge next time!

The assertive approach

Assertive influence is the use of clear and unambiguous language. By expressing your feelings you ask directly, calmly and confidently for what you want (or don't want). Being assertive does not involve aggression, simply firmness and resolve on your part. Maintain good eye contact, and speak in a level and unemotional tone, expressing your needs unequivocally and concisely.

Assertive influence works effectively with autocratic people or those who least expect assertion from you. You believe in yourself, you act and initiate, rather than react. Coupled with assertiveness, persistence can work wonders. This is a technique widely known as 'broken record'. You make your statement and, depending on the response you receive, you repeat it in a slightly different form. You keep doing this until the other person fully understands what you mean. Example: 'Can you process this by 12 o'clock, please?' 'I appreciate what you are saying but this document must be ready for this afternoon's board meeting.' 'Well, in that case your other work will have to be delayed.' 'That is not good enough. I will leave it with you and call back in an hour to see how you are getting on.'

The passive approach

At first glance, being passive seems at odds with exerting influence over others. The passive approach suggests that the rights and needs of others take precedence over yours. The option of influencing outcomes through submission is certainly viable as long as you can live with any feelings of low self-esteem or frustration it may engender. Do not dismiss the possibility of using passive or submissive behaviour to achieve the outcome you want. There will be many incidents in your life when submission can pay positive dividends.

Suppose you are stopped by the police for a minor traffic violation? What are you likely to achieve by aggression, or even assertion? The expectation is that you will remain passive and submit. Any other approach is likely to be counterproductive.

The persuasive approach

There is often a case to be made for good, old-fashioned salesmanship in management. Although most people claim that they do not like the sales 'type', we are, after all, perpetual 'buyers'. In a typical year we might make purchasing decisions to buy a car, a holiday or even a job. In most cases we expect and receive a certain amount of 'salesmanship' – we are all buyers, and buyers need salespeople.

The open and straightforward sales approach works well with anyone who expects to be sold to. A carefully planned sales case clearly shows how the benefits of your suggestion match the needs and wants of others. Objections and resistance can be overcome, and reaching a positive decision makes sense. The influencing style known as 'bridging' is an approach which works particularly effectively with people who cannot stand the overtly persuasive technique. There are three main paths to successful bridging:

1 Draw out the other person's point of view through careful questioning. Check their values and beliefs, needs and wants.
2 Using rapport skills, demonstrate that you understand and empathize with their point of view.
3 Lead them towards agreement by offering credit and praise in response to their good ideas and suggestions. Show clearly how these fit in with your own proposals.

The bargaining approach

Adam Smith, the eighteenth-century economist, suggested: 'Man is an animal that makes bargains. No other animal does this – no dog exchanges bones with another.' When we try to influence others there is often an imbalance. Yes, they may agree to our suggestions, but there is something which they would like in return. At this point the bargaining starts. It may be possible to add value to your idea through creative negotiation – not just sharing the cake but making the cake a bigger one. Given common needs and outcomes which complement one another, it will be your greater skills as a negotiator which lead to an acceptable 'win–win' resolution.

The one question which should be at the forefront of your mind before you embark on the bargaining or negotiating approach is: 'To what extent do I need to maintain this relationship?' If the answer is 'very little', then it may not be necessary to conduct an equal negotiation. However, most managers recognize the need to sustain an ongoing relationship with others, and a flexible approach allows them to trade concession for concession.

For the time when you find yourself having to negotiate, here are a few suggestions:

1 Set your sights high. You will probably have to lower them at some stage so it makes sense to aim at a higher outcome than you expect to achieve.

2 Find out what others want before you commence your negotiation. They will have a 'package' of needs, a shopping list, and unless you understand these needs *before* you start talking, they will probably spend the entire negotiation producing one demand after another. If this happens and you run out of concessions to trade, you will be forced to concede to their remaining demands in order to reach a final solution.

3 Do not *give* anything away – always try to trade one concession for another. Give something away that the other person wants only in return for something that you would like to have or retain. Even the most unlikely elements can be traded for one another: for example, time concessions for cost reductions, or agreeing to a better grade of company car in return for a smaller salary increase. Take care when you evaluate the apparent worth of a concession. It is tempting to say 'yes' immediately if the concession holds little value for you. Ask yourself: 'This may be of little value to me – but how much is it worth to the other person?'

4 Remain flexible at all times. Continue to seek even the most improbable way out of any impasse. Both sides want to negotiate a solution, so there should not be any need for the discussion to founder on any apparently insoluble sticking points.

Summary

- Different people and different circumstances demand flexibility of influencing style.
- Depending on the outcome you seek you will need to choose the style most suitable and follow it through.
- Change style only when you notice that you are unlikely to achieve your outcome if you continue the way you are going.
- The influencer who possesses the widest range or choice of style has the greatest flexibility of operation.
- The person who has the greatest flexibility will be the most successfully consistent influencer.
- Behavioural flexibility provides the maximum opportunity for eventual success.

MODELS OF STRATEGIC INFLUENCE

There are several well-known strategies used by influential managers. Here are three: the systematic (or ten-step) strategy; the soft strategy; and the harder strategy. Experiment with these models and notice the results they achieve. Which one do you feel the most comfortable using? Which one stretches you?

Model 1   The ten-step strategy

Use or adapt the following check list to help plan your approach to influencing in a more systematic fashion:

- *Step 1*   Prepare the background details of my forthcoming situation. (Who will I be influencing? Are they the decision maker or one of a group of decision makers? What will I be influencing them to do or think? When will I carry out my influencing ? Will it take one meeting, or many? Where will I conduct the meeting? What will be the advantages/ disadvantages of different locations?)
- *Step 2*   My specific objectives. (What outcomes do I want? What is the best? Worst? Likely outcome?)
- *Step 3*   What do I know about the values and beliefs, needs and wants of the decision maker?
- *Step 4*   How will the other person benefit from my proposition?
- *Step 5*   What influencing style will work best? Which style will be least productive?
- *Step 6*   What are the other person's typical (or probable) decision-making strategies?
- *Step 7*   What is their personality and how might it affect my strategy and tactics?
- *Step 8*   How will I develop and maintain good rapport?
- *Step 9*   What objections do I anticipate? How do I plan to overcome them?
- *Step 10*   How will I go about getting a decision?

Model 2   The soft strategy

Stage	*Skills necessary*
State your view of the problem	Agenda setting Presentation (do it tentatively) Seeking feedback
Clarifying others' perceptions	Listening Reflecting Questioning Summarizing
Get agreement to existence of problem	Handling of information Use of evidence Handling feedback

Seek solutions:
- propose solutions (see Model 3 below);
- invite their solutions;
- jointly seek compromise/best solution.

Model 3   The harder strategy

Stage	*Skills necessary*
Make proposal	Agenda setting Assertiveness Presentation
Get reactions	Listening Questioning Reflecting
Summarize and check	Summarizing
Deal with objections	Choice of appropriate influencing style or level according to whether commitment or compliance is required Resistance handling
Outcome	Summarizing Closing

Source: (for the softer and harder approaches) Purbooks.

FURTHER READING

Argyle, M., *The Social Psychology of Everyday Life*, Routledge, 1992.
Buzan, T., *The Mind Map Book*, BBC Books, 1993.
Carnegie, D., *How to Win Friends and Influence People*, Cedar Books, 1938.
Charvet, S. R., *Words that Change Minds*, Kendall/Hung Publishing, 1995.
Hopkins, T., *How to Master the Art of Selling*, Warner Books, 1982.
Laborde, G., *Influencing with Integrity*, Syntony Publishing, 1987.
Lambert, T., *The Power of Influence*, Nicholas Brealey Publishing, 1995.
Knight, S., *NLP at Work*, Nicholas Brealey Publishing, 1995.
Pease, A., *Talk Language*, Simon & Schuster, 1989.
Rackham, N., *Spin Selling*®, Gower, 1995.
Richardson, J., *The Magic of Rapport*, Meta Publications, 1987.
Storey, R., *The Art of Persuasive Communication*, Gower, 1997.

20 Communication

Krystyna Weinstein

Why do we discuss the issue of communication so much these days? Why do we become concerned when employee attitude surveys in companies tell us that staff receive most of their information through the grapevine and rumour, that no one tells them anything in time, that they don't recall what they have been told, or that they have little opportunity for 'upward' communication to tell management what they think?

WHY IS COMMUNICATION IMPORTANT?

Communication has been called the life-blood of an organization. Without it, little would be achieved. Until robots take over from us entirely at work, therefore, we will need to communicate with each other in order to do our individual jobs. In a sense, then, communicating is sharing.

We also communicate with each other because using each other as a resource is the most effective way of running any organization. It has taken many managements many years to recognize that people who do the day-to-day tasks in a company are likely to know more about that work than anyone else. Involving them, and hearing what they have to say, is therefore crucial. More importantly, communicating with people is recognizing their worth as human beings.

In a corporate setting, this means that we value people not merely as 'role people' but as 'whole people'. It is in everyone's interests that we all develop and make use of our varied skills, interests, and insights. Everyone, including the company, ultimately benefits. Tom Watson, who built IBM into a highly successful global corporation, believed that: 'the basic philosophy, spirit and drive of an organization have far more to do with its relative achievements than do technological or economic resources, organizational structures, innovation and timing.'

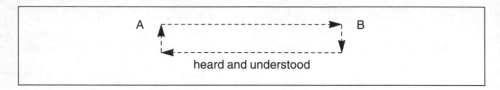

heard and understood

Figure 20.1   A simple communication model

Thus the quality of communication in an organization will affect staff motivation and job satisfaction, their sense of commitment and energy, and their performance and productivity. Staff will react to the 'climate' in the organization – and the main contributing factor to this climate is managers' values and styles.

A corporate philosophy that believes in openness, and in using all the human potential within its metaphorical four walls rests on, and must by definition be sustained by, good communications – upward, downward, and horizontal. Everyone must be involved and must be encouraged not only to communicate in all directions, but also to listen and be prepared to receive feedback.

WHAT IS COMMUNICATION?

Communication is about conveying 'messages' to others: it is both a 'process' (how do I communicate) and a 'content' (what do I communicate), though in fact they are often inseparable.

Two definitions encapsulate the simplest notions of communication:

1   Communication is social interaction through messages. The word 'interaction' focuses on a vital ingredient: the opportunity for feedback, without which there is no real communication. Only by checking back, asking for clarification, and feeding back one's own interpretations and understanding, are we truly communicating (see Figure 20.1); the alternative is a monologue. This 'interaction' involves three elements: the use of language (our prime, but not sole means of communicating with one another), our behaviour, and other symbols (e.g. status symbols that also communicate). The 'message' is the content: that is, what we are trying to convey, and what we inadvertently convey.

2   Communication is about creating shared meaning and understanding. By communicating – interacting – we are creating an opportunity to share our view of something with others and to hear about their views. We are building a common understanding. It gives us the opportunity to ensure that our words in particular, but also our behaviour, are not misunderstood or misinterpreted, as can so easily happen. For example, a shrug of the shoulders, or the use of a word such as 'responsibility', can be open to many interpretations.

WHY COMMUNICATION IS NOT SIMPLE

No organization is a gathering of homogeneous people. It is a mix of employees with different backgrounds and different levels of education. They bring to work different abilities and aspirations. Their past experiences differ, as do their present needs. Each performs a different job – exciting and demanding, or mundane and routine. Each plays a different role in the company, and views events and information from a different perspective and angle. Each will therefore require slightly different information/communication, in different forms and at different times. One of a manager's main jobs is to understand and cater for these differences.

Thus, what starts out as a simple model becomes complicated, with layers of potential confusion (see Figure 20.2). This chapter sets out to unravel at least some of the complexities of communication.

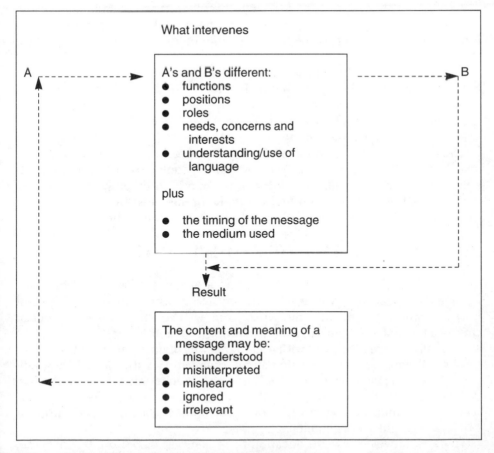

Figure 20.2   What can complicate communication

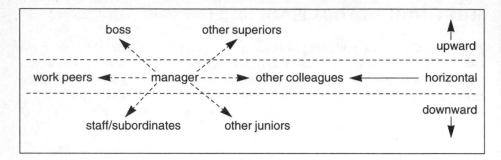

Figure 20.3   The manager as hub of a communication network

A MANAGER'S JOB IS ABOUT COMMUNICATING

It is by talking and listening that managers get most of their work done.[1]

Managers talk most of the time, and mostly face to face.[2]

As the quotations point out, communicating is a vital part of any manager's job. He or she is, in fact, at the hub of a communication network (see Figure 20.3).

Each contact made by the manager requires a differing form of communication. What a manager says to his or her boss, the language in which it is couched, where and how it is conveyed, will differ from what he or she says to subordinates or to other colleagues. The nuances are endless.

In order to perform the variety of roles that are required of a manager,[3] he or she needs various communication skills: to be able to express him- or herself clearly; to be both a good mixer and a good listener; to be aware, supportive, persuasive; above all, to be fair and open, and to be prepared to talk to everyone in this network. In other words, he or she must be able to manage the complex web of communications that surrounds him or her.

HOW CAN YOU MANAGE YOUR COMMUNICATIONS?

Communicating encompasses how we relate and interact, and how we behave and speak. It concerns what we say and to whom, how we say it, and how we convey it. (This includes what 'form' we use – the spoken or written word – and what 'medium' we use – a meeting or a memo.)

Journalists have long lived with a similar series of unstated 'questions' that they ask themselves when writing an everyday story with the right ingredients. These are: *who, why, where, when, what* – commonly known as the five Ws. These same five Ws apply to all communications. If you, as a manager, bear them in mind, no matter what communication you are involved with, you will have a useful set of guidelines.

There is, however, a sixth question to remember: *how*. Do I, for instance, communicate with my staff at a meeting, or by means of a memo? That choice is important, for as Marshall McLuhan said many years ago, 'the medium is the message', or at least an important part of it. And what does my language and behaviour communicate?

Although in this chapter we shall look at each of these six questions separately, in everyday life they are interlinked and inseparable: who you are communicating with determines what you will communicate, how and possibly even where.

Who you are communicating with

In everyday life, a conversation with our grandmother or our child will differ from one with a friend in a pub or winebar. The same is true in an organization.

The 'whos' in organizations will vary on a number of dimensions:

- *Who are they?* What is their position in the organization? Are they senior managers, supervisors, clerks or secretaries? This will begin to tell us about their needs, their interests, their level of knowledge, the questions they may ask us, the detail we need to give them, the language to use with them. In other words, every bit of organizational information has to be 'translated' to suit their needs, to be made relevant to them in their work or their position.
- *What is their role?* Are they from sales, production, personnel, research, finance, advertising? Again, their needs will vary and will be geared to their specific roles, activities, and perspective – for example, to produce more, save money, or ensure good working conditions.
- *Are they all from your own department?* Then at least they probably all speak the same or similar internal language or jargon. But that is still no guarantee that they will be interested in the same detail or angle.
- *How many different 'whos' are you communicating with* at any one particular time (e.g. at a meeting or when writing a report)? If many, you need to tell your story in different ways – while ensuring it is still the same story. You may even have to run several separate meetings, or prepare additional separate written pieces.

Your awareness of people's differing needs, and being prepared to cater for them, is a powerful message to those you communicate with.

Why are we communicating?

'Why?' is a vague question, not precise enough to elicit specific information. A more fruitful way is to ask: What has 'prompted' the need to communicate, and what 'outcome' am I seeking?

In organizations, any communication has a final purpose or 'outcome'. Something has to be done, or achieved (e.g. a particular task has to be performed, to ensure delivery of an item). That outcome has itself usually been *295*

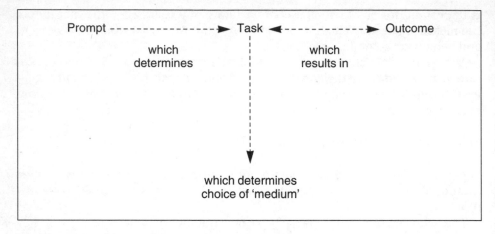

Figure 20.4   Why are we communicating?

'prompted' by something happening – or not, as the case may be. To continue our simple example, delays are being caused in another department.

Thus 'why we communicate' has two parts to it: a prompt, and a required outcome. Between them, the prompt and the outcome tell us what the 'task' of our communication is. It may be to teach, persuade, suggest, inform, motivate, establish good rapport with, and so on. Knowing what our task is, we can then decide 'how' best to go about it, that is, what medium to use: a memo, a training session, a pep talk, or greater involvement in the work of the department (see Figure 20.4).

We should also remember that when we communicate with someone in our organization on a work issue, the main outcome is an organizational one. Managers who observe this point are more likely to be fair in their interactions with others than managers who 'personalize' these organizational relationships.[4]

This is not to deny that we often have 'hidden agendas' when we communicate. The attractive man in the marketing department may be able to help me with my task, but I may also be interested in getting to know him better for other reasons! Nothing wrong in that. But I need to bear in mind that the organizational outcome is the one that dictates our communication, even when the marketing man has abandoned me for someone else.

Where will you communicate?

Where will you be communicating: in a one-to-one encounter, in a lecture hall, in your room, on the shop floor, at a meeting? Will the encounter be formal or informal? Will the other party to the interaction have notice of your 'communication'? Will they be prepared or caught unawares?

The answers to these questions will have implications not only for 'what' you can communicate, but also 'how' you communicate it. A personal reprimand on the shopfloor, or by memo, is less likely to achieve the desired effect than a face-to-face meeting in a quiet room. The 'task' gives us clues about where we can best communicate.

When will you communicate?

This is a perennial question for corporate communications. Rumour and the grapevine travel with an amazing speed and efficiency – with implications for managers. Get there first, or at least respond to them fast and honestly. We come back to management style and philosophy.

Not having time is used as a frequent excuse for not communicating. Yet not communicating is itself a powerful form of communication. It conveys messages about how unimportant the person not being communicated with is, how undervalued and mistrusted, and how important and scarce the information is ('information is power'). It also sends messages about the degree of commitment there is in the organization to 'open communication', in spite of all the protestations in corporate mission statements and board pronouncements.

Consider the issue of a possible plant closure. Conveying and sharing this information earlier rather than later, in an open way, would lead to a greater understanding of the issue, and a commitment to explore and find the best solutions.

What am I communicating?

The 'what' of communication is about content. What is the subject matter, the detail, level, slant and angle? What is relevant, and what is my 'task'? The answers to these issues will be derived partially from asking the questions 'who' and 'why'.

There are four categories of corporate communication, as follows:

1 *Job- or task-related* Without it, individual jobs and tasks would not get done.
2 *Organizational/work-related* Relevant, but not immediately vital, and the result of a cross-fertilization of ideas, which sparks off thoughts, and leads to developments or changes.
3 *Integrational* Involving people in the larger 'whole' of an organization, its values, vision and sense of purpose. It adds a perspective and meaning to their work, and gives them a greater sense of commitment.
4 *Housekeeping* Less job-, and more people- and place-related: who has moved where, who has joined, how the canteen is being renovated, an office party.

Be clear about which category any particular communication falls into, for each of these four should be conveyed by different means. It is a strange (but authentic) organization that one day used a memo to communicate the introduction of a new computer system which would revolutionize everyone's *297* work, and the next week used the same medium to ask employees not to throw orange peel into wastepaper bins.

Returning to the four categories:

- The first type would involve face-to-face communication, or possibly memo.
- The second would occur at meetings, and through other two-way communications (e.g. suggestions schemes), or focused and thought-provoking articles in a company newspaper.
- The third possibly through the well-written and thoughtful articles in a company newspaper but, crucially, backed up by everyday attitudes and behaviour, and further enhanced through training and other face-to-face communications, such as quality circles.
- The last by noticeboard, or in a section in the company newspaper (see 'What medium to use?' below).

By thinking about, and carefully deciding, what to communicate and to whom – provided you have assessed your recipient and his or her interests correctly – you are conveying your own understanding and sensitivity to your listener/recipient.

How shall I communicate?

Put simply, 'You can't not communicate'. Virtually everything we do when in the company of others communicates something to them. So, considering the five questions posed in the preceding sections, and creating the most appropriate 'communication', is a considerable step in the direction of good communications.

But there is obviously more to it than that. There are two further elements you have to consider: what 'medium' to use; and what impression you yourself give to others.

What medium to use?

There are a number of different way of communicating, as follows:

- *Orally* One-to-one; small groups; committees; larger meetings; telephone; training sessions.
- *In writing* Letter; memo; note; report; research study; noticeboard; text on a computer screen.
- *Visually* Using a variety of visual materials when writing or speaking (e.g. charts, diagrams, photographs, and film or video).

You can thus vary your communication. But you need to ask a number of questions. How important is the information? Which is the best or most appropriate means for the task in hand? Should the recipient be given the opportunity to respond, or ask questions?

Can the information you want to convey be sufficiently simplified and clari-fied to be passed on by the written word? Or is it more important or complex, and therefore better conveyed orally, giving your recipients the chance to ask for clarification?[5]

It is not possible in a short space to discuss which medium is most appro-priate for each occasion. But there is one simple test which will help: ask yourself which you would prefer yourself, if you were in the position of being a listener/receiver of the item you are planning to 'communicate'. If you have questions to ask, then the medium you need to use is a two-way, face-to-face one, rather than a written one.

The catch, however, is that as a manager you are likely to be more comfort-able with the written word than some of the other people with whom you deal and communicate. Your own preference in this case should be carefully con-sidered. Is your audience as literate as you?

If you opt for a face-to-face setting, you still have to decide whether a larger, more formal meeting is best, or a small discussion group. And that depends on whether the issue in hand is one which would benefit from a discussion, or whether it merely involves you imparting information.

	Downward communications			Upward communications		
	Used %	Prefer %	Prefer as % of used	Used %	Prefer %	Prefer as % of used
Noticeboard	57	17	24	n/a	n/a	n/a
Informal conversations with your immediate boss	55	33	44	62	39	52
Internal memoranda/letters to staff	49	17	25	24	10	30
Grapevine/gossip	45	3	5	26	2	8
Department/group meetings	39	30	46	34	27	48
Company newspaper/house journal	39	13	23	n/a	n/a	n/a
Briefing groups/team briefings	36	27	48	30	26	54
Formal appraisals on how well you are doing	33	20	34	27	18	39
Newsheet	32	12	21	n/a	n/a	n/a
Pre-arranged meetings with your immediate boss	32	25	43	37	30	48
Conversations with more senior employees than yourself	32	19	36	29	18	38
Meetings with people from other departments/areas of company	29	18	35	n/a	n/a	n/a
Video	28	9	28	n/a	n/a	n/a
Trade union meetings	23	8	26	21	8	30
Employee version of annual report	21	13	26	n/a	n/a	n/a
Via employee representatives	15	8	34	20	11	30
Letters column in company newletter	n/a	n/a	n/a	11	5	20
Via surveys of employee opinions	n/a	n/a	n/a	8	10	29
Some other method	3	1	19	2	1	38

Base: All respondents (1063)

Figure 20.5   Table of communication media (*Source:* IMS)

Employee preferences

Employees are frequently asked how they prefer to 'hear' information. Figure 20.5 illustrates the result of one typical survey. Most favoured were the various forms of face-to-face and two-way communications such as team briefings and regular, short departmental or section meetings – a method used successfully by Japanese firms here in the United Kingdom.

What also stands out from this and most other similar surveys is that employees want their manager to be their prime source of information.

The importance . . . and the intention

The importance of the communication will to a large extent dictate the medium. In the example given earlier, announcing a new computer system by memo is clearly using a totally inappropriate medium. Something as important as a change in work practices must involve many meetings and discussion groups – as well as written information – with all concerned.

The 'intention' or task will also dictate the medium. It is not possible, for instance, to motivate individuals by writing to them. The issue is too complex, needing insights into what motivates them, and why they are demotivated. You can only find this out by having some form of two-way communication.

The 'channel'

You also need to consider the 'channel' (see Figure 20.6). Do you wish to communicate something to everyone? Will you do this by meeting people individually, or in a group? Or will you inform representatives, who then pass on the information? And if you choose the latter, will the information get distorted en route? And will it matter?

Spoken communication

Spoken communication – if well planned, sympathetically conducted, and if the number of people is kept small (no more than ten people) – allows for discussion, sharing, and generally for productive communication, since people have the opportunity of contributing. Meetings (or team briefings) are an

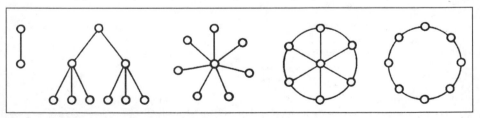

Figure 20.6   Varieties of channels of communication

excellent means of discussing work procedures, introducing changes, or resolving other work-related issues. For personal and individual issues, face-to-face communication is the best, possibly preceded by a letter to alert the other person.

So, consider: will you be better able to convey your message, and is it more likely to be heard and understood, if it is presented by you in person, in a discussion group, in some written form, or visually – or by a combination of all of these? And if the subject matter merits a discussion, what type of gathering do you think will be best?

Written material

Written material, being one-way, does not allow the recipient much opportunity to reply. Where a large amount of information has to be conveyed, the written form allows the reader to assimilate at his or her own pace. However, ask yourself whether your audience is as used to reading as you are; and if not, the shorter the message, and the simpler the language, the better.

For quick communication of a straightforward, uncontroversial nature (and as a manager you need to decide whether this is the case), the memo or letter is the easiest and most direct.

What impression do I give to others?

So far this chapter has looked at the 'mechanics' of how to communicate. But the other single most important element in any communication is yourself: the language you use; and your behaviour and body language.

Status . . . and subordinates

Whether we like it or not, another person's status frequently influences how we communicate, and particularly how we behave.

Plush office or open plan, great expanses of carpet or lino, which floor people inhabit, what they wear (dirty overalls or a dark pin-striped suit) influence how we behave – and in return how they behave towards us. Being told what a person 'does' also influences how we speak to them, involve them, and what we expect of them.

Being aware of this, and of how precisely any one of them influences you, is the first step to overcoming any 'distortions' that occur. 'Downward' communications (see Figure 20.2) are particularly prone to these distortions.

Clerks doing routine, mundane tasks, often feel their work has little or no significance. Others' behaviour towards them often reinforces this. Consequently, they make errors and mistakes which bring down the wrath of those who depend on their work being done methodically. Yet a simple explanation to them of how their work is important, because it is part of a chain and affects the work of many others, could improve their standard of work, not to mention their motivation.

301

Inevitably, one such gesture is not enough, but it may be a beginning.

SEPARATION, DISTANCE ... AND PERSPECTIVE

In most organizations, communication is further complicated by separation and distance. Distance is not only geographic – at the other end of the country. It occurs much closer to home, in the same building, separated by floors. Frequently, being separated means not meeting, not talking, not knowing, not understanding, and not communicating.

Distance may also mean working in a different department, that is, with a different perspective on the organization. Yet bringing together people from the various disciplines within a company may not only be vital to the organization's continued productivity: it would also be 'integrational' and reinforce people's sense of belonging, of being part of a coherent whole.

It is this growing realization that has resulted in many organizations creating suggestion schemes, team briefings and quality circles, as part of their overall corporate communication strategies.

Suggestion schemes ... by any other name

A suggestion scheme is a structured two-way communication system. It has old-fashioned connotations, but is being revived, for it has the potential to tap into the accumulated knowledge and insights of employees, and gain their commitment and involvement. It has been variously renamed as Brainwaves (British Airways), Winning Lines (British Rail), or Ideas Unlimited (BBC).

Such a scheme requires a highly formalized system to fulfil the following functions:

- Enable employees (individuals or teams) to spend the time on developing an idea; possibly the company can have a 'problems in search of a solution' file.
- Let them know exactly how to present ideas, and what criteria will be used to assess them.
- Inform them of the procedures by which their contribution will be accepted and assessed.
- Tell them who will assess the ideas, and how it will be done.
- Reward employees in a recognized way.
- Publicize the winners and their ideas, as well as others who also contributed.
- Market the idea widely, throughout the company, using all the various media available.
- Run the scheme efficiently, possibly even appointing someone to run it on a full-time basis.

If well administered, it may become a stepping stone to gaining more employee commitment. (*Note:* When, in the 1980s Ford asked their hourly people to suggest easier ways of building one of their models, they received over 1400 suggestions, of which they incorporated 500.)

Team briefings

Team briefings are used by over 500 organizations throughout the United Kingdom. A briefing is a two-way communication system, though the impetus for holding briefings comes from managers. Their prime purpose is to communicate corporate policies and other information that staff need to be aware of.

They underline a basic element in a manager's job: to keep his or her staff informed of important issues within the company. Briefings should be held regularly, no more than six weeks apart, in work time, for no more than 15 people at a time, and lasting for 30–40 minutes. The manager gives his 'briefing', which is then followed by questions and answers.

It is a 'cascading' system: senior managers inform those below them; they in turn brief their own managers; and finally section heads or their equivalent inform members of staff. Everyone in an organization must get the same information, although sometimes the slant of that information may differ, given the differing departmental perspectives, and the differing needs of employees at various levels and locations of an organization.

First, a manager must him- or herself be well briefed, with back-up written notes to assist him or her. He or she should be trained in listening and presentation skills; and prior to the briefing needs to spend time working on anticipated questions, and the answers.

Quality circles

Quality circles are a Japanese 'invention' that has grown in popularity in the United Kingdom in recent years.

Their main aim is to bring together on a regular basis a group of people from different parts of an organization, and representing the same or different departments, to tackle a 'quality' issue for the organization. The questions quality circles ask are: 'How can we ... ?' and 'What can be done to ... ?'

Each circle is given authority to call for any information it needs, is able to question others, makes presentations, and offers recommendations.

The by-products of quality circles are at least as useful as the quality-related recommendations. Participants talk of feeling more involved in their work and in the company and its activities. They say their communication skills improve, and they develop more participative ways of working. Their self-confidence grows, and they find their opinion carries more weight with their colleagues. They also become aware that everyone has a different style and a different contribution to make at work, and to the business.

House magazines and newsletters

It is unlikely that a manager, on his or her own, will be required to produce a house magazine or newsletter. But they are a medium frequently used for conveying information.

They are excellent for 'integrational' material, possibly work-related ideas being shared, and certainly 'housekeeping' information (see 'What to communicate' above). Being a one-way form of communication, however, they have their limitations, and are at their best when dealing with relatively straightforward 'information'. The question remains: Is it simply 'management' generated and approved information, or can employee comments and dissatisfactions also be included? If the answer to the latter is 'no', their function is narrowed. Yet if they fail to publish controversial material, or what employees already 'know' (e.g. the difficulties encountered on a new shopfloor production line; or the results of an employee survey with negative feedback), their credibility will be limited.

When creating house magazines and newsletters, however, managers have to decide what their 'task' is – to inform, to persuade, or to influence – and hence, how the material is to be written and presented ... and what material would best be treated by 'oral' means, and should therefore be omitted.

Such publications are no substitute for real communication, which is two-way sharing and has more to do with attitudes and behaviour than information.

The noticeboard ... or talking board

The noticeboard is an underused medium. With the possibility of using eye-catching layout and design, and given the speed with which information can be placed there, added to, or changed – and its accessibility to all – it is a company's nearest equivalent to a daily newspaper, and a good deal cheaper. But its usefulness is – as is that of a newspaper – for conveying information of a non-controversial nature only.

Such a board needs a careful and well-arranged display of items, perhaps differentiated by colours, and monitored daily for material that needs to be removed and/or updated. It can have allocated spaces for regular features, and could become a place for a 'letter to the editor' style of communication, a talking board in fact (not dissimilar to graffiti!).

MANAGING YOURSELF ... YOUR BEHAVIOUR

Our behaviour gives us away all the time: 'actions speak louder than words'. Old adages have a great deal of truth in them!

It follows that part of managing your communications is about managing yourself.

- 'An ear is as good as – or better than – any other communication channel.'

- 'A wise man encourages you to find out what you know for yourself.'
- 'Silence is golden.'
- 'If all else fails, try talking.'

These four maxims are not mutually exclusive, but are indispensable elements in how you communicate.

Listening ... is communicating

Listening is a skill which is sorely neglected. Yet by listening to others we inform them that we think they are important. We are showing them that what they have to say is worth hearing, and that they are valuable. Listening can also take a lot of the effort – or drudgery – out of your own thinking. By listening you discover that others are already doing it for you!

Questioning ... is communicating

Asking the right questions – not interrogative and accusing 'why' questions, but ones which open up a discussion, enabling the other person(s) to reflect and analyse, and to take initiative and responsibility – also sends positive messages. Questions such as 'What would you do ...?' or 'How would you go about ...?' gives back to individuals their 'power', which is taken away from them when they are issued with instructions and orders.

... and so is silence

Silence is another skill well worth developing. Not the silence associated with 'not telling', but that associated with giving others the time and space – in any conversation and interaction – to reflect and decide what to do or say next. It is part and parcel of interacting with them creatively and positively. People who are given space and the encouragement to think will normally discover energy and commitment to work, and obviate the need for managerial interference.

Talking ... establishing rapport

Managerial 'walkabouts', stopping to talk to staff, getting to know them as people and not simply as role fulfillers, discovering their strengths and what they can offer, how they think and what they value: these are all ingredients that go towards creating a 'communicating culture' in an organization. They are often more powerful than the 'communication initiatives', such as suggestion schemes and house magazines, that normally form part of a formal corporate communication strategy.

Body language ... and tone of voice

Body language is our giveaway. Most of us are not aware of our gestures, postures and quirks that tell the person with whom we are interacting: whether we really are listening – while thinking we are giving that impression; whether we do feel confident and relaxed – in contrast to our brave verbal claims; whether we have heard what we have actually been asked; and whether we do intend to keep our promises.

Eye contact, a nod of the head, the supportive 'aha' murmurs, and not shuffling papers or looking at your watch as someone is speaking ... these are just some of the ways in which you can improve your own communication. By doing so, you signal to others that you mean what you say when you claim to want better communication and contact with them.

Similarly, more can be communicated by the tone of your voice than by the words that accompany it. A brusque 'That's interesting' communicates the listener's true state of mind.

Language ... and words

When communicating, we tend to concentrate on the words, but they lay endless traps for us. Are we sure we are saying the 'right' thing? As one manager, anxious to assure his employees that the computers about to be installed in his office were nothing to be afraid of, reassured them: 'There is no need to worry, since the computers can only do what you do.'

Language also traps us in other ways. We use abbreviations, shorthand and jargon; or we indulge in long, abstract and increasingly imprecise words – on the principle that 'the weightier the word, the weightier the argument, and the more knowledgeable we appear'. This is a particular vice for writers, though speakers have been known to indulge in it (see Chapter 5, on Writing). Worst of all, though, we frequently fail to check that what we have said, or written, has been both heard and understood: that is, we fail to receive 'feedback'.

The words of Confucius uttered hundreds of years ago still make sense:

> If language is not correct, then what is said is not what is meant. If what is said is not what is meant, then what ought to be done remains undone.

THE IMPORTANCE OF FEEDBACK

We began this chapter by pointing out that interaction was an indispensable part of communication. This means giving and receiving feedback. The person or persons you are communicating with must have the opportunity, and be encouraged, to respond. You must also listen to their responses, and be seen to be acting on them.

Whenever you are communicating, consider which medium to use, for it is
important and beneficial – for everyone – that there should be an opportunity

for 'feedback', whether in the form of agreement, disagreement, questions, other points of view, or clarification.

We frequently shun feedback because we are afraid of what we will hear. Yet from such feedback we can always learn something new which we can apply in the future. As another old adage has it: 'There is no such thing as failure, only feedback.'

CHECK LIST OF KEY POINTS

1 Remember, you can't *not* communicate.
2 Communicating is sharing.
3 Work through the six questions: who – why – where – when – what – how.
4 Check that your 'listener' has heard and understood.
5 Make sure there is a genuine opportunity for feedback.
6 Be aware that you communicate with language, behaviour and other symbols.
7 Listen yourself, ask questions . . . and then talk.

NOTES

1 Rosemary Stewart has carried out extensive research into managers' jobs, and how they spend their time. In her highly readable book, *Managers and Their Jobs*, 2nd edn (Pan Books, 1988), she states that:

It is by talking and listening that managers get most of their work done. The amount of time that managers spend with others depends upon the job and its context, and the individual's inclination. The 160 managers in this study spent two-thirds of their time in conversation. Other studies have found an even higher proportion . . .

2 J. H. Horne and T. Lupton, 'The work activities of middle managers', *Journal of Management Studies,* February, 1965:

Managers talk most of the time, and mostly face to face. They seem not to be overwhelmed by paper or formal meetings. They swop information and advice and instructions, mostly through informal, face-to-face contact in their own offices . . . [this] calls for the ability to shape and utilise the person-to-person channels of communication, to influence, to persuade, to facilitate.

3 In his book, *The Nature of Managerial Work* (Harper & Row, 1973), Henry Mintzberg has listed ten roles that the average manager performs, of which six are active 'communication' roles:

● *three interpersonal roles:* as a figurehead, representing his or her department; as a liaison with other departments; and as a leader of his or her own staff; and

- *three information roles:* as a monitor, scanning for and receiving information; as a disseminator, passing on information; and as a spokesman for his or her department.

4   In this context, Alistair Mant, in his thought-provoking book *The Leaders We Deserve* (Blackwell, 1983), has created a useful image. He talks of the 'binary' and 'ternary' manager. The binary manager tends to see relationships and communicating with another person in personal terms. A ternary manager sees that relationship, and any communication, as having an organizational/task outcome. By bearing this in mind, he or she can avoid becoming embroiled in highly personal and often emotional communication. For what may seem tough in personal terms becomes fair in organizational terms. (This in no way, of course, excuses thoughtlessness, inconsiderateness or other elements that creep in to destroy our communicating.)

5   Max Boisot, in *Information and Organizations* (Fontana, 1987) – a book full of insights – has added another useful dimension to the 'what' and the 'how'.

    He has devised a method for classifying 'information' that we convey to others along two dimensions:

- Can it be coded easily, where one end of the continuum is highly structured and can be symbolically represented (e.g. by numbers) while the other is vague and full of intangible ideas?
- Can it be easily disseminated – by what means, and relevantly, to an appropriate audience?

If the information can be easily codified, in understandable language or numbers, the written word may be a means of transferring it to others. If, however, it is not easily codifiable, the sole means of conveying it to others may be face-to-face in a meeting, where there are opportunities for discussions and questions.

    For example: motivating staff. This is a difficult, person-specific type of communication. Every one of us is motivated by something specific to ourselves and our needs: that is, it is not 'information' that is easily codifiable. Trying, therefore, to motivate me in a large lecture on motivation may give me some intellectual insights, but will probably do little to actually motivate me. What I would need is a face-to-face discussion, to uncover the reasons why I am feeling demotivated.

    By contrast, sales figures are easily codifiable, will be widely understood, and thus lend themselves to being communicated by a process of dissemination such as a booklet, or even a lecture with slides.

FURTHER READING

Adler, A., *Communication at Work*, McGraw-Hill, 1993.

Argyle, M., *Bodily Communication*, Methuen, 1988.

Bland, M. and Jackson, P., *Effective Employee Communications*, Kogan Page, 1990.

Bone, D., *Practical Guide to Effective Listening*, Kogan Page, 1988.

Collard, R., 'The quality circle in context', *Personnel Management,* September 1981.

Decker, B., *How to Communicate Effectively*, Kogan Page, 1988.

Drennan, D., 'Are you getting through?', *Management Today,* August 1989.

Ivey, A., *Managing Face to Face Communication*, Chartwell-Bratt, 1988.

Leeds, D., *Smart Questions for Successful Managers*, Piatkus, 1987.

McConville, J. and Wood, A., *Suggestion Schemes*, Industrial Society, 1990.

MacKay, I., *Asking Questions*, IPD, 1995.

MacKay, I., *Listening Skills*, IPD, 1995.

Robertson, A., *Listen for success*, Irwin, 1994.

Rogers, C. and Roethlisberger, F. J., 'Barriers and gateways to communication', *Harvard Business Review,* November 1991.

'Team briefing: practical steps in employee communication', *Industrial Relations Review and Report,* no.361, February 1986.

Weinstein, K., 'The communication syndrome', *Personnel Management,* June 1969.

Wicks, R. J., *Helping Others: Ways of Listening, Sharing and Counselling*, Souvenir Press, 1994.

21 Meetings

John Gregory

Managers spend a great deal of time in meetings – often ineffectively, and usually with a growing sense of frustration. This chapter looks at meetings and at why so many are ineffective, and suggests some steps to be taken to make them more effective, concluding with a simple seven-point guideline for the chairman and the meeting member.

GOOD MEETINGS MEAN MORE PROFIT

It is popular to grumble about meetings; indeed, this pastime can become a dangerous obsession, so that, in some organizations, the climate is such that managers find it very difficult to conduct effective meetings. Jokes and 'laws' about meetings proliferate and the well-known video, *Meetings Bloody Meetings,* although admirable, may have unwittingly contributed to the myth that meetings are a nuisance. Perhaps the typical management attitude to meetings is best summed up by a story told to me by a financial manager. He recounted the final act of a long and difficult meeting when, after $2\frac{1}{2}$ hours, little had been achieved and the only decision that they were about to make was a time for the next meeting so that they could continue their fruitless endeavours. After much diary searching the chairman thought he had found a consensus and announced, 'How about next Wednesday?' To which one of those present replied with a groan, 'Oh no, not *Wednesday* – that ruins two weekends!'

What, then, is the message? It is that senior management should encourage and cultivate a 'good meetings climate', because in doing so they will improve:

- *Communication* A business organization is, by definition, two or more people engaged in commercial pursuit. Organizations cannot cohere or achieve goals without communicating, and effective meetings play an essential part in this process.

- *Policy formulation and planning*   These activities require ideas, discussion and debate on key issues and on alternatives. They benefit from the collective wisdom of the management team and carefully considered proposals and options. This process can only take place in meetings.
- *Decision making*   Some decisions have to be made in formal meetings (or endorsed by them) because of constitutional or statutory requirements; for example, Cabinet, council and boardroom decisions. But there are many circumstances in which the quality or durability of a decision will be enhanced if it is subjected to careful (and urgent!) consideration in a meeting at which those responsible for its implementation or affected by it are present.

Better communication, better planning and improved decision making will have a positive effect on the bottom line, and this is a justification for giving thought and energy to improving meetings.

Do we need a meeting?

If so many managers express the view that they spend too much time in meetings, perhaps they should not be there in the first place. It is undoubtedly the case that some meetings should never have been called, so it is worth exercising the discipline of asking, 'Do we need a meeting?' before setting one up. Figure 21.1 is a useful check list which can be used to determine whether there is a need for a meeting.

A positive answer to one of the questions in the check list suggests that a meeting is needed. However, just by calling a meeting you do not communicate better, build teams, make good decisions or solve problems. Many meetings which undoubtedly should have been held, fail. Let us now consider why this happens.

WHY DO MEETINGS FAIL?

Meetings can be broadly classified into formal and informal. The formal category embraces all those meetings that are required by some written constitution, Articles of Association, or statute. The conduct of formal meetings is usually governed by rules or custom and the membership controlled by election or some form of qualification.

By far the more frequent and managerially important meeting is the informal type, which may be a regular or ad hoc problem-solving type of meeting. Whatever the type, the chances are that they fail from time to time or, in some cases, all the time! But why?

Do the rules require a meeting?
So many formal meetings are required by statute or constitution and they have to be called and held in accordance with the rules. Although they often seem tedious and pointless, such meetings are consistent with open, democratic administration and provide some reassurance to those with an interest in the organization concerned.

Is there a need to communicate?
How often do you hear the complaint 'nobody tells us anything'? When a business is proposing change there may be a strong case for holding briefing meetings in order that a positive attitude can be encouraged. The great advantage of a meeting over a written briefing is the two-way nature of the communication. So if you want to avoid rumour and distortion, you want to change attitudes or you want to take people with you, consider the case for a meeting or series of meetings.

Is there a need for team building?
Well conducted meetings can do much to build a good team. Leaders of the best sports teams, and winning generals, have recognized the benefits of the 'Here's how we win' meeting, and the same thing can work in business.

Do I need advice and guidance before making a decision?
It doesn't follow that if the answer is 'Yes', a meeting is required, since a few phone calls or a one-to-one discussion may achieve the desired result. However, collective advice reviewed and weighed in a meeting will often lead to a better decision. It has to be recognized, though, that some managers who are poor decision makers use meetings as a device for delaying or compromising when they would have been better to take speedy action.

Have we got a problem or crisis which can be better dealt with by a group solution?
Not quite the same as the last point because in this instance there is a crisis and a need for urgent action – but there are many circumstances in which a 'war cabinet' approach is needed. For example, an unexpected takeover bid, a lightning strike, a serious accident. The crisis may involve several departments or call for a range of specialist views or skills; the sooner they are all brought together in a meeting the better.

Figure 21.1   Check list: do we need a meeting?

People problems

Since a meeting is a social group it is not surprising that they reflect the weaknesses and idiosyncracies of their members. For example:

- An incompetent chairman.
- An idle committee secretary.
- Interpersonal conflict between members or departmental rivalries (the 'point scoring' syndrome).
- An anti-meeting culture (the 'this is going to be a waste of time' syndrome).
- Mistrust or envy by those outside the meeting (the 'what are they up to' syndrome).
- Ill-conceived membership (e.g. a vertical or diagonal slice, when a peer group is demanded).

Planning problems

The varied and awkward nature of human beings does not mean that meetings are always going to be difficult and ineffective, provided someone gives some thought to the structure and content. More typically, what happens is that there is:

- Insufficient notice of a meeting or silly timing.
- No understanding of the aim: 'Why are we here?'
- No agenda or a badly structured agenda.
- Poor paperwork: 'These figures don't add up!'
- A feeling that 'we've discussed all this before'.

Progress

It is a common complaint that after a meeting, even a productive meeting, nothing happens. For example:

- No record or minute is circulated.
- No action or follow-up on decisions is taken.
- There is no continuity between meetings.
- No upward reporting occurs.

It follows, therefore, that to achieve better meetings something has to be done to change managers' attitudes towards meetings. This can be achieved by attention to the three 'P's: people, planning and progress.

PEOPLE

It is worth giving attention to three 'people' factors: attitude, selection, and training. Let me explain.

Attitude

Much damage is done because managers lack a positive approach to meetings. To encourage a positive view:

- *Avoid the word 'committee'* Bureaucracy and inactivity are too closely associated with the word 'committee', so where possible, stop using it. Consider alternatives, using active descriptions such as working party, task force, and action group, or using descriptions which emphasize efficiency or excellence like quality circle, profit improvement group, and so forth.
- *Emphasize importance and urgency* Senior managers have a key role to play in emphasizing the importance of the work done in meetings, and through encouraging their own staff to take a positive attitude by, for

313

example, arriving at meetings on time, preparing for meetings, and constructive contribution.

Selection

We rightly take time and care to recruit managers, but rather less concern is shown when assembling a group to perform some managerial task. It seems that the 'least busy' or 'buggin's turn' principle is often applied. When forming a meeting group, such matters as intellectual ability, experience, seniority, need for confidentiality, and representational and personality factors all need to be considered. The group will have an aim similar to a manager's job description and there is, therefore, a case for preparing a 'group specification'. Obviously, in some circumstances, the group task preselects the group, but there will be many occasions when members of a working party or task force should be carefully selected.

If care in picking members is important, the choice of chairman is often critical to the effectiveness of a meeting. There are occasions when seniority or status leave no room for consideration, but when there is a choice, personality and skills such as listening, managing time, prioritizing, summing up, fairness, firmness, impartiality, and so on, must be taken into account.

Training

Once the importance of meetings is recognized, the need for simple but effective training follows. There are short courses on effective meetings, training films and videos, and useful booklets. Any training aimed at improving the effectiveness of meetings will also help change the attitude to them. Do not overlook the special training needs of the chairman and the secretary (e.g. preparing agendas, taking notes, writing action reports).

PLANNING

Once management attitudes are positive, the climate is right for effective meetings, but this will not happen unless the chairman and the secretary give some thought to what they want to achieve and how they intend to set about it – in other words, planning. Specifically, they will need to:

- Time meetings to be cost effective and acceptable to the members.
- Fix the location to be convenient and free of interruption and distraction.
- Clarify their terms of reference or aim.
- Plan and prepare an agenda. Some informal meetings may not need a written agenda as long as everyone knows why they are there and what is to be covered.
- Consider the need for supporting papers, which should be well written, up to date and accurate.

- Consider the need for prior consultation and discussion on difficult issues in order to prepare the ground and save valuable time at the meeting.

In crises, meetings have to be called at short notice and little preparation is possible. In these circumstances the chairman's role becomes even more significant, as does the post-meeting progress, of which more below.

PROGRESS

If I had to nominate one single factor which has contributed to the 'bad press' that meetings enjoy it would not be easy, but post-meeting inactivity would be high on my list. Nothing will have a greater potential for convincing managers that they are wasting their time if they can see no cause-and-effect relationship between the outcome of the meeting and subsequent action, or if they are continually covering old ground. If something positive happens they will soon begin to change their attitudes to meetings. What needs to be done?

- *Circulate a record of the meeting* Call them minutes if you like, but, if you are free of procedural requirements, it might be better to describe them as an 'action and information report'. In any event, it is preferable to have an 'action column' in the record so that the names of those responsible for carrying out the agreed decisions can be noted. This puts the action manager on the spot and goes some way towards avoiding the 'I didn't realize I was supposed to do anything' reaction.

For the chairman
1   Know your committee (terms, rules, members).
2   Prepare (compile agenda, plan meeting).
3   Consult before the meeting (i.e. prepare the ground).
4   Be firm but fair.
5   Convey sense of urgency/importance.
6   Listen.
7   Seek consensus/agree the action.

For the member
1   Prepare/know your facts; consult subordinates before the meeting.
2   Don't be late.
3   Accept the chair.
4   Be constructive.
5   Don't lose your cool.
6   Question if in doubt.
7   Fight your corner – but don't waste time.

Figure 21.2   Check lists for better meetings

- *Take managerial action*   This means taking an interest in what happens post-meeting – asking for a progress report, and generally encouraging and prodding to ensure that matters are progressed.
- *Report post meeting progress*   Let those at the meeting and others know what has happened. This may encourage others and it will enhance the status of meetings.

CHECK LISTS OF SEVEN WAYS TO BETTER MEETINGS

Given that the priority is to produce a better meetings climate by encouraging a positive attitude, there is much that the individual manager can do to improve his or her own performance in meetings, whether as chairman or just a member. As a reminder, and as a guide to better practice, two check lists (Figure 21.2) are provided, one for the chairman and one for the member. Use these lists as a reminder. More thought and some effort could do much to improve the effectiveness of your meetings.

FURTHER READING

Carnes, W. T., *Effective Meetings for Busy People: Let's decide it and go home,* McGraw-Hill, 1983.

Fletcher, W., *Meetings, Meetings: How to manipulate them and make them more fun,* Hodder, 1985.

Janner, G., *How to Win Meetings,* Gower, 1991.

Melrose Films, *Complete Communication,* 1989. Training package which includes a section on meetings.

Melrose Films, *Impact at Meetings – with Greville Janner,* 1990. Video training film.

Part III
MANAGING THE BUSINESS

Introduction: understanding the business

Last, but not least, you need to understand the business. There are enormous differences between industries and between individual businesses within an industry, but there are also skills and knowledge held in common. The secret of success as a manager is to broaden your skills and knowledge base to include something of all these, instead of sticking narrowly to your technical specialism, accounting, production, marketing, and so on, which earned you your promotion to management. Great managers are generalists.

Understanding the business provides answers to such fundamental questions as: Why are we here? What do we think we are doing? What should we be doing? How do we do it? If you feel these questions are perhaps a little metaphysical for a manager, consider how even the great seat-of-the-pants operators can also come unstuck. Prevention *is* better than cure.

In Part III we offer ways of thinking about these matters as well as guidelines for developing your own business skills. It begins with an introduction to accounting, written to dispel the non-accountant's bafflement. A chapter on the whole process of project management, from project concept to post-completion audit, applies to every function of management, but may perhaps be seen to add a production viewpoint.

Three techniques chapters follow in areas which are crucial to the business: decision making and problem solving; negotiating; and finally creativity.

22 Financial information and management

Neil Garrod and Bill Rees

Accounting is often described as the language of business, and a number of surveys have suggested that accounting information is probably the most influential source of information for investment analysts. One such study, by Arnold and Mozier, reported that the Income statement was ranked first, the balance sheet second, half-yearly results were third, the chairman's statement fourth, and the source and application of funds fifth. Following Financial Reporting Statement 1 issued by the Accounting Standards Board in 1991, the funds statement is now a cash flow statement which is, according to the Accounting Standards Board, even more informative. Given the subjectivity of many accounting processes, this dominance of accounting information as a basis for these specialists' decisions is very encouraging for accountants, but also requires further investigation and explanation. In addition, one must be cautious that the less well informed do not interpret the value of accounting information as equivalent to numerical exactitude or an uncritical and reverential awe of the alchemy employed by the fiscal wizards who produce them.

Our purpose in this chapter is to give those unfamiliar with the use of accounting information a balanced view of the reliability of the information produced by accountants, to convince them that a knowledge of the detailed methods of accountancy is unnecessary to its understanding, to explain and illustrate the techniques of financial interpretation, and to show how accounting information is used in management decision making. Throughout, the level of technical explanation is elementary, whereas a relatively sophisticated discussion of the implications is considered important to business managers. Jargon is kept to a minimum, but the occasional technical term cannot be avoided.

This chapter is divided into four sections. In the first section, the process used by accountants to establish measures of income and wealth from a vast array of transactions is examined. The explicit focus is on the formal reporting system for the preparation of published accounts, but in most organizations the same technical principles are employed for the internal reporting system. The second section examines the accounting statements of two competing organizations to illustrate the information that can be extracted from these data and the degree of reliance that can be placed upon them. The later part of this section concentrates on the technique of ratio analysis. The third section drops the emphasis on external reporting and considers the managerial uses of accounting data, either for evaluating decisions or for monitoring progress. Although in many instances the accounting system will be part of this managerial process the information used is less formal or prescribed. The final section concludes the discussion.

THE ACCOUNTING PROCESS

Accounting attempts to measure two interrelated concepts: income and wealth. It should be emphasized that as concepts these are not directly observable phenomena, as they can be, and often are, defined in multiple ways. Consequently, a set of rules has become generally accepted or enforced, via professional pronouncements and regulation, to try to impose some measure of standardization on the assessment of these two ephemera. This is best illustrated by an example, focusing on one of the many transactions which might make up the activities of an organization.

In this example a contract for the manufacture and sale of two identical articles is won in month 1, and the raw material is immediately ordered and received. In month 2, the supplier of the raw materials is paid £500 in full settlement and the labour force completes manufacture of both articles and is paid £500 for their work. One article is delivered in month 2, the second in month 3, and full payment of £3000 is received in month 4. In addition, monthly overheads of £150 are incurred and an asset costing £2400 with an expected useful life of 24 months is being utilized. The transactions involved, together with the conventional accounting representation of these transactions, are shown in Figure 22.1.

While this is a naive and simplified example it does illustrate many of the problems involved in accounting:

- Notice that there is no correlation between profit and cash flows. In the very long run, profits and cash flows will be equal. The problem arises when reports are created for the short or medium term, when the timing of cash payments and receipts falls out of step with income and expense recognition. This difference, or time lag, has been the downfall of many a profitable and expanding company.
- The income is taken to the profit and loss account not when the order is received or when cash payment is made, but (usually) when the product is delivered.

	Opening values	Month 1	Month 2	Month 3	Month 4
Cash flows					
Purchases		0	(500)	0	0
Labour		0	(500)	0	0
Payment		0	0	0	3000
Overheads		(150)	(150)	(150)	(150)
		(150)	(1150)	(150)	2850
Profit and loss					
Sales		0	1500	1500	0
Opening stock		0	(500)	(500)	0
Purchases		(500)	0	0	0
Labour		0	(500)	0	0
Closing stock		500	500	0	0
Cost of sales		0	(500)	(500)	0
Gross profit		0	1000	1000	0
Overheads		(150)	(150)	(150)	(150)
Depreciation		(100)	(100)	(100)	(100)
Net profit		(250)	750	750	(250)
Balance sheet					
Fixed assets	2400	2300	2200	2100	2000
Stock	0	500	500	0	0
Debtors	0	0	1500	3000	0
Bank	0	(150)	(1300)	(1450)	1400
Creditors	0	(500)	0	0	0
	2400	2150	2900	3650	3400
Opening capital	2400	2400	2150	2900	3650
Profit/loss		(250)	750	750	(250)
Closing capital		2150	2900	3650	3400

Figure 22.1   Example of the conventional representation of accounting transactions

- Expenses are taken to the profit and loss account either when incurred, in the case of general expenses, or when the revenue for the produce they have created is accounted for. Thus expenses are matched to the relevant income.

    This point is especially significant in the case of the depreciation charge for the asset purchased. The cost of the asset is gradually accounted for, or expensed, over the expected productive life of the asset. This means that the balance sheet figure representing fixed

323

assets is simply that proportion of the cost of the asset which has not yet been written off as an expense, and not, as is used in everyday parlance, an estimate of the asset's current market value. Strictly speaking, depreciation costs incurred in producing the articles should be added to the stock value in a similar manner to the labour costs.

● There is no necessary link between accounting measures of income and wealth and the underlying economic values. The asset values in the balance sheet are neither an assessment of the realizable value nor the replacement cost of the asset. Even if they were, the value of the firm as a whole may well be very different from the value of its constituent parts. In our example, a valuation of the firm would have recognized the impact of the contract when it was won, not as it was completed.

This dichotomy between accounting and economic values can be shown by example if we accept stock market capitalization of a company's shares as their economic value and compare this with the accounting measure of shareholders' equity (see Figure 22.2). It can be seen that the accounting measure of value is very different from the market's. More crucially, the relationship between the two is unstable. However, while absolute values are different, the importance of accounting information to market participants, such as the investment analysts described above, highlights that accounting procedures do result in useful summary data. The important issue is how these various accounting numbers can be used in combination to present a comprehensive picture of company performance.

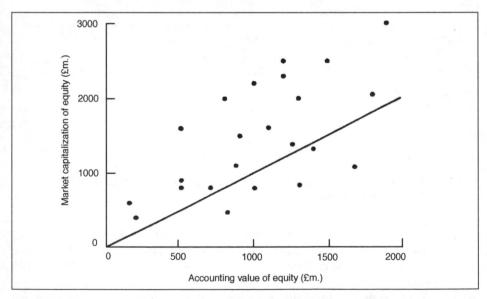

Note: The data refer to a cross-section of companies from the FT 100. Companies whose accounting value is equal to the market capitalization would lie on the line shown.

324 **Figure 22.2 Accounting value of equity *vs* stock market capitalization**

- Because there is a difference between the date at which inputs are purchased, notably fixed assets and stock, the date at which they are used in the production process, and the date at which the product is sold, the original measure of the cost of these expenses is no longer accurate. This is due to the change in the purchasing power of sterling as a result of general price level inflation, and to the change in the value of these costs in relation to other items. Both these factors will tend to distort and, in the case of productive as opposed to financial companies, usually overstate any traditional accounting measure of income. Furthermore, if assets or liabilities are held which are measured in monetary amounts, such as debtors, creditors, loans, and bank balances, a company can incur a holding gain or loss during inflationary times. This element of income is not measured by traditional accounting systems.

- When accounts are prepared for any company there will be a great many transactions in various stages of completion at the accounting date and many more that will have been completed during the period under review. The sheer magnitude of the task involved in collating and valuing the myriad transactions presents a serious practical problem in measurement for the accountant, and the degree of subjectivity involved complicates the auditor's task of verification.

Accounting tries to measure income and wealth by applying a set of standard procedures. For the United Kingdom, these are laid down in the Companies Acts, by the Stock Exchange for quoted companies, and in Financial Reporting Standards issued by the Accounting Standards Board. These requirements attempt to standardize a vast range of accounting practices, but they must leave room for sufficient flexibility to accommodate differing circumstances. It is this scope for subjectivity which periodically excites a considerable degree of criticism of (creative) accounting practices. While there is some truth in the complaints, the alternative of a more regimented system may lead to less meaningful accounting statements and will certainly impose additional costs on the firm and its shareholders. The main general conventions which guide the decisions of accountants are:

- *The accruals (or matching) convention* This refers to the process whereby expenses are accounted for in the same period as the revenues which they helped to create. This results in profit measurement differing from cash flows and, generally, leads to reported accounting profit generation preceding cash inflows. This can cause companies significant difficulties and, often, an unwelcome surprise. The vast majority of companies which become bankrupt do so not because of a lack of profitability (a longer-term measure), but rather, because of a lack of cash (a shorter-term measure). Look again at the example illustrated in Figure 22.1. Change the months to years and the problem becomes quite acute: the project becomes profitable in year 2, but cash flow is negative until year 4. Thus bridge financing is required for the first 75 per cent of the duration of the project. If the company cannot find willing lenders, then the firm will become bankrupt while still indicating an accounting profit.

- *The prudence convention*   This governs the timing of the realization of income, and hence expenses, in the accounts. As prospective losses are more readily allowed than future profits, a pessimistic bias is reflected in the accounts.
- *The consistency convention*   Given the choices available from a wide spectrum of accounting practices, it is desirable that a company should be restrained from switching between alternatives to suit its own convenience.
- *The going concern convention*   This assumes that the company will persist for the foreseeable future. This has two major consequences: first, that the value of assets on liquidation, or market values, are not normally relevant; and secondly, that the accounts must incorporate, to some extent, expectations about the future as well as events in the past.

Further to those specified, a number of implicit but not necessarily trivial conventions apply. First, we measure and aggregate diverse items in monetary amounts, though the value of money is not stable. Second, we define and report on an entity, but the specification of that entity can be problematical when groups of companies are involved. Finally, we define and report on a specified period of time, and it is the attempt to allocate transactions to particular periods that creates many of our problems.

It is interesting to speculate why these conventions and the multiplicity of more detailed rules have come into being. We have seen that they fail to produce measures that are consistent with economic reality, that they fail to cope with the distorting effects of inflation, and that flexibility in the accounting rules, together with the subjectivity required in applying them, allows considerable scope for 'creative accounting'. This does not sound like a strong recommendation. However, the source of these conventions lies not in any deep and consistent theory, but in a pragmatic trade-off between economic relevance and practicality. As such, they represent the distillation of experience. Many times in the last twenty-five years, commentators have suggested that accounting measurement is flawed and that alternative financial statements are required. Yet no alternative has yet proved viable and analysts still pay more regard to accounting information than to other variables. Recent empirical and theoretical research work is beginning to unravel the complex web of relationships between accounting and market values that make the former invaluable in the estimation of the latter. Thus it is conventional historic cost statements which are currently utilized by the business world for external reporting and within an organization for decision making and control procedures.

UNDERSTANDING ACCOUNTING INFORMATION

As a language, accounting numbers create an image of the economic wellbeing of an organization. However, in common with any language, different nuances can be placed on the same words. There are now, as we have said, a number of constraints on how the language can be used, but in an uncertain and ever-changing world it would be counterproductive to overconstrain the role of the accountant in creating the image portrayed. In these circumstances, the value of the accounting numbers comes not from their absolute value, but from their comparison with others. The problem is to find valid comparisons. Difficulties arising from measurement problems and general uncertainty about the future mean that the performance of a company in any one year cannot necessarily be directly compared with the results of a different company or even the same company in different years. To illustrate, the accounts of two typical companies will be described and compared.

Further problems are the mass of data presented and the difficulties involved in making comparisons between organizations of differing size. Both of these problems can be countered, to some extent, by the use of ratio analysis, which attempts to remove the effect of size from the accounting numbers and concentrates the information contained in the accounting statements.

The accounting statements

The exhibits here are simplified and adjusted data from two large quoted companies operating across a diversified range of activities (see Figure 22.3). The accounts are prepared for the group as a whole with subsidiaries (more than 50 per cent owned) 'consolidated' into the totals. Other partly owned companies, associated companies or investments are accounted for by a variety of methods which only take account of the relevant proportion of the investment.

In the Accounting Standards Board's Statement of Principles it is stated that 'the balance sheet delineates the enterprise's resource structure (major classes and amounts of assets) and its financial structure (major classes and amounts of liabilities and equity)'. The format shown in the example is prescribed by the Companies Act of 1985 *et al* which incorporates the requirements of the European Union (EU) 4th Directive on company reporting. Most categories would be supported by notes to the accounts expanding on the detailed composition of the entries or their method of computation. It is by far the easiest way to think of a balance sheet as a list of the values of the assets and liabilities of a company with the net difference represented by the shareholder's investment in a company. We already know this to be a naive approach, as the valuations attached to each category have little to do with their cost of replacement or their disposal value. Furthermore, even if the individual asset and liability values are accurate, the value of the company as a whole could be very different from the component parts. This is partly due to the asset values excluded from the balance sheet, such as human resource

CONSOLIDATED BALANCE SHEETS (£m.)

	Alpha		Beta	
	1995	1996	1995	1996
Capital employed				
Fixed assets				
Property, Plant and Equipment	122.2	114.7	158.5	135.0
Investments	27.8	25.0	50.0	39.7
	150.0	139.7	208.5	174.7
Current assets				
Stock (inventory)	94.2	84.3	62.8	68.3
Debtors (accounts receivable)	111.7	100.2	49.7	54.3
Investments	3.3	12.3	0.7	0.0
Cash	16.7	11.0	21.0	18.2
	225.9	207.8	134.2	140.8
Creditors due within one year	(153.3)	(142.5)	(120.8)	(126.2)
Net current assets	72.6	65.3	13.4	14.6
Total assets less current liabilities	222.6	205.0	221.9	189.3
Creditors due after one year	(69.9)	(80.3)	(89.5)	(79.0)
Provisions for liabilities and charges	(5.2)	(3.5)	(1.2)	(0.5)
	147.5	121.2	131.2	109.8
Financed by:				
Capital and reserves				
Called up share capital	22.2	22.0	11.0	11.0
Share premium account	69.0	68.5	18.5	18.5
Revaluation reserves	22.7	10.0	72.2	48.3
Profit and loss account (retained profit)	27.5	14.7	4.3	9.0
	141.4	115.2	106.0	86.8
Minority interests	6.1	6.0	25.2	23.0
	147.5	121.2	131.2	109.8
Creditors payable within one year				
Loans and overdrafts	42.7	45.2	32.0	38.4
Trade creditors	60.8	54.3	29.8	27.0
Other creditors	23.5	23.0	31.7	33.2
Taxation and social security	17.7	12.7	16.0	16.3
Bills of exchange	2.3	3.3	7.0	7.3
Proposed dividends	6.3	4.0	4.3	4.0
	153.3	142.5	120.8	126.2

328 **Figure 22.3   The balance sheet**

	Alpha		Beta	
	1995	1996	1995	1996
Creditors payable after one year				
Loans	67.0	75.0	88.5	77.8
Taxation	1.7	1.5	0.5	0.7
Other	1.2	3.8	0.5	0.5
	69.9	80.3	89.5	79.0
Provisions				
Pensions	2.6	3.5	0.0	0.0
Taxation	2.6	0.0	1.2	0.5
	5.2	3.5	1.2	0.5

Note: There would be many further notes to the accounts relating to other items, giving further detail or explanations, but as these are not necessary for this explanation they have been omitted for the sake of clarity.

Figure 22.3   The balance sheet (concluded)

assets, and partly the synergistic operation of individual assets. However, bearing in mind the limitations of the valuations used, we can examine the individual items to discover what indications of performance can be deduced from the information contained on the face of the balance sheet. The listing of assets indicates that whilst Beta has slightly less invested in assets, 342.7 (208.5 + 134.2) as opposed to 375.9 (150.0 + 225.9), it apparently has a much higher percentage in fixed assets than Alpha, 61 per cent (208.5/342.7) against 3 per cent (150.0/375.9). The distinction between fixed and current assets rests on the nature of their role within the company and its operations. Fixed assets are expected to remain within the firm and to be used in generating future profits, while current assets arise as part of the trading cycle, or are intended to be used up in production during the next reporting period, or are incidental stores of surplus funds such as short-term investments. Overall growth in assets is much the same for both organizations at around 8 per cent, but while growth is a natural objective for management, it ties up capital and is therefore only beneficial if productive. Note, however, that in Beta's case, fixed assets apparently increased by £33.8m. while current assets fell by £6.6m. But this growth may be illusory. Fixed assets are originally valued at cost and, for most assets, this cost is gradually written off as depreciation. At the same time, inflation may well be increasing the net monetary value of an asset, and the unexpired historical cost becomes increasingly outdated as a surrogate measure of the economic cost of utilizing such an asset. Both Alpha and Beta have tried to adjust for this by revaluing property, in Alpha's case by £22.7m. and in Beta's by £72.2m. (see revaluation reserves). The amount of this revaluation, which occurred in the year under review, accounts for much of Beta's fixed asset increase. Thus the difference in asset structure could be explained either by differing revalua-   *329* tion processes or by genuine differences in asset structure.

The liabilities of the companies are not readily identifiable from the balance sheets as they are revealed as summary statistics that are elaborated in notes to the accounts. From the notes it can clearly be seen that a large section of creditors comprise a source of finance. Even using a narrow definition of finance, loans and overdrafts amount to £109.7m. in Alpha's case and £120.5m. for Beta (loans and overdrafts payable within one year plus loans payable after one year). The remaining creditors are either short-term debts due for expenses incurred, trade and other creditors, unpaid taxes and dividends, or bills of exchange.

Provisions represent distant liabilities which are expected to fall due in the foreseeable future as a result of the current activities of the company, although currently there is no legal obligation. The finance provided by the shareholders is divided into four sections. The nominal value of the shares sold is 'called up share capital', and any excess over the nominal value received for those shares is 'share premium'. There is no effective difference between these two, and together they represent the funds raised by the firm when they originally issued the shares to the market. The 'revaluation reserve' has already been discussed and represents the write-up of assets, normally property. As no profit has yet been realized, this adjustment is not taken through the profit and loss account but is recognized via this balance sheet adjustment. As we shall see, recent amendments in the reporting of company performance means that profit and loss values and reserve adjustments are now brought together into a new statement called the statement of total recognized gains and losses. The 'profit and loss account' is the residual value of all profits earned on behalf of the shareholders that has not yet been distributed to them in the form of dividends. Minority interests represent the shares of subsidiaries not owned by the group.

In the Accounting Standards Board's Statement of Principles, company performance is discussed not only in terms of the traditional profit and loss account, or income statement, but also in terms of statements of financial performance. These now include not only the profit and loss account but also a note of historical cost profits and losses, and also a statement of total recognized gains and losses, in each case with related notes. It is argued that together these statements disclose the chief components of an enterprise's gains and losses, of which income and expenses (i.e. the traditional income statement) are only a part. These statements of financial performance are expected to contribute to the purposes of financial reporting by:

1   giving an account of the results of the stewardship of management to enable users to assess the past performance of management and to form a basis for developing future expectations about financial performance; and

2   providing feedback to users so that they can check the accuracy of their previous assessments of financial performance for past periods and, if necessary, modify their assessments for future periods.

In assessing the overall financial performance of an enterprise during a period, all changes in equity of the enterprise from activities or events need to be considered. The total of such changes, excluding those deriving from capital contributed by or payments to shareholders themselves, is referred to as total recognized gains and losses. Profit or loss for a period is only considered as a component of this total recognized gain or loss, and focuses on revenues for its output (income) that the enterprise has earned and recognized and what it has sacrificed to obtain that output (expenses). Thus the total recognized gains and losses incorporates gains and losses which are recorded via changes in reserves as well as those recorded through the income statement. The main purpose of this expansion of performance reporting from just the profit and loss account is to bring together all aspects of company decisions to present a more rounded summary of company performance during the reporting period.

In addition, the profit and loss statement itself has been changed to require the separate reporting of continuing, acquired and discontinued operations. This reflects the underlying aim of the financial statements, which is to supply valuable information for the prediction of future cash flows. By separating out the ongoing from the discontinued operations it is hoped that the forecasting value of the information will increase.

To date, the information value of the statement of total recognized gains and losses is still very much untested, despite the claims of the Accounting Standards Board. As a consequence, we will consider only the performance measurement aspect of income statements. Another unanswered question is the information relevance of the separate recognition of continuing, acquisition, and discontinued operations. Sales of segments of a company are brought about for many reasons. Often the least important is that of performance. As such, there is a strong school of thought which indicates that past performance of the 'whole' company is more reflective of future efficiency than a selective view of what is considered the 'core', or continuing, business of the firm. We will, therefore, restrict our comments to an interpretation of the 'total' figures of the firm, rather than simply 'continuing' or 'continuing and acquisition' parts of the business. In addition, as is often the case, discontinued operations represent a very small percentage of total operations of the firm. If this is not the case, then it may well be worth asking the question why downsizing is taking place in such a significant way.

From the example accounts (Figure 22.4), it can be seen that Alpha's turnover has soared by 77 per cent whilst Beta's was relatively stable. In both cases, some allowance should be made for the effects of inflation. In the example, no breakdown of the operating costs is given, but company law does require firms to provide a simple analysis, and the management's internal accounts would be very much more detailed. The operating profit percentage earned by Alpha has dropped slightly (10.2 per cent from 11.3 per cent). Meantime, Beta's margin rose (10.6 per cent from 9.0 per cent), leaving them with a modest increase in income. The remaining costs and revenues allocated to this period are not dissimilar, apart from the higher income earned

CONSOLIDATED PROFIT AND LOSS ACCOUNT (£m.)

		Alpha		Beta	
		1995	1996	1995	1996
Turnover:					
Continuing operations		510.6	287.5	370.6	392.8
Acquisitions		96.3	52.8	36.5	0.0
		606.9	340.3	407.1	392.8
Discontinued operations		(25.7)	(12.1)	12.4	0.0
Total turnover		581.2	328.2	394.7	392.8
Operating expenses		521.7	291.2	352.9	357.3
Operating profit:					
Continuing operations	50.5	29.4		39.2	35.5
Acquisitions	9.6	6.2		4.3	0.0
Discontinued operations	(0.6)	1.4		(1.7)	0.0
Total operating profit		59.5	37.0	41.8	35.5
Share of associated companies' profits		1.5	1.3	7.8	11.0
Investment income		4.0	3.3	2.7	3.2
Finance costs		(14.7)	(10.5)	(14.2)	(14.3)
Profit on ordinary activities before taxation		50.3	31.1	38.1	35.4
Taxation		(14.0)	(9.0)	(11.0)	(9.3)
Minority interests		(5.3)	(2.7)	(2.8)	(4.6)
Dividends		(11.5)	(7.5)	(4.8)	(4.0)
Retained profit		19.5	11.9	19.5	17.5

Figure 22.4   The profit and loss account

by Beta's greater investment in associated companies (classified as fixed asset investment on the balance sheet) and the considerably higher proportion of income paid out by Alpha as dividends.

A final statement required under the Statement of Principles is a cash flow statement. The underlying rationale behind the preparation of accounts is assumed to be the provision of information regarding cash inflows and outflows to help with assessments of liquidity, financial viability and future cash flows. The cash flow statement, together with related notes, reflects an enterprise's cash receipts classified by principal sources and its cash payments classified by main uses during a period. It provides information about an enterprise's activities in generating cash through operations and its financing decisions, and its expenditure of cash in meeting debt interest and dividend decisions and its investment decisions. Important uses of information about an enterprise's current cash receipts and payments include helping to assess factors such as risk, the enterprise's liquidity, financial viability, financial adaptability, and the way in which profits are converted into cash.

However, a cash flow statement provides an incomplete basis for assessing prospects for future cash flows because of the effect of timing differences, as previously indicated in Figure 22.1. Many current cash receipts, especially from operations, result from activities of earlier periods, and many current cash payments are intended or expected to result in future cash receipts. As statements of financial performance are prepared using the accruals concept, they adjust cash flows to measure results for a period. For this reason, the Accounting Standards Board feels that statements of financial performance used in conjunction with balance sheets and cash flow statements, together provide a better basis for assessing future cash flow prospects of an enterprise than do cash flow statements alone.

Whether this is the case is still an open question. From the discussions above it could be argued that the value of cash flow statements is simply to indicate that the enterprise has sufficient cash to continue operating. As such, it is something of a blunt instrument that indicates a simple dichotomy: survive or not. On the other hand, a careful analysis of the balance sheet and statement of total gains and losses, particularly the profit and loss account, will provide a richer indication of the 'quality' of survival that might be expected.

Ratio analysis

Ratio analysis is a technique which has built up something of a mystique, and yet it is a simple attempt to produce summary statistics to save time in the perusal of a large number of accounting statements and to facilitate comparability by standardizing the results for size.

Thus our two companies have reported profits on ordinary activities in 1995 of £50.3m. and £38.1m. respectively. Yet these results are not comparable, because of the different scale of the two operations. It would be possible to standardize the results using a number of different scaling factors, for example, turnover, capital, or employees:

	Profit margin	Return on capital	Profit per employee
Alpha	50.3 × 100/581.2 = 8.65%	50.3 × 100/147.5 = 34.1%	50.3m./10,050 = £5005/emp
Beta	38.1 × 100/394.7 = 9.65%	38.1 × 100/131.2 = 29.0%	38.1m./15,453 = £2466/emp

Which of the many scaling factors to use and which of the multitudinous possible combinations of ratios to compute rather depends on the focus of the study in hand, but some general guidance can be given.

In various studies by British and American academics in which comprehensive sets of ratios for large samples of industrial or commercial firms have been analysed it has been shown that many of these ratios are substitutes rather than complementary. Once a different aspect of corporate performance has been identified most of the pertinent information can be derived from one or two ratios. Thus five ratios may well contain about 80 per cent of the information available from a set of forty or more. The five main characteristics, or factors, which are examined in more detail below, are: profitability, *333* financial leverage, working capital position, asset turnover, and liquidity. It must be emphasized that while these categories were distinctive in the academic studies, on average, it does not follow that they are universally applicable or necessarily significant. For instance, while the inventory/current assets ratio was found to contain most of the available information about short-term liquidity, liquidity is not necessarily a useful indicator for an analysis of efficiency. Nevertheless, these five ratios form a good starting point for a general review of corporate performance and will be examined and explained using the sample accounts for illustrative purposes.

Profitability

Alpha 25.3% (17.2%) Beta 20.8% (22.0%)

Return on capital is profit before interest and taxation, expressed as a percentage of total capital employed. For example:

$$100 \times (59.6 + 1.5 + 4.0) / (147.5 + 42.7 + 67.0) = 25.3\%$$

As such, this is a crucial ratio which measures a company's efficiency in earning a return on capital employed. In the example used, Beta's return suffered a marginal decline due largely to the revaluation of capital invested in fixed assets, whereas Alpha showed a marked improvement due to the remarkable increase in reported profits. Further evidence on these trends would be informative.

In inflationary times profit is often overstated and capital understated.

Financial leverage (gearing)

Alpha 60.8% (65.1%) Beta 61.7% (65.2%)

A complex ratio calculated as total liabilities expressed as a percentage of total assets. For example:

$$100 \times (153.3 + 69.9 + 5.2) / (150.0 + 225.9) = 60.8\%$$

The higher the proportion of relatively cheap capital in the form of liabilities, the greater the average return shareholders can expect, but the risk of large fluctuations in that return also increases. It is a moot point as to whether leverage is beneficial or not, even when there are apparent tax advantages. This ratio is heavily dependent on the dubious valuation of shareholders' equity in the balance sheet and is more reliable when the stock market valuation of equity is used.

The competitors here show little difference though both have slightly increased their reliance on equity capital.

Working capital position

Alpha 0.60 (0.60) Beta 0.39 (0.45)

This ratio is calculated as current assets divided by total assets. For example:

$$225.9/(225.9 + 150.0) = 0.60$$

It illustrates the relative importance of flexible and liquid current assets compared to long-term assets. A high level of current assets does imply the possibility of inefficient asset management. The fall in Beta's ratio is due to the revaluation, but there is still a substantial difference between our two competitors.

Liquidity

Alpha 0.42 (0.41) Beta 0.47 (0.49)

A slightly unusual method of computation is used here, as inventory is divided by current assets. For example:

$$94.2/225.9 = 0.42$$

However, the influence of current liabilities was examined in the leverage ratio and the statistic used here has been found to be influential in research studies. Our example shows Beta with a marginally higher proportion of relatively illiquid stock, but there is little evidence of any unhappy trends.

Asset turnover

Alpha 1.55 (0.94) Beta 1.15 (1.25)

This statistic measures how effectively an organization uses its assets to produce output and is calculated as turnover divided by total assets. For example:

$$581.2 / (150.0 + 225.9) = 1.55$$

Beta maintains a fairly stable level of output per unit of assets, though there appears to be a marginal decline. However, the increase in assets is largely accounted for by the revaluations which pushed up the reserve by £23.9m. Alpha again shows a startling increase in asset turnover. Something is going on!

The ratios examined are not definitive and many alternatives are available, but they are illustrative of the techniques that can be used to elicit information from formal accounting statements.

As with other accounting data, ratios must find a point of comparison. The ratio statistic in itself is uninformative and supposed benchmarks, such as a working capital ratio of 2.0, are misleading. A convenient way of obtaining both a time series and cross-sectional perspective would be to lay out the statistics as follows:

	1986	1987	1988	1989	1990	1991
Sales growth %						
Gamma (examined company)	12.2	15.5	18.9	23.0	17.2	25.3
Delta (competitor 1)	14.7	15.9	19.7	21.8	22.0	20.8
Epsilon (competitor 2)	17.5	18.5	20.1	23.4	18.2	17.0
Industry average	15.1	16.2	18.5	20.0	18.2	16.2

Thus this example shows the industry and three of its constituents making a substantial recovery during the second half of the decade, tailing off in the 1990s for all of the series save for Gamma. It is best to compare corporate performance with a company's closest competitors, as industry groupings cover such a wide range of products and organizational sizes. In the same way, considerable caution should be employed when contrasting different industries or firms from different countries, as accounting practices can result in considerable variation. For example, the return on equity of British firms often appears to be slightly higher than their American rivals and considerably above that of continental competitors, even when the reality is the reverse.

When using ratio analysis or attempting to interpret accounting statements, it must often be left to the analyst's experience of the industry to arrive at informed conclusions. One exception where a more general approach has become accepted is in the use of Z scores to try to predict corporate bankruptcy. This statistic is an amalgam of various ratios which have been found to have a significant relationship with impending failure. Thus commercial organizations publish the Z score trends for companies in comparison with sector averages. It should be noted that some commentators are sceptical of this approach, and more subjective attempts to identify corporate difficulties or managerial incompetence have been suggested.

ACCOUNTING INFORMATION AND MANAGERIAL DECISION MAKING

The information produced by the accounting system is not only of importance to outsiders via the medium of financial reports. Management use accounting data to evaluate current performance in order to establish whether or not corporate objectives are being met, to assess the contribution that alternative decisions are likely to make towards reaching those objectives, and to monitor the progress of previous decisions. This managerial decision-making process and the role of accounting information is illustrated in Figure 22.5.

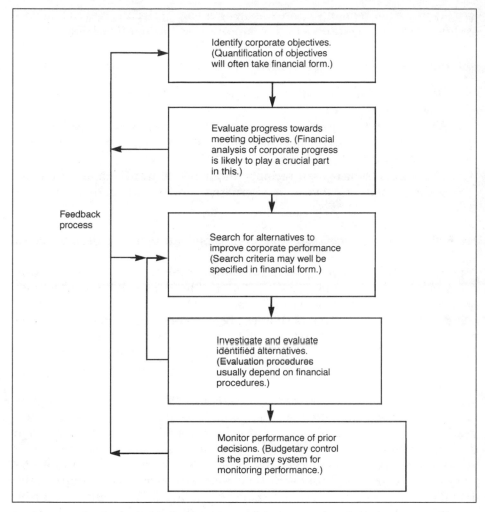

Note: Throughout this process the environment, and changes therein, will be observed. In many cases the clearest information source is financial.

Figure 22.5 The role of accounting information in the decision-making process

The two areas that we will focus on here are the decision-making process and monitoring the effects of the decision via the budgetary control process. Brief mention is also made of the technique of financial modelling, which is a valuable aid to both of these functions.

Managerial decision making

Although accounts are a measure of past events, they are important for what they tell us about the future. The presumption is that the results and trends identified by the accounting statements of the last few years can be suitably   *337* modified by management's appreciation of changing circumstances to give a useful forecast of the future. This is important as business decisions should primarily be evaluated by their effect on 'the future differential cash flows' of the company:

- *Future,* as we cannot affect past cash flows, though we must live with their consequences.
- *Differential,* because it is the expected change induced by a decision when compared to the next best alternative that should be the focus of the decision-making process.
- *Cash flows,* as it is cash receipts and expenditure which affect a company's ability to invest in alternative projects to earn interest or income.

Thus the effect of a decision on the profit is only incidental to the cash flows generated.

Long-term decisions require consideration of the timing of the cash flows generated by the decision. Early receipts can be reinvested to earn further returns, while later receipts are still tied up in the project. Under these circumstances, the differential cash flows, both income and expenditure, must be 'equalized' by discounting the cash flows by an appropriate interest rate. This is a 'net present value' computation with which any manager concerned with long-term decisions should be familiar, and a simple example is worthwhile.

In this example (see Figure 22.6), the early investment in productive equipment and working capital creates an immediate net cash outflow. The first year's cash flow is also negative followed by a build-up of net positive cash inflows before they start to decline. A terminal cash outflow is created by taxation residues and cessation cost. The appropriate discount rate to be used – here 15 per cent – depends on the risk of the project rather than the actual cost of the particular source of capital utilized. This technique can be applied to any decision which is expected to alter the cash flows of a company, be it increasing sales revenue, disposing of assets, or reducing expenditure. The effects of inflation and tax can be confusing and are best dealt with by estimating after-tax actual cash flows and discounting by the after-tax actual, as opposed to real, cost of capital appropriate to a project of this risk.

In Figure 22.6 it can be seen that the net cash flows resulting from the decision to invest are positive. After adjustment for the timing of the cash flows, however, a negative net present value is calculated indicating that the project should not proceed. The reported accounting profit could be expected to average £3333 per year, with higher profits in the years where sales peak. Clearly, profitability of a long-term decision is not a suitable assessment criterion as it ignores the costs of raising sufficient capital in the form of investment funds.

Short-term decisions often drop the emphasis on cash flows in order to focus on the contribution to profit of a particular decision. This is an

£000	Time 0	Year 1	Year 2	Year 3	Year 4	Year 5	Year 6	Year 7
Cash flow	−25	−12	6	16	22	14	4	−5
Discount factor	1.000	0.870	0.756	0.658	0.572	0.497	0.432	0.376
Present value	−25	−10.440	4.536	10.528	12.584	6.958	1.728	−1.880
Net cash flow	=£20,000							
Net present value	= −£986							

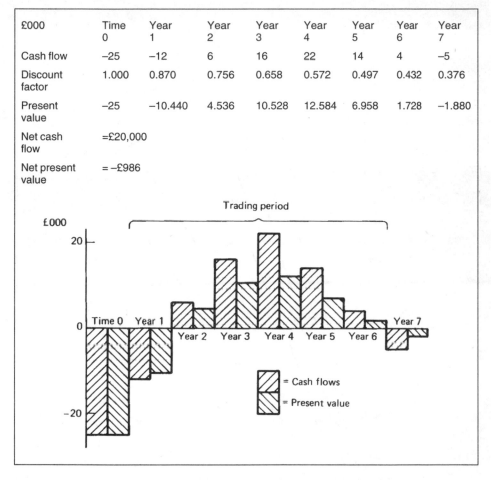

Note: The discount factor allows for the effect of interest at the appropriate rate over the time involved (e.g. Year 3 = 1/C1 +0.15)^3 = 0.658)

Figure 22.6   Actual and discounted cash flows for project evaluation

approximation as it is still the cash flows that are crucial, but where the timing differences are minimal the contribution towards profit is an acceptable compromise. The essential requirement is to separate out the costs and revenues that affect contribution from those that are fixed costs for the purposes of the decision under review. Many costs appearing as relevant to a product on traditional accounting statements are, in fact, beyond the influence of the decision maker and are therefore irrelevant to the decision. As a general rule, those costs which require arbitrary allocation to distinct products or are unaffected by the volume of output of a product, should be ignored in short-term decision making. Examples are depreciation charges, administration and overhead expenses, and production costs unaffected by volume, even that proportion of production wages that is fixed in the short

339

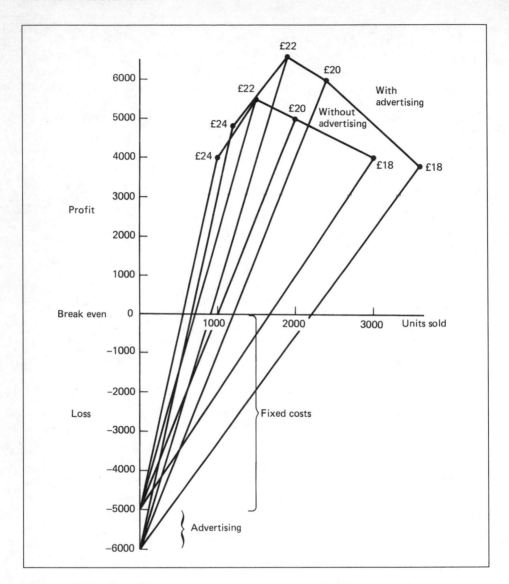

Figure 22.7   Graphical representation of contribution analysis

term. All costs are variable in the long term and most are at least sticky, if not fixed, in the short term, and thus considerable thought should go into the classification of company costs for short-term decision-making purposes.

When variable costs and revenues have been identified, decisions can be based on the maximization of contribution towards fixed costs and profit. The example here (see Figure 22.7) is based on a pricing and advertising decision for a product whose fixed costs are thought to be £5000 per month and variable costs £15 per unit. Alternative prices under consideration are £18, £20, £22 and £24 for which demand figures are estimated at 3000, 2000, 1500 and

1000 respectively. The demand could be increased by 20 per cent by an advertising campaign costing £1000.

It can be seen from Figure 22.7 that the option of selling at £22 each, supported by the advertising campaign, is the preferred decision. The graph includes the fixed-cost element for illustrative purposes, but it is apparent that the same decision would be arrived at whether the fixed costs were £0, £5000 or £50 000, assuming that the costs are genuinely fixed and that the option of closing down is not available.

Two points arise from this example. First, the graphical presentation is unnecessary, as the result can easily be calculated. However, the presentational benefits of the graph and the ease with which changes in expectations can be evaluated make this form of presentation very useful. Second, the decision was arrived at after considering the total contribution, which requires the incorporation of the effects on demand of the alternative pricing possibilities. Thus the traditional approach of pricing at cost plus a mark-up is deficient where demand depends on price, and can lead to ridiculous decisions. In one example, an engineering firm allocated expected costs across its workforce and priced its product using labour costs plus a mark-up. A decline in demand led to an upgrading of the costs to be borne by each labour hour and a consequent increase in prices, the first step in a classic price rise–demand fall vicious circle.

Financial modelling

Financial modelling is a use of accounting data that is closely related to the internal decision making of a company. A computer-based replication of the accounting statements is produced, usually utilizing 'spreadsheet' software. The relationships between inputs, outputs, costs and revenues are carefully specified, and the forecasts and decision variables obtained from management. The expected results from this complex set of interrelationships are then produced, allowing management to investigate readily the effect of changes in forecasts, decision variables, and the environment, and to react accordingly. While it will normally require a financial specialist to produce a sensible computer-based model, once it is completed, non-specialists should be able to alter parameters such as prices, costs, product mix, growth and inflation forecasts, and tax regulations, and immediately examine the results occasioned by such alterations.

Budgetary control

Accounting information is used for control as well as for decision making. Not only can the information feedback enable corrective action when necessary, but also the process of reviewing the outcome of earlier decisions may help to improve subsequent ones. It may also identify areas where individuals have been overoptimistic in their claims. However, it is difficult to provide more than a very brief and general insight into budgetary control systems. *341*

These systems are usually unique, being designed with a particular firm or set of circumstances in mind, and a meaningful explanation would fill this chapter. As an overview, it is apparent that the budgetary control system is one of the key methods used by management to try to ensure that the decisions previously made are being carried out effectively and are having the desired results. Significant deviation from budget should trigger an investigation and remedial action, while providing feedback to the decision makers. The budgetary system is also sometimes seen as part of the (de)motivational process and it probably represents the non-financial specialist's most common brush with accounting data. Budget statements are usually produced by the financial accounting system and, as such, are similar in appearance and concept, though often only showing a subsection of the full results. The clearest difference from normal accounts is the three categories of information reported: the results for the period; the intended results for the period; and the variance between the two.

Some important points should be borne in mind when dealing with budget statements, either as perpetrator or victim. The reporting entity is often a subsection of the company and this presents troublesome allocations. Costs applicable to the whole organization are allocated to budget centres, often on arbitrary bases, and as these are beyond the control of the budget centre managers they are irrelevant to the budgetary and decision-making process. The inputs and outputs of goods and services by the centre require pricing if the profit or loss is to be computed, yet when this is not an arm's-length transaction, the transfer price used can often be misleading.

The responsibility for the results of a budget centre should be matched by the power to affect those results. Thus a cost centre manager can often affect the volume but not always the price of the costs; profit centre managers may find aspects of the revenue-generating process beyond their control, and investment centre managers would often have to live with the actions of their predecessors.

The budgetary regime which is designed to induce a congruence of goals and coordination within the organization can often promote suboptimal behaviour by managers. There is many an apocryphal story in which short-term remedies to meet budget constraints have a damaging long-term effect. Given today's emphasis on multiple career changes, however, those who implement such remedies will have benefited from the short-term benefit but be long gone before the longer-term problem is realized.

The setting of budget targets can be a useful short-term planning process and provides a motivational tool, but this will not come cheap. If a budget is set easily it has probably been done improperly. It is essential that the managers who have to meet budgets should be consulted about, and preferably agree to, their targets. It is also necessary to ensure coordination between the budgets of different centres, and this can be aided by the use of financial models as previously discussed.

Budgets are not popular but they are essential, both as an aid to planning and as an early warning system when those plans start to fail.

CONCLUSION

In one brief chapter it is impossible to give more than a flavour of the accounting process and its uses. However, it will be apparent to most managers or investors that financial data provide some of the most important sources of information available, the misreading of which can be fatal for a company's progress or a manager's career prospects. It is hoped that this chapter has illustrated that ignorance of accounting systems does not preclude a general understanding of accounting reports. Perhaps the most subtle insight is the required balance between unfounded faith in the numeric exactitude of accounting and sceptical rejection of its relevance to decision making.

Some examples of the uses of financial information have been alluded to. Although rather more experience would be required before one would feel confident applying these techniques, perhaps the reader will now have a greater understanding when subjected to them. Indeed, there may perhaps be a future opportunity to point out to the perpetrators some errors in their ways.

CHECK LIST OF KEY POINTS

1   Whatever its failings, financial information is pervasive in business. This suggests that it is seen as being useful by management practitioners and that a working knowledge is essential for career development.
2   There is no single correct set of accounting results. Financial statements are a product of the choice of accounting methods, a number of subjective decisions, and the underlying transactions.
3   If managers are aware of the limitations of financial statements, a considerable amount of valuable information can be derived from them. Ratio analysis is one technique which is often utilized to this end.
4   When analysing long-term decisions it is advisable to take account of the timing of cash flows. It is the future differential cash flows, discounted by an appropriate cost of capital, which are relevant.
5   Short-term decisions concentrate on marginal costs and revenues. The interrelationships between prices, demand and costs are difficult to estimate but are fundamental to effective decision making.
6   Financial information can play a valuable role in budgetary control. Such systems are often pervasive within the firm and it is advisable to understand their motivational and social impact as well as their accounting and feedback roles.

FURTHER READING

Basic

McKenzie, W., *The Financial Times Guide to Using and Interpreting Accounts*, FT/Pitman, 1994.

Advanced

Rees, W. P., *Financial Analysis*, Prentice Hall, 1995.

23 Project management
John Lewington

Projects are the main mechanism used by management for coping with the introduction of new systems, products and processes, and any changes outside the normal day-to-day operations of the organization. Projects inevitably bring about change to some facet of the organization and often all of the skills embodied in this book will be necessary to complete a project successfully. A project may be as small as the implementation of a word-processing system, or as large as the building and equipping of a new factory. Large organizations will have highly developed bureaucratic systems of project submission, appraisal, presentation, approval and resourcing. Small organizations with short communication chains will often have very simple decision-making processes and informal systems of project appraisal.

In this chapter I will define the main phases of project management and show how a manager may tackle each phase in a professional manner (see Figure 23.1). All projects involve elements of risk. The level of risk can be very high if the size of the project is large in relation to the size of the organization carrying it out. Successful projects should enhance a company's profitability, market position and self-esteem. However, projects often fail through poor appraisal of potential problems, inadequate organization, lack of technical expertise and underfunding.

Good project management systems should embody the following aims:

- Ensure that the organization reacts to environmental pressures and changes in a rational manner.
- Accurately estimate the resources required to complete the project successfully, and ensure that no resource needs are hidden or forgotten.
- Fully appraise the total expenditure of resources in terms of the economic and organizational benefits.

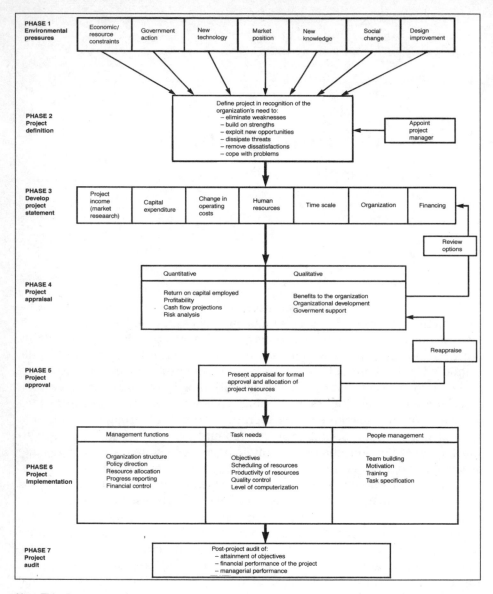

Note: This diagram provides an overview of the main phases and components of project management.

Figure 23.1   The main phases of project management

- Implement the project through a coordinated plan on a timescale appropriate to resources availability and organizational needs.
- Develop the organization's current systems and resources to be able to cope with the changes that the project will bring.

ENVIRONMENTAL PRESSURES

346   The main skills in this phase of project management are perceptual. Change

must be seen as possible or necessary due to internal or external opportunities. The ability of the organization to respond to environmental stimuli will depend on a number of factors such as:

- attitude of mind of management to change;
- internal politics and management's perception of the relative importance of the problem or opportunity;
- organization's size and structure;
- bureaucratic complexity and internal inertia in launching new ideas; and
- perceived threats/risks of the change.

Small organizations may be quick to perceive new opportunities, but will sometimes lack the financial resources to exploit fully the environmental change. Large organizations will have the resources, but internal politics, bureaucratic systems and organizational inertia may stifle innovation. Most projects will be appraised on their economic justification. The stronger the economic justification, the more likely the project is to be raised to reality. The four main areas likely to generate new projects are: increased productivity; resource constraints; new products, services and markets; and government action.

Increased productivity

Some projects may present obvious advantages and indisputable need through clear economic viability. Cost savings through increases in resource (labour, materials, space, equipment) productivity are vital to the survival of any organization. The application of new knowledge and technology will provide the driving forces for change. Replacement of old facilities should also provide the opportunity to improve methods and implement new systems.

Resource constraints

Many projects are forced upon management through shortages of labour, raw materials, space and equipment. Successful products and services may outgrow their operational resource provisions. Therefore, projects are devised to provide additional capacity, the cost of which must be balanced by cost savings and additional revenue generation. Other projects will be developed to cope with physical shortages of raw materials and office/factory space that are constraining operations.

New products, services and markets

The introduction of new products, services and markets will generate projects which define the resources, timing and expenditures involved in the venture. The organization will need to assess the impact of the new product on existing products in determining the possible viability of the project. The *347* expenditures on R & D, new facilities and market launch must be matched by future forecasts of sales revenues.

Government action

New legislation often initiates new projects in order that an organization's facilities and systems comply with government requirements. It is unlikely that these projects will generate cost savings or additional revenues. Therefore, organizations may use the project as a mechanism for controlling and minimizing costs.

PROJECT DEFINITION

Projects must be accurately defined, as the research involved in the development of a project statement may involve substantial investment of resources. Therefore, a project may be categorized under one of the following headings:

- Cost savings.
- New products and services.
- Replacement of plant, vehicles and buildings.
- Product research and development.
- Exploration for mineral reserves.
- Expansion of product/service capacity.
- Marketing campaign to increase sales.
- Organizational development/training programme to enhance an organization's human resources.
- Environmental, health and safety enhancements.

All of the above categories would be expected to produce long-term economic benefits, except for environmental projects which might be necessary to comply with legislation.

The initial sponsors of the project must clearly define their aims and objectives. This will require intense discussions about the 'fit' of the project with existing policies, resources and skills of the organization. If the project is beyond the scope of the organization's current skills, then it may be necessary to employ consultants or approach specialists to frame the project appropriately. The rationales and hypotheses should be submitted to senior management for formal approval before starting the next project phase.

DEVELOPING A PROJECT STATEMENT

When an idea, concept or suggestion seems worth considering, then the approval of senior management will generally be sought. The data collection will involve considerable time in the compilation of a large project statement. Therefore, a presentation of the objectives, rationales and potential benefits may be necessary before starting the study. The technical and business research involved in this phase may involve several of the following activities in order to make accurate estimates of expenditures and revenues:

- Market research – estimates of selling price, market share, market size, selling costs.
- Technical research – experimental products and model plants.
- Patent surveys and searches.
- Development of synthetic time and work standards.
- Preliminary negotiations with government, local government and unions.
- Computer simulations to aid the design of systems.

In many projects with a long gestation period and high technological uncertainty, these estimates will be little more than guesstimates or 'ball park' figures. A diagram of the main cost factors that can arise is given in Figure 23.2. From Figure 23.1 you will see that there are a number of areas to be considered in this phase to ensure that a comprehensive project statement is compiled.

Project income

Most projects will stand or fall on their ability to increase the organization's net income, either through new revenue generation or cost reduction. The increase in 'cash flow' will be the sole justification for the capital expenditure. Any of the following sources of income generation may be used individually or in combination to justify the project's capital expenditures:

- Sales revenue from new products or services (or royalties).
- Release of capital through disposals of existing assets.
- Increase in revenue from expansion of capacity.
- Reduction in costs of existing operations.
- Government grants and special contracts.

Capital expenditure

Every project statement will contain a listing of the capital expenditures (long-term assets) necessary. A wide variety of funding methods (see Financing, page 352) may be feasible/desirable for different facets of the project depending upon the size of the expenditure, corporate policy and attitude to risk. Expenditures may be categorized according to their economic life in order to make some forecasts of depreciation.

There is always a tendency to *underestimate* capital expenditure on projects. This is particularly true of long-term projects where the problems of delays, inflation, technical change and new factors (e.g. pollution control) may surface as the project progresses. Therefore, the inclusion of a 'contingency allowance' to cover unforeseen eventualities and problems may be justified. The main areas of project expenditure can be stated as follows:

349

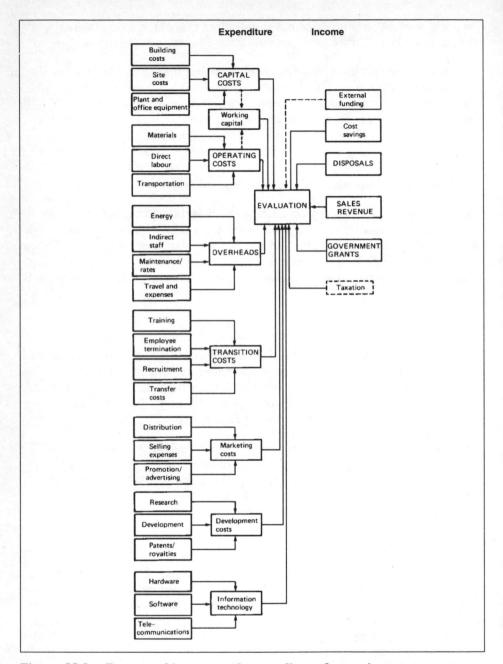

Figure 23.2   Factors of income and expenditure for project statements

- Land and buildings.
- Plant and equipment.
- Tooling and storage facilities.
- Working capital.

- Vehicles and materials handling equipment.
- Computers (hardware and software) and telecommunications networks.

Changes in operating costs

Most projects will result in some changes in operating costs. The main focus of a project may be cost savings in materials or labour through increasing capital investment. The result of this is a higher-risk situation in terms of changes in the level of activity.

Productivity increase projects can be focused upon the following areas:

- Improved material utilization.
- Increased labour productivity.
- Overhead reduction or faster absorption.
- Reduction in telecommunications or energy costs.
- Reduction in sales or distribution costs.
- Improved information systems and decision making.

Human resources

A project may require special technological or managerial skills to be completed successfully. These skills may be in short supply. Therefore, the utilization of these skills will either be expensive in terms of their actual or opportunity (internal to the organization) costs. The creators, innovators and entrepreneurs who will be crucial to the success of the project must be coordinated and scheduled carefully. The project manager must consider the task needs in selecting and blending an effective team to solve potential problems. The 'real' cost of the man hours that will be required for the project must be accurately assessed.

Timescale

Some consideration must be given to an outline plan of the main activities to establish an overall duration for the project. There may be a tendency to *underestimate* the timescale in order to encourage project selection. Judgements about timescale are always partly subjective and there is always senior management pressure to reduce the total timescale of the project to a minimum. This will encourage the 'crashing' of activities, that is, the pouring in of resources to reduce activity timescale. Conversely, the delay and late completion of activities will have harmful effects on a project. If the cumulative loss of benefits (financial) and the overall cost of the project on different timescales are considered together, then the sum of loss of benefits and project cost may provide an optimal timescale (see Figure 23.3). Ultimately, product life cycles and other environmental stimuli (competition) may have the most profound effects on management's perception of an appropriate   *351*

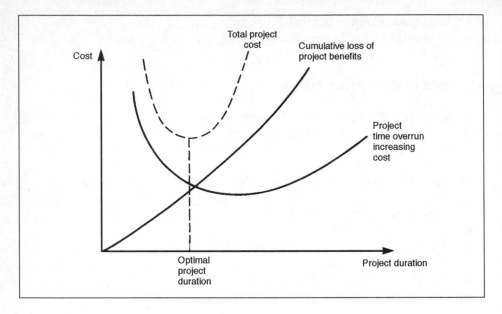

Figure 23.3   Total cost of project

timescale. If it is feasible, some consideration should be given to phasing the project in such a way that the first phase will generate funding for subsequent phases.

Organization

A preliminary assessment of organizational problems must be made. The way in which a project is organized and operated after completion will have cost implications in terms of expenditure and revenue. The person appointed as project manager will have to answer several key organizational questions:

- How should the personnel be organized in order to maximize communication, motivation and task completion?
- Should the whole project be handed over to a subcontractor on a turnkey basis?
- What sort of organization will be required to operate the new system in order to plan for training and staffing?
- What information and computer systems will be of benefit to the project team?

Financing

Most projects will be financed internally using current cash flow or borrowing capacity. However, large and/or high-risk projects may require alternative funding strategies. One of the following alternatives may be used to reduce the impact of adverse risks on your organization:

- Venture capital funding.
- Joint projects in the form of partnerships or consortia.
- Royalty and licensing agreements.
- Locating to obtain government employment grants and subsidies.
- Leasing and renting buildings and equipment.

Once these issues have been decided the project is ready for appraisal. The estimates, guesstimates and 'ball park' figures will form the basic budget for the project. Some updating, review and changes will undoubtedly occur from feedback during the appraisal.

PROJECT APPRAISAL

In this phase, management are concerned with appraising the information and rationales stated in the project statement. Several alternative options should be appraised to allow for choice. However, this is not always practicable. The appraisal may result in feedback on management's attitude to facets of the project which will result in revisions of the project statement and reappraisal. As the project statement may have been gathered from a wide variety of sources the information must be screened for consistency.

Surveys reveal that great emphasis is placed on the quantitative factors in project appraisal. However, it should be remembered that these are only *estimates* and *forecasts*. In addition the qualitative factors expressed in the objectives, rationales and non-quantifiable benefits should fit with current strategies and business policies. Therefore, the main objectives of this phase are as follows:

- To determine whether the project meets the organization's criteria for financial return on the investment.
- To ensure that the estimates present an accurate/practical/realistic view of the project.
- To appraise the risks in relation to the economic returns.
- To determine the fit and effects of the project on the organization's future strategies and policies.

Project appraisal may require considerable management accounting and computing skills; you should therefore consult Further Reading at the end of the chapter for the detail behind these techniques.

Profitability

Most projects will be undertaken because they promise to improve the economic position (wealth) of the sponsoring organization. One problem in   *353* selecting projects is to define an appropriate rate of return for any given risk. Many organizations ignore this problem and set one rate of return for all projects. Deciding on an appropriate rate of return can be affected by many factors such as the organization's cost of capital, returns from other similar projects, or returns from other investments outside the organization. Other factors such as inflation, current interest rates and taxation may have some bearing on the figure. Profitability criteria can be expressed in a number of ways, but payback period and rate of return on investment predominate.

Payback period

This is the time taken to repay the investment out of the cash flow from the investment:

Payback period (years)	1	3	5	7
Projects	Computers	Vehicles	Property	Government

Payback method is very easy to understand and widely used by a variety of organizations.

Rate of return on investment

This is expressed as a percentage rate per annum.

Generally, organizations set a minimum rate (sometimes called cut-off rate) of return to be obtained from their projects:

Minimum rates of return (%)	10	20	30	40
Projects	Government Property	Vehicles		Computers Pharmaceuticals

Several techniques are used for assessing rate of return, all of which give different answers. Some employ formulae (accounting rate of return); others attempt to forecast cash flows, then apply discount factors (discounted cash flow DCF). There are two kinds of DCF technique: net present value (NPV) and internal rate of return (IRR). Net present value utilizes the organization's minimum rate of return and determines the result on a 'go'–'no go' basis. Internal rate of return attempts to determine the exact compound rate of return for the project over its entire life. The result is then compared with the minimum rate of return. Both techniques lend themselves more to computer models of sensitivity than manual calculations.

Projects not meeting the organization's criteria for profitability will rarely be progressed. If a project makes good basic business sense, then it might be recycled through the statement and appraisal phases for investment trimming and rethinking.

Cash flow projections

Expenditures, forecasts of income and timescale projections should be combined into a cash flow projection. This will provide management with an overall view of cash commitments and the rate at which loans might be paid off. Using a spreadsheet will enable a model of project cash flows to be developed. This will allow management to appraise the effects of inflation and taxation.

Risk analysis

A spreadsheet cash flow model will greatly ease the burden of examining the risk aspects of the project. The relative significance of the investment decision is dictated by the size of the investment in relation to an organization's net assets. Failure of a small project can be absorbed, but failure of a large project could be disastrous. Therefore, risk analysis should make management aware of the 'downside' risks which might evolve under certain environmental conditions.

One technique of risk appraisal is *sensitivity analysis.* The approach is to take each main factor in the project (e.g. sales income, materials cost) and vary it by +10 per cent and –10 per cent, one at a time. This should give some indication of the most sensitive variables which will provide a concentration of attention. This awareness of potential problem areas may result in some reorganization of the project or hedging of risks.

Another method is to examine the project through a variety of scenarios. This may provide some insights into how the project should be managed in different environments. Computerization is an essential feature of this process.

Generally, risk should be related to reward. If a project has high risks, then a high rate of return should be expected. However, most organizations have one rate of return for all types of projects. This rate of return is set relatively high, on the basis that those projects which work out will pay for those which fail.

Benefits to the organization

In project appraisal the decision-making process will undoubtedly be affected by some qualitative factors which cannot be expressed in economic terms. In cases where accurate estimating of costs and revenues is difficult, then these may be the most important decision-making variables. Any one or a combination of the following factors may be used to provide project justification:

- Improvement of product/service market position.
- Stronger cost structure of products or services.
- Security of employment for the workforce.
- Release of non-productive assets.

- Improvements in the organization's financial structure.
- Implementation of new technology to meet competition.
- Establish technological lead over the competition.
- Establish a position in a high-growth market.
- Development of new products or services.
- Comply with health and safety regulations.
- Improve corporate image.
- Develop new skills and expertise in the workforce.
- Improve managerial control and decision making.
- Fit with the firm's business plan.

Organizational development

Projects may be a catalyst for organizational development. They may determine many new directions to the organization's task systems, a focus for change, learning, conflict resolution and a new set of working relationships.

Government support

In most industrialized countries the government plays a significant role in providing financial support for high-risk and economically marginal projects. This support may be through taxation relief, direct loans, grants or contracts. Intangible government support may make funding easier to obtain or provide an opening in export markets. The effect of government funding is to reduce risk and provide a market for products and services. In return, the government will require job creation and stability of employment for a specific region.

PROJECT APPROVAL

In this phase, the project statements and appraisals should be combined into one summary document for presentation to senior management. In large organizations, this will involve the completion of standardized forms covering the factors to be considered by their specific type of organization and business. The summary report may be accompanied by a presentation, 'selling' the project to senior management. Good project management software packages assist in generating presentation graphics.

The report and/or presentation should contain the following elements:

- Main objectives of the project.
- Main rationales supporting the project.
- Models, pictures and outline designs of new products or services.
- Market information – strategy, size, share, pricing, promotion and advertising.
- Proposals for the organization and staffing of the new system.
- Outline of information systems and data-processing support networks.
- Product/service cost data.

- List/summary of main capital expenditures.
- Profitability statements.
- Cash flow forecasts.
- Financing proposals.
- Potential risks and environmental problems.

If the project is not approved, then senior management should provide their reasons for rejection. This might then involve further research and appraisal before resubmission.

PROJECT IMPLEMENTATION

The implementation phase involves the planning, scheduling and coordination of a wide variety of resources. The physical activities must be paralleled by the development of appropriate human resources to implement and operate the new system. The integration of activities will involve the mobilization of resources on both an internal and external basis. The organization of the project must evolve around clear lines of responsibility and communication married to an integrated set of activities with a time-phased plan.

Task objectives

In general, the aim is to minimize project duration. However, while this may be an important consideration in many projects it is not the sole criterion. Projects may be implemented using one or more of the following objectives as a guide to planning:

- Minimize total project duration.
- Minimize the total systems cost of the project.
- Minimize cost for a given project duration.
- Provide an even (steady) loading on scarce resources.
- Minimize time for a given project cost.
- Maximize the use of available resources.

Organization structure

Project management requires both a vertical and horizontal flow of work, which cannot be achieved through rigid formal authority. Three basic structures exist for managing projects. However, none provides a perfect solution and each has its strengths and weaknesses.

Functional structure

Where projects are confined to one specific function (e.g. production, marketing) in the organization, then this approach may be appropriate. Where projects cut across functions, control becomes difficult.

357

Project structure

Teams of specialists are formed to carry out a specific project. Responsibility and lines of communication are very clear in this type of organization. However, the costs of maintaining this type of structure in a multiproject environment can be very high.

Matrix structure

In this structure, the project manager maintains a team against a background of functional activities. This structure promotes learning and a strong technical base, but may sometimes evoke a conflict of priorities with functional managers.

Policy direction and resource allocation

Projects often create new operating systems, but managers have to maintain the existing systems. This will cause conflict between the project manager and functional managers if priorities are not clearly stated by senior management. Resource requirements should be identified, related to tasks, and provision made to ensure that the resources will be available at the required time.

Financial control and progress reporting

Most organizations will operate their main controls through the finance department. The simplest way is to plot a cumulative forecast of expenditure and then monitor the actual expenditure against it. The purpose of this is to highlight possible overspending before it gets out of control. Expenditure forecasts are generally broken down into spent (bills paid), committed (orders placed), and to be committed. Written reports and occasional presentations will be required on some projects.

Scheduling of resources

The scheduling of resources will be accomplished using a network to link activities logically (Figure 23.4). Organizations use a variety of names for this approach: for example, critical path method (CPM) or analysis (CPA), and precedence network or programme evaluation and review technique (PERT). Once the network has been drawn logically, relating the completion of activities, then a bar chart can be drawn or produced from a computer package (Figure 23.5).

First, management must make a decision on the detail in which they plan to schedule each task. The basic information required on each task is:

- a brief description of the task;

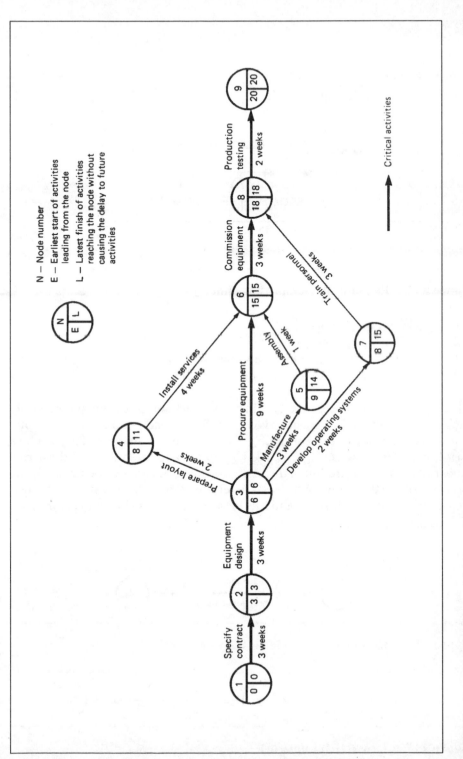

Figure 23.4 Example of a simple network

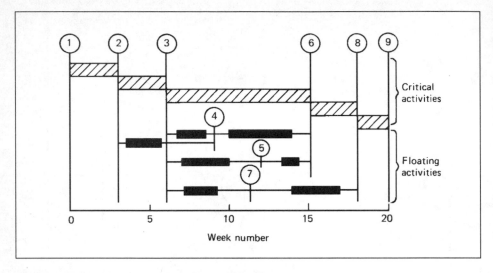

Figure 23.5   Example of a simple bar chart

- a time duration of the task;
- a responsibility for the task;
- a list of tasks that must be complete before the task can start; and
- a specification of resource needs for each task.

An arrow is used to represent a task in the project and this is most commonly known as an 'activity'. The activity is bounded at each end by a circle commonly known as an 'event' (or node). An example of a single activity such as 'write report' is shown in Figure 23.6. The length and orientation of the arrow is *not* related to the duration of the task. However, the arrow does point in the direction of the time flow for the task. After the activity 'write report', the next task may be word processing, and this is represented as shown in Figure 23.7.

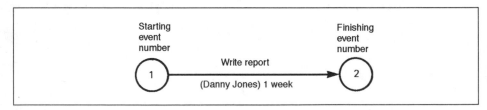

Figure 23.6   Example of a single activity network

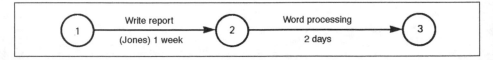

Figure 23.7   Two-activity network

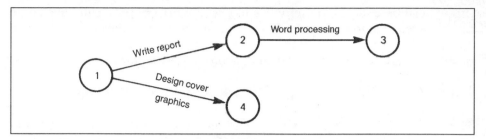

Figure 23.8   Example of how concurrent activities are represented

The numbers at the tail and head of the arrow are called 'event' numbers. Therefore, activity 1–2 is 'write report'. If the report were a long one, then it might be worth commencing word processing before it was completely finished. However, for this example we will assume that word processing cannot start until the writing is finished. The cover of the report could be designed while the report is being written; such concurrent (or parallel) activities are represented as shown in Figure 23.8.

Once the report and cover are ready, then they may be printed, bound and distributed. Figure 23.9 shows the complete sequence. The arrow connecting event five and event six is a 'dummy' activity with zero time duration and it is used to maintain proper logical order and unique numbering (for computer input purposes) within the network diagram.

The network is not only a plan, but is also a communication device for ensuring that all departments understand how their contribution fits into the whole picture. A main network may have to be broken down into a series of sub-networks to be used within individual departments.

Even small projects justify the drawing of a network and construction of a simple bar chart. Larger projects will justify the use of computers for control and updating purposes. If computers are to be used, then schedules of resources associated with each activity may also be required. If activities are delayed or get ahead of schedule, then the impact on later activities can clearly be seen. A wide variety of commercially manufactured aids for displaying projects and plans is also available.

Some activities will have to be completed to an exact time schedule; these are called the 'critical path' activities and set the shortest time in which the

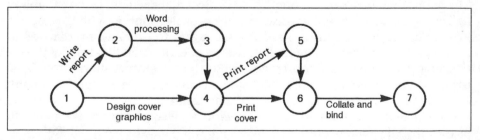

Figure 23.9   A complete network, showing logical order and unique numbering

project can be completed. Activities not on the critical path will have some free time referred to as 'activity float'. This means that management will have some limited discretion on the start and finish of non-critical activities. This discretion may be used to level demands on scarce resources.

Computerization of the project management process

The level of computerization will depend on the size of the organization, and project complexity. While some organizations may choose mainframe computers for processing project data, most will choose microcomputers for their flexibility and ease of updating. Simple projects may be managed using simple scheduling software or spreadsheets. More complex projects will require the use of powerful software packages specifically designed for project management (e.g. Time Line, Microsoft Project – see WorldWideWeb references). These packages are constantly being updated, but specifically, their common features include:

- Calculation of start, finish and float times for all activities.
- Development of Gantt (bar) charts for each activity.
- Preparation of individual activity schedules by manager responsibility.
- Production of calendar and milestone charts, with facilities to include public holidays.
- Tracking of multiple (5+) resource demands and costs per activity.
- Individual and multiproject histograms of resource usage for smoothing and levelling.
- Colour graphics and data outputs for project progress presentations.
- Export/import data from/to main spreadsheet and database packages.
- Support multiple access through local area networks (LAN).

Capabilities to import and export data among a variety of spreadsheet and database packages increases in importance as the number of management participants grows. In national and international projects, this facilitates E-mail and direct interchange of data files across the Internet.

Productive management of resources

The main advantage of computer-based project management is the capability to review time, cost and critical resource projections as changes occur. Project management software enables managers to examine alternatives to future plans using 'what if' modelling. Using one, or a combination, of the six task objectives given earlier provides a guide for generating alternative plans. Greater understanding of potential trade-offs between resources (see Figure 23.3) should improve overall economic management.

Project managers should review a wide variety of alternative plans to ensure the efficient scheduling of scarce and high-cost resources. Resource peaks (see Figure 23.10) can be managed by developing plans that 'smooth' or 'level' demands on critical resources. Where scarce resources are shared

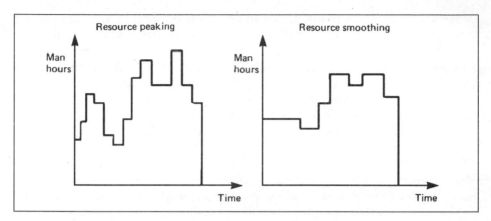

Figure 23.10   An example of resource smoothing

across a number of projects, efficient scheduling and allocation will generally require the use of sophisticated project management software.

Quality control

This may present substantial problems, particularly on large projects involving complex subcontractor interrelationships. Therefore, the quality of work must be constantly monitored by designers, surveyors and architects. The information and reports should be stored using a database computer package for cross-referencing. This will enable project management to keep comprehensive control and records of all quality control reports. Quality circles can be set up to provide a constant dialogue on quality problems and project progress.

People management

Many aspects of personnel management are effectively dealt with in other chapters of this book. However, it is very easy to forget about human resource development when the task aspects (getting things finished) appear to predominate. But individuals and groups must be *motivated* to achieve project objectives. In technically complex projects, there may be a high element of *training* taking place both formally and informally. Therefore, it is necessary to build effective *teams* capable of supporting and assisting each other (see Chapter 18 for team building). This involves good communications, mutual respect, and an ability to resolve conflict effectively. There is no such thing as delegation in the management of a project. Every activity must have an owner who is committed to resolving problems, so that the task is completed successfully.

AUDITING PROJECT PERFORMANCE

To improve future performance it is not unusual to carry out a post-project   *363* audit. The main focus of an audit should be on the accuracy of the project statement, the adequacy of the project appraisal process, and finally, the effectiveness of the implementation. All large projects should probably be audited one year after full implementation. Smaller projects may be sampled and appropriate examples of good and bad results examined. The results of the audit may assist management in formulating an effective organizational development programme aimed at greater effectiveness in project management for the future. The main areas of examination are listed below.

Objectives

Has the project achieved its objectives in terms of performance, resolving problems, exploiting opportunities and provided an appropriate return on investment?

Project statement

How accurate were the forecasts of costs, expenditure, income and time-scale? Could/should more accurate estimates have been prepared?

Appraisal

Did the appraisal process properly consider all of the practical alternatives, risks and organizational implications? Were effective strategies developed for coping with potential problems and reorganization?

Implementation

This will undoubtedly come in for the greatest scrutiny in the following areas:

- Planning and scheduling of resources.
- Procedures for contracting and tendering.
- Labour, materials and equipment utilization.
- Adequacy of financial control mechanisms.
- Progress reporting and communication systems.
- Analysis of delays and lost time.
- Organization structures and personnel policies.

Use of the check list

The check list that follows is designed as an *aide memoire* for the busy manager and should be used in conjunction with Figures 23.1 and 23.2 to ensure the rounded consideration of a project. Most large organizations will have their own systems, procedures and project peculiarities; it may also be useful to develop an internal check list of factors for your own organization's environment.

PROJECT MANAGEMENT CHECK LIST

Environmental pressures

1 Does the organization have sensing mechanisms and communication channels in order to:
   - spot market changes;
   - recognize new business/service opportunities;
   - adopt new technology and systems;
   - reduce costs and be more competitive;
   - incorporate employee suggestions;
   - resolve customer problems;
   - respond to social change?
2 Who is responsible for project initiation?
3 How are potential projects formulated for project definition?

Project definition

1 Can the project be adequately categorized (i.e. R & D, cost saving, replacement, expansion, etc.)?
2 Which person/group/department/committee is responsible for defining the terms of reference/objectives/constraints of the project?
3 Is the potential project consistent with the current policies of the organization?
4 Is it likely that top management will support the project?
5 Are the technical expertise/skills requirements within the scope of the organization or should consultants be employed?

Developing a project statement

1 Has the project been approved in principle by senior management?
2 Have the rationales/objectives/constraints/importance of the project been adequately defined for costing and estimating purposes?
3 Can the income/sources of revenue for the project be adequately defined/guesstimated/forecast?
4 Have all of the following items of expenditure been properly considered:
   - land, new buildings and site facilities (roads, etc.);
   - machines, office equipment and computers (hardware and software);
   - training costs for completion of the project and implementation of the new system;
   - employee recruitment and termination;
   - relocation of employees and facilities;
   - research and development costs;
   - marketing and sales?

5　What changes in annual operating costs will occur after the project is completed?
- materials and staffing;
- transportation, distribution and energy costs;
- rates, building and equipment maintenance;
- computing and telecommunications costs;
- staff travel and expenses;
- marketing and sales?

6　Will any specialized scarce human resources be required to complete the project successfully?

7　Does the estimated timescale for the project conflict with the required completion date? If so, how can the two be reconciled?

8　Will a special organization structure be needed to complete the project?

9　Will a new organization structure be required after the completion of the project?

10　Can the project be financed internally? If not, where will the external financing come from?

11　Can appropriate measures of profitability be calculated from the information available?

Project appraisal - quantitative

1　Does the project meet the organization's criteria for profitability in terms of payback and/or return on investment?

2　Will the project/investment enhance the long-term profitability and security of the organization?

3　Will the cash flow projections for the project affect other projects and/or the normal operational requirements of the organization? If yes, how can this problem be coped with?

4　Will the project involve cost savings and stronger market position?

5　Can any limits of accuracy be placed upon the market size, market share and product life?

6　Will inflation have a significant impact on the larger items of expenditure?

7　Can the relative risks be assessed in quantitative terms through 'sensitivity analysis'?

Project approval

1　At what level in the organization can the project be approved (department manager/area manager/managing director/board)?

2　Are you satisfied that the project statement represents the 'best' solution to the problem?

3　If the project cannot be approved in present form what areas need changing to make the project viable?

4 Are the contingencies for cost overruns sufficient on large items of expenditure?

5 Can resources be allocated in step with the current timescale for the project?

6 Is the project too large/risky for the present organization? If so, should a partner/venture capital be found to form the project as a separate venture?

Project implementation

1 Has an appropriate balance been defined between resources–timescale projected expenditure?

2 Have responsibilities/organization structures been defined to ensure successful completion of the project?

3 Has senior management provided appropriate policies for the conduct of the project?

4 What progress reporting will be required in terms of frequency/detail/format/expenditure?

5 What financial controls should be implemented to ensure successful completion of the project?

6 What mechanisms exist for coping with cost overruns and expenditures not originally forecast?

7 Have the main task activities been clearly defined and responsibilities allocated?

8 Are the milestone dates and activity completion times clear to the whole team?

9 Is the frequency of scheduling/rescheduling of resources and activities complex enough to justify computerization?

10 Do the current plans maximize the productivity of project resources?

11 Who is responsible for controlling/monitoring the quality of the work completed?

12 What processes are planned into the organization structure for developing the project team and/or the team to operate the new system?

13 What incentives exist to encourage the team/contractor to complete the project on time?

14 What training will be required for the project team members and/or the people operating the new system?

15 Have appropriate task specifications been prepared for individual members of the project team?

Project audit

1 Is the project sufficiently important to warrant an audit? If so, how long should elapse before an audit is meaningful?

2 To what extent has the project achieved its objectives?

3   Did the project attain its financial performance objectives in terms of return/ project budget?
4   Was management of the project effective and were resources used efficiently?
5   What can be learned to improve future projects?

FURTHER READING

General

Briner,W., Hastings, C. and Geddes, M., *Project Leadership*, 2nd edn, Gower, 1996.
Drigani, F., *Computerized Project Control*, Dekker, 1989.
Heizer, J. and Render, B., *Production and Operations Management*, Prentice Hall, 1996, chs 16 and 17.
Lock, D. (ed.), *Project Management Handbook*, Gower, 1987.
Turner, J. R., *The Handbook of Project-Based Management*, McGraw-Hill, 1993.

Project management for specific tasks

Barkley, B., *Customer-Driven Project Management: A new paradigm in total quality implementation*, McGraw-Hill, 1994.
Craig, S., *People and Project Management For Information Technology*, McGraw-Hill, 1995.
Leavitt, J. S., *Total Quality through Project Management*, McGraw-Hill, 1994.
Roseneau Jr., M. and Moran J., *Managing the Development of New Products*, Van Nostrand Reinhold, 1993.

Project appraisal, implementation and auditing

Dinsmore, P. C., *Human Factors in Project Management*, American Management Association, 1986.
Kharbanda, O. P., *What Made Gertie Gallop: Lessons from project failures*, Van Nostrand Reinhold, 1996.
Souder, W. E., *Project Selection and Economic Appraisal*, Van Nostrand Reinhold, 1983.
Turner, W. S., *Project Auditing Methodology*, North-Holland, 1980.
UNESCO, *Project Evaluation*, HMSO, 1985.

Useful addresses on the WorldWideWeb

MSProject Software: http://www.microsoft.com
Timeline Software: http://www.symantec.com

24 Decision making and problem solving

Peter Walker

The fortunes of large corporations depend on the quality of decisions made by their management. Despite this, many managers have little formal training in decision making and little understanding of how they finally arrived at a decision and made a choice.

Certainly, literature is available on many specific techniques which can aid decision making, but to be useful these techniques must be applied within an overall framework. The purpose of this chapter is to look at such an overall framework which may be used to make any decision.

Effective decision making will often require inputs from problem solving and contingency planning and hence these processes are also discussed. Because creativity is required in all the other processes it is also referred to.

DECISION MAKING, PROBLEM SOLVING, CONTINGENCY PLANNING AND CREATIVITY

The purpose of decision making is to make the best possible choice, based on sound information. However, if the information is either inaccurate or incomplete, the decision may fail. The purpose of problem solving and contingency planning is to improve the quality of information being processed.

Problem solving looks at the past with the purpose of understanding the causes of any problem that needs correcting. Contingency planning looks to the future with the purpose of anticipating future problems.

Problem solving, when required, must precede decision making because the decision must be based on the best understanding of the past and present situation. In contrast, contingency planning will be conducted after a decision has been made in order to refine or improve the chosen course of action before implementation.

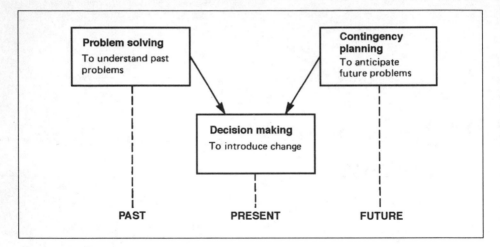

Note: The causes of past problems and an understanding of possible future problems are information necessary for an effective decision.

Figure 24.1   Relationship of decision making with problem solving and contingency planning

Thus decision making can be seen as the process of bridging from the past to the future when the manager wants to change the present (see Figure 24.1).

CREATIVITY

Applied creativity is essential to each of the three processes outlined above. For example, creativity will be needed in problem solving to develop possible causes of problems. It may also be needed in decision making to develop new alternatives or solutions from which to choose. In contingency planning, creativity will be used to develop ideas about future problems which could occur and possible reasons for those problems.

There are several techniques to enhance creativity, of which brainstorming is the best known. However, one thing which is common to these techniques is that judgement is suspended while the new ideas are being generated. In other words, we should not try both to create and to evaluate an idea simultaneously. Rather we should create first and evaluate second.

This is illustrated in Figure 24.2, where a concern is used to focus on creative generation of possible approaches to resolving that concern. Next, an analytical approach is used to select and implement the best approach to reach a solution. A simple example of this could be the situation in which you need to establish a rapid transport link between two towns. As a result of creative thinking, some 'possible approaches' might be generated: scheduled airlines; private helicopter; private car; carrier company; and railway transport. Evaluation of these ideas is delayed until after they have all been gener-

ated, when criteria such as cost, time, reliability, and so on, can be used to

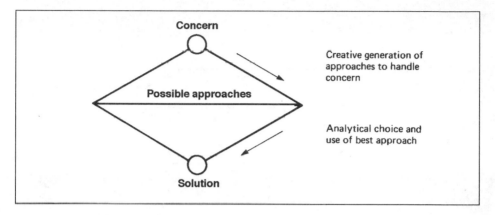

Figure 24.2   Separation of creativity and analysis

evaluate them and a detailed schedule established for the chosen means of transport.

Each of the processes of problem solving, decision making and contingency planning use this two-step approach, where ideas are first generated and then analysed, and it is this separation of creativity and analysis which helps to make the process so effective.

Where the phrase 'brainstorm ideas' is used in this chapter it means 'creatively generate new ideas without stopping to criticize or evaluate at this stage'.

PROBLEM SOLVING

The purpose of problem solving is to discover what caused a current situation, so that this knowledge may be used to decide how to handle it. If the causes are already fully understood, or there is no desire for change, there is no need for problem solving.

The formal use of problem solving is badly neglected for the simple reason that many managers fail to recognize that their problems require analysis. Rather, when something goes wrong they make an assumption about the cause and then act upon that assumption without checking it. If the assumption is correct, then all is well, but too often the hoped-for improvement fails to occur and this triggers another idea on problem cause which is once again acted upon. In this way, time, effort and resources may be wasted while the problem continues.

The definition of a problem

We have a problem when 'an object or a system has a defect and the cause of that defect is unknown'. In turn, a defect can be defined as a deviation in performance from the required standard (see Figure 24.3). The first step in

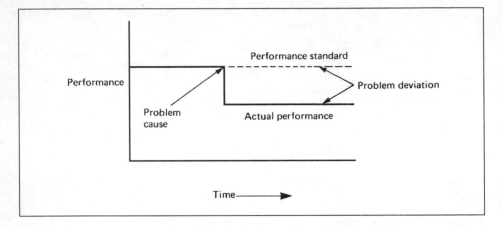

Note: The deviation could be a step function as shown or a gradual deterioration.

Figure 24.3   Deviation diagram

problem solving is to write down a problem statement. This is particularly important in group problem solving when agreement on the statement ensures a common understanding of the problem. A good problem statement will be a short sentence which specifies the object and its defect.

Thus, for example, if the floor in part of the factory becomes particularly dirty and the reason for this is unknown, then the problem statement could simply be: 'Floor in area B gets dirty'. Note that the required standard is that the floor should be 'clean'.

A common mistake is to phrase the problem statement in terms of the expected solution. Thus an incorrect problem statement would be: 'How to clean the floor in area B'.

Use of the incorrect problem statement will focus people's thinking on solutions about how to clean the floor, while at the same time tending to exclude the types of solutions aimed at preventing the floor becoming dirty in the first place. Certainly the group will give little thought to *why* the floor is getting dirty.

Getting to the root cause

Often problem solving will not stop when the immediate cause of the problem has been uncovered. Rather, the cause of the immediate problem can become the focus of further problem solving to uncover the cause of the cause.

For example, the initial problem might be 'sales revenue below target'. Investigation shows the cause of this to be poor sales of product X. In turn, poor sales of product X are caused by a salesman leaving the company as the result of bad supervision. This can be illustrated in Figure 24.4.

Of course, we can go further than 'bad supervision' and ask what caused the supervisor to perform poorly. The point at which we stop and cut the

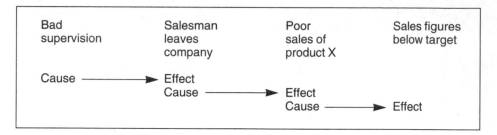

Figure 24.4   Cause/effect staircase

cause–effect chain is when we reach a cause where we can take effective action. For instance, if only one supervisor is performing badly, we may choose to replace him, while if a number of supervisors were inadequate, we might need to go back further and find out why.

Methods of problem solving

Brainstorming

Used on its own, brainstorming is the simplest technique for generating ideas on the cause of a problem. Here the problem-solving group simply generates a list of possible causes which are written down without criticism by the group leader for all to see. Ideas from one person trigger other ideas from group members. In this way, a very comprehensive list of possible causes can be generated, which significantly increases the possibility that the true cause will be recognized.

The weakness of this approach is that it offers no way of testing the ideas that are generated, and also, there is no segregation of causes from causes-of-causes.

In the previous example, brainstorming would show 'bad supervision' and 'salesman leaves company' both as causes of 'below sales target', rather than 'bad supervision' as the cause of 'salesman leaving'. However, it is possible to reorganize the brainstormed list after it has been generated in order to identify causes-of-causes.

The Ishikawa diagram

Sometimes called the 'fishbone' or 'cause and effect' diagram, the Ishikawa diagram is widely used in the quality circles movement.

It provides a simple way to structure brainstorming of problem causes in a manner which has a good visual impact, and also segregates each level of cause from the preceding one by introducing a branch in the diagram between each effect and its cause. It is common to start the diagram by assuming that all causes can be included under the headings of manpower, methods, machines and materials. This is illustrated in Figure 24.5. Once the   *373*

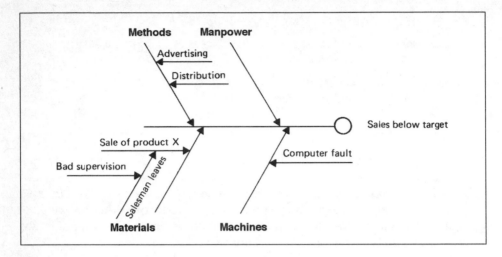

Figure 24.5   Partially completed Ishikawa diagram

Ishikawa diagram has been used to identify possible causes, other tools are used to collect and analyse data to confirm whether the problem causes are correct.

The Ishikawa diagram, together with other data collection and analysis tools, are collectively known as the seven QC tools. They are most useful in solving chronic or long-term problems where quantitative or numerical data can be collected about the problem for analysis.

Difference analysis

Management level problems often involve qualitative or non-numeric data, while sporadic problems that occur unexpectedly may not provide the opportunity to collect much data. Difference analysis is a particularly useful approach in these situations as it may be used to analyse both qualitative and quantitative data.

Difference analysis is a data stratification tool which provides new insights into the problem situation by stratifying the data along different dimensions. Its advantages may be summarized as follows:

● It narrows the area within which the problem cause may lie and hence provides a focus for brainstorming possible causes.
● It helps identify missing information which may be important.
● It aids the process of disproving possible causes which are in fact incorrect.

However, while the method has significant advantages for particular types of problem, it is also more difficult to use and requires practice to become profi-

cient. Working with a skilled consultant or attending a training course are probably the simplest ways to acquire the skill and get feedback on how to improve.

The application of difference analysis may be explained as follows. If an object has a defect, then, by definition, it is not performing to the expected standard. The reason you believe the expected standard to be 'expected' or 'reasonable' is because somewhere, at some time, you have seen the problem object or something similar to the problem object meet the expected standard or a similar standard.

If you have a new and unique object that has never performed to the required standard, then it is important to ask if the standard is reasonable and realistic. If you decide the standard is reasonable, the judgement will be based on your experience of the most similar object and situation you know. Thus if you have two identical objects in identical situations, then, by definition, they must behave in an identical manner. Hence the statement 'this object has a fault' means that it must in some way be *different* from a similar object without a fault, and further the difference provides us with a clue about why the fault exists.

Putting it another way, this means that when we are looking for the cause of a problem we can eliminate from consideration all those features of the faulty object which are identical with objects not having the fault. This is exactly what the service engineer does when repairing faulty equipment. If, when he looks at the faulty equipment, he can see anything which is different from the way he knows good equipment to be, then he will focus on that difference in looking for the cause of the fault.

The principle is obvious in the case of the service engineer, and when we are problem solving in a familiar situation we instinctively use the technique. We have a clear mental image of a non-defective object which we use to identify (and hence examine) differences which exist in the defective object compared to the non-defective object.

The principle may be illustrated by the following example. A hotel has purchased new cups and saucers. After a while, the hotel manager notices that the new cups are getting chipped more frequently than the old ones used to, and also more frequently than the new saucers.

To learn more about the chipping he may compare the new cups with the old cups. Also he may compare the new cups with the new saucers. Dependent upon this comparison he may identify a number of things which are unique or different about the new cups (i.e. shape and decoration). Using 'shape and decoration' as a focus for further examination he may find that the new shape results in the cups knocking together in the dishwasher and hence chipping. Here a *change* (i.e. the dishwasher action) has acted on a *difference* (the cup shape) to cause the *problem effect* (cup chipping).

This is illustrated in Figure 24.6 where the 'set of objects with the problem' are the new cups and the 'set of objects without the problem' can be taken as the old cups. Then one of the 'differences unique to the problem set' is the new cup shape. Because the dishwasher action affects or acts upon the *difference* (i.e. the new cup shape) it may be the cause of the problem. Note that it

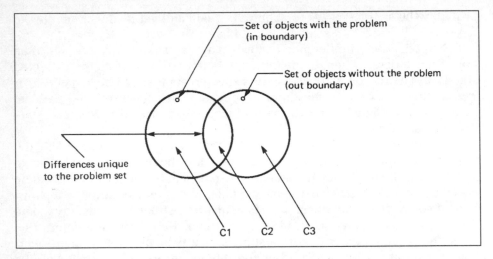

Set of objects with the problem
(in boundary)

Set of objects without the problem
(out boundary)

Differences unique
to the problem set

C1   C2   C3

Note: C1 is a change that acts on a difference unique to the problem set, while C2 is a change acting on features common to both problem and non-problem sets and C3 is a change which acts on differences unique to the non-problem set. Here, C1 is the only change which *may* be the cause of the problem because it is the only change acting on something which is *different* about those objects which exhibit the problem.

Figure 24.6   Differences unique to the problem set lead us to the problem cause

is irrelevant whether or not the dishwasher action also affects features common to objects without the problem.

As a shorthand, we will talk about objects within the problem set as being 'in boundary', while any object not having the problem is 'out boundary', or outside the boundary of the problem set.

It will be clear from the above example that the technique of difference analysis is most obvious and easy to apply when we have very similar objects 'in boundary' compared to objects 'out boundary'. This is because the number of differences will be small and hence they should lead us quickly to the cause of the problem. Thus the 'old cups' are probably a more useful 'out boundary' set than the 'new saucers', and both are clearly more useful than knives or forks, both of which are valid 'out boundary' sets but too far removed from the problem set (i.e. too many differences) to be really useful. However, even when a close 'out boundary' set cannot be found, the method can be remarkably successful if systematic questioning is used to uncover the differences.

When looking for useful 'out boundary' sets, look for the element of surprise. If you are surprised that the old cups chip less often than the new, then they are likely to be useful in the difference analysis. Because you are less surprised that the knives or forks do not chip, then they are likely to be less useful.

Good questioning skills are crucial in the effective use of difference analy-

sis. Kipling summed it up in the following verse:

I keep six honest serving men
They taught me all I knew);
Their names are What and Why and When
And How and Where and Who.

In order to uncover all the differences between the 'in boundary' problem and the 'out boundary' situation where the problem does not exist, questions must be asked systematically to cover all aspects of the case.

A common sequence in which to ask the questions is as follows:

- *What* What is the object with which we are having difficulty? What is the defect?
- *Where* Where is the object when the difficulty is first seen? Where on the object is the defect?
- *When* When (time and date) does the problem occur? When in the object's life cycle does the problem occur?
- *How* How much of the object is affected by the problem? Is there a pattern to the defects?

The full set of questions which must be asked is shown on the problem-solving worksheet Figure 24.7. To explore the problem in sufficient depth, follow-up questions should also be asked to each of the questions shown.

For example, if we ask, 'Where are the chipped cups first seen?', the answer may be 'preparation area'. This leads us into the follow-up question, 'Where in the preparation area are the chipped cups seen?' By narrowing down the area in which the problem is known to exist we eliminate equipment, personnel, and so on, not used in this more narrowly defined area.

At some point, the follow-up questions will become so detailed that we do not have the requested information. If we still lack sufficient information to determine problem cause, then the follow-up questions point to the additional information required. When we have sufficient information, the 'differences' column will lead to a solution.

As we saw earlier, the problem cause must be a 'change' acting on a 'difference'. Hence we can first identify 'changes' to the 'differences' and then identify which of those changes could be the problem cause. In practice, people often find it helpful simply to use the 'differences' and 'changes' columns as a focus for brainstorming possible causes.

If we have an object that has always been defective, or defective over the time period that information has been available to us (i.e. a chronic problem), then the 'changes' column will not help us and we must brainstorm problem causes from the 'differences' column.

Disproving possible causes

Following brainstorming, there will often be a significant list of possible problem causes, with only one of them being the true or correct cause.

Typically, people only try to verify theories about cause by checking to see   *377*

PROBLEM-SOLVING WORKSHEET			PROBLEM STATEMENT: *New cups chipping*	
	In boundary	**Out boundary**	**What is different in the boundary?**	**Have any changes occurred related to these differences?**
What object	What is the object with which you are having difficulty?	With what other objects would you expect to have a similar problem, but are not?	Is there any feature which is common to the objects in boundary, which is in no way true of objects outside the boundary?	
	New cups	*Old cups* *New saucers*	*Shape* *Decoration*	*New shape and decoration on cups introduced one month ago*
What problem	What problem is occurring that should not be occurring?	What other problems might you expect to have with the object, but have not?	What is peculiar about the problem in boundary which doesn't apply to problems outside boundary?	
	Chipping	*Large cracks*		
Where	Where geographically is the object when the problem is seen?	Where geographically might the problem be expected to occur, but is not seen?	Is there anything peculiar to the place in boundary which doesn't relate to other places outside boundary?	
	Preparation area for laying tables	*Laid tables*	*Washing and storage*	
	Where is the problem seen on the object?	Where on the object might the problem be expected to occur, but is not seen?	Is there anything peculiar to the part of the object in boundary which doesn't relate to other parts outside boundary?	
	Rim	*Handle* *Base*	*Thinnest part*	
When	When do these problems occur in calendar or clock time (not relative to events)?	When might they occur, but do not?	Is there anything happening during the time in boundary which doesn't apply to any other stages outside boundary?	*Introduced one month ago*
	Last month	*Before this*	*New cups introduced*	
	Within what stages (parts) of the life cycle do these problems occur?	Within what stages might you have expected the problem, but have not found it?	What is peculiar about stages in boundary which doesn't apply to any other stages outside boundary?	*Dishwasher action* *Dishwasher loading procedure*
	After washing	*After evening clear up* *Before dishwasher loading*	*Dishwasher action* *Dishwasher loading procedure*	
How much	How much of the object is affected by the problem?	How much of the object might you expect to be affected, but is not?	What is peculiar to the affected area in boundary which does not apply to areas outside boundary?	
	10% of all new cups *One or two chips per cup*	*100% of all new cups* *Multiple chips*		
	How frequently do the problems occur?	How frequently might the problems occur but do not?	What is significant about the frequency in boundary which wouldn't apply to other frequencies outside boundary?	
	One or two per day	*Weekends only*		
	What is the trend of these occurrences?	What trend might normally have been expected but does not occur?	Is there anything significant about the trend in boundary which wouldn't apply to other trends outside boundary?	
	Level at one or two per day	*Varies with people on shift*		

Note: A partially completed worksheet illustrating its use on the problem of the chipping cups. Note that everything changes with time, which means that any time differences (like dishwasher action) are automatically repeated in the changes column.

378 **Figure 24.7   Problem-solving worksheet**

if they can cause the problem in the defective objects. This is only half the story. Another key test is to see if the theory can also explain why the problem does not occur in all those objects in 'out boundary'. For example, our theory may be that high humidity has caused the sudden outbreak of rusting on certain metal parts in stores. A key question to ask is, 'How does the high humidity theory also explain why other metal parts in stores are free from rust?'

In general, most people try to prove their theories correct by looking for supporting evidence that can only make the theory more probable. However, if you look for evidence to prove your theory wrong but cannot disprove it, then there is a good chance you may be correct.

The method of trying to disprove possible causes is as follows. Each of the possible causes from the brainstormed list is examined in turn against the 'in boundary' and the 'out boundary' information. For each piece of 'in boundary' information we ask, 'Can the cause explain why we see that this problem exists in this way?', and for the 'out boundary' information we ask, 'Can this cause explain why this problem does not exist in this situation?' Any possible cause which cannot explain all the facts may be rejected, leaving perhaps one or two possible causes to be checked out through actual test.

Separation of individual problems is necessary in difference analysis because it is an analytical process designed to link a specific cause to a specific problem. This can be contrasted with simple brainstorming or Ishikawa diagrams, which may link a number of causes to a generalized problem.

For example, if you have an ongoing reject rate of 5 per cent in a production process (due to machine tolerances) which suddenly jumps to a total of 12 per cent (caused by a batch of faulty materials), then you have two problems. Thus if you brainstormed the general problem of 12 per cent reject rate, both 'machine tolerances' and 'faulty materials' could appear on the list and be seen to contribute to the overall problem. However, with difference analysis, the problems of 5 per cent reject and 7 per cent reject should be treated separately or the information on one problem will blur the information on the other: that is, it is more difficult to link the start of the 7 per cent problem to the receipt of the faulty materials, when our information also shows rejects occurring (due to the 5 per cent problem) before the faulty material was received.

While a simple problem may not require completion of a formal worksheet as shown in Figure 24.7, it is always worth checking what we believe to be problem cause by mentally checking if it explains all the 'in boundary' and 'out boundary' information we can think of.

DECISION MAKING

To be successful a decision must have:

- *Rational quality* To the extent that there is a difference between the available choices it will be important that the alternative offering the most benefit is chosen.

- *Commitment to implement*   To the extent that the commitment of the people involved is necessary for effective implementation, it will be important to gain that commitment.

When choosing who to involve in a decision, you should consider who can contribute to requirements for quality and commitment. Although most managers give overriding consideration to achieving a high-quality decision, more decisions probably fail through lack of a real commitment to follow them through and make them work.

The decision-making process described here is ideal for use individually or with a group. Because it offers a clear and logical approach to selecting a high-quality alternative while actively involving the group in the decision-making process, it is also excellent as a means of gaining group commitment.

Every decision will contain three elements:

1   *Objectives*   The things we wish to achieve as a result of the decision.
2   *Alternatives*   The choices available to us.
3   *Risks*   The uncertainty that a particular alternative will actually deliver the objectives we want or has unplanned side effects.

The ideal decision maker will be someone who clearly identifies his or her objectives, creatively generates new choices or ways of meeting those objectives, and is prepared to make choices involving risk where the benefit/risk pay-off of a choice makes it the most appropriate solution.

However, our flesh and blood manager frequently behaves very differently from the ideal model. Typically he or she adopts an approach which may be called incremental analysis in which he or she moves a minimum distance from the existing situation when change is required.

First, the manager may have no clear idea of his or her objectives. Rather, he or she finds that something has gone wrong and simply wishes to get out of trouble or make some improvement. Thus he or she is looking for an acceptable rather than the best solution.

Next, the manager may have spent little time creatively generating new approaches with the result that the choices available to him or her only represent small changes to the existing situation.

Finally, the manager may not be working in an environment in which risk taking is encouraged. Too many people may have an investment in the current situation and be unwilling to exchange it for the uncertain future associated with a significantly different approach.

The process for decision making discussed helps to overcome these difficulties because it is structured in the following way. It starts with a discussion of the objectives (rather than an argument over the alternatives). By doing this we can:

- Improve understanding of what an ideal solution could achieve.
- Generate commitment to more than a minimum solution.

- Avoid the politics of 'hidden objectives' because every individual knows that an undeclared objective will not be available to give weight to his or her choice at a later stage.

Following agreement on the objectives, a brainstorming session can take place to creatively generate new solutions or choices if this appears appropriate (i.e. existing choices appear lacking in some respect). The brainstorming can be creative and avoid criticism because it is understood that evaluation against objectives is the next step.

After alternatives have been generated, they are scored against each objective in turn with the purpose of finding the maximum overall benefit (achievement of objectives). This avoids the 'information overload' and fruitless argument that can result from a direct overall comparison of alternatives against each other.

Having identified the alternative which offers the best overall benefit, we then evaluate that alternative for risks. What are the unknowns and what could go wrong if that choice were adopted? If the alternative offering the best benefit also has significant risk, then other alternatives must be evaluated and the one offering the best risk/benefit pay-off chosen. This allows an open discussion on the level of risk people are prepared to accept.

Decision level

Decisions can occur at three levels and it is important to be clear at what level you are acting:

1 *Decisions you can make* are those decisions where you have the authority to act.
2 *Decisions you can recommend* are those decisions where you can only recommend to the person having the authority to act.
3 *Decisions you must accept* are those decisions made by others which will not be changed by any recommendation of yours. Here, you can only make subsidiary decisions on how to come to terms with a situation which will not change.

If we try to act at too high a level, then time is wasted in planning a decision that will not be acted upon. If we act at too low a level, then we may be accepting unnecessary constraints which result in a sub-optimum choice.

The decision statement

The decision-making process should start with a single-sentence decision statement to specify the decision to be made. Care should be taken to ensure that the decision level is correct and that there are no unnecessary modifiers. Take, for example, the decision statement, 'Buy a new car for my wife'. Is the word 'new' an unnecessary modifier and would you consider a second-hand *381* car? Do you really have the power to act or will your wife be unhappy if you choose a car for her, without her involvement?

Decision objectives

The extent to which an alternative meets an objective is the benefit that the alternative provides. In addition, some objectives may have limits which must not be violated or the decision will have failed. For example, if you can raise a maximum of £20,000 to buy a car, but you would like to buy as cheaply as possible, then the benefit graph would look as in Figure 24.8. By breaking the cost requirement into two parts, it can be described as follows:

1 *Essential objective* Cost not to exceed £20 000.
2 *Desirable objective* Cost to be as low as possible.

However, not every requirement will have an essential and desirable objective within it. For example, we order from a supplier a shipment of goods, but our plant is shut down until 10 August and our customer contract will be cancelled if the goods are not available by 20 August. Between 10–20 August it makes no difference when the goods are received. In this case, we only need specify an essential objective: that is, delivery must be between 10–20 August. Note that if it were an advantage to have the goods early, then there would also be a desirable objective – 'Goods delivered as soon as possible after 10 August'.

An example of a desirable only objective could be the plant colour scheme: that is, a colour scheme which is liked by staff and promotes effective work practice. While it is possible to imagine a colour scheme so grotesque that people stop working or leave the company, it is so unlikely that an essential objective need not be framed in these terms.

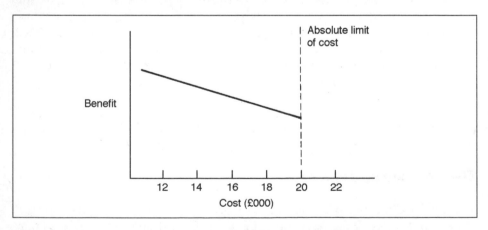

Note: Within a defined limit, there is a relationship between cost and benefit. Beyond this limit the graph is discontinuous and no effective decision can be made.

Figure 24.8   A benefit graph for car cost

Setting objectives

The first step is to brainstorm all the possible objectives and examine them to ensure that all aspects of the decision are covered. Next, examine the objectives for overlap, and combine any objectives which are saying the same thing in different ways. Then separate the objectives into those which are essential and those which are desirable:

- *Essential objectives* should then be worded so that the limit is clear and measurable, because it will be important to know if an essential objective has been violated and that choice is a 'no go'.
- *Desirable objectives* should be worded so that it is clear how alternatives can be measured against those objectives.

The achievement of some objectives will be more important than that of others, and it will be necessary to weight the objectives so that the final choice will be focused on satisfying the most important objectives.

The method of weighting desirable objectives is chosen for two practical considerations:

1 People are much better at making comparative than absolute judgements. For example, few people have 'perfect pitch' and can tell you the frequency of a musical note. However, most people can tell if one note is higher or lower than another.
2 The ability to discriminate is limited and the weighting scale used must be comparable with our ability to use that scale. A scale of 1–10 appears practical and convenient.

In order to weight the desirable objectives, first identify the most important desirable objective and 'benchmark' it with a weighting of 10. Each of the other desirable objectives is then compared with the benchmark and given a weighting from 1 to 10 depending upon how important it is seen to be compared with the benchmark.

It is quite acceptable to have two or more objectives with the same weighting. Be careful not to finish up with a large number of low-weighted objectives that in total outweigh a single high-weighted objective which is, in fact, more important.

An example of what our objectives might be if we were considering a job offer is as follows:

Essential objectives
- Salary greater than £30 000.
- House move not necessary.

Desirable objectives	Weight
Offers interesting work.	10
Salary as high as possible.	8
Opportunities for advancement.	4

Note that if you only have one job offer, then you are faced with a binary decision, so that you can either accept or refuse that offer. Your decision will depend upon how well your present job and the offer compare against the objectives.

Observe also how the essential objectives are clearly measurable, allowing a determination of whether an alternative meets the requirements and is a 'go' or 'no go'.

Generating alternatives

In some situations, the alternatives are fixed and there is therefore no need to pursue new alternatives or attempt to improve existing ones. Choosing a new car might be an example where you are limited by what is available on the market within your price range, and generating additional alternatives will not be possible.

If none of the alternatives available meets your needs very well, this is an indication that you should look for new ideas. Even if existing alternatives are satisfactory, this should not blind you to the possibility of an even better alternative.

Brainstorming or other creativity techniques may be used to generate new alternatives, using your objectives as a focus for creating the new ideas.

In certain situations, the alternatives will be different plans or approaches to achieving a particular outcome. Planning tools may be used to develop a robust plan which meets the objective of the decision. The seven management tools (or seven new QC tools) may be used for this purpose. However, the use of these tools is outside the scope of this chapter.

Where the decision objectives are used to creatively develop better alternatives, then it is common for one alternative to be developed to the point where it is clearly better than the other possible approaches. If this occurs, then the subsequent step of evaluating alternatives becomes simple.

Evaluating alternatives

Once alternative solutions have been identified, they must be evaluated against the objectives in order to determine which one offers the most benefit. First, any alternative that fails to meet an essential objective can be eliminated. Second, all the alternatives should be scored against each objective in turn.

Say, for example, you have received four job offers and were evaluating the salary objective, then the evaluation might be as in Figure 24.9. Note that the job offering £28 500 has been eliminated because it does not achieve the minimum requirement of £30 000. Note also that the score need not have a simple relationship to salary: that is, because of current debts, house mortgage or other reasons, a salary of £32 500 might be much more valuable than a salary of £31 000; while a salary of £35 000 might be only marginally more useful than £32 500. The questions the score should be answering is 'What does this (salary) mean to me? What is it worth?'

Objective	Job 1	Job 2	Job 3	Job 4
Salary as high as possible	Salary offer £28 500 Score N/A	Salary offer £31 000 Score 6	Salary offer £32 500 Score 8	Salary offer £35 000 Score 10

Figure 24.9   Evaluating job offers

Also be careful to ensure that what you measure is what you want. For example, if one job also offers a car, will you give that a cash value and add it to salary? If another job involves a long journey to work, will you deduct travel costs to determine net salary?

Once the alternatives have been scored for an objective, the weighted scores are calculated as a product of the objective weighting and the alternative score. Thus, where the salary objective has a weighting of 8, we get weighted scores for salaries in each job as in Figure 24.10.

By summing up the weighted scores that an alternative has for each of the objectives, we come up with an overall score which represents the 'benefit' delivered by that alternative. The alternative with the highest score is then the 'best initial choice'. This is illustrated in the case study below, 'Choosing an office copier', and in the worksheet in Figure 24.11 which shows the Premiere copy machine being the initial choice with a score of 180.

Risks

When we make a decision, our initial choice is based on what we think is most likely to happen if the alternatives were implemented. However, making any choice involves some risk. The choice we make might not work out the way we expect, or its introduction may have unplanned side effects. Thus we have to make a final decision based on the benefits and the risks of the alternatives.

We all take some risks. For example, we will cross a road without concern

Objectives	Job 2	Job 3	Job 4
Highest salary possible	Salary £31 000 Score 6	Salary £32 500 Score 8	Salary £35 000 Score 10
Objective weighting 8	Weighted score: 48	Weighted score: 64	Weighted score: 80

Figure 24.10   Weighted scores for salaries in each job

DECISION-MAKING WORKSHEET

Decision statement: Purchase an office copier

OBJECTIVES	Zenith MK1		Premiere		Alpha Copy King	
Essential	Info.	Go/No	Info.	Go/No	Info.	Go/No
Delivery by 1 June	Ex stock	Go	Promised 30 May	Go	Immediate delivery	Go
Sorter capability	Sorter available	Go	Sorter available	Go	No sorter	No Go
Down time 2 days maximum	Contract available	Go	Contract available	Go	Contract available	Go

Desirable	Wt.	Info.	Sc.	Wt.Sc.	Info.	Sc.	Wt.Sc.	Info.	Sc.	Wt.Sc.
Lowest cost	10	£2800	10	100	£3200	8	80			
Minimum down time	8	Replacement service	6	48	Good repair service	10	80			
Reduction capacity	2	Limited capability	4	8	Full enlargement and reduction	10	20			
INITIAL CHOICE (TOTAL)				156	Initial choice		180			

RISKS		Pr.	Se.		Pr.	Se.		Pr.	Se.
Probability/Seriousness				Missed delivery date	M	H			
				Dealer bankrupt	M	H			

FINAL CHOICE	Best overall choice					

Figure 24.11 A convenient format for information when making a decision

despite the risk of death associated with a car accident. When crossing the road the high seriousness of an accident is offset by the low probability of its occurrence. As traffic builds up, accident probability increases and we delay crossing for a while. At the other extreme, people will risk a high-probability loss (of cash) in a fruit machine because the seriousness of that loss is low. Hence the size of a risk (and our willingness to accept it) is a function of probability (of occurrence) and seriousness (if it does occur).

When evaluating risk, the elements of probability and seriousness may be conveniently evaluated on a three-point scale of high, medium and low. Risks with high probability and seriousness will be most significant, while those with a low probability or low seriousness will be the least significant. If the initial choice also has little risk, then clearly it is the one to adopt.

However, if the initial choice has significantly more benefit than the others but also has substantial risk, then the final choice is more difficult. Here we need to ask two questions: Is this a level of risk I would be prepared to accept in any circumstances? Is this a level of risk which is justified by the superior benefits of this alternative? If the risks associated with the first initial choice are too great, then the next alternative must be evaluated, and so on.

Some people are temperamentally greater risk takers than others, and there is no correct degree of risk to accept. Thus risk cannot be subtracted from benefit in a mathematical sense to arrive at the best overall choice. Rather, the final choice is a matter of judgement. While an effective manager may be a high-risk taker, he will also work to reduce risk to a minimum in a given situation and only take risks to achieve worthwhile benefits.

An example of where risks may rule out an alternative is given in the office copier case study which follows.

Case study – purchasing an office copier

Imagine you have just opened a branch office and need to purchase a small copier, which is essential to the operation. While cost is an important consideration, you will have to pay whatever price is necessary to obtain one. The essential requirements are that it can be installed by 1 June, and it must include a sorter or sorter option to handle the planned growth of multipage documents.

You require a minimum down time for repairs and it is essential that the copier is never unavailable for more than two days. Any down time will disrupt office routine to some extent. While a reduction capability – and other special features – would be nice to have, they are not essential for the work you expect.

The following copy-machines have been examined.

Zenith Mk 1

This machine is available ex-stock at a price of £2800 and has the capability to take a sorter, which may be added later. From your past experience, it is a   *387* reliable machine. However, the manufacturer's service organization can only offer you a next-day repair service. They have an excellent and reliable loan scheme that offers an immediate replacement machine if any repair exceeds 48 hours. This is a basic machine, and the reduction feature is not very easy to use. Also it cannot enlarge documents up to A3 size.

The Premiere

This machine is new on the market and you are very impressed with the performance of the demonstration model, which produces really first-class copies. Because it is new, delivery is a problem and the dealer was very reluctant to commit to a 30 May delivery date. It will be repaired by an independent service organization who can offer an excellent eight-hour repair time. However, you happen to know that this service organization is in financial difficulties and if it went bankrupt your repair contract with them would lapse. The machine has a number of excellent features, including zoom, reduction, and enlargement up to A3 size. It looks good value at £3200, and can accept a sorter, which is very easy to fit.

The Alpha Copy King

This produces good, high-quality copies and at £1600 it is by far the cheapest machine. The manufacturer has its own repair organization and offers a 'guaranteed next day' repair service. Immediate delivery is available, and this machine would do all of the jobs expected at start-up. However, it lacks the convenience of a good reduction capability and unfortunately cannot take a sorter attachment.

In this case study, the Alpha Copy King must be eliminated because it does not have a sorter capability, and hence it fails to meet an *essential* objective. The Premiere then becomes the initial choice because it offers the most overall benefit (i.e. out of the remaining alternatives, it offers the highest score of 180 against the *desirable* objectives). However, the Premiere also has risks of missed delivery and a bankrupt dealer, which are both seen as medium probability with a high seriousness, and which are not outweighed by its marginal advantage. Hence the Premiere is eliminated on the basis of *risks*, and Zenith Mk 1 becomes the best overall choice.

This evaluation of the alternative copiers against both *essential* objectives, *desirable* objectives and *risks* is shown in the worksheet in Figure 24.11.

Other points to note in the office copier case study are as follows:

- The decision was to *purchase* an office copier, which effectively rules out lease options. If this is intentional, that is fine. If, however, it is an unintentional constraint, then the decision statement has caused us to ignore potentially beneficial lease options.

- It will also be seen that the cost objective relates to the price of the machine, and ignores the running costs which may be significant over the life of the machine. Thus the way the objectives are worded can significantly affect the evaluation.

CONTINGENCY PLANNING

When a choice is made the implementation of that choice can be seen as an action plan. Contingency planning is the process of protecting a plan against what might go wrong in future.

Without a plan, nothing can go wrong and hence contingency planning can only start once a plan has been developed (in contrast to problem solving which should occur first to provide the information needed to make a plan). Contingency planning may be needed because there is a weakness in a new plan or to protect an existing plan where the situation is changing. It can be seen as a number of brainstorming steps designed to uncover possible future problems which then become the focus of subsidiary plans either to prevent those problems occurring or to reduce their effects. Steps in contingency planning are as follows:

1 List all the steps in the plan and identify key areas which include unknowns or which are particularly critical to plan success.
2 Using 1 as a focus, brainstorm possible problems and then identify those on your list having a high seriousness and high probability of occurrence.
3 Using 2 as a focus, brainstorm possible causes of major problems and identify causes with a high probability of occurrence.
4 Develop plans aimed at preventing problem causes identified in step 3 and which have a high probability of occurrence.
5 Using 2 as a focus, identify problems still likely to occur (despite steps 3 and 4) and list the negative effects that would happen.
6 Develop plans to handle serious negative effects identified in 5. Ensure a warning mechanism if those effects could start suddenly or unexpectedly.

Because people are anxious for their plans to succeed, they often fail to examine them critically and hence miss flaws which could easily have been corrected. In the same way it is easy to be defensive about criticism of a plan, rather than thinking how we can use the information to our advantage.

In contrast, Napoleon is said to have mentally rehearsed every battle he fought weeks before the event. He would go over his own tactics, visualizing the enemy defences, their reaction and the terrain. In the same way, we can significantly increase the success of our own plans by mentally rehearsing them both to eliminate possible problems and to prepare our defence should these problems arise.

CHECK LIST

1 *Decide what to work on first:*
   - List all the issues you face on a sheet of paper.
   - Prioritize list on the basis of seriousness and urgency of each issue.
   - Work first on most important issue.

2 *Determine if problem solving, decision making, or contingency planning, is required:*
   - If something has gone wrong, use problem solving as necessary to understand root causes.
   - If you need to take action to resolve a current problem or capture a current opportunity, and root cause is already known, use decision making.
   - If you are concerned that something may go wrong in future, use contingency planning to protect your plans.

3 *If problem solving is required:*
   - Specify the problem as a deviation between actual and expected performance.
   - Collect 'in boundary' and 'out boundary' data about the problem.
   - Test possible causes against the data and through experiment.
   - Confirm root cause.

4 *If decision making is required:*
   - Specify the overall purpose with a one-line decision statement.
   - List objectives, separate 'essential' and 'desirable' objectives, and give a weighting to those that are desirable.
   - Evaluate possible alternatives against the objectives.
   - Check best alternatives for associated risks.
   - Make the best overall choice.

5 *If contingency planning is required:*
   - Imagine the plan in action.
   - List all the possible problems which could occur.
   - Develop preventative and protective actions to prevent problems occurring and to reduce the impact if they do still occur.
   - Establish measurements and monitor plan for problem occurrence.

FURTHER READING

Buzan, T., *Use Your Head*, BBC Publications, 1974.

Cesarani, J. and Greatwood, P., *Innovation and Creativity*, Kogan Page, 1995.

Kepner, C. H. and Tregoe, B. B., *The Rational Manager*, McGraw-Hill, 1965.

Leatherman, R. W., *Quality Leadership through Empowerment*, Human Resource Development Press, 1992.

Mizuno, S., *Management for Quality Improvement: The Seven New Q.C. Tools*, Productivity Press, I 988.

Prince, G. M., *The Practice of Creativity*, Macmillan, 1972.
Robert, M., *The Essence of Leadership*, Quorum Books, I 991.
Simon, H. A., *The New Science of Decision Making*, Harper & Row, 1960.
Wilson, G., *Problem Solving and Decision Making*, Kogan Page, 1993.
Yetton, P. W. and Vroom, V. H., *Leadership and Decision Making*, University of Pittsburgh Press, 1973.

25 Negotiation

Nicholas Jeffery

We negotiate all the time – whether it is with our children and our partners, as a customer or supplier of goods and services, or with our staff at work or colleagues from other departments. It is a key skill for all managers, but particularly for those who have to manage without formal authority, but need to get work done through influence, project groups and subcontractors. In any circumstances where our needs and aims are different from the people with whom we are in contact, *and yet on whom we are dependent in some way*, we have to negotiate.

This chapter is about the concepts and skills of negotiation. It has five sections covering: reasons for negotiating; preparation; styles of negotiation; structure of negotiations; and interpersonal skills of negotiation. It provides a series of questions and prompts to help you in your own negotiations. The ideas and examples here are based on a Western cultural view of negotiation and human relations. There may be different customs and protocols you should be aware of when negotiating with people from other cultures or countries. Therefore, treat this chapter as a guide and always be sensitive to local traditions and customs. Good manners are an asset in negotiations wherever you are!

WHY NEGOTIATE?

Negotiation is just one method of resolving differences between people. There are other ways of solving problems or achieving what you want, such as formal authority, persuasion or more formal means of resolving differences such as arbitration, mediation or litigation. Hence negotiation should be a conscious choice on your part.

Although negotiation takes time and effort, it is usually more efficient and less costly than the alternatives. These can be strikes or industrial tribunals (in the case of employee relations) or litigation (in the case of customers or suppliers) or war (in the case of international relations).

There are two key questions you need to ask before deciding to negotiate:

1   Can I reach a better outcome through negotiation than by some other means?
2   Is it worth it: that is, is the outcome or stake important enough to invest time and effort in negotiating with the other side?

If the answer to either of these questions is 'no', you may want to consider other ways of attaining what you want, or prefer just to accept the terms that are offered.

It is worth negotiating if the other side have something significant that you want or is important to you. This need not necessarily be something tangible, such as a price reduction or a service agreement: it could, for example, be your desire for a productive long-term relationship or to be perceived as acting fairly in the eyes of a wider audience such as consumer groups or the press.

Having decided to negotiate, how do you do it?

PREPARATION

The key to successful negotiation lies in thorough groundwork and preparation. The following is a short check list of points to consider in advance of meeting face to face.

Outcomes and success criteria

Negotiation is a means to an end, so consider carefully what you are trying to achieve:

My desired outcomes

- What agreement do I want to be in place at the end of the negotiation?
- What is the most I would expect? What is the least?
- What would a good bargain look like?
- What criteria will I use to judge the success of the negotiation?

Their desired outcomes

- What are my opponents' desired outcomes?
- How much do I know about their needs and motivations?
- What criteria will they be using?

The relationship

Negotiation takes place within the context of a relationship. The nature and   *393* quality of this relationship will have a significant influence on your ability to reach agreement, the type of bargain you want to conclude, and the *likelihood of it being implemented afterwards.*

Relationships may be *independent*: that is, once the business has been completed both parties go their separate ways (e.g. a one-off deal with a supplier, or when you buy a used car). In business, however, relationships are likely to be *dependent*, where the negotiation takes place between two parties who are bound together in some way. Here, the relationship will endure beyond the specific matter you are negotiating about, and the memories of past bargains will be carried into this and later negotiations, for example with trade unions, long-term customers or suppliers (or your spouse!). The need for 'win – win' negotiations (see below) in this context is considerable. Therefore, consider the following factors:

- What sort of relationship do I need after the negotiation is finished?
- Are we likely to do business again?
- How important are good relations to making what is agreed work in practice?
- How much trust is there between the parties?
- In what context is this negotiation taking place?

Mandate

Often you will be negotiating on behalf of an organization or group who will set limits to your authority and will be affected by any agreement that you reach on their behalf. You must, then, be fully briefed on the following points:

- What are the things I can negotiate about? What is outside the negotiation, i.e. non-negotiable?
- What are the limits to my authority?
- Who sets these limits and what are my options should I need to deviate from them?
- Who else has an interest in the outcome of this negotiation and how aware am I of their views?

Assumptions and expectations

Sometimes negotiations go badly wrong because one or both parties make assumptions about the situation that are not valid or have unrealistic expectations (e.g. that a customer has a limited budget, or that there is no support for industrial action). In this case:

- What assumptions am I making about my own position and that of my opponent?
- How clear am I about the difference between what I *know* about the situation and what I *assume?*

- What expectations do I have about my opponent?
- What information do I have or could I obtain to check the validity of my assumptions?

Reality check

Once you have done your preparation, you need to subject your plans to a reality check:

- How realistic are my desired outcomes for this negotiation?
- What do I know about similar settlements in the industry or the organization?
- What does past history suggest will be a realistic and fair agreement?
- How does what I want match with what either side can reasonably deliver (e.g. in terms of cost, time and quality)?

Assessment of negotiating power

Assessment of negotiating power is such an important part of a negotiator's preparation that it merits a section to itself. Your assessment of your own and your opponent's negotiating power will affect your whole approach to the preparation and conduct of the negotiation.

The key to assessing your negotiating power lies in understanding your *best alternative to a negotiated agreement* or BATNA. The questions to ask yourself are: What is the best outcome I could achieve if I do not negotiate with this party? What other options do I have if I do not negotiate? The more options you have and the more attractive they are compared with what you can agree through negotiation, then the greater your negotiating power. Working out your BATNA also helps you judge the acceptability of the deal on the table: namely, if the agreement you are heading towards is worse than your BATNA, then it is time to break off negotiations.

You also need to make an assessment of your opponents' BATNA to understand their negotiating power. What alternatives do they have to a negotiated deal with you? How attractive do these alternatives look?

A weak BATNA does not mean that you have to accept without question whatever terms your opponents offer. Good negotiators take active steps to improve their BATNAs. Some have been known to lead their opponents into thinking that their BATNA was stronger than it actually was! So, for example, if you are trying to negotiate better credit terms from an existing supplier, your negotiating power will be increased if you have a quote from a competitor offering you what you want. If you are trying to negotiate a pay rise with your boss, your power will be increased if you have a firm offer from another employer offering you a higher salary.

Work out your variables

In any negotiation there will be a range of elements or variables that go to make up the issue or problem under discussion. They are called 'variables' because they can be changed through negotiation, and they can be added to or subtracted from any package that will constitute the final agreement.

For example, in most sales negotiations, not only the price of the goods or service on offer is at issue. The specification, delivery date, credit terms, volume of purchase, warranty, after-sales service, training, and so forth, could also be included as part of any negotiated package. Similarly, in an employment negotiation with trade unions, not only the size of any pay increase has to be decided, but also other elements such as annual leave allowance, health insurance, sick pay, pensions, notice periods, overtime allowances, working practices, and so on, which all go to make up the employment relationship.

These, then, are examples of types of variables the negotiator has to play with – variables in so far as they may have a value to one side and can be traded for variables that may be of value to the other side. Skilled negotiators seek to create the widest range of variables possible in order to give themselves room to make creative and mutually satisfying bargains. They also have a sound knowledge of the value (monetary or otherwise) that they can place on each variable, and ensure that they do not trade high-value for low-value variables.

- What are the different variables that you have to play with?
- Which are negotiable? And which are non-negotiable?
- How important or valuable is each variable to you?
- What is your assessment of the importance or value of each variable to the other side?

STYLES OF NEGOTIATION

The style of negotiation you should adopt will depend on the relationship between the two parties.

Win–Win

In 'win – win' negotiation, the intention is to conclude a deal in which *both* parties achieve all or most of what they want. Negotiation is seen as a *problem-solving* activity, where the ultimate aim is a fair and reasonable agreement, based on objective criteria. It seeks to contribute to a sustained and positive relationship because both parties feel they are benefiting from the deal – hence 'win–win'.

'Win–win' negotiation does *not* mean that soft, submissive postures need be adopted or that the realities of negotiating power do not come into play. But the underlying philosophy is one of *abundance*: namely, that with goodwill and creativity we can increase the size of the cake so that there is enough for everyone to have what they want.

Independent advantage

When you negotiate for independent advantage, you are concerned solely to achieve as many of your own objectives and interests as possible – regardless of the condition in which that leaves the other side, the feelings of resentment and bitterness that may result, or the good opinion of third parties. It is a high-risk strategy that is worth employing only if the following conditions apply:

- the relationship is short-term;
- you are unlikely to do business again;
- you do not need the cooperation of the other side for implementation;
- you are certain of your superior negotiating power; and,
- your organization's survival is at stake.

You have therefore to determine with care:

- What style is appropriate to the context you are in?
- What style is appropriate to your own style and personality?

KEY NEGOTIATING PRINCIPLES

Win–win

These principles provide the foundation on which to prepare and conduct your negotiations. They are based on that excellent book, *Getting to Yes*, by Roger Fischer and Bill Ury.

Separate the people from the problem

This principle suggests that negotiation should be seen as a problem-solving activity, with the aim of achieving the best deal for all sides, rather than a clash of wills or personalities where the intention is to humiliate or overcome the other side. Avoid making personal remarks or 'point scoring', and ignore such remarks made to you; they rarely contribute towards a good agreement.

Treat the negotiation as an objective issue to be resolved, independent of the people involved. You may need to empathize and acknowledge that people feel strongly about the matter, but always keep returning to the problem as a separate entity.

Focus on interests, not positions

People will approach negotiations with specific ideas and demands about what they want. For example:

- 'We must have a 10 per cent pay rise.'
- 'We will only accept 7 days' credit terms.'
- 'The system must be able to guarantee 99.9 per cent up-time.'
- 'I want a holiday in Majorca next year.'

These are called positions. The skilled negotiator looks for the *interests* that a position represents: that is, the *underlying need* or satisfaction that the position is trying to achieve, which is a more general value and *can be met in several ways*. For example, the underlying interests behind a 10 per cent pay increase could be the need to maintain a standard of living, or to match other awards in the same sector. But if these are the underlying interests, there are many other options or combinations of options that can meet that need than simply a 10 per cent pay increase.

By focusing on satisfying interests, the negotiator gives both parties room to create solutions that will meet both their needs, rather than engaging in a tug of war between narrow positional stances.

The questions to ask to discover interests in the face of a positional demand are:

- What would that give you?
- Why is that important to you?
- What need does that satisfy?
- What else would give you what you are looking for?

Invent options for mutual gain

Working with interests rather than positions creates much greater space where an agreement can be found. This is because the range of options and variables open to the negotiator is much wider. Once the views and needs of both parties have been discovered, the skilled negotiator should generate different options and possibilities for solving the problem. The negotiation then becomes a search for the best combination of options or 'package' that satisfies both sides, rather than a trading of positions using one or two variables.

There is an old negotiator's saying: 'If you change the price, change the package.' For example:

CUSTOMER: We can only confirm the order if you give us a 5 per cent discount off the list price. [*Position statement*]

SALES NEGOTIATOR: If cutting costs are important to you, [*Focusing on interests*], then there are several options we could look at: If you ordered twice as many we could offer a 5 per cent discount, or if you paid cash in advance and were prepared to forgo the warranty, then that would probably be worth 5 per cent to us. [*Generating options*] Which of those are of interest to you? [*Testing for a reaction*]

The key questions in inventing options for mutual gain are:

- How else could we solve this problem?

- What are the different elements or variables in this package that we could trade?
- What else might be of interest to us or the other side?

Use objective criteria

Making any deal conditional on meeting objective, independent criteria agreed by both sides is a good way of bringing fairness and reasonableness into the negotiation. Objective criteria are those that are independent of both sides. For example, pay increases could be measured against the retail price index or the industry average.

Independent advantage

When you negotiate for independent advantage, a different set of principles and values apply. If 'win–win' negotiation is about helping everyone achieve what they want, then negotiating for independent advantage is about gaining the biggest slice of the cake for ourselves. The following principles pertain in this approach to negotiation.

Positional bargaining

No attempt is made to identify underlying interests or invent ways of mutual gain. Your aim is to set out your position (i.e. what you want) in the fullest possible terms and move slowly from that position.

Open with the highest defensible bid or lowest defensible offer

By opening high, you create a position from which any movement will be measured. The emphasis is on the word 'defensible' because you will need to be able to justify your position in a way that appears credible to the other side. Opening high (or low) also means that you are likely to have exceeded any point the other side would have considered settling at, and therefore they will be shifting in your favour their own assessment of where the final bargain will be struck.

Move slowly

Concessions are made grudgingly. Any concession by your side should only be made if a concession of equal value is made by the other side. You are constantly pressuring the other side to make concessions in your favour, while offering lower-value concessions in return. Seek to trade concessions that are of higher perceived value to the other side, but are of low value to you.

Convince the other side of the merits and justice of your position

Throughout the negotiation, there is a need to persuade and justify the merits   *399* and reasonableness of your position, while at the same time minimizing and neutralizing the arguments and claims of the other side.

STRUCTURE OF A NEGOTIATION

Assuming you have done your preparation and are now sitting face to face, how does a negotiation proceed? Typically a negotiation will have five phases, that will lead you to a bargain. These are: open; explore; propose; bargain; and close. Depending on the complexity of the issues to be negotiated and the relationship between the parties these five phases can take from five minutes to several years. Each will be described briefly in turn.

Open

The opening sets the scene for the negotiation. It is the time for people to settle, introductions to be made, and the roles of various individuals in the negotiation to be made clear. The arrangements for the meeting may be discussed (e.g. how long it is expected to last, times for tea and coffee, who is taking notes, and so forth).

Most importantly, during the opening the agenda for the negotiation must be clarified: that is, what is to be discussed and what, in broad terms, you are trying to reach an agreement about. You will also find it helpful to agree what is *outside* the agenda or scope of this negotiation, namely what will *not* be discussed. This may save much time and misunderstanding during the later stages.

Explore

In the exploration phase, both parties take turns to describe how they see the problem, what they consider to be the important issues, and what sort of settlement they are looking for. If the exploration phase is conducted well, both sides will raise questions, listen carefully to the replies, and reflect back in detail, so building the fullest possible picture of the other side's views and concerns, and in particular, what is important to them, and which issues they see as central to the problem and those they consider only peripheral.

Generating options and alternatives will also happen at the end of the exploration phase, and this will signal the move into the proposing phase.

Proposing

Having explored the issues, the next phase is to make some tentative proposals towards an agreement. Proposals will often be made cautiously and hedged with conditions and caveats. Both sides will be looking for reactions to their proposals, either in terms of acceptability or as counterproposals. Frequent breaks or adjournments may be taken to allow each side to consider their next moves in private.

At this stage, proposals that do not receive a favourable reaction can be withdrawn without risking the outcome of the negotiation.

Bargain

As both sides judge the acceptability of the proposals on offer and assess them against their objectives and their bargaining power, the proposing phase will merge into the bargaining phase. This is the point at which the deal is made and firm specific agreements are reached. The caution and tentativeness of the previous phases is replaced by more direct and specific language: for example, 'We will agree to x if you will agree to y. Do we have a deal?'

Summarizing at each stage of the deal is a key skill here. Also any offer that has been made and agreed in the bargaining phase cannot be withdrawn or repudiated by either side without risking the whole negotiation and jeopardizing the trust and goodwill of the other side.

Close

At the end of the negotiation, you must summarize exactly what has been agreed, tie up any loose ends, and then shake hands on the deal! Equally important, you must clarify what has yet to be agreed or what business remains for another time.

Make sure you keep a written record of what has been agreed.

THE SKILLS OF NEGOTIATION

This section deals with the interpersonal and communication skills you will need at the negotiating table. All your preparation will come to nothing if you are not able to communicate assertively what you want and to listen purposefully to the other side.

Listen, listen, listen!

Listening is the key skill of effective negotiators. It is an active skill that demands giving your full attention to the other side and then reflecting back to them what you have heard, however unreasonable it may sound to you! For example:

TRADE UNION OFFICIAL: What we demand is a 10 per cent pay increase, luncheon vouchers and two extra days holiday a year.
MANAGER: Let me check I've got all that. You're saying you would like a 10 per cent pay rise, luncheon vouchers and two more days holiday a year.
OFFICIAL: That's right.

Reflective listening has the following advantages for the negotiator:

● It helps you clarify what the other side are saying.

- It buys you time to think about your response.
- It creates trust and rapport because the other side can hear that you are interested in what they have to say.

Questioning

Reflective listening should be combined with questioning skills. Questions are particularly important in the exploration and proposing phases of a negotiation. They help you understand what the other side want and, skilfully used, will help the other side clarify their own outcomes. Questions also enable you to check the other side's reaction to your proposals, and they assist both sides in developing alternative proposals that will move you towards an agreement. For example, in the exploration phase:

- 'How do you see the problem?'
- 'What is important to you?'
- 'Is there anything else of concern?'
- 'How else could we approach this problem?'

And in the proposing phase:

- 'What would your reaction be to this idea?'
- 'If we agreed to this proposal, what would you be able to offer in return?'
- 'How would we have to change these proposals for them to be acceptable to you?'
- 'How does that sound to you?'

Empathy

Using empathic words and phrases can be a great help in building a constructive dialogue with the other side. For example:

CUSTOMER: We demand that the computer system is totally operational by the 14th, when we move into the new offices.
IT MANAGER: I can appreciate that. If I was in your position I would want that too. [*Empathy*] However, our production schedule is so full that we would not be able to go fully operational until the 18th. Why don't we discuss how we can minimize the disruption for those four days? [*Problem solving*]

Proposing - useful words and phrases

The most useful word in the negotiator's phrase-book is 'If'. As a prelude to making proposals or responding to the other side, it communicates the conditional nature of the deal and does not commit you to anything. For example:

MANAGER: *If* we accepted your proposal for a five per cent price increase, we would want to reduce the delivery time by a week for each batch.

SUPPLIER: That would be difficult for us now, but *if* we said four days now and aim for a week in three months' time, would that be acceptable to you?

Other useful words and phrases to use in the proposing phase are:

- 'What if . . .'
- 'How about . . .'
- 'What would your reaction be to . . .'
- 'That's an interesting idea.'
- 'We'd like to think about that.'

Words and phrases to avoid or use with caution are those that convey judgement or inflexibility:

- 'But . . .' (Substituting 'and' for 'but' is a better approach.)
- 'No way.'
- 'This is a fair offer.'
- 'You can't be serious.'
- 'You won't get a better deal than this.'

These are likely to antagonize the other side and cause them to become as inflexible in their thinking as you are!

Summarizing

Skilled negotiators use frequent summaries to take stock of the point reached in the negotiation and to clarify what has been said. A detailed summary is particularly important at the end of the negotiation when a bargain has been struck, so that all parties are absolutely clear about what has been agreed to. It can save a lot of misunderstanding and bad feeling afterwards.

When in doubt or lost for something to say, summarize.

Take a break

In lengthy and complex negotiations, it is always useful to take a break in order to collect your thoughts, reflect on what you have heard, develop new options and plan your next move. This ploy is particularly important in team negotiations when you may need to check out the views and reactions of other members of your side. Taking a break can also help to calm the atmosphere if emotions are running high between the sides.

If you are undecided what to say or do next, take a break – if only for a couple of minutes. Never negotiate 'on the hoof' – you will end up with an agreement you will regret.

Body language

Your body language and posture will communicate as much of what you are thinking and feeling as words ever will, so pay close attention to your own and to that of the other side. In general, it helps to adopt a relaxed, alert and open posture which conveys confidence in yourself and respect for the other side. Eye contact is important, but avoid intense eye contact, as it may appear as if you are trying to stare your opponent out. Avoid slouching or slumping in your seat – this will convey mixed messages to the other side and may prompt aggressive responses.

CHECK LIST OF KEY POINTS

- Prepare thoroughly. Work out your aims and the variables you have to play with.
- Assess your negotiating power. What is your best alternative to a negotiated agreement (BATNA)?
- Think of the other side. What are their aims? What is their BATNA?
- Think 'win – win'. How can we both get what we want?
- Separate the people from the problem.
- Focus on interests rather than positions.
- Invent options for mutual gain.
- Use objective criteria to assess the fairness of any deal.
- Listen carefully, ask questions, summarize frequently.
- Take a break when the going gets tough.

FURTHER READING

Fischer, R. and Ury, W., *Getting to Yes*, Century Hutchinson, 1982.
Kennedy, G., *Everything is Negotiable,* Arrow, 1984.
Ury, W., *Getting Past No,* Business Books, 1991.

26 Creativity

Victor Newman

Creativity, or the ability to make something new, is a double-edged organizational sword. Although it can generate new opportunities and competitive advantage, its very novelty and risk can also be a source of potential instability to an existing formula for business success. Conversely, without creativity it is impossible to manage change. One of the most useful contexts for creativity is in terms of creative problem solving, and most books on the subject deal with how to use creativity to solve problems. The practice of creativity is further complicated by the need to involve groups of individuals in developing and implementing solutions.

CREATIVITY, RISK AND INSTABILITY IN ORGANIZATIONS

This concern for potential instability through creativity can take extreme forms. For example, a world-class automotive manufacturer wanted help in retaining their highly talented European designers who had become disenchanted with continually optimizing existing products and components in conventional configurations instead of creating new products containing genuinely novel technologies and materials. This automotive manufacturer wanted better, but not novel products. Japanese researchers admit that their industrial culture of optimizing stable products and processes carries its own risks: especially where these product families are coming to their end without having developed new, innovative successor products.

In another case, a public relations company wanted to design and document a bidding development process for winning new clients that would distinguish between those activities within the process that were routine, and those that really needed to be creative to capture their client's attention and win the account. In both cases, bringing creativity into the workplace was seen as a risk to a stable or, as in the latter case, unstable formula for success.

As a result, we can begin to see that the ability to apply creativity, the ability to create something new, is a fundamental aspect of managing change in organizations.

CREATIVE PROBLEM SOLVING

Creative problem solving is subject to the issues of convention, recognition, expression and exposure. Novelty or creating something new requires an understanding of what is conventional. Recognition, expression and exposure means we must consider the political level within the organization at which the problem happens to be recognized: who sees it, how it is expressed, and whether recognizing and expressing the problem will expose the individual or group involved to political sanctions. Sometimes the culture of the organization may not provide the language to express the problem. The greatest enemy of problem solving is the way we can distance ourselves from seeing the real problem: that is, the way our mind-sets – frozen perceptions, stereotypes or personal myths of cause and effect – can mean we institutionalize problems by continuing to deal with symptoms, and reinforce the reappearance of these same symptoms by ignoring fundamental causes coming from systems operating in the environment.

These problem-solving levels can be illustrated through looking at organizations in terms of which issues are seen as organizational 'dead cats', or problems which no one wants to touch in the game of pass-the-parcel because, when the music stops, the problem may end up in your lap, and attempting to resolve it will mean confronting powerful people or values within the culture.

Often a problem is initially seen as a mere task (see Figure 26.1). A team is formed to manage the task of dealing with a problem. It works together and realizes that the task itself is a symptom of a deeper problem. The team then begins to redefine the problem. The problem starts to have a life of its own, and, in the form of a symptom, escapes out of its original functional 'task' frame, reframing through the 'process' level that manufactures it as a by-product down to that of 'system' – where the problem is not to bury the dead cats you and your colleagues receive, or to improve on the burial process or necessary teamworking involved, but to find out where the dead cats come from, and just *who* is being paid to make and introduce waste in the form of dead cats into the system of the organization? And what assumptions are the decision makers making about the environment their organization is operating in to justify their decisions? Someone, somewhere, is being paid to make decisions that are driving you crazy, but to solve problems at this level means becoming involved in politics – and remember, all they asked you to do was to deal with this simple task.

Sometimes, organizations choose to undergo complete redesign of the way they do business in the form of a *business process re-engineering* exercise, because, politically, it is easier to take the pain of a major change than to admit to the reality that they are not in control of their processes and, that as

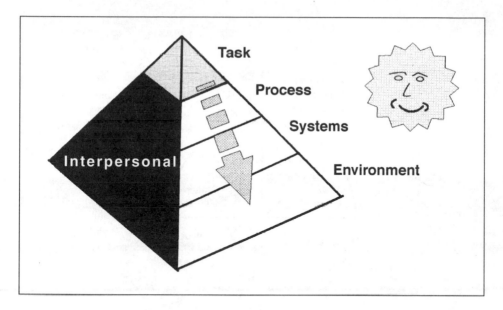

Figure 26.1   Levels of problem solving

a result, they are too busy fighting fires to solve their own problems. Transforming the problem into money with techniques like 'cost of quality' can help to transcend the problem-solving levels by connecting profit to the problem. Small wonder that problem solving remains at the level of task, and keeps organizations busy.

INTRODUCING 'PROBLEM SOLVING FOR RESULTS'

'Problem Solving for Results' is an approach designed to provide a self-assessment profile to help individuals understand their personal problem-solving style, and to locate and introduce some key techniques with accompanying illustrative cases which, if applied, could help to develop a broader, more balanced style of problem solving. The structure of Problem Solving for Results follows the problem-solving model shown in Figure 26.2, as well as explaining the principles of, and the obstacles to, creative thinking. Figure 26.2 provides a map of potentially useful techniques and their approximate locations within the problem-solving process.

THE IMPACT OF PROBLEM-SOLVING STYLES

Individual problem-solving styles

We all have a characteristic problem-solving style. Understanding this personal style is a key to managing oneself and working with others in teams to solve problems. The problem-solving styles profile locates individuals between three useful problem-solving stereotypes (see Figure 26.3). We are   *407*

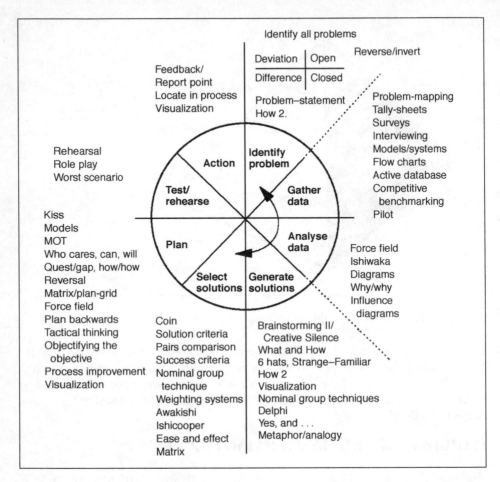

Figure 26.2 Problem-solving techniques covered in Problem Solving for Results

all Coyotes or Competitors, it just depends on the situation. But to think like the Eagle means that we recognize the problem situation which is different and out of the ordinary, the special occasion that requires escaping from old repertoire in order to work on this singular problem in such a way that we will never have to face this kind of problem again.

The significance of thinking about developing and discussing these style stereotypes is that individuals often cannot choose their problem-solving style because they are not aware of what they are doing. This confusion is all the more damaging when a team of individuals is formed to solve a problem. In this situation, three forms of problem-solving behaviour become obvious to the sensitive observer (see Figure 26.4).

Existing team development models serve only to document the progress of this battle, regarding conflict as inevitable and even healthy. This is rather like developing the assumption that being in hospital is part of being a skier if

The Coyote	The Competitor	The Eagle
Coyotes like to grab the first idea that appears and seems to fit, and apply it. If that doesn't work, they grab a successor, and another, and so on, until either they succeed or are themselves destroyed.	Competitors work out of a fixed repertoire of solutions. They see every problem-solving situation as an opportunity to demonstrate and test their own personal collection and values: their 'right stuff'.	Eagles fly over the complete thinking process much like a helicopter, keeping it in sight and deliberately working forwards, and sometimes deviating backwards when necessary. Eagles know that it's OK to say stop and to ask 'What are we doing, now?'

Figure 26.3   Three problem-solving stereotypes

Style	Characteristics
Combat	Where typical problem-solving behaviours combine to reinforce and exaggerate each other, leading to conflict and instability, which is resolved by the formation of . . .
. . . Cliques	Where a dominant individual forms a clique of like-minded members who impose their personal repertoire onto the team, and potentially develop . . .
. . . Subsistence	Satisfaction with a way of working that reinforces the power and stability of a clique, producing mediocre but politically satisfactory results without ever challenging the status quo of the group.

Figure 26.4   Three forms of problem-solving behaviour

you ski so badly that you always end up there. Under these conditions, there is a strong possibility that individuals may only be learning how to choose the wrong option and may never learn how to manage a creative problem-solving process within a group.

CREATIVITY AND TEAMS

More people can mean less creativity

After years of using and observing brainstorming in groups, I agree with Weisberg and others that groups tend to produce fewer ideas in total than the individuals within those groups working on their own. Why do groups apparently produce fewer ideas in total when brainstorming as a group than they do as individuals? This is due to the combination of four 'c' words: *clues, cues, correctness* and false *consensus*, sheltering under an umbrella labelled *fear of exposure* (see Figure 26.5). When new or transitional groups with a short life span are asked to brainstorm, individuals' fear of making a public mistake means that they hang back from contributing until the first ideas have been expressed and captured on the flipchart by the facilitator.

409

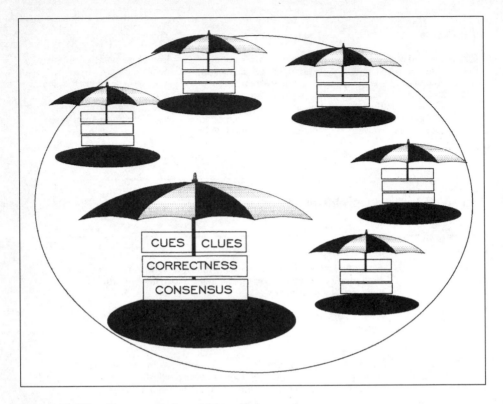

CUES | CLUES
CORRECTNESS
CONSENSUS

Figure 26.5   Team members' fear of exposure

Once these ideas have appeared, individuals' fears of public exposure are reduced because the cues or clues for solution 'correctness' in this social situation are clearer, and individuals can go on in relative confidence to produce ideas that are stereotypical of the first ideas. In other words, this fear of exposure supports the tendency in traditional brainstorming sessions for individuals within a group to adopt prematurely a convergent style of solutions, and is otherwise complemented by the unscheduled arrival of the first idea which someone inadvertently introduces before a brainstorming has been formally announced. The impact of the inadvertent, early solution or idea is heightened by this fear of exposure. Our education and social approval systems reinforce the idea that there is a single, correct solution to a problem – that there is *an* answer. Creativity then becomes the ability to optimize or build variations on these early ideas, developing ideas that fit. The ambiguity necessary to creative thinking means that we find the absence of strong cues or clues for correct solutions daunting, and we hang back waiting for the more socially confident individuals who believe that they can recognize the problem and apply an existing piece of repertoire to break the ambiguity of the silence and demonstrate their recognition. It is this aspect of recognition that is central.

For the not-so-confident, waiting for these correct solution cues means running the risk of appearing autistic in not having recognized the problem, and letting slip that you do not have a comparable repertoire from which to select a working solution. It is this comic fear of exposure, the fear of not recognizing the cue and applying inappropriate responses or repertoire in a social context that is the basis of many of the modern comedies of manners, typified in John Cleese's 'Fawlty Towers' series. It is as though we run the risk of proving to everyone that we are imposters, of having to admit that the social game is up: you have been found out and must retire shamefaced.

Similarly, once people have developed some ideas, our evaluation may be influenced by their status within the group or larger organization, and we need to be able to discuss and discard ideas without laying the foundation for conflict and revenge. I believe that it is no great exaggeration to say that our ideas are like our own children. They may behave badly but we tend to feel that only we, as parents, are allowed to intervene in public with our children; an onlooker's comment or implicit criticism, however justified, will never be forgotten or forgiven. Our ideas are our babies – we made them. Criticize or discard them and you criticize me, and though I smile on the surface of my public, adult behaviour, in my heart I will neither forget nor forgive.

Better brainstorming: the use of creative silence

If you want an effective brainstorming session, consider planning to include the following:

1 Generate and display a clear and open *problem statement.*
2 Issue everyone with a pad of Post-it stickers and a black flipchart pen.
3 Announce a high-volume target for ideas and suggest that you either have no preconceptions, or, conversely, that you know of at least five or more completely different ways of approaching the problem.
4 Announce a period of *creative silence* (2–5 minutes) in which everyone privately develops and records their own ideas, one idea per Post-it, and each person generating as many Post-its as they can. Ask everyone to avoid glancing at each other's Post-its.
5 Everyone then puts their Post-its containing their ideas onto a whiteboard. If the group is more than, say, four individuals, encourage people to put up and briefly explain no more than three ideas at a time without comment or analysis, working round the group until all ideas are displayed. This provides the opportunity to group ideas together into themes, and for new ideas to be triggered as people listen. This discipline keeps everyone involved and listening. When identical ideas are generated, they can be superimposed over each other.
6 Encourage the group to come forward to the whiteboard and formally collect and arrange the ideas into families, giving each family a title. This will involve some active discussion (see arrangement in Figure 26.6).

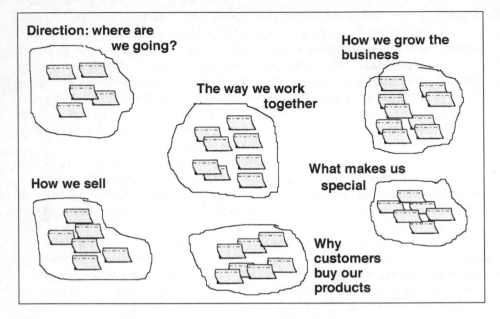

Figure 26.6   Creating the families of ideas and filling the gaps

7   Encourage the group to identify gaps in the families of ideas and fill these in with spontaneous Post-its.

8   Make connections between groups of ideas and/or deliberately connect unlike ideas, and ask: Why not connect them up?

The key technology for successful brainstorming is a single point of focus: *creative silence*, supported by Post-its and one-colour pens.

Although groups using traditional brainstorming produce fewer and usually narrower ideas in total than those applying the creative silence technique, the surviving ideas will have gone through a fairly rigorous process of evaluation, which makes the point that groups are very good at seeing what is defective or missing in an idea. The cautionary story about the camel being a horse designed by a committee is worth remembering.

FUNDAMENTAL APPROACHES

Creative problem solving uses creativity to understand the problem as well as to generate new solutions and implement them. Whenever you suspect that the way you are thinking about a problem is stereotypical or routine, you may wish to escape from your old repertoire and apply some creative thinking. The fundamental approaches to developing creative ideas involve achieving a playful or investigative frame of mind so that we can create, manipulate and escape from patterns in the following ways.

Capture

When we capture the problem, we think like a hunter. We can only stalk a creature if we understand it. We begin by trying to capture the essence of the problem by building an accurate model of it, including its key components, their relationships, and the environment in which it operates. In my own experience, for example, one of the key lessons learned in implementing IT systems within a company is that each director has a different view of how the business works, a view that is usually functionally based. A useful exercise is to ask them to work together to build a working model of the business. In making the model, they develop a shared understanding that takes them out of their specialist knowledge.

Move

When we construct models, we may inadvertently locate ourselves inside our models. Movement means deliberately positioning ourselves *outside* the problem in order to view it from different perspectives. This is outside-the-box thinking typified by the traditional solution to the nine-dot problem whereby the problem is posed of just how to connect an arrangement of nine-dots using four consecutive lines (see Figure 26.7). The figure illustrates how drawing our lines *outside* the box created by the dots, and then looking back into the box, allows us to escape our self-imposed limitations.

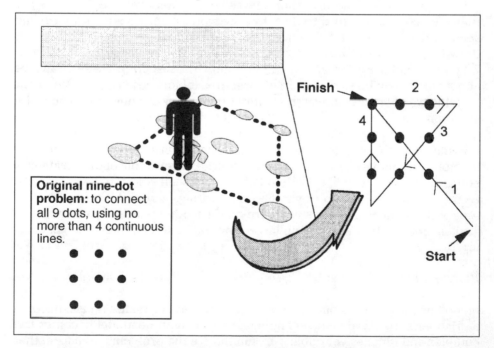

Figure 26.7   The nine-dot problem and outside-the-box thinking

These different perspectives include anyone who may be influenced directly or indirectly by the problem, including customers, competitors, historians, or anyone who has a different viewpoint.

Useful variations include: de Bono's coloured hats, where you put on a different emotional perspective 'hat' to think differently about the problem; and developing a personal 'buddy' relationship, where one can refer back to a colleague who does not own the problem that you are up against, and who can therefore take a step back from that problem and ask open questions about it. It is the difference in viewpoint, the detachment, that allows us to see the model and the problem differently.

Connect and compare

Here we consider both the familiar and the unfamiliar within the problem. A deliberate comparison with an apparently unconnected problem can provide an opportunity to understand the original problem through contrast and similarity.

Working with what is familiar may trigger alternative ways of expressing and solving the problem. This familiarity can be expressed in the form of analogies which, if we develop them, allow us to work within a parallel universe of analogy, and then return with solutions developed within the parallel analogic universe that we can translate back to the concrete and original situation.

In one business, workforce morale was so low that even the directors felt that they could not afford to discuss how worried they were without being seen as troublemakers. I conducted an exercise that involved all staff each drawing a picture of how they would explain the business situation to a 7-year-old child. By extracting the common themes from these drawings and feeding them up to the board of directors, it became acceptable to admit to being worried and, ultimately, to initiate plans to do something about the situation.

Combining all three elements – capture in model form, movement, and connection and comparison – can be very powerful. An example of this strategy is contained in the story of how Ben Rich of Lockheed sold the idea of stealth technology to the Pentagon, by rolling ball bearings across the generals' desktops and announcing, 'Here's your airplane!' (In other words: we can make an airplane for you that will look no larger on a radar screen than this ball bearing.)

Play and reverse

Modelling the problem can become a trap or an end in itself. You can become a prisoner of the modelling technology, especially if the model becomes too complex and reduces your ability to summarize the problem into a form that allows you to progress. In this situation, it may be useful to challenge the logic of the problem by deliberately playing and experimenting with the model. This can mean disassembling and putting it together again several times, under different and unusual conditions, to discover redundant functions or properties of components that you had missed.

The second form of play is to view the model as a machine or process and run it backwards to see what happens. I led an assembly improvement project in an automotive plant by asking the project team to develop a plan for quickly disassembling the vehicle faster than it took to assemble it. Then we videoed the way this was accomplished. By running the video tape backwards, we gained some radically new ideas about saving time and simplifying the assembly process.

Cheat

When we 'cheat' in creativity, we deliberately choose to forget or ignore the limitations of the present situation in order to construct a new pattern, or way of thinking about the situation, based on escape.

Cheating can involve making outrageous demands with a straight face. In other words, asking people to abandon their mind-sets about how they do things, and instead, to develop a completely different strategy. This can be achieved to some extent through competitive benchmarking, but if you really wish to cheat, I believe that a new form of benchmarking may be necessary: that is, fantasy benchmarking to take you to a leading position in your field of endeavour. If you want to be the best, dream your own dream about what being best would be like, what it would mean. The moral is: you will never lead if you follow someone else!

In business process re-engineering, modelling the existing way of doing business can create an incrementalist mind-set that leads to the new process becoming just an improvement on the original. A way of escaping from this incrementalist mind-set can be to challenge dramatically the original specification for performance by asking 'Wouldn't it be nice if we could ...' (WIBNIWC).

As a project leader of a team redesigning a corporate procurement process, I felt that we were not being sufficiently challenged. I reset the design goal from a process lasting four weeks and involving 400 people, down to two hours and driven to support new, customer-facing product teams involving no more than six procurement specialists across the corporation, demystifying procurement by making it a fundamental process skill. Initially, this was seen as impossible by team members, but once we built a model of this visionary process and defined the competences and supporting infrastructure and technology, it all began to look possible, and we moved ahead.

A variation on this approach is to cheat or use directional psychology through, first, visualizing what success would mean to the business or team, and then working backwards by identifying obstacles to that vision and, ultimately, developing strategies to overcome those obstacles. By ignoring the limitations of the present and working backwards from where we want to be,   *415* we have the additional advantage of knowing where we are going, instead of becoming paralysed through analysing our existing difficulties.

SUMMARY

It is important to understand the threatening nature of creativity to established formulas for business success. Creativity is vital to the understanding as well as the solving of problems. There is no point within an organization in trying to solve a problem that no one else recognizes or wants to solve. We can use an eight-stage problem-solving process wheel (see Figure 26.2) to manage our deployment of problem-solving techniques and develop a balanced problem-solving style across a team. Creative silence (the silent generation of individual ideas on Post-its) is a useful way of overcoming a team's initial fear of exposure. Being creative is like visiting another country where they speak a different language. The more you go there, the more relaxed you become and the more fun you can have.

CHECK LIST

- Problem ownership: Whose problem is it? Who wants to solve it? Who will gain? Who does not want to solve it?
- Problem-solving styles: Coyotes, Competitors, and Eagles; Combat, Cliques, and Subsistence styles.
- Obstacles to brainstorming in groups: fear of exposure; cues, clues, correctness, and false consensus.
- Creative silence: Post-its and pens; involving everyone in sharing a few ideas at a time.
- Fundamental creative approaches to escape existing patterns of thinking include: capture; move; connect and compare; play and reverse; and cheat.

FURTHER READING

Adams, J. L., *The Care and Feeding of Ideas: A guide to encouraging creativity*, Penguin, 1988.

de Bono, E., *The Mechanism of Mind*, Penguin, 1981.

de Bono, E., *Serious Creativity*, HarperCollins, 1992.

Chaharbaghi, K. and Newman, V., 'Innovating: towards an integrated learning model', *Management Decision*, **34** (4), 1996.

Kaufmann, K., 'Problem solving and creativity', in: J. Henry (ed.), *Creative Management*, Sage, 1991, pp.103–34.

Kirton, M. J., 'Adaptors and innovators at work', in *Adaptors and Innovators: Styles of creativity and problem solving*, Routledge, 1994, pp. 51–71.

Kondo, Y., 'Creativity in daily work', *Human Systems Management*, **9**, 1990, pp. 7–13.

Newman, V., *Problem Solving for Results*, Gower, 1995.

Rich, B. R. and Janos, L., *Skunkworks: A personal memoir of my years at Lockheed,* Little, Brown, 1994.

Weber, R. J. and Perkins, D. N., *Inventive Minds: Creativity in technology,* Oxford University Press, 1992.

Weisberg, R. W., *Creativity and Other Myths,* Freeman, 1986.

Index